CITIES DIVIDED

Cities Divided

Politics and Religion in English Provincial Towns, 1660–1722

JOHN MILLER

OXFORD

UNIVERSITY PRESS

OXFORD

UNIVERSITY PRESS

Great Clarendon Street, Oxford OX2 6DP

Oxford University Press is a department of the University of Oxford.
It furthers the University's objective of excellence in research, scholarship,
and education by publishing worldwide in

Oxford New York

Auckland Cape Town Dar es Salaam Hong Kong Karachi
Kuala Lumpur Madrid Melbourne Mexico City Nairobi
New Delhi Shanghai Taipei Toronto

With offices in

Argentina Austria Brazil Chile Czech Republic France Greece
Guatemala Hungary Italy Japan Poland Portugal Singapore
South Korea Switzerland Thailand Turkey Ukraine Vietnam

Oxford is a registered trade mark of Oxford University Press
in the UK and in certain other countries

Published in the United States
by Oxford University Press Inc., New York

© John Miller 2007

The moral rights of the author have been asserted
Database right Oxford University Press (maker)

First published 2007

British Library Cataloguing in Publication Data

Data available

Library of Congress Cataloguing in Publication Data

Data available

Typeset by Newgen
Printed in Great Britain
on acid-free paper by
Biddles Ltd., Kings Lynn, Norfolk

ISBN 978-0-19-928839-7

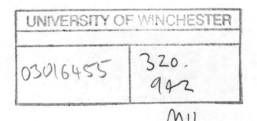

FOR SOPHIE AND WILLIAM

Preface

This book brings together the study of two normally separate topics—popular politics and urban governance; the former has been more widely studied in this period than the latter. It reflects my continuing interest in the nature of political division and the means by which communities and their rulers sought to limit the impact of that division. It seeks to build on the work done by both social and political historians on power relationships, the nature of government, and the working of communities. My background in political history meant that I perhaps came to the study of urban history with a rather different approach from that of many urban historians. I have devoted relatively little attention to economics or the occupational background of urban rulers, and more to what urban government actually did and its social and political significance. Here again I hope that I have been able to build on the insights of urban historians like Peter Borsay, Perry Gauci, Jonathan Barry, and Phil Withington. I suspect that my lack of a specific training in urban history may have led to some lacunae or misunderstandings, and for this I ask the reader's indulgence. I have also extended my normal chronological range, in order to examine continuities as well as change within what I increasingly think of as the long seventeenth century: one needs to ask why Tory crowds under George I shouted 'down with the Roundheads!'

In working on this book I have contracted many debts of gratitude. I am most grateful to the duke of Beaufort and the Marquess Townshend for allowing me to work on manuscripts at Badminton House and Raynham Hall respectively. My thanks are due to the British Academy, for two grants for research in a variety of provincial archives, and to the Arts and Humanities Research Council for part-funding a year's sabbatical leave, in which the book has been written. I should like to thank Beverly Adams, Justin Champion, Stuart Handley, Jason Peacey, and Stephen Roberts for information and advice; and, more generally, the members of the seminar in seventeenth-century British history, at the Institute of Historical Research, for comments on those parts of the book which were given as papers, for a wide variety of information and for showing that rigorous historical debate can also be fun. I am also grateful to Oxford University Press's anonymous reader for very full and helpful comments on the first draft. Last but not least, I should like to thank my son Nik for invaluable advice on computing and my wife, for putting up with my absences on research trips and my imperviousness to everyday things when writing.

J. M.
July 2006

All dates are old style, but with the year starting on 1 January. Spellings have been modernized.

Contents

Abbreviations

BCL	Bristol Central Library, Reference Section
Besse	J. Besse, *A Collection of the Sufferings of the People Called Quakers*, 2 vols., London, 1753
BIHR	*Bulletin of the Institute of Historical Research*
BL	British Library
Bodl	Bodleian Library
BRB	Hull City Archives, Bench Books
BRL	Hull City Archives, Letters
BRO	Bristol Record Office
Browning, *Docts*	A. Browning (ed.), *English Historical Documents, 1660–1714*, London, 1953
BRS	Bristol Record Society
Campana	E. Campana de Cavelli, *Les Derniers Stuarts à Saint Germain en Laye*, 2 vols., London, 1871
Carte MSS	Bodleian Library, Carte MSS
CCSP	*Calendar of Clarendon State Papers*, 5 vols., Oxford, 1872–1970
C (H)	Cambridge University Library, Cholmondley (Houghton) MSS, Correspondence
Church of Christ	R. Hayden (ed.), *The Records of a Church of Christ in Bristol, 1640–87*, Bristol Record Soc., 1974
CJ	*Commons Journals*
CKS	Centre for Kentish Studies, Maidstone
Clarendon MSS	Bodleian Library, Clarendon MSS
Collection	*A Collection of the Addresses which have been Presented to the Queen since the Impeachment of . . . Sacheverell*, London, 1710
Coventry MSS	Longleat, Coventry MSS (consulted on microfilm)
CPA	Archives des Affaires Étrangères, Paris, Correspondance Politique, Angleterre
CSPD	*Calendar of State Papers Domestic*

CSPV	*Calendar of State Papers Venetian*
CUHB, ii	P. Clark (ed.), *Cambridge Urban History of Britain*, ii: *1540–1840*, Cambridge, 2000
DAM	Dover Corporation Records, Assembly Minutes, James I to Charles II, rear of volume (consulted at Centre for Kentish Studies, now at East Kent Record Office, Dover)
Defoe, *Letters*	D. Defoe, *Letters*, ed. G. H. Healey, Oxford, 1955
Defoe, *Tour*	D. Defoe, *A Tour through the Whole Island of Great Britain*, 2 vols., Everyman edition, revised, 1962
Duckett	Sir G. Duckett (ed.), *Penal Laws and Test Acts 1687–8*, 2 vols., London, 1882–3
DWL	Doctor Williams' Library
East	R. East (ed.), *Extracts from the Portsmouth Records*, Portsmouth, 1891
EHR	*English Historical Review*
EKRO	East Kent Record Office, Dover
Ellis	G. J. W. Ellis (ed.), *Ellis Correspondence*, 2 vols., London, 1829
FAB	Norfolk Record Office, Norwich Civic Records, Case 16d, Folio Assembly Books
FHL	Friends House Library
Fiennes	C. Fiennes, *The Journeys of Celia Fiennes*, ed. C. Morris, London, 1949
FSL	Folger Shakespeare Library
Grey	A. Grey, *Debates in the House of Commons 1667–94*, 10 vols., London, 1763 (can be accessed via **www.british-history.ac.uk**)
Halliday, *Body*	P. D. Halliday, *Dismembering the Body Politic: Partisan Politics in England's Towns 1650–1730*, Cambridge, 1998
HJ	*Historical Journal*
HLQ	*Huntington Library Quarterly*
HMC	*Historical Manuscripts Commission Reports*
HP 1660–90	B. D. Henning (ed.), *History of Parliament: The Commons 1660–90*, 3 vols., London, 1983

HP 1690–1715	E. Cruickshanks, S. Handley, and D. Hayton (eds.), *History of Parliament: The Commons 1690–1715*, 5 vols., Cambridge, 2002
HP 1715–54	R. Sedgwick (ed.), *History of Parliament: The Commons 1715–54*, 2 vols., London, 1970
HR	*Historical Research*
HUO, iv	N. Tyacke (ed.), *History of the University of Oxford*, iv: *The Seventeenth Century*, Oxford, 1997
JBS	*Journal of British Studies*
JEH	*Journal of Ecclesiastical History*
JSAHR	*Journal of the Society for Army Historical Research*
Latimer, i	J. Latimer, *Annals of Bristol: Sixteenth and Seventeenth Centuries*, Bristol, 1970
Latimer, ii	J. Latimer, *Annals of Bristol: Eighteenth Century*, Bristol, 1970
LHB	Leicestershire Record Office, BR II/1 (Leicester Hall Books)
LHP	Leicestershire Record Office, BR II/18 (Leicester Hall Papers)
LJ	*Lords Journals*
LPL	Lambeth Palace Library
Luttrell	N. Luttrell, *A Brief Historical Relation of State Affairs 1678–1714*, 6 vols., Oxford 1857
Lyon Turner	G. Lyon Turner, *Original Records of Early Nonconformity*, 3 vols., London, 1911–14
M636	British Library, microfilms of Verney correspondence
Marvell	A. Marvell, *Poems and Letters*, ed. H. M. Margoliouth, rev. E. Duncan Jones, 2 vols., Oxford, 1971
MCB	Norfolk Record Office, Norwich Civic Records, Case 16a, Mayor's Court Books
Millerd	J. Millerd, *An Exact Delineation of the Famous City of Bristol*, 1673, facsimile, Bristol Museums and Art Galleries, n.d.
Morrice	Dr Williams' Library, Roger Morrice's entering book, MSS 31 P–R
NCR	Norfolk Record Office, Norwich Civic Records
NLI	National Library of Ireland

Norf Arch	*Norfolk Archaeology*
Norths	R. North, *Lives of the Norths*, ed. A. Jessopp, 3 vols., London, 1890
Norwich since 1550	C. Rawcliffe and R. Wilson (eds.), *Norwich since 1550*, London, 2004
NRO	Norfolk Record Office
NRS	Norfolk Record Society
'Oates's Plot'	Warwickshire Record Office, CR 1998, 'Large carved box', item 17, unfoliated volume entitled 'Oates's Plot'
OCA, ii	M. G. Hobson and H. E. Salter (eds.), *Oxford Council Acts 1626–65*, Oxford Historical Soc., 1933
OCA, iii	M. G. Hobson (ed.), *Oxford Council Acts 1666–1701*, Oxford Historical Soc., 1939
OCA, iv	M. G. Hobson (ed.), *Oxford Council Acts 1701–51*, Oxford Historical Soc., 1954
P & P	*Past and Present*
PC	National Archives, Privy Council records
Pol of Rel	T. Harris, M. Goldie, and P. Seaward (eds.), *The Politics of Religion in Restoration England*, Oxford, 1990
Pol State	A. Boyer, *The Political State of Great Britain*, 60 vols., London, 1710–40. For vols. i–viii, 2nd edn., London, 1718–19
Prideaux	H. Prideaux, *Letters to John Ellis*, ed. E. M. Thompson, Camden Soc., 1875
PSP	A. J. Willis and M. J. Hoad (eds.), *Portsmouth Sessions Papers 1653–88*, Portsmouth Record Soc., 1971
PwA	Nottingham University Library, Portland MSS
RBL, iv	H. Stocks and W. H. Stevenson (eds.), *Records of the Borough of Leicester*, iv.(1603–88), Cambridge, 1923
RBL, v, vi, vii	G. A. Chinnery (ed.), *Records of the Borough of Leicester*, v–vii (1689–1835), Leicester, 1965–74
Ref and Revival	J. Barry and K. Morgan (eds.), *Reformation and Revival in Eighteenth-Century Bristol*, BRS xlv, 1994
Reresby	Sir J. Reresby, *Memoirs*, ed. A. Browning, rev. M. K. Geiter and W. A. Speck, London, 1991

Schellinks	W. Schellinks, *Journal of Travels in England 1661–3*, ed. M. Exwood and H. L. Lehman, Camden Soc., 1993
SGCR	Norfolk Record Office, Norwich City Records, Case 17b, St George's Company, Rules etc, vol. 3, 1602–1729
SP	National Archives, State Papers
SR	*Statutes of the Realm*
Stilling	L. Davison, T. Hitchcock, T. Keim, and R. B. Shoemaker (eds.), *Stilling the Grumbling Hive: The Response to Social and Economic Problems in England, 1689–1750*, Stroud, 1992
Tanner MSS	Bodleian Library, Tanner MSS
TNA	The National Archives
TRHS	*Transactions of the Royal Historical Society*
V & A	Victoria and Albert Museum, National Art Library
VCH	*Victoria County History*
VN	text reproduced on **www.virtualnorfolk.uea.ac.uk**
Wake MSS	Christ Church, Oxford, Wake MSS
Walsh et al.	J. Walsh, C. Haydon, and S. Taylor (eds.), *The Church of England c.1689–c.1833: From Toleration to Tractarianism*, Oxford, 1993
Whiteman	A. Whiteman (ed.), *The Compton Census of 1676*, London, 1986
Williamson	*Letters Addressed from London to Sir Joseph Williamson, 1673–4*, ed. W. D. Christie, Camden Soc., 1874
Wood	A. Wood, *Life and Times*, ed. A. Clark, 5 vols., Oxford Historical Soc., 1891–1900
WYAL	West Yorkshire Archives, Leeds

Introduction

I. THE NATURE OF POLITICAL DIVISION

In April 1722, Coventry prepared for a general election, with some trepidation. Recent elections for the city had been marked by violence and accusations of electoral fraud. This was the first general election since the maximum interval between elections had been increased from three years to seven: some of the crowd were to shout 'no seven years Parliament!'[1] The election quickly came to resemble a civil war. Lord Craven, the brother of one of the Tory candidates, who lived near the city, was said to have given a large crowd unlimited quantities of drink. They continued to drink on their way back and were said to number as many as 4,000 countrymen, apprentices, and journeymen. They marched in a military manner, armed with sticks and clubs, with drums and trumpets, colours flying, and green leaves in their hats.[2] The Whig candidates and the Whig mayor and aldermen had been expecting trouble. They had brought in many freemen who were serving in the army; they had also raised extra constables, armed with spiked sticks. The soldiers appeared in their regimental uniforms armed with swords, and attacked the Tory crowd, wounding several. It was said that one soldier refused to draw his sword against men armed only with sticks, until positively ordered to do so. After a while, the soldiers were driven back by sheer force of numbers. Six men were committed to gaol by the magistrates, none of them soldiers.[3] When the poll began, the Whigs claimed that the crowds broke the windows and heads of those who would not shout Tory slogans, wounded the mayor, and threw missiles at his house; they also threw stones into the booths where votes were being taken. The sheriffs polled 106 for the Whig candidates and five for the Tories and then adjourned for an hour, claiming that the violence made it impossible to continue.[4] When the hour ended, the Whigs claimed that the sheriffs did not dare

---

[1] *HP 1715–54*, i. 340.

[2] Ibid.; *Flying Post*, 12–14 Apr. 1722; *Weekly Journal or British Gazetteer*, 14 Apr. 1722. These three sources number the crowd as 2,000, 4,000, and 1,000 respectively.

[3] *Weekly Journal or Saturday's Post*, 14 and 21 Apr., *Post Boy*, 5–7 and 14–17 Apr. 1722; *HP 1715–54*, i. 340.

[4] *Flying Post*, 12–14 Apr., *Weekly Journal or British Gazetteer*, 14 Apr. 1722.

resume the poll, the Tories that the Whig candidates and mayor carried the sheriffs off and kept them incommunicado until they agreed to make a return on the basis of the votes cast thus far. According to the Tories, there were still 2,000 freemen waiting to vote, of whom 1,500 had promised to vote for the Tory candidates. The Tories petitioned against the return; in November the Commons, despite its Whig majority, agreed that there had been 'outrageous riots, tumults and seditions'. The election was declared void. The corporation prepared for a fresh election by creating many new Whig freemen, but carried it by only a narrow margin.[5]

The Coventry election of 1722 showed the depth of local division in a period which, in national politics, was coming to enjoy 'political stability'. If the Whig dominance of the central government and Parliament was unshaken after the election of 1722, at the grass roots, and especially in towns, there were deep and violent animosities.[6] There were several significant features of the Coventry election. First, many in the Tory crowd would have been ineligible to vote. The city's franchise was restricted to the freemen; countrymen and apprentices would not have been freemen; some journeymen (daily paid workers) may have been. Being ineligible to vote did not prevent active participation in elections. Second, in the seventeenth century, Coventry had the reputation of being strongly Puritan (later Nonconformist) and Parliamentarian.[7] By Anne's reign the corporation was strongly Whig and contained many Dissenters, but the majority of citizens were Tories. The corporation used all sorts of ruses to ensure the return of Whigs to Parliament; the Tories responded with violence.[8] Third, much of the rhetoric used by the Tory crowds harked back to the Interregnum: they cried 'Down with the Roundheads! Down with the Rump!' and (allegedly) 'no Hanoverians'.[9] Slogans and rhetoric dating back to the civil wars continued to be used well into the eighteenth century. There were frequent references to the 'murder' or 'martyrdom' of Charles I. For generations after 1660, Tories and Churchmen depicted their opponents—Whigs and Dissenters—as the lineal and ideological descendants of those who had 'rebelled' against,

[5] *Post Boy*, 5–7 Apr. 1722; *HP 1715–54*, i. 339–40. A Whig newspaper agreed that only 100 out of about 1,800 had been able to vote: *Weekly Journal or British Gazetteer*, 14 Apr. 1722.
[6] See J. H. Plumb, *The Growth of Political Stability in England 1675–1725* (London, 1967); L. Colley, *In Defiance of Oligarchy: The Tory Party 1714–60* (Cambridge, 1982); K. Wilson, *The Sense of the People: Politics, Culture and Imperialism in England, 1715–85* (New York, 1995).
[7] J. J. Hurwich, 'A "Fanatick Town": The Political Influence of Dissenters in Coventry, 1660–1720', *Midland History*, iv. 1977, *passim*.
[8] *HP 1690–1715*, ii. 623–32; *HP 1715–54*, i. 339–40.
[9] *HP 1715–54*, i. 340; *Weekly Journal or British Gazetteer*, 14 Apr. 1722. A Tory newspaper referred to the Whigs as the 'Rump faction': *Weekly Journal or Saturday's Post*, 14 Apr. 1722.

and executed, Charles I.[10] The annual commemoration of the regicide, established by Act of Parliament, used a form of service that compared the king's 'martyrdom' to the passion of Christ.[11] Whigs, especially under Charles II, hotly denied that they advocated rebellion or approved of the regicide. The people's right to resist a tyrant, advanced unequivocally by John Locke in 1690, initially found few supporters among his Whig contemporaries.[12] Only after the publication of Clarendon's *History of the Rebellion*, under Anne, was there a widespread Whig attempt to justify the Parliamentarians' resistance to Charles I; most still professed to abhor the regicide, although many may privately have felt he deserved his fate.

Many who had lived through the civil wars believed that they had profoundly changed England; the phrase 'before the civil wars' ran like a tremulous mantra through John Aubrey's *Brief Lives*, as he recounted one change after another. Old orthodoxies and authorities had been overthrown and the world had been turned upside down, which was why those who made the Restoration were determined to set it the right way up again; there remained a constant nagging fear that these orthodoxies and authorities might not survive a second assault. We can see with hindsight that anxious Royalists and Tories exaggerated their fragility. However sincerely the Tories might believe during the Exclusion Crisis[13] that 'Forty-one is come again', civil war was not likely, as the Whigs lacked either the military resources or the will to fight—but their posturing scared the Tories and the king.

By no means all the rhetoric used at Coventry harked back to the civil wars. There were references to the recent Septennial Act and the House of Hanover. Cries of 'no Hanover' may have been designed to be offensive to the

---

[10] For a thoughtful discussion of who 'rebelled', see D. H. Pennington, 'The Rebels of 1642', in R. H. Parry (ed.), *The English Civil War and After, 1642–58* (London, 1970), ch. 2.

[11] A. Lacey, 'The Office for King Charles the Martyr in the Book of Common Prayer, 1662–85', *JEH* liii (2002), 519–26.

[12] See J. P. Kenyon, *Revolution Principles: The Politics of Party 1689–1720* (Cambridge, 1977); M. P. Thompson, 'The Reception of Locke's *Second Treatise of Government*, 1690–1705', *Political Studies*, xxiv (1976), 184–9.

[13] Jonathan Scott has argued that the crisis of 1679–81 was not mainly about exclusion, partly on the grounds that little time was actually spent on it in the Parliament of 1680–1: *Algernon Sidney and the Restoration Crisis, 1677–83* (Cambridge, 1991), 20. The reason for this was simple. Once the exclusion bill had passed the Commons and been rejected by the Lords, it could not be reintroduced unless the king could be persuaded to wipe the slate clean by proroguing Parliament, which he refused to do. I would add that how MPs voted on exclusion was seen, especially in elections, as an indication of party allegiance. Mark Knights, *Politics and Opinion in Crisis 1678–81* (Cambridge, 1994), 4–5 and ch. 2 preferred to talk of a 'succession crisis'. Tim Harris, *Restoration: Charles II and his Kingdoms 1660–85* (London, 2005) continues to use the term 'exclusion crisis'.

corporation (and the government), they may have been genuine expressions of Jacobitism, or they may have been invented, or exaggerated by the Whigs. Since the Exclusion Crisis a new type of political vocabulary had developed, based on the divisions between Whig and Tory. If the Tories depicted the Whigs as hostile to monarchy and friendly to Dissent, the Whigs claimed that the Tories were willing to contemplate a Catholic on the throne. In the last years of Anne and the early part of George I's reign, Whigs referred to their opponents as 'Jacks' (Jacobites) rather than as Tories.

But how much did these issues matter to 'ordinary people'? Events at Coventry suggest that they mattered a great deal. Since 1640 England had seen an unprecedented explosion of political news and comment; attempts to re-establish pre-publication censorship at the Restoration were only partially successful. Moreover, the dissemination and discussion of political news were never dependent solely on print and continued vigorously, especially in the increasingly numerous coffee houses.[14] From the Exclusion Crisis there is evidence of wider popular participation in politics, not only in parliamentary elections, but in petitions, addresses, and associations, many of them printed in the official *Gazette* and elsewhere.[15] Although contemporaries argued that these addresses—or at least those produced by their opponents—were meaningless and unrepresentative, the sheer number of people who subscribed them would suggest that they were not. They also implied that 'the public', a body of people wider than the electorate, should have a voice in politics.[16]

With the end of censorship in 1695, the volume of publication increased substantially. Newspapers became a regular part of the political scene; the end of the ban on presses outside London and the two universities opened the way for provincial publishing. The papers contained a variety of foreign and domestic news, and advertisements.[17] As in the 1640s and the Exclusion Crisis,

---

[14] J. Miller, 'Public Opinion in Charles II's England', *History*, lxxx (1995), 359–81; Harris, *Restoration*, passim.

[15] M. Knights, *Representation and Misrepresentation in Later Stuart Britain* (Oxford, 2005), chs. 3–4.

[16] *Pol State*, iv. 32; Knights, *Representation*, 117, 159–61.

[17] The one big omission was news of parliamentary debates: the Commons regarded them as secret, although it did at times authorize publication of its 'votes': J. Miller, 'Representatives and Represented in England, 1660–89', *Parliaments, Estates and Representation*, xv (1995), 125–32; Knights, *Representation*, 195–204. The only publication to include debates was Boyer's *Political State*. This was in stark contrast to the very sophisticated newspaper reports on political manoeuvring in Parliament in the 1640s: J. Peacey, 'Hocus-Pocus Politics', paper given to the London seminar in seventeenth-century British history, to be published shortly. There was rather more parliamentary news in manuscript newsletters: Knights, *Representation*, 227 and n. 29.

some newspapers provided comment on political events, some of it polemical and scurrilous. There were also satirical prints and ballads to carry the issues beyond those who could read.[18] Above all, there were elections, especially parliamentary elections. The electorate was much larger in this period than was traditionally thought—larger, indeed, in percentage terms than after the reform bill of 1832.[19] However, the number of voters varied enormously between constituencies. There were 'rotten boroughs', with only a handful of voters, which became more numerous after 1715, as successive Whig Houses of Commons opted for the narrower franchise in election disputes, and Whig borough patrons sought to reduce the number of electors that they had to deal with. Even so, boroughs with very small electorates could see vigorous contests.[20] Contests were more likely in larger constituencies, and the unenfranchised, as at Coventry, could influence the outcome by their physical presence.

Not all elections were contested, but from 1679 an increasing number were contested, many on political issues, which acquired party labels.[21] The politicization of elections owed much to three general elections in 1679–81, encouraging candidates who had served earlier to campaign on their record. The timing of elections became predictable after the Triennial Act of 1694 laid down that there had to be a general election at least every three years; there were ten between 1695 and 1715. Party issues spilled over into municipal elections, especially where the right to vote was vested in the corporation, or the mayor was the returning officer. The more sensational contests (which usually meant the most violent) were reported in the press, possibly encouraging violence elsewhere.

---

[18] It is possible to arrive at a reasonable estimate of the percentage of people who could write: D. Cressy, *Literacy and the Social Order in Early Modern England* (Cambridge, 1982). But reading was taught before writing and there were many who learned to read without learning to write, often because they wished to learn from print, or to be entertained by it, but had no functional reason for learning to write: M. Spufford, *Figures in the Landscape: Rural Society in England 1500–1700* (Aldershot, 2000), chs. 10–11; M. Spufford, *Small Books and Pleasant Histories* (London, 1981), esp. ch. 2.

[19] J. H. Plumb, 'The Growth of the Electorate in England, 1600–1715', *P & P* 45 (1969), 111; D. Hirst, *The Representative of the People? Voters and Voting under the Early Stuarts* (Cambridge, 1975), 104–5; G. Holmes, *The Electorate and the National Will in the First Age of Party* (Lancaster, 1975), 23–4; W. A. Speck, *Tory and Whig: The Struggle in the Constituencies 1700–15* (London, 1970), 16.

[20] See, for example, Buckingham, with its thirteen electors: *HP 1660–90*, i. 139–42; *HP 1690–1715*, ii. 35–8; M. Kishlansky, *Parliamentary Selection: Social and Political Choice in Early Modern England* (Cambridge, 1986), ch. 8.

[21] J. Miller, *After the Civil Wars: English Politics and Government in the Reign of Charles II* (Harlow, 2000), 83–93, 257–61.

Historians of the period 1689–1715 have stressed that England's was a 'divided society', rent by the 'rage of party'.[22] Tim Harris and others have advanced similar claims for the reign of Charles II—or at least 1678–85—and historians of the civil wars now generally accept that there was widespread popular participation and commitment on both sides. When Parliamentarian forces entered Cornwall, they were shocked by the hostility—and violence —of the local women towards them.[23] David Underdown and Mark Stoyle have demonstrated the strength of committed popular Royalism: it was not just based on obedience to social superiors.[24] Similarly, Knights and Harris have stressed the importance of popular Toryism during the Exclusion Crisis. Both Royalist and Tory journalists soon overcame their reluctance to appeal to the people: Sir Roger L'Estrange more than matched the Whigs in polemic aimed at a popular audience.[25] Tory polemicists were supported by High Church clergymen, some of whose sermons used language every bit as blood-thirsty as that of militant Puritans of the 1640s. Nowhere was the strength— and extremism—of popular Toryism more evident than in the reaction to the trial of Dr Sacheverell.[26]

II. URBAN SOCIETY AND GOVERNMENT

In earlier work, I studied the extent and nature of political division under Charles II. I am now trying to do the same between 1660 and 1722. In 1722 the Whigs comfortably won the general election, despite nationwide anger at the scandal of the South Sea Bubble less than two years before. This suggested that they had gained an unshakeable hold on the electoral system as well as the government. I am looking particularly at provincial towns, because they

---

[22] G. Holmes, *British Politics in the Age of Anne* (London, 1967); Plumb, *Political Stability*, ch. 5; Speck, *Tory and Whig*; G. Holmes and W. A. Speck (eds.), *The Divided Society: Parties and Politics in England, 1694–1716* (London, 1967).

[23] M. Stoyle, *Loyalty and Locality: Popular Allegiance in Devon during the English Civil War* (Exeter, 1994), 234.

[24] D. Underdown, 'The Problem of Popular Allegiance in the English Civil War', *TRHS*, 5th series, xxxi (1981), 69–94; D. Underdown, *Revel, Riot and Rebellion: Popular Politics and Culture in England, 1603–60* (Oxford, 1985); Stoyle, *Loyalty and Locality*; J. Morrill, *The Nature of the English Revolution* (Harlow, 1993), 281–2.

[25] Knights, *Politics and Opinion*, chs. 9–10; T. Harris, *London Crowds in the Reign of Charles II* (Cambridge, 1987), ch. 6. In *Restoration*, ch. 5 (especially 285), Harris is more sceptical about popular Toryism.

[26] G. Holmes, *The Trial of Dr Sacheverell* (London, 1972).

contained a manageable and defined group of people, and because many generated extensive records. The nature of these records means that I have focused mainly on larger corporate towns at the expense of small towns and non-corporate towns, some of which (like Manchester or Birmingham) were very large. Most importantly, to a considerable extent they ran their own affairs. Town governments were, of course, far from fully autonomous. They were subject to competition from other bodies within the town and to intervention from outside by powerful landowners and the central government.[27] One major reason for this intervention was that many towns returned members to Parliament—five-sixths of the Commons sat for boroughs. Having to contend with such formidable intervention, they needed powerful patrons and friends at court, but on a day-to-day basis towns were generally run by men who did not belong to the landed elite or aspire to a seat in Parliament. This meant that they could not wield the authority that came with great landed wealth, exalted rank, and the leading offices in county government. They thus had to find ways of legitimizing their authority in the eyes of the townspeople.[28]

The one urban area which I have chosen not to discuss in detail is the London conurbation. Its population was so much larger than any provincial town, and its social and institutional make-up was so much more complex, as to make it a different entity. London's influence on provincial towns was enormous. It was the home of the national government, Parliament, and the law courts. It played a dominant role in the printing industry and the dissemination of news. It offered a range of entertainments and shops that no provincial town could match; where London led—in fashions for clothes, consumer goods, and architecture—provincial towns followed. The greatest compliment a travel writer could pay to a provincial town was to describe it as 'another London'. Its demands for food and goods stimulated agriculture and industry in the provinces and helped break down traditional regulations governing urban markets and manufactures. It drew in aristocratic families, for business and pleasure, and delegations from towns, seeking benefits or fearful of threats. London dominated English urban life. The only exception was in the Commons: the London conurbation returned only ten members. This led rich Londoners with political ambitions to build up electoral 'interests' in provincial towns.[29]

---

[27] See below, Ch. 5. [28] See below, Chs. 2–4.
[29] Four for London, two each for Westminster, Southwark, and Middlesex (only part of which was in the conurbation): *HP 1690–1715*, i. 731–40 and *passim*.

In order to analyse political and religious divisions within towns, it is necessary to consider the nature of towns and the working of town governments,
which means adopting a rather different perspective from most studies of early
modern English towns. Historians working on the century before the civil wars
focus mainly on economic and social problems. Many towns experienced long-
term economic decline. Overseas markets for England's main industry—
cloth—were disrupted by war or protectionist tariff policies. Population
growth led to increased food prices and reduced the purchasing power of the
poor; the unemployed rural poor flocked to the towns in search of work and
relief, adding to the towns' problem of coping with their indigenous poor.
Although some accepted that England was overpopulated, others believed that
much of the problem of poverty was brought about by the moral inadequacies
of the poor themselves. The law provided for the punishment of 'vagrants', and
those who were 'loose, idle, and disorderly'. Magistrates decided whether an
individual fell into either of these categories, with Puritans proving particularly
rigorous.[30]

In the century before 1640, then, towns struggled to cope with economic
decline, overpopulation, and poverty. After 1660 the economic position of
many towns improved markedly. Overseas trade and shipping grew rapidly,
manufactures expanded and diversified. The population ceased to expand,
food production rose. Food prices fell; more and more people had money
to spend on consumer goods, if they chose. And many did so choose: people
began to buy goods, not because they needed them, but because they wanted
them—ornaments, china, mirrors, and clocks; style and design now mattered
as much as functionality. Consumers also wanted more diverse and exotic food
and drink—coffee and tea became fashionable—and spent more on leisure
pursuits, on entertainment and learning, clubs and societies. The rapid expansion in the range of consumer goods, increasingly sold in specialist shops, and
leisure facilities, was apparent first in London, but soon spread to provincial
towns. Developments in the West End of London popularized new architectural fashions, which were followed, at varying rates, in provincial towns.
Thus the prevailing historiographical view of the century after 1660 is far
more optimistic than that of the previous century. From an era of economic
decline, poverty, and moral repression, English towns moved into a period

---

[30] P. Clark and P. Slack (eds.), *Crisis and Order in English Towns 1500–1700* (London, 1972);
P. Clark and P. Slack, *English Towns in Transition 1500–1700* (Oxford, 1976); P. Slack, *Poverty and
Policy in Tudor and Stuart England* (London, 1988).

of prosperity, an improved built environment, and the pursuit of material gratification and pleasure.[31]

In neither of these historiographies does politics or religion have a place, except where the disciplining of the poor was seen as driven by Puritanism.[32] Historians of religion have analysed the impact of godly reformation on towns in the century before 1640,[33] but less has been written on religion in towns after 1660—partly, no doubt, because urban magistrates' response to religious diversity was often benevolent non-intervention.[34] Politics (in the sense of nationally based, ideologically driven politics) played only a limited role; parliamentary elections were rarely contested before the 1620s, when some began to be fought on political lines, a development that became more marked in the two general elections of 1640.[35] By contrast, from 1679 many elections in towns showed clear party divisions. The most sophisticated studies of urban party politics consider the period after 1715,[36] although there are some perceptive studies of individual towns before then.[37] But while partisan conflict is interesting, and often exciting,[38] it was far from universal. Many towns avoided electoral contests and managed to limit the potentially divisive impact of political and religious difference. Relations between Quakers—the most obviously 'different' of the new sects—and their neighbours changed after the Restoration. In the 1650s their behaviour was extremely provocative and they suffered

[31] The classic exposition of this view is P. Borsay, *The English Urban Renaissance: Culture and Society in the English Town 1660–1770* (Oxford, 1989). See also A. McInnes, 'The Emergence of a Leisure Town: Shrewsbury 1660–1760', *P & P* 120 (1988), 53–87, and his 'Debate' with P. Borsay in *P & P* 126 (1990), 189–202; A. McInnes, *The English Town 1660–1760*, Historical Association (London, 1980).

[32] I shall discuss the connections (if any) between Puritanism and social control in Ch. 3.

[33] See for example, P. Collinson and J. Craig (eds.), *The Reformation in English Towns 1500–1640* (Basingstoke, 1998).

[34] See P. Gauci, *Politics and Society in Great Yarmouth, 1660–1722* (Oxford, 1996); J. Miller, 'Containing Division in Restoration Norwich', *EHR* cxxi (2006), 1019–47.

[35] Kishlansky, *Parliamentary Selection*, claimed that elections were first fought on political lines in 1640, but for evidence of political contests in the 1620s, see Hirst, *Representative of the People?*, 137–53; R. Cust, 'Politics and the Electorate in the 1620s', in Cust and A. Hughes (eds.), *Conflict in Stuart England* (London, 1989), ch. 5. It is worth remarking that the frequency of general elections in the 1620s made it more likely that issues would be carried over from one election to the next.

[36] Wilson, *Sense of the People*; also N. Rogers, *Whigs and Cities: Popular Politics in The Age of Walpole and Pitt* (Oxford, 1989); N. Rogers, *Crowds, Culture and Politics in Georgian Britain* (Oxford, 1998).

[37] Gauci, *Yarmouth*; J. T. Evans, *Seventeenth-Century Norwich* (Oxford, 1979). There are also many excellent studies in the *History of Parliament* volumes on the period: *HP 1660–90*, and especially *HP 1690–1715* (also David Hayton's splendid 'introductory survey' in the latter).

[38] See for example, the essays in *Pol of Rel*. Paul Halliday's fine study, *Dismembering the Body Politic* (Cambridge, 1998), emphasizes conflict rather than consensus largely because it is based heavily on King's Bench records: had there not been conflict, these cases would not have come to court.

widespread violence. After 1660, they remained distinctive in dress, language, and behaviour; they still refused to observe the fasts and feasts of their neighbours; but they no longer disrupted church services or harangued their fellow townsmen in the street. The differences between Quakers and non-Quakers became tolerable rather than intolerable, and their sufferings earned them considerable sympathy.[39]

Political and religious divisions could be contained because politics (in the sense of ideologically driven party politics) and religion were not the only things that mattered to townspeople. To understand why, we need a broader definition of 'politics', based on individuals and groups pursuing interests and getting things done. Those seeking benefits, favours, or protection approached those in positions of power; if the latter delivered what was requested, they expected acknowledgement in the form of courtesies, political support, or money.[40] Historians of the *ancien régime* in France routinely see 'politics' as consisting of struggles about power and policy conducted largely within the administration. Similarly, historians of both government and society in England have recently come to embrace a wider understanding of politics, in terms of power relationships and how government *worked*.[41] One result of this broader, more socially based approach to politics has been to blur the boundaries between 'rulers' and 'ruled'. Government, at all levels, depended partly on the authority that came with office, and partly on negotiation. Government— and law enforcement—needed to be seen to be fair and conducted according to accepted rules. The extensive participation of ordinary citizens in the government of parish, town, and county enabled them significantly to shape the content of government. With few exceptions, offices were open only to adult males, and often only to freemen. Senior places in the corporation of a large town went to the wealthier freemen, but more modest offices (such as jurymen) were filled from a wide spectrum of the 'middling sorts' and some, like parish constables or watchmen, from the comparatively humble. Office conferred power. Grand juries told magistrates what needed to be put right, reporting aldermen who failed to keep the street in front of their houses in good repair. Trial juries decided whether an accused person was guilty, and of what offence.

---

[39] J. Miller, ' "A Suffering People": English Quakers and their Neighbours, *c*.1650–*c*.1700', *P & P* 188 (2005), 71–103; A. Davies, *The Quakers in English Society, 1655–1725* (Oxford, 2000).

[40] See Miller, *After the Civil Wars*, ch. 3.

[41] See, for example, K. Wrightson, 'The Politics of the Parish in Early Modern England', in P. Griffiths, A. Fox, and S. Hindle (eds.), *The Experience of Authority in Early Modern England* (Basingstoke, 1996), ch. 1.

Participation—and the rotation of office-holding—meant that many individuals both exercised authority over others and had others exercise authority over them: gentlemen accused of criminal offences came up before juries of their social inferiors, while the villager who (as constable) could arrest his neighbour during his year in office might find their roles reversed the following year.[42]

Rather than a simple distinction between 'rulers' and 'ruled', one should think in terms of a cascading series of power relationships, in which the position of individuals shifted from one year to the next. These relationships involved negotiation, conducted partly through legal processes, partly through petitions and appeals for justice; such appeals were cast in deferential language, but rested on a clear sense of the obligations that went with rank and authority. This was a society with profound inequalities, but their impact was reduced by participation in government and law enforcement, and by the practical realization that both functioned better with a degree of negotiation, restraint, and common sense on both sides. People generally preferred redress and restitution to insisting on the utmost rigour of the law. Even for humble people, the law was a resource which could be used to secure redress:[43] often legal action was started in order to persuade an adversary to seek a compromise. In criminal cases, the decision whether to prosecute was often influenced by the desire of the 'better sort' to maintain communal harmony.[44] Not everyone shared this culture of 'reconciliation' —godly magistrates saw no scope for flexibility when doing the Lord's work— but many did, especially in a tight little community like a provincial town.

Although some of the most interesting work on the 'politics of the parish' has focused on rural communities,[45] there have been attempts to apply similar

---

[42] See the excellent essay by Mark Goldie, 'The Unacknowledged Republic: Office-Holding in Early Modern England', in T. Harris (ed.), *The Politics of the Excluded, c.1500–1850* (Basingstoke, 2001), ch. 6. See also P. Withington, 'Views from the Bridge: Revolution and Restoration in Seventeenth-Century York', *P & P* 170 (2001), 128–32; P. Withington, 'Citizens, Community and Political Culture in Restoration England', in A. Shephard and P. Withington (eds.), *Communities in Early Modern England* (Manchester, 2000), 139–41; J. Barry, 'Introduction', in J. Barry (ed.), *The Tudor and Stuart Town: A Reader* (Harlow, 1990), 29–32. See also below, Ch. 2.

[43] Counsel were often retained by both sides in settlement cases. Those claiming to be wrongly committed to the house of correction could sue out a *habeas corpus* and have their case heard in the courts at Westminster: J. Innes, 'Prisons for the Poor: English Bridewells, 1555–1800', in F. Snyder and D. Hay (eds.), *Labour, Law and Crime* (London, 1987), 85–6.

[44] See for example J. A. Sharpe, *Crime in Early Modern England* (Harlow, 1984); C. Herrup, *The Common Peace: Participation and the Criminal Law in Seventeenth-Century England* (Cambridge, 1987); R. B. Shoemaker, *Prosecution and Punishment: Petty Crime and the Law in London and Rural Middlesex, c.1660–1725* (Cambridge, 1991); S. Hindle, 'The Keeping of the Public Peace', in Griffiths, Fox, and Hindle (eds.), *Experience of Authority*, ch. 7.

[45] Apart from Wrightson's 'Politics of the Parish', see also S. Hindle, *On the Parish? The Micropolitics of Poor Relief in Rural England, c.1550–1750* (Oxford, 2004).

insights to towns and to investigate the ways in which towns can be seen as 'communities'. The word can too easily suggest an idealized, harmonious state which may never have existed. Towns were tough, competitive places, in which life for many was hard. They did not welcome incomers—described as 'foreigners'—unless they had something advantageous to offer to the town: contrast the hostile reception given to destitute Huguenot refugees in Norwich and Bristol in the 1680s with Norwich's calculated targeting of skilled Flemish clothworkers under Elizabeth.[46] Yet the profound inequalities and frequent conflict in early modern towns did not mean that they could not function as communities, nor that talk of 'community' was empty rhetoric. A 'community' possessed institutional forms, a sense of geographical place and of membership (through either inclusion or exclusion), a rhetoric of community (or civic identity), and a range of actions or artefacts through which to express that rhetoric.[47] One mark of the viability of a community was the extent to which it could contain and resolve conflict.

The viability of a town as a 'community' had less to do with formal structures of representation than with the content of urban government. Most town constitutions were profoundly undemocratic, with existing members of the corporation filling vacancies by co-option, but often this seems to have occasioned little complaint.[48] It may well be that participation in the lower levels of government enabled townsmen to achieve what they wanted without needing political representation.[49] Oligarchy reflected the realities of urban government: office was more a burden, or duty, than something actively sought, and the pool of potential corporation members was limited to wealthy businessmen, who could afford to devote time (and sometimes money) to the town's affairs.[50] Such men could usually be relied upon to promote the town's economic interests. Thus the worsted weavers on Norwich corporation

---

[46] J. Miller, 'Town Governments and Protestant Strangers, 1560–1690', *Proceedings of the Huguenot Society*, xxvi (1997), 578–80, 585–6; J. Miller, 'The Fortunes of the Strangers in Norwich and Canterbury 1565–1700', in B. Van Ruymbeke and R. J. Sparks (eds.), *Memory and Identity: The Huguenots in France and the Atlantic Diaspora* (Columbia, SC, 2003), 112–14. For the hostile reception in the 1680s, see BRO, JQS/M/5, fo. 10, JQS/M.6, fos. 259, 257, 255; *CSPD Jan.–June 1683*, 363.

[47] P. Withington and A. Shephard, 'Introduction', in Shephard and Withington (eds.), *Communities in Early Modern England*, 2–12.

[48] There was more likely to be argument about the franchise for parliamentary elections, but this was often instigated by defeated candidates petitioning against the return of their opponents.

[49] In this context, see V. Pearl, 'Change and Stability in Seventeenth-Century London', in Barry (ed.), *Tudor and Stuart Town*, 152–65.

[50] See below, Ch. 2.

were active in defending the city's textile industry, while the merchants of Great Yarmouth accepted that their prime responsibility was to ensure that the harbour did not silt up. Similarly, corporation members paid the poor rate and, like other ratepayers, wished to keep payments as low as possible, and drive out incomers who might become a burden. Senior corporation members who served as magistrates were concerned to maintain order and protect property, and to discipline the poor, by punishing the 'loose, idle, and disorderly', or those who invited the wrath of God by failing to keep the sabbath holy. In this, they could be confident of the backing of the 'better sort', defined in both moral and economic terms. The values of the 'respectable' majority were upheld and reinforced by the punishment of the marginal and deviant.[51]

Urban rulers lived close to their fellow townsmen and came across them continually in their daily lives. The means of coercion at their disposal were flimsy; they could keep order only with the help of townsmen, as parish officers or in the watch and the militia. Even if the corporation did not formally consult the townsmen, it might do so informally. Civic rulers tried to emphasize their dignity and authority through civic ritual, ceremony, and celebration, but such occasions were sometimes appropriated for partisan purposes.[52] Unity of values and of purpose within the town could create a solidarity that proved stronger than the forces of political or religious discord, although most towns succumbed to such corrosive forces at times during this period. But at other times, religious differences proved less powerful than ties of neighbourliness, as more people came to accept religious pluralism and treat belief as a personal matter (even if they would not wish their child to marry a Catholic or a Quaker). From the point of view of magistrates in Hull or Norwich, religious persecution was disruptive of order and business. Similarly, many town magistrates and citizens were reluctant to allow political divisions to disrupt their lives; conflicts were often triggered by outside intervention, especially in parliamentary elections.[53] When such intervention occurred, towns which had earlier contained or avoided division became polarized; neighbours and friends exchanged insults and blows and civic celebrations became expressions not of unity but of hatred.[54] Perhaps the most bitter partisan conflicts of this period were seen in the 1710s, when at times the state met violence with violence. If

---

[51] See below, Ch. 3.   [52] See below, Ch. 4.

[53] Also in the early 1680s by attempts to persuade corporations to surrender their charters: see below, Ch. 8.

[54] See below, Chs. 12–13. A modern example of celebration designed to maintain divisions and to cause offence can be found in Orange marches in Northern Ireland.

clashes became less frequent thereafter, this was because parliamentary elections became less frequent and the Whigs tightened their grip on many small boroughs. But although parliamentary politics became less dramatic, politics in many towns remained volatile, especially at election time. Political division had become an established feature of urban, and national, life.

1

The Nature of Towns

I. WHAT WAS A TOWN?

Seventeenth-century England was not highly urbanized. It has been estimated that in 1700 less than 20 per cent of the population lived in towns with more than 2,500 people—and half of those lived in London. The population of London's eastern suburbs in 1700 has been estimated as 91,000, substantially more than the two largest provincial towns, Norwich and Bristol, combined.[1] Yet towns were very numerous—contemporaries put the number at almost 800.[2] The majority were small market towns, which dealt mainly in local produce. What distinguished them from villages were a concentration of population and a specialist economic function, in this case a market, and perhaps a fair. In most small towns marketing was more significant than manufacturing, as many industries were located in the countryside.[3] Larger towns had a more complex social structure, a political order more elaborate than those of parish and manor, and an influence on the surrounding area. The larger the town, the more complex its social and political structures were likely to be, and the wider its influence.[4] Any attempt to categorize towns is fraught with pitfalls, not least because towns' fortunes changed over time. At the bottom of the scale were simple market towns, with populations as low as 600. These were much the most numerous. In the second rank were towns with a wider impact and larger population, some of them county towns. These would have a rather more extensive marketing and distribution role, a greater range of trades and

---

[1] P. Corfield, *The Impact of English Towns, 1700–1800* (Oxford, 1982), 2; M. J. Power, 'East London Housing in the Seventeenth Century', in Clark and Slack (eds.), *Crisis and Order in English Towns*, 237.

[2] McInnes, *English Town*, 2 n.   [3] Barry (ed.), *Tudor and Stuart Town*, 9.

[4] Clark and Slack, *English Towns in Transition*, 4–6; McInnes, *English Town*, 10–11. For the increasing diversity of goods, services, and cultural and leisure facilities in county towns, see A. Everitt, 'Country, County and Town: Patterns of Regional Evolution in England', in P. Borsay (ed.), *The Eighteenth-Century Town, 1688–1820: A Reader* (Harlow, 1990), 97–111.

shops, possibly significant manufactures, or a port. At the top were towns with a regional influence, such as Norwich, Bristol, York, Exeter, and Newcastle, all with populations of over 10,000 by 1700.[5] These were all long established, but in the later seventeenth century, new towns came to the fore. These included manufacturing centres, like Manchester and Birmingham, naval dockyard towns like Plymouth and Portsmouth, and leisure towns, notably Bath. At the same time, many older towns grew, extended their traditional functions, and developed new ones.

In general, towns fared much better after the Restoration than in the century before the civil war, when rural unemployment drove people off the land into already overcrowded towns. The Tudor textile industry produced a limited range of cloth, geared to northern Europe; the industry lagged behind that of the Low Countries in terms of product range and finishing. Although the cloth industry of many towns was declining, a few turned the religious wars on the continent to their advantage. Norwich revitalized its cloth industry by attracting several thousand clothworkers from the war-torn southern Netherlands, who brought new skills and a reputation for high standards of workmanship. The corporation handed over responsibility for quality control to the newcomers, and so secured for Norwich cloth a reputation for good workmanship; the Dutch Bay Hall helped create a similar reputation for Colchester.[6] But at the same time Norwich expelled many poor people from the surrounding countryside who did not have the marketable skills of the 'strangers'.[7] In general, however, the story was one of stagnation, or decline, and a growing poverty problem, exacerbated by poor harvests and outbreaks of plague.

By contrast, as we have seen, the century after 1660 was one of growth, in terms of overseas trade, manufactures, and consumption at home. Food prices fell. The government had earlier tried to keep food prices down, by regulating the markets; now Parliament (which consisted mostly of landowners) tried to keep them up, by paying bounties on exports and banning imports until the

[5] E. A. Wrigley, 'Urban Growth and Agricultural Change: England and the Continent in the Early Modern Period', in Borsay (ed.), *Eighteenth-Century Town*, 42–3; McInnes, *English Town*, 6. Wrigley's figures for 1700 have been used by Paul Slack in *CUHB*, ii. 352. For another set of figures compiled by J. Langton, some of which are very different, see *CUHB*, ii. 473–4. My hierarchy of towns is based on Clark and Slack, *English Towns in Transition*, 8–11.

[6] Defoe, *Tour*, i. 132.

[7] J. Miller, 'Town Governments and Protestant Strangers, 1560–1690', *Proceedings of the Huguenot Society*, xxvi (1997), 577–89.

price of grain rose above a certain level.[8] People had more money to spend, and spent it on consumer goods of all kinds. Consumers became more demanding; entrepreneurs and wholesalers worked hard to give them what they wanted, and to influence their choices. England remained a country of small producers, working in small workshops or the home. But more and more now worked to the specifications of entrepreneurs, producing for customers who were conscious of new fashions, from Europe and beyond. Already in 1698, the intrepid traveller Celia Fiennes visited Newcastle-under-Lyme, hoping to see the making of 'fine teapots, cups and saucers . . . in imitation and as curious as that which comes from China'.[9] Traditionally, most shopkeepers had combined manufacture and retail, making goods in the back room and selling them from a board in the front window. Some types of shop had always drawn goods from many sources, such as drapers, grocers, or booksellers. Now there were far more specialized shops, with glass windows for display and assistants (and mirrors) to help the customers. The new types of shop, and the demand for a wider range of consumer goods, foods, and leisure services, spread from London to the larger provincial towns.[10] The range of shops, and the variety of trades, increased, as periwig makers and clockmakers appeared alongside tailors and shoemakers.

The growing diversity of retail and leisure facilities formed part of what Peter Borsay dubbed the 'English urban renaissance'. It had its origins in London, where more and more of the landed elite spent part of the year, on business, attending Parliament (which met for several months each year from 1689), but also socializing, seeking marriage partners for their children, and enjoying themselves. Shops and other facilities (theatres, pleasure gardens, clubs) were developed to cater for this growing body of affluent customers (and affluent Londoners); many of them came to expect to find similar facilities in their local provincial centres. They also came to expect a different urban environment. The West End of London contained, alongside quite narrow streets in areas like Soho, elegant squares, built round gardens; these served as a model for provincial developments, like Queen Square in Bristol. The new developments of the West End generally followed building regulations laid down in the City after the Fire. These included a minimum width for streets, an insistence

---

[8] R. B. Outhwaite, 'Dearth and Government Intervention in English Grain Markets, 1590–1700', *Economic History Review*, 2nd series, xxxiii (1981), 389–406.

[9] Fiennes, 177.

[10] For the range of foods available in Shrewsbury, see McInnes, 'Leisure Town', 65, 79–80. For shops, see McInnes, *English Town*, 12–13.

on using brick, stone, and tile (instead of wood), and a stipulation that the fronts of building should be flat, without the jetties (upper floors jutting over the street) common in Tudor towns.[11] There was also a growing concern for style—for large, symmetrically arranged sash windows, and central front doors in ornamental surrounds. These new styles could be imposed on new developments (or by great landowners, like Lord Brooke at Warwick). More often, they spread by emulation, as individual houses were rebuilt, or re-fronted, according to the latest fashions.[12] In many towns there was neither the space nor the demand for new development. Some of the earliest squares were in rapidly growing towns, such as Birmingham or Liverpool, but even in overcrowded Bristol, space could be found if the demand was there, either by building up the ground on a site formerly subject to flooding (Queen Square) or building on hitherto undeveloped land (St James's Square). Meanwhile, many corporations provided leisure space for visitors, laying down gravel walks and planting trees, for shade. Enterprising businessmen, especially innkeepers, provided entertainments, including stage plays, balls, and concerts. Purpose-built facilities— assembly rooms, concert halls, theatres—appeared rather later.[13] There was a growing appreciation of the aesthetics of urban life and pride in both civic buildings and domestic architecture.

The 'urban renaissance' reached its zenith between the 1720s and the 1760s; this was the time that John Wood the elder established a model of polite and genteel urban living at Bath. But there are many signs of such developments during the period covered by this book, and occasionally earlier. Towns with a substantial marketing role, or which were the venues for county business, had long appreciated the benefits of attracting affluent custom: indeed, towns lobbied to secure meetings of the assizes and quarter sessions at the expense of their rivals. Chester, Durham, Winchester, and Leicester had established race-meetings (which attracted wealthy custom) well before 1640.[14] The competition to host county meetings reminds us that there were losers as well as winners. Small market centres lost out to larger ones, as did those which were not located on major roads and rivers, or lacked a significant hinterland:

---

[11] E. L. Jones and M. E. Falkus, 'Urban Improvement and the English Economy in the Seventeenth and Eighteenth Centuries', in Borsay (ed.), *Eighteenth-Century Town*, 123–7.

[12] McInnes, 'Leisure Town', 74–5, 78–9.

[13] Borsay, *Urban Renaissance, passim.* The dates of the building of squares, theatres, assembly rooms etc. can be found in Borsay's appendices, from p. 321. See also P. Corfield, 'From Second City to Regional Capital', in *Norwich since 1550*, 151; J. Ellis, *The Georgian Town, 1680–1840* (Basingstoke, 2001), 22–4, 100.

[14] Borsay, *Urban Renaissance*, 356–67.

Lincoln, for example.[15] Some towns continued a long-term decline. At Sandwich and Rye, the harbours had silted up: Fiennes found Sandwich 'a sad old town', in which most buildings appeared about to fall down.[16] The new spa towns were at the mercy of fashion. Tunbridge Wells did not exist in 1600; by 1700 it was a significant town, with a church, numerous shops in an attractive pedestrian area, the Pantiles, shady walks, a market, and a wide range of leisure facilities. Instead of a corporation, it was run by 'the company', an assembly of those who came to drink the waters, and it was by any standards a successful town. Defoe thought that it lacked nothing that could make a man or woman completely happy. But other spas, such as Wellingborough, enjoyed a brief vogue and then fell out of favour.[17] Some towns stood little chance of attracting a fashionable clientele, or were not interested. Portsmouth, as a dockyard town, had little to offer the fashionable visitor, and some Bristolians claimed that theirs was a working city and did not need to pander to the nobility and gentry. This did not, however, prevent some citizens from trying to compete with Bath, by developing the Hotwell.[18]

In this book, I have chosen to focus (with varying degrees of detail) on seven towns; all have good and some have excellent records. They offer a variety of urban types and a significant geographical spread, although four are in the south of England and only one in the north. They include the largest provincial towns: Norwich, a manufacturing centre, and Bristol, a major port. Both were cathedral cities, as were Winchester and Oxford; the former depended on attracting the gentry, while the latter was above all a university city, attracting many wealthy young men and their parents, although it also had a significant marketing and trading role. Portsmouth was one of the emergent 'dockyard towns'—Chatham and Plymouth were others. It was also a garrison town, as was Hull, although its traditional economic role was as a port. Situated in 'a corner of the world, surrounded by water, and no use' (as one gentleman from York put it), Hull did not attract much aristocratic custom and did not need to; its trade prospered.[19] Leicester owed its revival in this period mainly to manufacturing; it would have liked more aristocratic custom than it could

[15] Ibid. 20–1, 23; Defoe, *Tour*, ii. 91–4.

[16] Fiennes, 129. For the decline of Grimsby, see A. Delapryme, *Diary*, ed. C. Jackson (Surtees Society, 1870), 153–5.

[17] P. Hembry, *The English Spa, 1560–1815* (London, 1990), chs. 5–6 and *passim*; Defoe, *Tour*, i. 126–8; Fiennes, 131–3. For Epsom, see Defoe, *Tour*, i. 159–62.

[18] *Flying Post*, 26–8 Dec. 1704; V. Waite, 'The Bristol Hotwell', in P. McGrath (ed.), *Bristol in the Eighteenth Century* (Newton Abbot, 1972), 112–21.

[19] WYAL, MX/R, 18/124.

attract. Norwich was not only a textile centre; it had a long-established role in marketing and distribution, and was a venue for county business and aristocratic social life. Thus my seven chosen towns had a variety of economic roles and their rulers and inhabitants interacted with a variety of other groups inside and outside their boundaries—cathedral clergy, one of the two universities, garrisons, and the county landed elite.[20] I would not claim that they were 'typical': all were corporate and larger than the great majority of towns. But large corporate towns generated the fullest records, making it possible to examine their government and politics in depth.[21] In the remainder of this chapter, I shall attempt to sketch the character of four of the seven—Norwich, Bristol, Leicester, and Hull.

II. SCENES FROM URBAN LIFE

In 1660 Norwich was England's second city, with a population of some 21,000, rising to about 30,000 by 1700.[22] The great majority lived within the ancient city walls, largely intact, which surrounded the city on three sides, with the river Wensum on the fourth.[23] Together the walls and river were estimated to be 3 miles long and enclosed a substantial area. Whereas Bristol and Hull were hemmed in and congested, at Norwich there were pastures, trees, and gardens within the walls (not to mention the cathedral close), and ample room for expansion.[24] There were many flower gardens, thanks perhaps to the 'strangers' from the Low Countries, who liked growing tulips; there were florists' feasts as early as the 1630s.[25] Because there was so much space within the walls, Norwich did not develop substantial suburbs, although the 'county' of the city included several hamlets outside the walls, covering an area a little larger than the present conurbation.[26]

---

[20] See below, Ch. 5.

[21] I have been able to write substantial accounts of the politics of Norwich and Bristol under Charles II: see Miller, 'Containing Division'; below, Ch. 9.

[22] J. F. Pound, *Tudor and Stuart Norwich* (Chichester, 1988), 28–30; Wrigley, 'Urban Growth', 42. However, Langton puts Norwich's population in the later seventeenth century at a little over 14,000: *CUHB*, ii. 473.

[23] Fiennes, 147.

[24] Defoe, *Tour*, i. 63; C. Barringer, 'The Changing Face of Norwich', in *Norwich since 1550*, 5–17.

[25] J. Evelyn, *Diary*, ed. E. S. de Beer, 6 vols. (Oxford, 1955), iii. 594–5; P. Clark, *British Clubs and Societies, 1580–1800* (Oxford, 2000), 48–9.

[26] See the map in W. Hudson and J. C. Tingey, *Records of the City of Norwich*, 2 vols. (Norwich, 1906–10), facing i. 46.

Visitors to the city commented on the many churches—in the late seventeenth century there were thirty-four parishes[27]—and the markets. Celia Fiennes visited the hay, hog, and fish markets, the separate shambles for the town and country butchers, and the main market square. Here was the market cross and hall, where one could buy fruit and 'little things', and a covered area under pillars, the corn market, with scales and measures chained to the pillars. The market was always busy, especially on Saturdays, and the market place (which also contained the guildhall) was the centre of the city. It contained several leading inns and was the normal venue for public whippings and medicine shows. Its importance as a centre for leisure and entertainment was highlighted by 'the gentlemen's walk or walking place', which was kept free of stalls.[28]

As well as a marketing and distribution centre, Norwich was the county capital. The summer assizes for Norfolk and some meetings of quarter sessions were held there. These attracted large numbers of the county gentry, and their wives and daughters, as did major civic occasions (notably guild day, on which the new mayor was sworn) and the period around Christmas. The gentry came to Norwich to socialize, to see and be seen, and to shop. They also came to consult doctors and lawyers and to exchange news and gossip.[29] The cathedral, its clergy, and its courts added to the social mix and the pull of business, drawing in tenants of ecclesiastical lands, litigants, and gentry families who wished their sons to study at the cathedral school.[30]

The influence of Norwich's cloth industry spread into the countryside. In the 1720s Defoe claimed that 120,000 people depended on woollen and silk manufacture, probably a substantial exaggeration.[31] In the early eighteenth century the industry went through a major crisis, faced with competition from cheap calicoes and other textiles from India. A petition of 1713 claimed that only one master weaver in eight had any apprentices and most of those had only one. Demand had fallen to a level where it was impossible to employ even half the available workmen. In 1721 an Act of Parliament banned the wearing

---

[27] See Hudson and Tingey, *Records*, facing i. 130.

[28] Fiennes, 147–8; *HMC Portland*, ii. 269–70; Corfield in *Norwich since 1550*, 152–3.

[29] At Launceston, a decayed town, the assizes, quarter sessions, and county elections provided a major part of the town's income; it had no manufactures but many attorneys: Defoe, *Tour*, i. 257–8.

[30] The cathedral played an even more significant role at Winchester: A. Rosen, 'Winchester in Transition, 1580–1700', in P. Clark (ed.), *Country Towns in Pre-industrial England* (Leicester, 1981), 172–3, 177–9.

[31] Defoe, *Tour*, i. 61–3; P. Corfield, 'A Provincial Capital in the Late Seventeenth Century: The Case of Norwich', in Clark and Slack (eds.), *Crisis and Order in English Towns*, 279; Corfield in *Norwich since 1550*, 147–8.

of such textiles. The Norwich cloth industry revived and went from strength to strength.[32] However, prosperity was not broadly spread. The hearth tax returns of the 1670s show that 59 per cent of households in Norwich were exempt from paying, on the grounds of poverty, as against 21 per cent in Bristol and 27 per cent in supposedly impoverished Leicester. Similarly, of those who were required to pay, 52 per cent were assessed on only one hearth as against 20 per cent at Bristol (and 11 per cent at Ipswich).[33] The people of Norwich had to work hard for their living. There was always a substantial poverty problem and any fall in the demand for Norwich cloth, due to war or foreign competition, had serious economic and social consequences.

Norwich's corporation was keen to attract wealthy outsiders to the city, but disapproved of entertainments that might corrupt public morals, distract people from their work, or encourage them to spend more than they could afford.[34] As a result, the development of leisure facilities in the city was largely a matter of private enterprise, as the proprietors of inns, taverns, or coffee houses sought to enhance their profits. Some activities of which the corporation disapproved, particularly if they involved gambling, took place outside the city. At Catton, the nearest village outside the city's jurisdiction, three alehouses advertised cockfights.[35] Men were also invited to wrestle for a prize, with spectators able to bet on the outcome.[36] By 1709 Norwich had a 'new' 4-mile racecourse, although it may have taken a while to establish regular meetings.[37] 'Gamesters' were also invited to play at ten pins in a number of villages, but also at venues within Norwich, including the Tailors' Arms in St Andrew's and the Man in the Moon in St Mary's.[38]

Not all leisure activities involved gambling. Sports popular among young men included football, regarded by the respectable as an excuse for a brawl, and its local variant, camping, which was even more violent.[39] For the less energetic,

[32] Defoe, *Tour*, i. 62–3; BL, Add MS 61649, fos. 202–3; F. Blomefield, *An Essay towards a Topographical History of Norfolk*, 11 vols. (London, 1805–10), iii. 347; MCB 28, fo. 3. The ban came into effect at the end of 1722.

[33] Pound, *Tudor and Stuart Norwich*, 42. Slack gives the same figures for exemptions, but gives the percentage of those assessed on either one or two hearths: *CUHB*, ii. 360.

[34] See below, Ch. 3.

[35] *Norwich Gazette*, 13–20 Mar., 10–17 Apr., 1–8 May, 17–24 Dec. 1709, 30 Dec. 1710–6 Jan. 1711, 15–22 Mar., 17–24 May 1712.

[36] Ibid. 16–23 Oct. 1708, 26 Apr.–3 May, 10–17, 17–24 May, 31 May–7 June, 14–21 June 1712.

[37] Ibid. 22–9 Oct. 1709, 8–15 July 1710.

[38] Ibid. 27 Aug.–3 Sept. 1708, 8–15 July 1710, 26 Apr.–3 May 1712. The word 'gamesters' was used of a meeting for ten pins at Lyng, ibid. 15–22 Mar. 1712.

[39] Ibid. 23–30 Oct., 27 Nov.–4 Dec. 1708; R. W. Ketton-Cremer, 'Camping, a Forgotten Norfolk Game', *Norf Arch* xxiv (1932), 88–92; for a reference to camping from 1671, see MCB 24, fo. 171.

clubs and societies abounded. The florists' feast continued to flourish.[40] A society of bell ringers was established in 1716, although bell-ringing competitions had been advertised some years earlier.[41] In the 1730s the city boasted 'very many' clubs, including several musical societies.[42] For a while, from 1700, the city also had its own Exchange, in imitation of the Royal Exchange in London. It was to be open from 11 a.m. to 1 p.m. each weekday, 'for all such as would, to meet freely and consult about their public affairs'.[43] In 1703 the assembly voted to close it; it was later alleged that it did so much damage to the traders of the city that 800 had petitioned to have it suppressed.[44] Other centres of conviviality were inns, taverns, alehouses, and coffee houses; Norwich boasted as many as three newspapers, the first appearing in 1701. Not much of the news which appeared was local—most was taken from London newsletters and newspapers—but the advertisements were of local interest.[45]

The development of open spaces and walks (with the exception of the 'gentlemen's walk' in the market place) depended on the generosity of individuals. The sixth duke of Norfolk was renowned for his hospitality. Visitors to his garden, with its bowling green and fair walks, were made welcome and regaled with good liquors and fruit. In assize week gentlemen and ladies paraded there. Even after the dukes had left the city, the gardens were preserved for the pleasure of the citizens and the bowling green was open to the public.[46] The other major centre of hospitality was Chapel Field House, which had extensive grounds. Its owners, the Hobarts of Blickling, leased it out, but retained the use of it for a few days each year. The gardens became a popular walking place and balls were sometimes held there in assize week.[47] By 1720 it was a venue for private assemblies and masquerades, with admission by invitation or ticket.[48]

[40] *Norwich Gazette*, 21–8 June 1707.

[41] Clark, *Clubs and Societies*, 76; *Norwich Gazette*, 8–15 Mar. 1712.

[42] NRO, MS 79, pp. 218–20.

[43] MCB 26, fo. 95; NRO, MS 453, 'A Description', under 25 Nov. 1700.

[44] Blomefield, *Norfolk*, iii. 431; FAB 8, fo. 255; NCR, Case 8h/1, 'Observations on the Charters' and draft of same.

[45] M. Knights, 'Politics 1660–1835' and A. Dain, 'An Enlightened Society', in *Norwich since 1550*, 178, 194–5. Unfortunately the only complete run of Henry Crossgrove's *Norwich Gazette* was destroyed in a fire at the Central Library in the 1990s. However, a microfilm of the issues from 1706 to 1712 had been made before the fire and this has been used here.

[46] *HMC Portland*, ii. 270; Sir T. Browne, *Works*, ed. G. Keynes, 4 vols. (London, 1964), iv. 156; Defoe, *Tour*, i. 63; *Norwich Gazette*, 6–13 Mar. 1708, 26 Mar.–2 Apr. 1709.

[47] B. Cozens-Hardy, 'The Norwich Chapel Field House Estate since 1545', *Norf Arch* xxvii (1941), 377–8; R. W. Ketton-Cremer, 'Assize Week in Norwich in 1688', *Norf Arch* xxiv (1932), 15–16.

[48] C. W. Branford, 'Powers of Association: Aspects of Elite Social, Political and Cultural Life in Norwich, 1680–1760', Ph.D. thesis (University of East Anglia, 1994), 101–3.

No public assembly rooms were built in the city until 1754, but in the 1730s there were assemblies, with dancing, drinking, and gaming in assize and sessions weeks. The ladies organized raffles and attended concerts or plays, then went on to 'the assembly', where they might stay until 4 or 5 a.m. A group of gentlemen and wealthy tradesmen, and their wives and daughters, formed a 'Friendly Society', which met monthly (for members only) in Chapel Field House.[49]

The corporation's main contribution to entertainment (apart from civic ceremony) was employing the waits. These were expected, in return for their salaries, to accompany the mayor and aldermen on civic occasions. They alone were allowed to charge money for playing music in public, and at gatherings such as weddings, but their activities were circumscribed—to play at the market cross they needed the mayor's express permission.[50] The mayor's court supported them when they complained that unauthorized musicians infringed their monopoly.[51] Their rivals soon reappeared and were given permission to perform during guild week, sessions week, assize week, or during parliamentary elections, but they played at other times as well.[52] In 1714 the waits became one of the city companies, with its own by-laws, and were instructed to hold monthly meetings for music lovers.[53]

Although they were servants of the corporation, the waits were a private enterprise. (One of the waits at Leicester claimed that he made up for his inadequate salary from the corporation by playing in other towns, where people were more generous.[54]) Similarly the city library, although housed in the New Hall, owed more to the city clergy than to the corporation. It contained mainly works of divinity and history and the clergy seem to have been the main users. It became a circulating library, by subscription, in the 1730s.[55] The corporation also made only a limited contribution to the built environment. It was too poor to contemplate ambitious civic building. The castle was 'ancient and decayed', the guildhall had last been refurbished in the 1530s, and the New Hall was the church of the former Blackfriars convent, granted to the city at the Reformation. The hall was still 'magnificent' in 1783, but the steeple fell down, through neglect, in 1712.[56] The adjacent St Andrew's

---

[49] NRO, MS 79, pp. 219–20.   [50] MCB 23, fo. 192, MCB 25, fos. 76, 134.
[51] MCB 24, fos. 214, 223, 224, 337, 338; NCR, Case 20a/15, 15 Jan. 1675.
[52] MCB 25, fos. 33, 139, 162.   [53] FAB 9, fos. 48, 49.
[54] LHP 34, nos. 29, 50, 56, 57, LHP 35, nos. 5, 7, 127; *RBL*, iv. 541.
[55] MCB 25, fo. 84, MCB 26, fo. 237*, MCB 27, fo. 218; NRO, MS 79, p. 215.
[56] Defoe, *Tour*, i. 63; NRO, MS 79, p. 142; C. Parkin, *History and Antiquities of the City of Norwich* (Norwich, 1783), 261–2; NRO, MS 79, p. 236.

Hall, used for the guild day feast, was a former church. It was surrounded by a number of rooms used for civic purposes.[57] The market cross was octagonal, built of freestone and flint, but its pillars were wooden and allegedly decayed, and it was demolished as dangerous in 1732.[58]

Unable to change their civic buildings, the city fathers embellished civic rooms with new portraits and coats of arms.[59] In 1701 the mayor's court considered how to make the city plate more 'fashionable'.[60] Norwich's citizens seemed far from eager to embrace new building fashions. The corporation showed little interest in building regulations, except to prohibit roofing with thatch.[61] Visitors acknowledged that the main streets were broad and well made and that many houses, especially around the market square, were tall and handsome. But most were made of traditional, local building materials (flint or lath and plaster) and Fiennes found the city's architecture old-fashioned.[62] In the city's fashionable centre, the dense streets around the market, there was little scope for new development. But if, in Fiennes's eyes, Norwich lagged behind in architectural fashion, and lacked the variety of entertainments available in London, Bath, or York, its citizens believed they enjoyed a good quality of life.[63]

Bristol was essentially a port, with manufacturing of secondary significance. Its role as an administrative centre was limited: situated partly in Gloucestershire and partly in Somerset, it was county capital of neither. Its bishop and cathedral were relatively impoverished and played a limited part in civic life. Traditionally Bristol traded primarily with western France, Spain, and Portugal, importing wine, sherry, and port. Selecting the right wines required knowledge and experience, and the Company of Merchant Venturers claimed a monopoly of overseas trade, arguing that only trained, specialist merchants could trade successfully. With the opening of the American and Atlantic trades, however, many smaller operators moved in, including shopkeepers with a part share in a ship. It took less skill to select sugar or tobacco than to evaluate sherry, and plantation owners sold to all comers. Bristol also had extensive seaborne and

[57] Parkin, *History of Norwich*, 264–5.
[58] NRO, MS 79, fos. 138–40. See *Norwich since 1550*, facing 194.
[59] MCB 25, fos. 153, 165–6, MCB 26, fo. 19, MCB 28, fo. 16; Parkin, *History of Norwich*, 265.
[60] MCB 26, fos. 109–10. In 1721 the mayor's court found that much of the city plate was useless and decayed: MCB 28, fo. 62.
[61] NRO, MS 79, p. 143; MCB 24, fos. 198, 212, 363.
[62] NRO, MS 79, p. 143; Fiennes, 148.
[63] NRO, MS 79, pp. 218–20; Corfield, in *Norwich since 1550*, 148–50.

coastal trade with Wales and Ireland and distributed goods of all kinds up the
Severn valley, and to many parts of southern England.[64] The port, on the rivers
Avon and Frome, was well protected from the storms in the Severn estuary,
but had to contend with tides which rose and fell 40 feet; piloting ships in and
out of the port was a complex and delicate skill.

Bristol was a bustling city, with a population of 20,000 in the late seventeenth century.[65] Visitors commented on its crowded streets, unlike at
Norwich, where, on weekdays, most people were indoors at their looms.
Whereas in Norwich there was room to expand within the walls, Bristol had
long since grown beyond them; Defoe remarked that there was 'hardly room to
set another house' in the city.[66] It was full of goods; space was at a premium.
The quays were stacked with building materials, as well as anchors. The Marsh,
even after the building of Queen Square, was a dumping ground for timber,
stone, millstones, and great guns. Timber was even dumped in the walks.[67]
Carts and building materials were kept in the streets, which were also full of
casks and piles of dung, coal, and ashes; Bristolians kept coal outside their front
doors. The streets, as in many towns, were continually pounded by overloaded
carts, many with iron-bound wheels.[68] Timber was supposed to be hauled on
sledges, to reduce the wear and tear on the roads, but often it was not.[69] Heavy
traffic also damaged the 'gouts' (or sewers), some of which ran beneath the
streets. The city's sewerage system was always overloaded. Gouts and 'low
ditches' became blocked; and sewage and storm water built up and stagnated,
or flowed from houses into the streets above ground. As in most towns, many
people kept pigs, adding to the general stench. To add to the hazards of
negotiating the streets, especially at night, they were ill lit (if they were lit at
all, which they were not in summer, or after 9 p.m. in winter). Many houses
had cellars without proper doors or which were entered by stairs without rails.

[64] For Bristol's trade, see Defoe, *Tour*, ii. 36–7; D. H. Sacks, *The Widening Gate: Bristol and the Atlantic Economy, 1450–1700* (Berkeley, 1991); W. Minchinton, 'The Port of Bristol in the Eighteenth Century', in McGrath (ed.), *Bristol in the Eighteenth Century*, 135–46; P. McGrath, *The Merchant Venturers of Bristol* (Bristol, 1975). The Merchant Venturers were far from exclusive: they were prepared to admit anyone who would renounce trading retail and tried, but failed, to force all specialist merchants to become members: McGrath, *Venturers*, 44, 51.
[65] Wrigley, 'Urban Growth', 42–3; McInnes, *English Town*, 6. Langton puts the figure at less than 14,000: *CUHB*, ii. 473.
[66] Defoe, *Tour*, i. 63, ii. 37.
[67] BRO, JQS/C/1, 2nd pagination, pp. 22, 33.
[68] BRO, JQS/M/6, fo. 15. For iron-bound wheels, see JQS/C/1, pp. 42, 116. For keeping coal in the street, see Defoe, *Tour*, ii. 38.
[69] BRO, JQS/C/1, 2nd pagination, pp. 22–3, 27; 04264/9, p. 158; Defoe, *Tour*, ii. 38.

The street surfaces were pitted and uneven, slippery, and often steep. Houses encroached onto the streets and some were structurally unsafe. On the waterfront, apart from the timber, carts, and dirt littering the quays, they were often in serious disrepair.[70] There were frequent complaints about the wall and steps near the weir, which was very unsafe; several had allegedly drowned there.[71]

Responsibility for cleansing, repairing, and lighting the streets was divided between householders, parishes, and the corporation, none of which was prepared to invest time or money in keeping them in good repair. Bristolians were busy, competitive people, who dumped goods where they could, if they could get away with it. But if the corporation's record on routine maintenance was poor, it made more effort to improve the built environment. In 1690 a 'Tolzey'[72] (covered walk) was constructed in St Thomas Street and in 1709–10 the council contributed to levelling and beautifying College Green, in front of the cathedral. New trees replaced the old and pitched walks were laid down.[73] In 1701–4 the old mayor's Tolzey was pulled down and a new council house built in its place. Some of the freestone from the Tolzey was given to the parishioners of St Nicholas, to make a covered walk on the Back.[74] In 1710 a new and bigger custom house was built and in the next few years two new bridges were constructed. One was nicknamed 'Traitor's bridge', because one of its promoters, Nathaniel Wade, had been in arms with Monmouth in 1685. The other, promoted by the city, crossed the Frome from the quay to St Augustine's Back.[75]

But the most important new development was Queen Square. In 1663 the council ordered that trees should be planted in the Marsh and level walks laid out. The initial plans for development extended only to a street, in which plots were to be leased out 'and the buildings to be uniform'. When the council considered further development in 1670, it again insisted on 'the uniform building of houses'. It also decided to build a new stone quay, for the convenience of the residents.[76] In 1699 the vicar of St Nicholas and others sought permission

---

[70] BRO, JQS/C/1, 2nd pagination, p. 7. See also Latimer, ii. 3–4, 18.

[71] BRO, JQS/M/4, fos. 106–7; JQS/C/1, 2nd pagination, pp. 5, 9, 20, 58–9.

[72] There were two Tolzeys in Bristol. One, the mayor's, was used for civic (especially judicial) business, the other was a meeting place for merchants—a 'mean and narrow' structure next to All Saints' church. Both were roofed and on pillars and open at the sides, so it was possible to walk there. See Latimer, i. 55–6, 67, ii. 17; A. Foyle, *Bristol*, Pevsner Architectural Guides (New Haven, 2004), 14, 134; Millerd.

[73] BRO, 07831, under 1690, 1709–10, 04264/9, p. 197.

[74] BCL, B10166, 'A Record' and 3rd 'calendar', 1704; BRO, 04264/9, p. 51; Latimer, ii. 59–60; W. Ison, *The Georgian Buildings of Bristol* (Bath, 1978), 90–1.

[75] BRO, 04264/9, pp. 221, 322–3, 07831, 1711–12, May 1714; BCL, B4502, p. 132.

[76] BRO, 04264/6, pp. 78, 80, 203.

to build in the Marsh. The council insisted that the houses should meet certain specifications: façades were to be of brick and minimum heights were established for each storey, with sash windows, and cornices. No standard design was imposed, so styles varied, but this was still the city's first attempt at urban planning.[77] By 1706 the square was in a reasonably finished state. It still had to contend with those who continued to dump timber and rubbish, and dry cloth and linen on the grass and rails.[78] Some who acquired houses there used them for rope-making and stored pitch and tar. The council tried to persuade the owners to move elsewhere.[79] In 1710 the new Custom House was built in the Square, which now had a salaried keeper. More trees were planted, so that they now extended round three sides of the square, and more walks were laid down.[80] The inhabitants still complained of dirt dumped on vacant ground behind their houses, and the problem of waste disposal seemed intractable, but the example was attractive enough for a second square, St James's, to be constructed between 1707 and 1716.[81] With the Hotwell emerging as a leisure venue, Bristol was becoming attractive and fashionable, but it was still primarily a working city. Bristolians rose and went to bed early and there was limited entertainment in the evenings.[82] There were proposals to establish an Exchange, in place of the old merchants' Tolzey (which was old and too small); several towns, including Chester, Liverpool, and Exeter, already had exchanges in the 1690s.[83] The proposal came to nothing, despite an Act of Parliament to facilitate it in 1722: the Tolzey site was too small, with too many adjacent buildings, and no agreement could be reached on an alternative site. An Exchange was eventually opened in 1743.[84]

---

[77] BRO, 04264/8, fo. 180; Foyle, *Bristol*, 19, 161–2; Latimer, i. 490–1; Ison, *Georgian Buildings*, 141–9.

[78] BRO, 04264/9, pp. 195, 202, 251; Defoe, *Tour*, ii. 115–16.

[79] BRO, 04264/9, pp. 276, 291: for the ropeyard walk, see Fiennes, 238. The corporation had laid down that no property in the square was to be let to tradesmen, especially those practising noxious or dangerous trades: Ison, *Georgian Buildings*, 142. Clearly the prohibition had been ineffectual.

[80] BRO, 04264/9, pp. 221–2, 254, 262, 276, 277; BRO, 07831, 1710–11.

[81] BRO, 04262/9, p. 623, 07831, 1715–16; BCL, B10154, 1716. Ison, *Georgian Buildings*, 149–52.

[82] BRO, 07831, 1697, 04264/9, p. 349; Latimer, i. 471–2, ii. 26; Waite, 'Bristol Hotwell', in McGrath (ed.), *Bristol in the Eighteenth Century*, 112–21; *Weekly Journal or Saturday's Post*, 4 Aug. 1722. The last offers an unflattering description of those attending the public room at the Hotwell, but leaves the reader in no doubt that they regarded themselves as fashionable.

[83] Fiennes, 178, 184, 247.

[84] BRO, 04264/9, pp. 445, 595, 600, 602, 607; Defoe, *Tour*, ii. 37, 115; Latimer, ii. 118–19, 246–7.

Leicester was substantially smaller than Norwich and Bristol, with a population of about 5,000 in the later seventeenth century.[85] Its economy traditionally depended heavily on marketing and distribution and, to a lesser extent, its role as county capital. It no longer had a resident noble family, and facilities for entertaining visiting dignitaries were limited.[86] Apart from the times when the gentry gathered for county business, its most obvious attraction was the horse-races, held since at least 1603. In around 1715 the Revd Samuel Carte bemoaned the lack of a stimulating intellectual life, the townspeople being preoccupied instead with faction and gossip.[87] It was a town of small shop-keepers and small craftsmen, and lacked an industrial base. It had suffered badly in the civil wars, being besieged and then sacked by the Royalists. In the late seventeenth century its fortunes changed, primarily as the result of the introduction of the knitting frame. Initially viewed with suspicion, the frames enabled the local hosiers to develop a stocking industry which, by the 1710s, was said to employ over 7,000 people. Even as its industrial role grew, it retained numerous rural features. Carte's map of 1722 shows that much of the area within the old walls consisted of orchards. The town fields extended over 2,800 acres, leased to townspeople in small parcels; the corporation voted in 1708 to enclose the South Fields and lease the land out in much larger units for higher rents, but abandoned the idea after stiff opposition. Many of the townspeople owned land further out. There was extensive employment in agriculture-related industries, such as butchery and dairying.[88] After a long period of poverty and decay, in the early eighteenth century there were signs of increased prosperity.

Some visitors to Leicester were unimpressed. In 1654 Evelyn described it as 'old and ragged', 'large and pleasantly seated, but despicably built', and very smoky. James Baskervile in 1675 conceded that it had once been handsome and had some fine churches, but described it as an old stinking town, on a dull river, inhabited mostly by tradesmen. When he visited, the corporation was attempting to clean the streets for the visit of the assizes judges, but the stench of stirred-up water and sewage made him feel sick.[89] In 1680 common

---

[85] Wrigley, 'Urban Growth', 42; McInnes, *English Town*, 6. It does not appear in Langton's list: *CUHB*, ii. 473–4.

[86] J. Simmons, *Leicester: The Ancient Borough to 1860* (Gloucester, 1974), 96.

[87] Ibid. 121; R. W. Greaves, *The Corporation of Leicester 1689–1835* (Leicester, 1970), 5.

[88] Bodl, Willis MS 85, fo. 49; RBL, v. 54–6; Simmons, *Leicester*, 71–3, 96–8, 112. The map is ibid. 108–9.

[89] Simmons, *Leicester*, 94; *HMC Portland*, ii. 308.

hall complained that walking the streets after dark was dangerous and that they needed to be improved, for the credit and convenience of the town. In 1698 it was reported that a gravel pit had been dug in Free School Lane so big that a horse and man could fall into it.[90] Although its record on street maintenance was poor, the corporation sought to improve the market, one of the keys to the town's growing prosperity. In 1713 the High Cross was cleaned and benches placed around it for people to sit on. In 1714–15 the corporation pulled down old shops and sheds in the Saturday market and built 'good' new rows of shops, with the ground in front properly paved. It laid down the dimensions of the shops and tenants promised to keep them in good repair, not to sublet, and not to set anything out in the street except what was on the shop 'windows'. Further new shops followed in 1716.[91] Other municipal initiatives included building a handsome new façade for the castle in 1698 (described not long before as a pitiful old fort) and a scheme of 1720 for building 'convenient small tenements' and houses on part of the town lands, at the town's expense, presumably to provide affordable housing for those working in the hosiery industry.[92] By the 1690s visitors' views of the town were more favourable. Delapryme noted numerous handsome buildings. Fiennes thought the market place large and handsome and liked the way 'ruined places' had been turned into gardens. Most houses were timber, but a few were brick and stone, and handsome.[93] Two decades later Carte wrote approvingly of 'fair' houses, the late medieval guildhall (not least its large kitchen) and the Gainsborough, where the mayor and aldermen met on market and fair days; it had a large balcony overlooking the market.[94] Carte was perhaps influenced by civic pride; Defoe had little to say about the town, other than the importance of its stocking industry.[95]

Hull was essentially a trading town; apart from shipbuilding and ship repairing, its manufactures were insignificant. Its main assets were the haven provided by the river Hull, where ships could anchor, protected from the savage tides of the Humber, and its geographical position: it had easy access to the Dutch Republic and the Baltic and excellent river links to Yorkshire and

---

[90] *RBL*, iv. 554, vii. 35.

[91] *RBL*, v. 65, 70, 73–4, 75, 77; LHB 4, fo. 124 (bis). In Oxford, the corporation was too poor to pay for enlarging the market place, so invited public subscriptions: *OCA*, iv. 59–60, 70–1, 80.

[92] Fiennes, 163; Delapryme, *Diary*, 34; Bodl, Willis MS 85, fo. 43; RBL, v. 88–9. For a similar proposal to build new houses in Oxford, see Wood, ii. 216–17. It is uncertain whether anything came of them.

[93] Delapryme, *Diary*, 34; Fiennes, 162–3.   [94] Bodl, Willis MS 85, fos. 45, 50–1.

[95] Defoe, *Tour*, ii. 88–90.

the East Midlands. During the War of the Spanish Succession, great fleets of over a hundred ships sailed from Hull to London, while the Dutch sent men of war to convoy Hull ships to and from Holland. Defoe thought more business was done in Hull than in any town of similar size in Europe. He added that Hull merchants were renowned not only for their wealth, but also for their fair dealing.[96]

Hull was still a fortified town, able to deny entrance to Charles I in 1642. To the south and east, it was protected by the Humber and the Hull and on the other sides there were two sets of fortifications, between which was a ditch with three drawbridges leading to three gates. There was also a ditch, spanned by drawbridges, outside the outer walls. The inner gatehouses had gates and portcullises and there were numerous guns on the gatehouses and walls.[97] Inevitably, the ditches were used as dumping places and sewers and could become very noisome.[98] The vast majority of the population—about 6,000 in 1700[99]—lived within the walls: Defoe found the town closely built and populous, with no room for expansion. The two major streets, the High Street and Lowgate, were relatively broad, but many side streets and lanes were narrow. There were signs of overcrowding, especially on market days; there were complaints in 1722 that there were so many carts and coaches in the market place that it was difficult to move.[100] Twenty years earlier, Celia Fiennes had found the buildings 'neat'. Defoe commented on the well-supplied market, the handsome Exchange (thronged with merchants), and above all Trinity House (which was to be rebuilt on an even grander scale in the 1750s).[101] The guildhall was much older, and had been extended rather than rebuilt in 1633. It was built on pillars with shops and a meeting place underneath. In 1679 the bench ordered that the façade should be beautified and a statue or picture of the king was to be set up. It was not demolished and replaced until 1813.[102] The old market cross, described by Delapryme as disgraceful, was replaced in 1682 by a 'magnificent' new cross, made of freestone, with a cupola on top, at a cost of £700.[103] The town spent heavily on its bridges. Those over the ditch at the gates needed

[96] Ibid. 242–3; E. Gillett and K. A. MacMahon, *A History of Hull* (Hull, 1980), 187–8. Defoe made a similar comment about the merchants of Great Yarmouth: *Tour*, i. 67–8.
[97] Fiennes, 88; *HMC Portland*, ii. 313.   [98] BRB 6, pp. 446, 694.
[99] Wrigley, 'Urban Growth', 42–3; McInnes, *English Town*, 6; *CUHB*, ii. 473.
[100] Defoe, *Tour*, ii. 244; BRB 6, p. 710.
[101] Fiennes, 88; Defoe, *Tour*, ii. 244. The Exchange had a clock by 1698: BRB 6, p. 435.
[102] Gillett and MacMahon, *Hull*, 108, 207; BRB 5, p. 622, BRB 6, pp. 178, 181.
[103] A. Delapryme, *A History of Kingston upon Hull* (Hull, 1986), 110; BL, Lansdowne MS 890, fos. 171–2.

occasional repairs, but the North Bridge, across the river Hull just north of the town, was a much larger structure. In 1676 the corporation, following a petition from ship-owners, resolved to rebuild it with two 'leaves', to allow ships to pass, but there were then complaints of inadequate passage for carts, horses, and cattle en route to market. A more substantial rebuilding in 1719–20 created a 'noble' stone bridge with fourteen arches, at a cost over £1,000.[104] Still more costly was the task of maintaining the fragile banks and the wharves and jetties along the river Hull, which suffered wear and tear from heavy use by ships and the fierce tides of the Humber. The building of the new citadel on the east side of the Hull in the 1680s added to the strains on the banks and there was a protracted dispute between the town and the crown as to who should maintain them; the town claimed in 1693 that it had spent over £2,000.[105]

How 'typical' were these towns? None was as dependent on the landed elite as Winchester or, in a different way, Oxford. However, few towns depended totally on their role as 'leisure towns'—Tunbridge Wells is the only obvious example—a role normally grafted on to those of marketing or distribution centres, county capitals, manufacturing towns, or ports.[106] Moreover, architectural improvement and the development of leisure facilities could occur without the landed elite; at Birmingham and Manchester most customers were wealthy townsmen; the same was probably true of Bristol—and later Hull.[107] Conversely, the gentry flocked to Bury St Edmunds, where the larger houses were mostly old, provisions were dear, and they made their own entertainment in assemblies.[108] That said, our four towns were relatively slow to show evidence of an 'urban renaissance'. On her tours in the 1690s, Fiennes picked out several towns as particularly fine. Nottingham was the neatest she had seen, with broad streets, fine stone houses, and a mile-long 'piazza'.[109] Newcastle, too, had broad streets and fine brick or stone houses, with a handsome Exchange. 'Their shops are good and of distinct trades, not selling many things in one shop as is the custom in most country towns and cities.' There were also pleasant walks and gardens. Newcastle was a major port, its economy dominated by the coal industry. It was extremely smoky, but the rich citizens did what they could

---

[104] BRB 5, pp. 465–6, 486, BRB 6, pp. 686, 693, 694; Defoe, *Tour*, ii. 245.
[105] BRB 6, p. 316.
[106] Borsay and McInnes, 'Debate', 192–4, 201.
[107] Borsay, 'Debate', 192; G. Jackson, *Hull in the Eighteenth Century* (Oxford, 1972), 262–73.
[108] Fiennes, 151–2; Defoe, *Tour*, i. 49–53; *HMC Portland*, ii. 265.
[109] Fiennes, 72. See also *HMC Portland*, ii. 308–9.

to make it an agreeable place to live.[110] Exeter was a major cloth-making and trading town, but Defoe found it full of gentry and good company. Fiennes found the streets broad; the Exchange, full of shops, reminded her of London; and she was impressed by the well-built houses and large market hall on stone pillars. She was also impressed by the walks and the quality of the water supply.[111] Other towns which won her approval were Durham and Shrewsbury, both county capitals in which gentry custom was important for the economy.[112] By contrast, she found Norwich's architecture old-fashioned and Bristol's streets narrow and dark, with jetties cutting out the light.[113] Neither she nor Defoe mentioned either city as attracting the gentry, although Norwich clearly did. Both were eventually to develop a range of leisure facilities; in Norwich, which had once enjoyed the patronage of the dukes of Norfolk, the money was raised by subscription—mainly from among the city's Tories.[114] Politics intruded even into the realm of leisure and pleasure.

[110] Fiennes, 209–12; Defoe, *Tour*, ii. 250–2. For shops at Bury St Edmunds, see *HMC Portland*, ii. 265.

[111] Defoe, *Tour*, i. 222.   [112] Fiennes, 213–16, 226–7; McInnes, 'Leisure Town', *passim.*

[113] Fiennes, 148, 237.   [114] Branford, 'Powers of Association', 59, 82–3, 104–5.

2

Rulers and Ruled

I. THE CORPORATION

Many towns derived the power to rule themselves from royal charters. A charter empowered the town to create a corporation, a body politic, which could hold courts, own and manage properties (including those belonging to charities), make and enforce by-laws, and impose local rates. The courts could hear a specified range of cases—in small towns, usually minor criminal offences, or civil actions involving property up to a certain value.[1] More serious cases were heard by the county quarter sessions or assizes, but some towns were 'counties' in themselves, had their own quarter sessions and (at least in theory) assizes, and were exempt from the jurisdiction of the county magistrates;[2] some also had their own militia, distinct from the county militia.[3] Most corporate towns had received several charters over the centuries; the polities these charters created were almost infinitely various. They had been issued on an ad hoc basis, in response to requests. Some very small towns had received charters. Queenborough, Kent, might be 'a miserable, dirty, decayed, poor,

---

[1] Halliday, *Body*, 37–9. For the difficulty of defining a corporation, see S. and B. Webb, *English Local Government: The Manor and the Borough*, 2 vols. (London, 1908), i. 262–70. For variations in jurisdiction, see ibid. 278–82, 288–9.

[2] Provincial towns which were counties in themselves in 1708 were York, Exeter, Canterbury, Coventry, Lincoln, Norwich, Bristol, Lichfield, Worcester, Poole, Hull, Newcastle, Nottingham, Southampton, and Haverfordwest: PC 2/81, p. 519. The larger towns held assizes once a year, as against twice in most counties. Hull held assizes approximately one year in two under Charles II but only one year in seven in the eighteenth century: *VCH East Riding*, i. 126; Jackson, *Hull*, 319. York's militia was commanded by the lord lieutenant of the West Riding: *VCH City of York*, 197. Southampton handed over the responsibility for gaol delivery and oyer and terminer to the circuit judges in 1725: A. T. Patterson, *A History of Southampton*, i.: *An Oligarchy in Decline*, Southampton Records Series xi (1966), 18.

[3] Hull was granted the right to have its own militia in 1661: BRB 4, pp. 342, 399; Marvell, ii. 18–20, 22. It soon ceased to function and in 1689 it was said that the town had not had any 'companies' for 'above twenty years past': *CSPD 1685*, no. 1451; BL, Egerton MS 3516, fo. 62. With a permanent garrison there must have seemed little point in having a militia as well.

pitiful fishing town', but it had a mayor and corporation and sent two members to Parliament.[4] Large towns which had not received a charter, such as Halifax and Manchester, were governed (like villages) by the officers of the parish, with the vestry fulfilling the role of the corporation.[5]

As populations and trade grew, towns requested more markets and fairs; inflation led to requests to increase the maximum value of cases that could be heard in their courts. In the middle ages, the crown had granted out many 'public' functions to private individuals or bodies. Under the Tudors the crown generally sought to weaken or abolish these 'liberties' or 'franchises', but in the case of towns new charters extended their authority. Many towns escaped from the tutelage of monasteries at the dissolution; some were able to purchase monastic land. New charters added to corporations' powers and responsibilities, while tending to concentrate power within the corporation in fewer people and make them less directly answerable to the townspeople.[6] The powers vested in civic rulers were designed to enable them to do the crown's bidding, and to maintain order. But those powers could also be used to resist, or negotiate with, royal authority. Enhanced power also fostered a stronger sense of corporate dignity and identity, which found expression in new town halls.[7] Not all was gain, however, from the towns' point of view. What the crown gave it could also take away. Charters enumerated the powers granted to corporations, but also laid down rules as to how they should use them—for example, setting out the quorum needed to make decisions, or the dates by which elections to office should take place. Infractions of the rules offered a pretext for a legal challenge against the charter; if it was declared forfeit, the king could either fail to issue a new charter, or grant a new one with more restricted powers, or allowing greater royal interference. Normally the monarch showed no inclination to take such measures, but it was always possible. Towns could never forget that their right to run their own affairs was, ultimately, dependent on the crown.

The structure of borough corporations varied considerably, as did the titles of their members. Many, like London, had two tiers—a court of aldermen and a common council. The aldermen dealt with day-to-day government; the

---

[4] Defoe, *Tour*, i. 110. See his similar comments on Sandwich and Saltash: ibid. i. 120, 231.

[5] Ibid. ii. 185–6, 197–200, 261. The same applied in the suburbs of London. In such communities there might also be a significant role for the county magistrates and (later) voluntary societies and statutory authorities: *CUHB*, ii. 532–7.

[6] R. Tittler, *The Reformation and the Towns in England, c.1540–1640* (Oxford, 1998), *passim*.

[7] P. Withington, 'Two Renaissances: Urban Political Culture in Post-Reformation England Reconsidered', *HJ* xliv (2001), 250–4; R. Tittler, *Architecture and Power: The Town Hall and the English Urban Community, c.1500–1640* (Oxford, 1991).

common council passed by-laws and voted rates. Many common councils also
approved leases and elected officials. The aldermen advised and supported the
mayor, who served for a year and was usually chosen from among them. He was
the chief executive, responsible for maintaining law and order. He normally
acted as a magistrate, assisted by some or all of the aldermen. A few towns
had more than one chief executive: Great Yarmouth had two bailiffs, until the
charter of 1684 vested power in a mayor. The cancelling of that charter in 1688
meant a return to two bailiffs, but the town switched permanently to a mayor
under a charter of 1703.[8] The selection of aldermen and councillors was rarely
democratic. At Norwich the common council was elected annually, by the
freemen, but this was unusual. The aldermen were also elected by the freemen
of one of the city's four great wards, but once chosen they served for life, unless
they were removed for misconduct. Elsewhere, as at Bristol, both aldermen and
councillors were chosen by co-option, by the existing corporation. Hull had
only a single tier, twelve aldermen. Candidates for office were selected by the
mayor and aldermen; a shortlist of two was then presented to an indeterminate
number of burgesses, or freemen—100 to 150 in the 1690s—who chose one.[9]
Berwick and Ipswich had more formal freeman assemblies.[10]

Charters empowered towns to appoint a range of officials. The town clerk,
who normally had legal training, took minutes, kept records, and gave legal
advice. It was a responsible and influential position; it was alleged that Bristol
corporation knew nothing of the law and took on trust what the town clerk
told them.[11] The recorder, who presided over some of the town's courts, was also
usually a lawyer and advised the corporation.[12] Some towns, however, appointed
noblemen as recorders, who appointed deputies to carry out their legal duties.
In some towns, there was an additional legal officer, the steward, who in Norwich
advised the sheriffs.[13] More often, the steward (or high steward) was a peer, who
acted as a friend at court (and in Parliament). Other offices held by members of
the corporation formed part of the *cursus honorum*, the series of offices which

[8] Gauci, *Yarmouth*, 28–9, 161, 170.   [9] *VCH East Riding*, i. 120.
[10] Webb and Webb, *Manor and Borough*, ii. 505–21, 558–60; M. Reed, 'Economic Structure and
Change in Seventeenth-Century Ipswich', in Clark (ed.), *Country Towns*, 90.
[11] *CSPD 1676–7*, 51.
[12] At Bristol, unusually, the recorder was ex officio an alderman. At Bedford, the recorder and
his deputy were voting members of the corporation: G. Parsloe, *Bedford Corporation Minute Book
1647–64*, Bedfordshire Historical Society xxvi (1944–5), 166. At Portsmouth Charles Bissell, town
clerk, resigned his post in order to be admitted as an alderman and then resigned as alderman when
he resumed his post.
[13] Evans, *Norwich*, 46, 58.

senior members were expected to fill before becoming aldermen or mayors. These included the chamberlains, who collected rents and fees and handled the town's finances. In most towns two chamberlains served for one year, but in Bristol the chamberlain was a permanent official; from 1698 he (like other city officers) was appointed for a year at a time, giving the assembly (aldermen and common council) an annual opportunity to remove him if his performance was unsatisfactory. He was responsible not only for the city's receipts and expenditure, but also for repairs to the city's infrastructure; grand jury present-ments contained frequent complaints of his failures and neglects.[14] The other major officer was the sheriff (some towns had two). They were responsible for serving writs and warrants and in some towns they held a court which heard minor civil and criminal cases. The outgoings of the office exceeded the profits and it was unpopular, a burden rather than a privilege.[15]

The political history of towns focuses mainly on the corporation, but there were other levels of government, especially in larger towns. The parish, as in the countryside, was responsible for highway maintenance and poor relief. Many urban parishes were small—Norwich had thirty-four. At the other extreme, Portsmouth had only one and the vestry at times played a significant administrative role.[16] In 1660 neither Holy Trinity nor St Mary's in Hull was technically a parish; the former was created a parish by Act of Parliament in 1661; the latter was treated for all practical purposes as a parish in its own right.[17] Larger towns were divided into wards for administrative and electoral purposes. Norwich had twelve 'small wards', grouped into four great wards. Common councillors and aldermen were elected by the freemen of the great wards and from 1663 aldermen were justices of the peace within their wards.[18] In many towns, aldermen were assigned a particular ward, for which they were responsible; they were reprimanded if they did not 'look after' their ward.[19] At York each ward had a wardmote court, which punished failures to clean and repair the streets, nuisances, and the like.[20]

Complaints about the negligence of aldermen offer a reminder that urban office was burdensome, requiring considerable expenditure of money and time.

---

[14] BRO, 02464/7, fos. 166, 168, 186. For twenty-three complaints in one presentment, see BRO, JQS/PR/1, Temple, 4 Apr. 1665.

[15] Evans, *Norwich*, 46–8.   [16] East, 195.   [17] Gillett and MacMahon, *Hull*, 190.

[18] Evans, *Norwich*, 51–4; Hudson and Tingey (eds.), *Records*, i. 48.

[19] MCB 24, fo. 50; BRO, JQS/M/4, fo. 151, JQS/M/5, fo. 61, JQS/C/1, 24 Apr. 1688. One suspects a certain sarcasm in an order at Hull to inform aldermen which were their wards: BRB 6, p. 461. Each year an alderman was assigned to each ward at Oxford: *OCA passim*.

[20] *VCH City of York*, 182–3. Quarter sessions dealt with most of these matters as well.

The Norwich mayor's court (consisting of the mayor, sheriffs, and aldermen) met twice a week; aldermen were also required to view city properties, attend committees, mediate in disputes, and attend the mayor to church on Sundays and festive occasions. Both aldermen and common councillors were elected by, and from among, the freemen. Under local by-laws only freemen could practise trades or sell retail in the city, but the freedom also brought liability to office and some avoided it for this reason. There were complaints that Dissenters, especially Quakers, avoided 'chargeable offices' by refusing to take the oaths and make the declaration required to qualify for office under the Corporation Act. Faced with refusals to serve, towns claimed a right to impose a fine; if the refuser would not pay, they tried to raise money by distraint or, if all else failed, appealed to the privy council. Leicester was an impoverished town, badly damaged in the civil wars. It found it hard to fill a governing body of twenty-four aldermen and forty-eight common councillors. Those who had been selected as councillors often pleaded that serving would take up too much time and ruin their business.[21] Others were allowed to fine, rather than serve; Thomas Worrall, elected chamberlain in 1701, said that his only apprentice was very sick, and that, if he died, Worrall would be unable to carry on his business.[22] Pleas to be allowed to resign on the grounds of ill health, old age, blindness, or deafness were more sympathetically received,[23] but even then some were asked to pay a fine in order to be released,[24] and some who offered to pay a fine were not allowed to.[25] There was more sympathy for those who claimed that they had sunk into poverty and so were unfit for office;[26] some were allowed a small pension, gift, or loan.[27] One sought a discharge on the ground that he was intellectually unequipped to cope with business; his spelling suggests that he may have had a point.[28]

    In all of these cases, the petitioners accepted that they could legitimately be called on to serve, but offered reasons why they should be excused—or, if they were already serving, discharged. The decision to serve was a weighty one. When Samuel Newton was elected an alderman of Cambridge, he asked for three days to consider. He prayed and opened his Bible, where he found a text which convinced him that he should serve.[29] Outright refusals to serve were less

---

[21] *RBL*, iv. 516–17, v. 24; LHP 39, fos. 97, 99.   [22] LHP 39, fos. 15, 24, 68.
[23] LHB 4, fos. 21, 117; LHP 34, no. 32, LHP 36, nos. 212, 215, LHP 39, fos. 159, 161.
[24] *RBL*, v. 37; LHP 38, nos. 232, 238.   [25] LHP 36, nos. 142, 162.
[26] LHP 32B, nos. 264, 270, LHP 39, fo. 245; LHB 4, fo. 78, LHB 5, fo. 65.
[27] LHP 34, no. 44, LHP 38, nos. 158–60; *RBL*, v. 20, 25.   [28] *RBL*, v. 8–9.
[29] S. Newton, *Diary*, ed. J. E. Foster, Cambridge Antiquarian Society (1890), 28–9; Cambs RO, Cambridge Common Day Book 8, fo. 223.

common, but more problematic. In 1665 Edward Billers, William Warburton, and Francis Noble, recently elected to the Leicester common council, refused to subscribe the renunciation of the Covenant. They were not Dissenters— they attended St Martin's and received communion. They claimed they should not have been elected because they were young and had no wife, servant, or apprentice to look after their businesses when they attended meetings.[30] The corporation claimed that they refused to subscribe in order to avoid office, and complained to the privy council, which twice ordered them to be sworn within fourteen days. They refused to swear or to give bonds to pay a fine of 100 marks for refusal. The mayor and aldermen had hoped that they would submit, and confessed that although they could legally impose the fines, they lacked the power, under the charters, to recover them by distraint.[31] They added that the three were shopkeepers with very good trades 'and there are very few of like ability with them, considering the late regulation'; forty of the seventy-two had been removed by the Corporation Act commissioners in 1662.[32]

Fines to avoid office could also be a useful source of income and there was a fairly clear distinction between those nominated for office because the corporation wanted them to serve and those nominated in the expectation that they would fine off. Most of those nominated were non-resident freemen, technically eligible to serve, who were warned that they would be elected sheriff and encouraged, more or less explicitly, to fine off.[33] There is also evidence, at both Hull and Norwich, of the election of Dissenters to office, either in expectation that they would fine, or in hopes of forcing them to accept their obligations as freemen.[34] At Hull, with a governing body of twelve, the burden on aldermen was heavy, and resident freemen who fined were still expected to attend the mayor on ceremonial occasions. In general, where those put forward for election were seen as suitable, in terms of wealth and residence, the bench tried to persuade them to serve. Similarly, it tried to dissuade those who sought to

---

[30] *RBL*, iv. 498, 505–7; LHP 32A, nos. 30–1.
[31] *RBL*, iv. 498, 505–7; LHP 32A, nos. 12, 13, 19, 21, 24; PC 2/58, pp. 291, 335–6, 367–8.
[32] *RBL*, iv. 507.
[33] BRB 6, p. 508; BRL 2759a, town clerk of Hull to John Rawson of Leeds and Elihu Jackson of Doncaster, 1 Sept. 1701 and 1 Sept. 1702. For similar proceedings at Norwich, see MCB 25, fo. 340.
[34] At Hull, Ralph Peacock and Jeremiah Shaw: BRB 6, pp. 447, 550, 580, 582, 584, 594. Both were trustees of a Presbyterian meeting house: W. Whitaker, *One Line of the Puritan Tradition in Hull: Bowl Alley Lane Chapel* (London, 1910) 100. At Norwich, John Barnham paid a total of £190 for two temporary and one permanent exemptions from office: FAB 6, fo. 259, FAB 8, fos. 8, 68, 70. On the other hand John Leverington agreed to serve as sheriff in 1672: MCB 24, fo. 214. At Coventry many Dissenters were elected to office and refused either to serve or to pay a fine: Hurwich, 'Fanatick Town', 18.

resign, sometimes expressing doubts whether they were as ill as they claimed.[35] (It could, however, treat sympathetically those whose health or wealth was clearly no longer adequate.[36]) In some cases, the persuasion worked.[37] Alderman Tripp, whose plea of ill health was initially treated with scepticism, was eventually allowed to resign, although he had admitted that resigning would 'be to my dishonour and my posterity'.[38] Alderman Ellis, who was allowed to resign on the grounds of ill health, admitted that his recent neglect of his duties had been 'an offence to you all'.[39] When Daniel Hoare resigned in 1712, because of his debts, he prayed to God to assist his brethren in discharging their trust—dispensing justice, encouraging virtue, discouraging vice, 'and promoting of love and charity amongst the inhabitants and in a hearty care and concern for the poor'.[40]

It would be naive to assume that all aldermen of Hull practised these principles, although they were reminded of them by an emblem and verses on the theme of 'mercy and justice' in St Mary's church.[41] Some, especially overseas merchants, were unable to spare the time, but almost all seem to have accepted that they had an obligation to serve. Very few refused point blank. Most pleaded either conscience or pressure of business—and some who initially pleaded conscience, or desired time to think about the oaths, eventually agreed to serve.[42] If some were elected in the hope that they would fine off, others were not allowed to do so.[43] William Crowle was put up for election for alderman in 1700. He asked to fine off; the bench, 'knowing his fitness', tried to dissuade him. Crowle said that he had to go abroad for several months. If he was let off on this occasion, he promised to serve in the future. The bench took him at his word. He was elected alderman in January 1701, and agreed to pay a fine of £200 when he failed to serve. He seems not to have paid the fine, and was finally summoned to be sworn in March 1704. He claimed that he was not duly elected or qualified. The recorder suggested a moderate fine. It was set at £200, but privately the bench was prepared to settle for £50, and accepted £80. It then had second thoughts and decided to prosecute Crowle at York assizes for £300—the maximum under the by-law which established fines for those refusing to serve. The judge thought the town's case strong, but, in view of

[35] BRB 5, pp. 177, 193–4; BRL 788, 791.
[36] BRB 5, pp. 568, 676; BRB 6, pp. 617, 618; BRL 1535.
[37] BRB 5, pp. 222, 565, 568.   [38] Ibid. 274–5.   [39] BRB 6, pp. 425–7.
[40] Ibid. 618, printed in J. Tickell, *History of the Town and County of Kingston upon Hull* (Hull, 1798), 597 n.
[41] T. Gent, *Annales Regioduni Hullini: or the History of the Royal and Beautiful Town of Kingston upon Hull* (York, 1736), 57.
[42] BRB 6, pp. 561, 586.   [43] Ibid. 435.

'contentions' in the town, offered to mediate. The bench agreed and the fine was fixed at £100.[44]

The great majority who did not wish to serve offered to pay a fine, which the bench normally accepted. This reduced the danger of disagreements and disharmony. It could also prove cheaper: taking a refractory burgess to court was expensive and the outcome was never certain. The by-law which required burgesses to serve if elected was generally accepted within the town, but the king's courts, in London or in York, might see it differently. Threats of prosecution for refusal were preceded by enquiries to the recorder or learned counsel. When Gilead Goch, elected sheriff in 1674, refused to renounce the Covenant, the bench consulted a London lawyer, Sir William Jones. He thought that the bench could impose a fine only if it was authorized by custom or the charter. He added that many corporations had made a by-law to that effect and that the sum levied should be reasonable.[45] The bench regarded Jones's opinion as a vindication of its right and fined Goch £100 (which he paid).[46]

Goch was a native of the town, amenable to community pressure. Non-residents elected sheriffs in order to exact fines could be less tractable. Bartholomew Towers of Leeds ignored a warning in 1697 that he might be chosen sheriff, so was declared elected. A messenger was sent to him, with an abstract of the by-law, to demand £200. When he did not pay, legal proceedings were started. When the case came to trial in 1699, the bench was prepared to settle for a lower sum. The judge decided that Towers should pay £20; the town's costs were £27.[47] Still more drawn out was the case of Elihu Jackson of Doncaster, who was elected sheriff in 1712 and refused to take the oaths. The trial finally took place in 1715. The court decided that, under the by-law, the fine should be £200. Jackson gave in a bond, but failed to make it good; it was not until 1717 that his wife handed over the money.[48]

The paucity of suitable men and the reluctance of some of them to serve meant that, however members of corporations were selected, the choice of

[44] Ibid. 465, 475, 522–3, 529–30. For the similar case of William Maister, who was let off, promising to serve in future, and then refused to be sworn, see ibid. 525, 558, 560. He declared that he was willing to pay a fine of £300, which he did.

[45] BRB 5, pp. 388–9. In 1663 the attorney general recommended that Coventry's new charter should give the corporation the power to impose such fines as they had usually done: SP 29/74, no. 56.

[46] BRB 5, pp. 387, 412. Jones was also consulted on the by-law of 1674 imposing a fine for refusing the office of chamberlain. He thought it was good in law: ibid. 414.

[47] BRB 6, pp. 419–23, 443, 448, 450; BRL 1186 (on rear).

[48] BRB 6, pp. 623, 624, 646, 652, 666, 670; BRL 1239a.

candidates was limited. Where they were selected by co-option, this seems to have aroused little resentment among the townsmen. At Hull most of the aldermen were merchants, who promoted the economic interests at the town, and sought to create an environment in which trade could thrive. There was also informal consultation with the wider body of burgesses (freemen).[49] At Great Yarmouth, all agreed on the need to prevent the haven from silting up, which would destroy the town's trade.[50] In Norwich, the most important economic group within the corporation was the worsted weavers, who promoted the city's interests, most notably when pressing for a ban on imported calicoes. In Bristol the position was complicated by a deep division between the Merchant Venturers and small independent merchants, but there were issues on which they agreed, such as the need to reduce the poor rate and a determination to move destitute Huguenot and Palatine refugees away from the city as quickly as possible.[51]

Apart from standing up for the town's interests in the wider world, mayors and aldermen were expected to provide good governance. Even if they were not formally answerable to their fellow townsmen through the need for re-election, in a wider sense they were. They were not like country gentlemen, living in large houses behind walls and fences. Aldermen lived cheek by jowl with their poorer neighbours; they passed them in the street and mixed with them in the tavern and the market place.[52] Moreover, they needed the co-operation of their fellow townsmen to make their government effective. Most corporations had a bevy of inferior officers: mace bearers, sergeants, bailiffs, market officials. At York 218 places had to be filled each year, in the corporation alone, not including officers of ward, guild, and parish; about half of these were quarter sessions jurors. Over 40 per cent of eligible men—freemen, paying the poor rate—held office of some sort each year.[53] This widespread office-holding and participation contrasted starkly with the oligarchic nature of most corporations and affected

---

[49] *VCH East Riding*, i. 125; Jackson, *Hull*, 309.

[50] Gauci, *Yarmouth*, 8–9, 19–20, 38, 78–83, 104, and *passim*.

[51] Sacks, *Widening Gate*; McGrath, *Venturers*. For Huguenots, see *CSPD 1680–1*, 609; BRO, JQS/M/5, fo. 210, JQS/M/6, fos. 259, 257, 255 (rear of volume). For the Palatines, see 04264/9, pp. 198, 200–1.

[52] The same was true in the towns of Holland and ensured that the civic rulers, or regents, who were perhaps more inclined to oligarchy than their English counterparts, paid heed to the views of their fellow townsmen: J. L. Price, *Holland and the Dutch Republic in the Seventeenth Century* (Oxford, 1994), 90–1, 95–7, and *passim*.

[53] K. Wrightson, 'The Politics of the Parish', in Griffiths, Fox, and Hindle (eds.), *Experience of Authority*, ch. 1; Withington, 'Views from the Bridge', 128. For the number of officers in the City of London, see Pearl, 'Change and Stability', in Barry (ed.), *Tudor and Stuart Town*, 154. There were more paid offices in the towns of Holland: Price, *Holland and the Dutch Republic*, 49–51.

the way the town government functioned at the grass roots; at the most basic level, officers would try to avoid acting on orders that they disliked, or that might upset their neighbours. The presentments of grand juries, of parish, ward, or town, told the corporation what the citizens thought was amiss: damaged streets, nuisances, dangerous structures, inmates. They also offered the possibility of dialogue, or negotiation, between rulers and ruled.[54]

Not all townspeople were eligible for such offices, although non-freemen and the poor might still have their role to play in the more menial parish offices and the watch. The participation of those below the civic elite, but above the poor, those who might see themselves as the 'better sort', gave them a sense of ownership of urban government. Those who participated most actively were inclined to see themselves as the 'better sort' in a moral sense as well, imbued with civic responsibility and driven by a commitment to good government and moral order, especially for the poor. There developed what one writer had called a culture of 'civic republicanism': participatory, hierarchical, and patriarchal, an expression of the citizens' confidence and pride in their ability to order their own affairs. Dealing with the rapidly changing demands from the centre, from the 1580s to 1660, helped to create self-reliance, civic identity, and, sometimes, solidarity. This was good government by the best men—and co-option could be seen as a way of ensuring that those who served were indeed drawn from the 'better sort'.[55] But if this mode of thought tended towards oligarchy, in the towns of both England and Holland, there were forces working against it. First, demography: this was an unhealthy age even for the landed aristocracy; mortality was higher in the towns than in the countryside. In addition, many families which had made fortunes in business subsequently lost them and were no longer 'substantial' enough to be considered for high civic office. Second, from the 1640s there were a series of purges designed to remove from the civic elites those deemed by the government of the day to be disaffected, ensuring a somewhat brutal rotation of office as political fortunes changed.[56]

[54] For an extremely thoughtful discussion of the significance of office-holding, see Goldie, 'Unacknowledged Republic'.

[55] Withington, 'Views from the Bridge', 129–32; P. Withington, 'Citizens, Community and Political Culture', in Shephard and Withington (eds.), *Communities in Early Modern England,* 139–41; Barry, 'Introduction', in Barry (ed.), *Tudor and Stuart Town,* 29–32; K. Wrightson, 'Sorts of People', in J. Barry and C. Brooks (eds.), *The Middling Sort of People, 1550–1800* (Basingstoke, 1994), ch. 1; J. W. Kirby, 'Restoration Leeds and the Aldermen of the Corporation, 1661–1700', *Northern History,* xxii (1986), 136.

[56] See J. T. Evans, 'The Decline of Oligarchy in Seventeenth-Century Norwich', *JBS* xiv (1974), 46–76; Kirby, 'Restoration Leeds'; Gauci, *Yarmouth,* chs. 1–2; Halliday, *Body, passim.* For Holland, see Price, *Holland and the Dutch Republic.*

We shall see in the later part of this chapter how far corporations' powers of coercion depended on the co-operation of the townsmen. To secure that co-operation they needed to maintain trust in the legitimacy and integrity of their government.[57] They did so partly by emphasizing the moral and even religious basis of their authority, through civic ceremonial and church attendance, and partly by the content of their government, by ruling in the manner expected by the 'better sort' among the townspeople, the honest and respectable. This implied certain standards of conduct in public life, in terms of both dignity and financial probity. By the time of the Municipal Corporations Act of 1835, many were bywords for corruption, but this does not seem to have been the norm in this period. In many towns probity was forced on the corporation: limited incomes and assets meant limited opportunities for self-enrichment. The mayor of Norwich was not supposed to spend more than £5 without the common council's consent, and he was not allowed to take anything from the poor box.[58] The general impression, in Norwich and elsewhere, is one of probity and competence.[59]

II. ORDER AND DISORDER

The body best equipped to maintain order was the army. At Hull the garrison had a guardhouse in the town. Patrols arrested those who were disorderly at night, taking them before the magistrates next morning.[60] But many towns—even large ones like Norwich and Bristol—were garrisoned only occasionally and the military never became part of the normal governance; at times, indeed, the soldiers constituted a major threat to good order. A few towns had their own militia. At Bristol, the common council voted in November 1660 to raise

[57] For legitimacy, see M. J. Braddick, *State Formation in Early Modern England* (Cambridge, 2000), 68–85.

[58] Hence there was outrage when Peter Thacker, mayor in 1705–6, was alleged to have taken £35 from the poor box: Raynham Hall, B2/2, bottom of box, 'misc ND', letter to Townshend endorsed 1707–8. The identification of Thacker comes from the reference to Sheriff Risborough: Blomefield, *Norfolk*, iii. 436.

[59] Pound, *Tudor and Stuart Norwich*, 108; Evans, *Norwich*, 52; K. Wilson, *Sense of the People*, 311–12; R. Sweet, *The English Town, 1680–1840* (Harlow, 1999), 105–7; Kirby, 'Restoration Leeds', 144; *CUHB*, ii. 245–6, 549–51. There is some evidence of political favouritism in the awarding of contracts in Norwich after 1717, but it was neither complete nor consistent: G. Guth, 'Croakers, Tackers and Other Citizens: Norwich Voters in the Early Eighteenth Century', Ph.D. thesis (Stanford, Calif. 1985), 189–95.

[60] Jackson, *Hull*, 317–18.

a regiment of foot, but Parliament had not yet settled the legal status of the militia and some doubted if it was wise to entrust the power of the sword to the city's magistrates.[61] In January 1661 some neighbouring gentlemen raised a volunteer troop of horse, which suppressed 'seditious' meetings.[62] Commissions to deputy lieutenants and officers arrived in July: the deputies included Sir Hugh Smyth of Ashton Court, a neighbouring gentleman, but not the mayor.[63] In the summer of 1662 the government feared disaffection; the militia was on guard during the fair in July. The horse (normally the best means of frightening people into submission) proved ineffectual and the deputies preferred to rely on the regiment of foot.[64] The authorities remained anxious for several years and responded to continuing concerns about disaffection in the city by commissioning more gentlemen; of nine deputies in 1665, only four were townsmen.[65] However, in 1672 thirteen deputy lieutenants were commissioned, almost all of them leading citizens. In the following year the marquis of Worcester replaced the duke of Ormond as the city's lord lieutenant. It was resolved to ask him to appoint deputies who were citizens rather than country gentlemen, which he did.[66] The citizens had regained control over their militia.

Norwich had one regiment of foot, commanded by a lord lieutenant (also lord lieutenant of the county) and six to eight deputies drawn from the civic elite. The commissioned officers were responsible for appointing the watch.[67] The militia searched the houses of suspicious persons (Dissenters or Catholics) for arms.[68] Serious disorders were rare until the early 1680s. In September 1682 'rude people' reacted to the cancellation of a hanging by besieging the gaoler's house and breaking his windows. A detachment of eighty-four militiamen, with muskets and pikes, dispersed the crowd, then stood in arms in the market place.[69] In 1683 there were major riots when a group of impoverished

[61] *CSPD 1660–1*, 293, 489, 571; BRO, 04264/6, p. 32.

[62] *Kingdom's Intelligencer*, 21–8 Jan. 1661.   [63] Carte MS 32, fo. 48.

[64] BRO, 04264/6, p. 59; *CSPD 1661–2*, 444, 507, 579, 595, 598.

[65] Carte MS 145, fo. 128. The four were Creswick, Knight, Cale, and Colston. Sir Humphrey Hooke lived only 4 miles away, and was nominated alderman in 1662, but played little part in the city's affairs.

[66] *CSPD 1672–3*, 101, *1673–5*, 116; BRO, 04264/6, p. 250. In 1676 the captains in the city regiment comprised Hooke, four current aldermen, and three future mayors. Six of the eight captains and six of the eight lieutenants were soon to join the artillery company: Badminton House, FmE 2/4/13. In 1683, the twelve deputy lieutenants included the mayor (ex officio) and nine aldermen; the only real non-citizen was Beaufort's son, the earl of Worcester: SP 44/164, p. 96.

[67] MCB 24, fo. 154.

[68] NCR, Case 13b, no. 7, Lieutenancy Order Book 1662–1704, fos. 11, 64–5, 83–4.

[69] Blomefield, *Norfolk*, iii. 418; NCR, Case 13bn no. 7, Order Book, fo. 79.

Huguenot weavers came to settle in the city. The citizens, many of them poor stocking weavers, drove them out of the house where they lodged. On 16 March ten weavers told a large crowd that the French had come to 'underwork' them and that they must be forced to leave. The crowd pulled the French from the houses where they were staying, dragged them around the streets and drove them out of the city; one woman later died of her injuries. The militia had not been able to prevent the riot, but it did prevent further disorder.[70] In October 1688 the militia dispersed a crowd that attacked a Catholic chapel; in December there were extensive attacks on Catholic property; the whole regiment was called out and prevented the disorder from getting out of control.[71]

Below the level of the militia, the authorities had to rely on the sheriff's officers, the constables, and the watch. Bristol tried various means of establishing an effective watch. In 1666 it established a 'common watch' of forty-eight, on duty each night from 5 p.m. to 7 a.m. In 1667 it reverted to requiring citizens to serve in turns and in person, although some paid substitutes.[72] In 1674 the common council allowed citizens to pay cash rather paying substitutes, many of whom proved inadequate. The money was to pay for twenty-six able watchmen, to serve through the night. Nineteen were allocated rounds and a constable was to remain at the Tolzey with the other seven, ready to respond to emergencies. They were to arrest night-walkers, disorderly persons, and those present at unlawful assemblies. Some 2,000 citizens were to contribute towards the cost (5*d.* or 7*d.* every seven weeks).[73] In 1676 it was ordered that a watch-house be provided in each ward and in 1678 men were appointed to visit them, to see if the watchmen were doing their duty. In 1693 some leading citizens refused to pay.[74] The watchmen were now supervised, on a ward basis, by constables, many of whom were allegedly negligent. There were still complaints that many watchmen were old and feeble or went home early.[75] In 1721 the magistrates ordered that two men should be added to the watch of every ward and that the constables should ensure watchmen were able bodied. Even though Bristol was said to be facing a crime wave, it seemed impossible to make the watch effective.[76]

[70] *An Appendix to the Chronological History of Norwich* (Norwich, 1728), 53–4; NRO, MS 79, p. 249, MS 453, 'A Description', 19 May; MCB 25, fo. 126; NCR, Case 13b, no. 7, Order Book, fo. 83 (refers to two riotous assemblies); BL, M636/37, John Verney to Sir Ralph Verney, 24 Mar. 1683; *CSPD Jan.–June 1683*, 363.

[71] *CSPD 1687–9*, no. 1715; Blomefield, *Norfolk*, iii. 424; NCR, Case 13b, no. 7, Order Book, fos. 98–9; *English Currant*, 29 Dec. 1688–2 Jan. 1689.

[72] BRO, 04264/6, pp. 142, 149, 162, 163, 185–6.   [73] Ibid. 261–2.

[74] BRO, 04264/7, fos. 86, 137, JQS/C/1, 2nd pagination, p. 30, JQS/M/5, fos. 81, 97.

[75] BRO, JQS/C/1, 2nd pagination, pp. 39, 43, 71–2.

[76] Ibid. 71; JQS/D/5, 13 Nov. 1721.

The reluctance to serve on the watch was understandable. Bristolians seem to have been volatile, aggressive, and insubordinate, especially when drunk. In 1699 a grand jury presented the landlord of the Three Tuns in Corn Street, for allowing people to drink excessively late one Sunday. Quarrels arose which (according to the grand jury) could well have ended in murder. (The Three Tuns was one of the city's leading inns, where aldermen often dined.) Nor was Bristol unusual. Portsmouth was both a naval and a dockyard town, with more than its share of violent people. Thomas Aldridge and Richard Harper, both seamen, fought and beat one another several times; on one occasion Harper claimed he was not well enough to fight, and one bystander tried to part them, but others would not let him and Harper ended with severe injuries to his nose and eyes.[77] Sometimes those accused of brawling were women.[78] Often the violence was fuelled by drink: John Voake was repeatedly in trouble for drunkenness, beating his wife, and threatening to set his house on fire.[79] At Norwich, there was limited respect for the lesser officers of the law. On 4 November 1699, the king's birthday, a constable was badly beaten while other men (and their wives) egged the assailants on.[80] In guild week in 1704 a constable and three of the watch of the small ward of St Peter Mancroft were escorting home Edward Randall, who was very drunk. When they met the watch of West Wymer ward, Randall became abusive, so the Mancroft men decided to put him in the stocks. The Wymer watchmen, also drunk, rescued Randall, severely beat the Mancroft men and set one of them in the stocks.[81]

Such incidents show the weakness of the machinery of order in towns. And yet, order did not collapse, which suggests that most townspeople were predisposed to behave peaceably most of the time. Many of the incidents just mentioned occurred when self-control was undermined by drink. Historians have emphasized that, far from being mindless challenges to authority, riots often had both an inbuilt discipline and strong sense of legitimization, based on values shared (at least in part) by those in authority.[82] By examining various types of riot, it is possible to show not so much the weaknesses as the inner strengths of urban society, which rested less on coercion than on self-restraint.

[77] *PSP*, 100–1.   [78] Ibid. 22, 31, 32, 35, 107, 111, 118–19.

[79] Ibid. 15, 20, 23. For other cases of drink-related domestic violence, see ibid. 36, 119, 142.

[80] NCR, Case 12b/1, bundle labelled 1690–9, informations of Randall King and Mary Burman, 5 and 6 Nov. 1699.

[81] NCR, Case 12b/1, information of George Allen and others, 18 June 1704.

[82] K. Wrightson and J. Walter, 'Dearth and the Social Order in Early Modern England', *P & P* 71 (1976), 22–42; K. J. Lindley, *Fenland Riots and the English Revolution* (London, 1982).

Not all disorders can be seen as either legitimized or self-disciplined. At Bristol in 1670 a large group of apprentices gathered on Shrove Tuesday with staves and clubs 'to fight'. It is possible that the tradition had already developed, well established in the eighteenth century, that groups of apprentices from different trades would fight on Shrove Tuesday.[83] Sometimes, they picked on a 'legitimate' target, as a pretext for (at least) violent horseplay. In Worcester in 1667 hundreds of apprentices pulled down bawdy houses.[84] At Bristol in 1685 apprentices attacked the house of a notorious bawd. She set her dogs on them, they burned her house down and carried her on a coal-staff to the house of her daughter-in-law, where they broke all the barrels in the cellar. They continued to carry her around the city until she was rescued by the constables.[85]

If some disorders seemed to involve violence for its own sake, others contained an element of criminality. Attempts to suppress smuggling sometimes led to violence[86] and there were attacks on deer parks well before those which led to the passing of the Black Act in 1723.[87] There were a series of similar episodes after James II's flight in 1688.[88] There were rumours that, the king having left the kingdom, all laws had ceased and people could take what they wanted.[89] It might be argued that ordinary people regarded the establishment of property rights over wild animals as unfair, but it is also clear that many deer-stealers were motivated simply by gain.[90] The same is true of those who plundered ships forced aground in Cornwall, although they may have claimed this as a customary 'right'. On at least one occasion, several people were killed or injured by the authorities.[91] There were also numerous riots against taxation —sometimes the excise, more often the hearth tax. At Bridport in 1668 the hearth money collectors were followed around the town by men, women, and children throwing stones. One was hit on the head and subsequently died.

[83] *CSPD 1670*, 76; Latimer, ii. 138; J. Barry, 'Popular Culture in Seventeenth-Century Bristol', in B. Reay (ed.), *Popular Culture in Seventeenth-Century England* (London, 1988), 74; J. Stevenson, *Popular Disturbances in England, 1700–1832*, 2nd edn. (London, 1992), 62–3.

[84] *CSPD 1666–7*, 560; Bodl, Rawl MS A74, fo. 37. This occurred in March, but some time after Shrove Tuesday.

[85] BRO, 07831, 17 Feb. 1685 (before Shrove Tuesday).

[86] BL, Add MS 61608, fo. 21; PC 2/74, pp. 54, 259, 2/76, p. 287; *Weekly Journal or British Gazetteer*, 1 Nov. 1718.

[87] *CSPD 1663–4*, 219, *1697*, 361, 394; Defoe, *Tour*, ii. 15–16; Latimer, i. 302–4, 357–8; J. Broad, 'Whigs, Deer-Stealers and the Origins of the Black Act', *P & P* 119 (1988), 59–61.

[88] *English Currant*, 26–8 Dec. 1688, 29 Dec. 1688–2 Jan. 1689.

[89] *HMC Beaufort*, 93.   [90] Broad, 'Whigs, Deer-Stealers', *passim*.

[91] *Loyal Protestant*, 11 Mar. 1682; PC 2/74, p. 55; *Flying Post*, 9–12 Dec. 1710.

The magistrates were nowhere to be seen.[92] At Kendal in 1696, coin was in very short supply, but an excise collector refused to accept what he regarded as unsound coins. Many alehouse keepers, half drunk, asked the mayor how they were to make a living if their money would not pass. He gave them fair words, but the crowd was not satisfied and rambled around ominously. The magistrates, realizing that the crowd was too strong for them, gave them drink and they promised not to molest the town that night, but would have a 'frolic' in the country. Next day, they searched for food and plunder in several villages, then attacked the town guard, injuring several. The recorder tried to appease them; he was knocked down, but he persisted and began to persuade them that the authorities had behaved reasonably. They calmed down and the guard arrested about twenty. The magistrates kept about fifty men in arms each night, until the county militia carried the rioters off to Appleby.[93]

There are signs here that obedience to authority was breaking down, but the crowd was prepared to listen and was partly persuaded by the recorder. The poor felt that it was unjust that they should be reduced to desperation by the deficiencies of the coinage. They had the numbers to take what they wanted, but confined their depredations to the villages. Underlying the crowd's behaviour was a sense of injustice. On other occasions, crowds enforced 'justice' when the authorities failed to do so. At Battle in 1693 fifty 'gossips', assisted by two young men in women's clothing, severely beat a vintner notorious for beating his wife.[94] At St Albans in 1700 a rumour spread that Amy Townsend, an old woman, had bewitched a boy. A crowd, not trusting the magistrates to act, decided to try whether she was indeed a witch, dragging her several times through the river until she was almost dead. They then took her home, but others claimed to have seen her swim, proving she was a witch 'and scandalous to that corporation'. They hauled her out of bed, set her on a chair, and carried her around the town. To appease them, a magistrate sent her to gaol, where she died two hours later.[95] An even more macabre example of popular 'justice' occurred at Denbigh in 1701. A woman was hanged for murdering her bastard child. When her body was taken down, it was discovered that she was still

---

[92] *CSPD 1667–8*, 224. For tax riots more generally, see M. Braddick, *Parliamentary Taxation in Seventeenth-Century England* (Woodbridge, 1994), 211–18, 252–66.

[93] *HMC le Fleming*, 343–4. See also P. Borsay, ' "All the Town's a Stage": Urban Ritual and Ceremony, 1660–1800', in P. Clark (ed.), *The Transformation of English Provincial Towns* (London, 1984), 242–6.

[94] Carte MS 76, fos. 219–20. See also Stevenson, *Popular Disturbances*, 64–5.

[95] *Post Boy*, 16–18 Jan. 1700.

alive. The hangman tried to hang her again, but the people rescued her and, allegedly, beat his brains out.[96] More common were riots provoked by recruiting, or 'kidnapping', young men for the armed forces. At Gravesend in 1699 a flotilla of small boats surrounded a ship, demanding that the captain hand over a 'kidnapped' boy.[97] At Deal in 1700 a 'kidnapper' was ducked in a well until he was almost drowned and then kicked up and down the street, before he was handed over to a magistrate, who sent him to gaol, possibly for his own safety.[98] In 1706, at Newbury, recruiting sergeants were beaten and shot at; one was badly wounded. At Abergavenny a large crowd rescued a man who was being enlisted; the authorities were too weak to support the recruiters or to bring the culprits to justice.[99] It is possible that the recruiters were trying to enlist men who by law should have been exempt; it is equally possible that the rioters did not want their fellow townspeople dragged off to the army; similarly, those imprisoned for riot were sometimes rescued from gaol by their fellow rioters.

Running through these incidents was a popular sense of justice, or rather injustice, not always shared by those in authority. Customs duties, which smugglers tried to evade, and the hearth tax, which the officials were trying to collect, rested on Acts of Parliament, although there were disputes about whether certain industrial hearths should be exempt from the latter. Those who attacked deer parks might claim loss of customary rights to take game and firewood, as well as stealing deer; the park owners claimed a right to use their land as they wished; from 1671 a series of Acts tightened the rights of landowners over game and annulled customary hunting rights. This might seem to be a rural rather than an urban issue, but Norwich corporation was determined to uphold the game laws. In 1698 a man was committed to gaol, until he found sureties, for having a greyhound which he was not legally qualified to possess.[100] In 1707 the sessions and mayor's court ordered that the 'good and wholesome' laws for the preservation of game should be enforced and in 1721 a gamekeeper was appointed for the city and county of Norwich.[101] A similar clash between claims of customary land use and landowners' insistence that they could manage their land as they chose had often led to enclosure riots

[96] *Post Man*, 9–11 Oct. 1701.   [97] Ibid. 24–6 Aug. 1699.
[98] *London Post*, 27–30 Sept. 1700. See also Stevenson, *Popular Disturbances*, 49.
[99] *HMC Portland*, iv. 279, 335; SP 34/8, fos. 73–4, 76–9.
[100] NCR, Case 20a/16, 7 May 1698.
[101] MCB 26, fo. 251; NCR, Case 20a/17, 18 Jan. 1707, 20a/19, 15 July 1721. Gamekeepers were also appointed by the lords of the manor of Lakenham and Hellesdon, both in the county of Norwich, and registered at quarter sessions: Case 20a/19, 15 July 1721, 7 Apr. 1722.

before 1640. These were now less common, rarely (as under Charles I) featured the crown as chief predator, and occurred mostly in rural areas, but there was a long-running dispute between the citizens of Coventry and the owners of nearby Cheylesmere Park.[102]

A somewhat different dispute over land use arose at York in 1672. On Shrove Tuesday, several hundred servants and apprentices were walking, talking, and allegedly doing 'much worse things' in the minster yard, disturbing those inside. One of the canons asked them either to come to the service or to leave; he seized the hat of one 'rude boy'. Others said that he provoked the youths, who may well have felt that they had a right to disport themselves in a public place on a holiday. After the service, the youths followed the canon to his house and broke his windows.[103] Here we have, not so much a conflict between order and disorder, but rather one between two kinds of order: the youths believed they were harmlessly enjoying themselves, the clergy that they were profaning sacred space.[104] In such cases, formal power rested with those in authority, but the people had numbers. Riot was the weapon of the weak, the mode of negotiation of those unable to aspire to responsible offices in parish or town. Often it was the weapon of last resort, used when attempts to secure redress through negotiation and appeals to the authorities had failed; and often it involved little or no violence.[105] Only when those in authority failed to respond, or powerful men wilfully abused their power, were riots likely to become more violent.

The most common cause of rioting was that people were unable to feed their families. Sometimes their livelihoods were threatened, by what were seen as unfair practices by their employers, or foreign competition. There were sporadic disputes between the Newcastle keelmen and the masters of the ships in which coal was transported.[106] In 1710 two judges thought the root of the problem was a restrictive contract between some of the colliery owners and the

[102] J. G. Kilmartin, 'Popular Rejoicing and Public Ritual in Norwich and Coventry, 1660–1835', Ph.D. thesis (Warwick, 1987), 87–8; M. Beloff, *Public Order and Popular Disturbances in England, 1660–1714* (London, 1963), 76–7.

[103] *CSPD 1672–3*, 546–7, *1673*, 36; BL, Egerton MS 3332, fo. 1 (misdated 1681). It would be interesting to know the nature of the provocation.

[104] See K. Wrightson, 'Two Concepts of Order: Justices, Constables and Jurymen in Seventeenth-Century England', in J. Brewer and J. Styles (eds.), *An Ungovernable People: The English and their Law in the Seventeenth and Eighteenth Centuries* (London, 1980), ch. 1.

[105] See Wrightson and Walter, 'Dearth and the Social Order'; J. Walter, 'Grain Riots and Popular Attitudes to the Law: Maldon and the Crisis of 1629', in Brewer and Styles (eds.), *An Ungovernable People*, ch. 2.

[106] *HMC le Fleming*, 79; Carte MS 239, fo. 97; *Weekly Journal or Saturday's Post*, 27 June 1719.

Thames lightermen.[107] There were a series of disputes in Colchester, as weavers sought higher wages. In 1675, at a time of drought and general stress (and following riots by weavers in London), the weavers marched round the town, led by a man blowing a horn. There were threats against the masters, but no violence.[108] In 1715 the weavers rioted after the employers and the Dutch Bay Hall, where cloths were sealed, ignored a number of complaints. These included the employers' refusal to provide the shuttles and other 'tackle' for their looms (the weavers provided the looms) as had been customary. Also the employers had changed the rates of payment and were not paying cash for woven cloth. The privy council deplored the weavers' riotous behaviour, but conceded that some of their complaints were justified.[109] The council's action did not bring peace for long. In 1719 the weavers complained that their masters expected them to produce a greater weight of cloth than they received in wool. They threatened to pull down the Dutch Hall and destroyed the weights there. They harmed nobody, but some who were arrested were freed next day by a large crowd.[110] The masters no doubt wanted to cut costs in the face of cheap imports. In Norwich, there were riots in July 1719, in which women had calicoes torn from their backs. The mayor's court pressed successfully for an Act of Parliament to ban the import of such fabrics.[111] In September crowds again attacked women wearing calicoes, seized them from shops, and destroyed them. They beat constables who tried to stop them and ignored the sheriffs' orders to disperse; they were eventually suppressed by the city's artillery company. In December there was a riot in Pockthorpe, just outside the walls. The rioters complained of lack of work and the wearing of calicoes and built a barricade of stones. Again they were dispersed by the artillery company.[112] The city's Whig rulers probably used the staunchly Whig artillery company because they feared that the militia would sympathize with the rioters.

The Norwich weavers' riots were by no means unique. In 1717 there were numerous riots in Devon, in protest against the treatment of weavers by the clothiers, who abused their monopoly position to drive down rates of pay.[113]

---

[107] SP, 34/12, fos. 141, 162, 170, 192, SP 34/13, fos. 24–6; Wilson, *Sense of the People*, 293–4.

[108] T. Glines, 'Politics and Society in the Borough of Colchester, 1660–93', Ph.D. thesis (University of Wisconsin, 1974), 150–4.

[109] PC 2/85, pp. 203–6.   [110] *Weekly Journal or British Gazetteer*, 14 Feb. 1719.

[111] MCB 28, fo. 3; FAB 9, fos. 79–80; NRO, Rye MS 18, pp. 1–2, 8.

[112] Blomefield, *Norfolk*, iii. 437; NRO, Rye MS 18, pp. 18–19, MS 79, p. 245, NCR, Case 20a/19, 14 Jan. 1721.

[113] *Post Man*, 28–30 Nov. 1717; *Weekly Journal or Saturday's Post*, 23 Nov. 1717; *Post Boy*, 19–21 Nov. 1717; Stevenson, 'Popular Disturbances', 104–5, 107–8.

But the most common cause of 'subsistence' riots was the dearness or scarcity of corn. These tended to focus on the movement of corn away from where it was grown, to a large town, or abroad. Following the very traditional analysis set out in books of orders issued by the crown between 1580 and 1640, the rioters blamed shortages on forestalling, regrating, and engrossing.[114] For much of this period there were few food riots. After protests in some south coast ports against the export of grain in the early 1660s,[115] there followed almost three decades of low prices. The next series of disorders came in 1692–3. They were blamed on foreign merchants, or those from seaports, buying up grain for export. In Colchester Dutch merchants bought large quantities.[116] At Worcester, dealers from Bristol bought up grain and other foodstuffs for export. In April 1693, crowds remained active for five days, carrying away all the grain from the market. Six rioters were rescued from prison and the crowd beat the magistrates, broke open houses, and carried away the corn. The mayor ordered all the freemen to appear in arms to keep order.[117] The government issued a commission of oyer and terminer to try the rioters and three were condemned to death; they were reprieved for a fortnight and it is not clear whether they were executed.[118] There were similar disorders in Weymouth, Shrewsbury, and Colchester, and widespread rumours that grain was being bought for export to France. To the rioters, the export of grain in time of dearth was totally illegitimate, doubly so if it was being sent to France. One expression of the rioters' sense of legitimization was the issuing of a 'proclamation' against carrying corn out of the kingdom by the rioters at Shrewsbury.[119]

In October 1693 the 'populacy' at Northampton forced the magistrates to act firmly against engrossing and forestalling, and the price of corn fell. There followed riots on several market days, in which sacks were cut and wagons thrown into the river. Women came to market with knives in their girdles 'to force corn at their own rates'.[120] The riots followed a royal proclamation against the export of grain.[121] There was another series of riots in June 1694, in which

[114] See P. Slack, 'Books of Orders: The Making of English Social Policy, 1577–1631', *TRHS*, 5th series, xxx (1980), 1–22; E. P. Thompson, 'The Moral Economy of the English Crowd in the Eighteenth Century', *P & P* 50 (1971), 76–136.

[115] *CSPD 1661–2*, 602, *1663–4*, 130–1; Southampton RO, SC 2/1/8, fo. 192; PC 2/56, fo. 163.

[116] Luttrell, ii. 629, iii. 20.   [117] Ibid. iii. 29, 91; *HMC Hastings*, ii. 229.

[118] Luttrell, iii. 111, 118; PC 2/75, p. 166; Carte MS 76, fo. 241.

[119] PC 2/75, p. 146; Luttrell, iii. 88.

[120] Carte MS 76, fos. 328, 341; (there is a copy of the second letter in *CSPD 1693*, 397); Luttrell, iii. 213.

[121] PC 2/75, pp. 260–1.

a crowd broke into an inn, beat the magistrates, and carried off two loads of corn; it was reported that two were killed and sixty or seventy injured.[122] There were grain riots in a variety of towns throughout the remainder of the 1690s. In October 1698 there was a proclamation against engrossing and an order to ban the export of grain; a few weeks before, forestallers had been beaten out of Brentford market.[123] In January 1699 Parliament banned grain exports for a year.[124] On Shrove Tuesday 1699 there were two incidents in Norwich where carts were stopped and sacks or corn and malt were taken; the mayor was allegedly informed, but took no action.[125]

There was even more widespread food rioting in 1709, when there was a serious famine in Scotland. The authorities and the crowds both blamed forestallers; at Colchester a crowd of over 200 threw stones and dirt at a grain dealer.[126] At Bristol, there were reports of large grain exports. Some 400 colliers from Kingswood appeared in the town on market day, 'under pretence of demanding bread'. Several warehouses were broken open and the magistrates' orders ignored; the rioters were appeased by the corporation's announcement that it would sell corn at low prices. When some rioters were imprisoned, they were rescued by their fellows. The militia was raised, along with volunteers from among the citizens, and order was soon restored, but not before several colliers had been wounded and the council house windows broken.[127] Later in the year there were renewed rumours of large-scale grain exports; the magistrates were at pains to deny them. They promised that they would enforce the queen's recent proclamation against forestalling and regrating, which must have strengthened the perception that the dearth owed much to the machinations of dealers and middlemen.[128] The lord mayor and aldermen of London told the council that the real problem was the large-scale export of grain, which the authorities had the power to discourage, but not to forbid. In November the Commons passed a bill to prohibit grain exports for nine months. The members' concern for their interests as landowners was, for once, outweighed by their fear of

[122] Carte MS 76, fo. 433; *CSPD 1694–5*, 227, 228, *1695*, 262–3.
[123] PC 2/77, pp. 250–1, 261; *Flying Post*, 13–15 Sept. 1698.   [124] Luttrell, iv. 470, 472.
[125] NCR, Case 12b/1, unlabelled bundle, information of Henry Thirkettle, 9 Mar. 1699, bundle marked 1690–9, informations of Henry Thirkettle and John Bowser, 7 Mar., Ann Smith, 25 Feb. 1699; *Post Boy*, 28 Feb.–2 Mar., 2–4 Mar. 1699.
[126] BL Add MS 61609, fos. 34, 38–9, 42, 61652, fo. 173.
[127] BL, Add MS 61608, fos. 165, 169, 172; *Post Boy*, 24–6 May 1709; BRO, 07831, 21 May 1709; BCL, B10163, 'A Catalogue of the Mayors'; Bodleian, MS Gough Somerset 2, pp. 84–5; Latimer, ii. 79.
[128] *Post Man*, 24–6 Nov. 1709.

disorder.[129] As the government was slow to take the necessary measures, towns-people took the law into their own hands. At Tewkesbury a crowd of 400 took corn off a boat bound for Bristol.[130] At Northampton there were a series of battles between the crowd on one hand and the magistrates and grain dealers on the other. The crowd was allegedly encouraged by attacks on grain dealers in a newspaper; it broke open houses, defied the magistrates and threatened to pull down the mayor's house and the town gaol.[131] The government took the complaints of the poor sufficiently seriously to order the mayor to do his utmost to prevent forestalling and regrating and to bring prices down.[132]

The frequent riots under William III and Anne show that, while towns-people normally respected and obeyed mayors and magistrates, they would defy them and even use violence against them if they failed to come up to the people's expectations of justice and fair dealing. At times, this was because the needs of government clashed with the people's views or interests, as in recruiting for the armed forces, the collection of unpopular taxes, and, in 1696, refusing to accept badly clipped coins. At other times, town authorities were simply unable to deliver what the people wanted. Grain dealers proved adept at avoiding market regulations, buying direct from farmers, selling corn in samples 'hugger mugger', rather than in the open market, or transporting grain in carts which claimed to be carrying something else; at Northampton, in 1709, they set up a 'by-market' just outside the town.[133] Towns might possess a sense of 'community', with a shared sense of identity and a common attitude to those outside. But that sense changed over time and was often contested, with at least the potential for violent conflict.[134] The limited power of the towns' rulers meant that authority was always fragile, obedience was always to some extent conditional on their delivering what the people expected. How they did so is the subject of the next chapter.

---

[129] Luttrell, vi. 503, 512, 516; BL Add MS 61609, fos. 34, 44.
[130] BL, Add MS 61609, fos. 44, 54, 56, 57.
[131] Ibid. 58–60, 114–15.
[132] BL, Add MS 61652, fo. 199.
[133] BL, Add MS 61609, fos. 60, 115.
[134] P. Withington and A. Shephard, 'Introduction', in Shephard and Withington (eds.), *Communities in Early Modern England,* 2–3, 6–12; Withington, 'Citizens, Community and Political Culture', in Ibid., 136; Borsay, 'Introduction', in Borsay (ed.), *Eighteenth-Century Town,* 35–6. For riots in the towns of Holland, see Price, *Holland and the Dutch Republic,* 94–5, 99–102.

3

Legitimizing Authority:
The Content of Government

An urban community needed to be governed, if ordered life was to be carried on. The streets needed to be maintained, water brought in, and sewage, ashes, and rubbish taken out. The poor needed to be relieved and standards of conduct, as defined by the respectable and hard-working, maintained. Trading had to be regulated, in order to ensure fair dealing and adequate provision of food. Guilds, or companies, still tried to confine the right to practise a trade to their members and to maintain standards of workmanship. Personal liberty and property had to be protected by effective enforcement of the law. Seventeenth-century towns had inherited from the middle ages a mixture of corporate regulation (of markets, manufactures, and retail) and individual responsibility (notably for the maintenance, cleansing, and lighting of the streets, although the corporation might play some part as well). The balance between corporate and individual responsibilities varied and was often disputed. In general, corporations were expected to fulfil their responsibilities, and to make householders fulfil theirs, with limited resources: modest revenues, personnel inadequate in both quantity and quality, and powers which rested on local by-laws rather than Acts of Parliament, and so could be questioned. Eventually a way was found to resolve these problems: Acts of Parliament enabling them to set up improvement commissions to pave, clean, and light the streets, levying a rate on householders to raise the necessary money. Towns began, in the 1690s, to secure Acts to establish corporations to manage the poor, but no improvement commission was set up, outside London, before 1737.[1]

---

[1] Sweet, *The English Town*, 42–3.

I. THE CIVIC FABRIC

In most towns, householders were responsible for paving and cleansing their half of the street in front of their houses. Parishes were responsible for the street next to churches and churchyards and the corporation was responsible for the street in front of civic buildings. As populations and trade grew, the pressures on the streets increased. Heavier carts and iron-bound wheels damaged road surfaces and there were numerous orders against them;[2] some towns encouraged the use of sledges in an effort to limit the damage.[3] Assigning responsibility for repairs to householders might make sense in theory, but proved difficult to enforce in practice. There were disputes as to who was responsible: some in Norwich involved three or four parties and took up to three years to resolve. At Leicester the corporation ordered an inspection of paving in 1716–17, to establish who was responsible for maintaining it, which implied that it did not know.[4] At Bristol, where space was at a premium, there were endless complaints that coal, timber, ashes, and building materials were piled in the streets. An Act of Parliament of 1700 reasserted the principle that Bristol householders were responsible for repairing and paving the street in front of their homes. The chamberlain was required to mend streets that were the city's responsibility and to scour gouts (sewers) and ditches, which might also involve work on the roads, and the common council was increasingly willing to make donations towards the cost of repairing major highways into the city, or other road repairs beyond the means of parishes.[5] At times grand juries were uncertain where the responsibility for repairs lay.[6] With monotonous regularity, grand juries presented householders for not repairing the streets outside their houses, failure to rail in cellars, dangerous structures, and the like. The civic leaders were among the offenders. Sir John Knight I was presented for not pitching (repairing) the street, not cleansing the doorway to his stables, leaving great marble stones on the quay, having a dangerous cellar

[2] BRB 6, pp. 347, 453, 680; *PSP*, 64; East, 6, 13, 97, 172.

[3] BRO, JQS/C/1, second pagination, pp. 22–3, 27, 04264/9, p. 158; Defoe, *Tour*, ii. 38; *RBL*, iv. 484, vii. 66, 81.

[4] NRO, NCR, Case 20a/15, 28 Apr. 1679, 11 Apr. 1681; FAB 8, fo. 81; MCB 25, fos. 34, 101, 105; *RBL*, v. 78–81, 84; Greaves, *Corporation*, 28–9.

[5] BRO, 04264/8, fo. 105, 04264/9, pp. 3–4, 39, 42, 50, 81, 136, 139, 170, 281, 349.

[6] BRO, JQS/C/1, 13 Apr. 1686, 24 Apr. 1688, second pagination, pp. 20, 57, 59.

door, and not repairing his house.[7] Sir Richard Crump and Alderman Day repeatedly failed to remove tons of stone and rubble which they had dumped in the river.[8] The largest volume of complaints was directed against the chamberlain. In 1665 there were twenty-three tasks that he was required to perform within a set time or face fines.[9] Some repairs—like the wall and steps by the weir (from which several had fallen and been drowned), the 'slip at the graving place', and the 'house of ease' on Aldworth's quay—remained unperformed for years.[10] (A slip was an artificial slope on which ships could be hauled out of the water; graving involved cleaning and re-pitching a ship's bottom.) These failures may have owed something to incompetence, but the basic problem was that the task of maintaining the civic fabric was too great. Bristolians carried on their businesses, stacked their building materials, and dumped their rubbish with little concern for their fellow citizens.

Other towns fared less badly than Bristol. Corporations assumed greater responsibility for rebuilding or widening at least the major streets and the market place.[11] Hull had the advantage of an ample supply of hard, round cobbles, which came in as ballast in Dutch ships or were given to the town by a local family.[12] Because the materials for repairs were freely available, the bench made frequent orders for repaving. In 1691 it ordered that the streets from the market place to Beverley Gate should be repaved, with a ridge in the middle and gutters on either side. In 1698 Celia Fiennes thought that the streets were in good repair.[13] In 1718–20 orders were given to pave High Street, part of Lowgate, and several lanes.[14] How far this was effective is uncertain; the orders given in 1720 were repeated in 1722. This may be explained by the tradition that, although the town provided the work materials, householders were expected to pay workmen for work done outside their houses.[15] A similar

---

[7] BRO, JQS/PR/1, St Thomas, Oct. 1664, St Stephen's and St Ewin's, 9 Oct. 1666, Temple and Redcliffe, same date; JQS/C/1, 4 Apr. and 11 July 1676, 8 Oct. 1678. (I use the titles Sir John Knight I and II following the practice in *HP 1660–90*.) For similar complaints from Portsmouth, see East, 6–7, 62, 75, 103, 729. In 1674 the town sought a private Act of Parliament for paving the streets: *CJ*, ix. 303, 308, 309.

[8] BRO, JQS/C/1, 2nd pagination, pp. 12, 13, 16, 19, 20.

[9] BRO, JQS/PR/1, Temple, 4 Apr. 1665.

[10] For the weir, see JQS/M/4, fos. 106–7, JQS/C/1, 24 Apr. 1688, 2nd pagination, pp. 5, 9; for the graving place see *CSPD 1680–1*, 441; JQS/C/1, p. 100, 13 Apr. 1686, 12 July 1687, 2nd pagination, p. 72; for the house of ease, see ibid., 2nd pagination, pp. 19, 22, 39. A presentment of 1681 suggests that the Merchants' Company was responsible for maintaining the graving place: ibid. 39.

[11] Jones and Falkus, 'Urban Improvement', 129–31, 135–6.

[12] Gillett and MacMahon, *Hull*, 201–2; Jackson, *Hull*, 310–11; BRB 6, p. 298.

[13] BRB 6, p. 269; Fiennes, 88. See also BRB 6, pp. 259, 298, 347.

[14] BRB 6, pp. 681, 694.   [15] BRB 6, p. 709; Jackson, *Hull*, 310–11.

arrangement existed in Winchester, using stone from the ruined castle to pave the streets.[16]

Street cleansing was also the responsibility of householders. Norwich corporation expected every household to have a privy and officials were ordered to prosecute those who did not.[17] Householders were supposedly responsible for having their sewage carted away, but much found its way into the streets, the common sewers (cockeys), and gutters (kennels). Cockeys included both natural streams and man-made drains, which carried away much effluent. The mouths and heads needed to be kept free, which was the city's responsibility; gates were used to help in their management and muck was sieved out in cisterns and sold. However, rubbish was often dumped in them, and in the streets. Sudden rains flushed all this dirt into the river, contaminating the water and obstructing navigation.[18] At Bristol there were complaints that some allowed their privies to overflow or to empty into the street. There were frequent complaints of the stench from pigsties. Two were presented for killing pigs and leaving the remains in the streets. In 1696 a grand jury expressed surprise that the city was so healthy, given the smell from a multitude of swine.[19]

Most corporations realized, sooner or later, that it was unrealistic to expect every householder to carry away their own rubbish and sewage, and to clean the street in front of their houses. Gloucester in 1679 expected them to do so every Saturday,[20] but most towns required them only to have it piled up, ready for removal by a scavenger, once or twice a week. London appointed a team of scavengers to collect and carry away the muck as early as 1672.[21] At Hull the traditional practice was for every householder to sweep the street in front of his house and carry the dirt and sewage to one of the gates or staithes, from which it would be removed by scavengers. In case of default, scavengers were to cart it away, charge the negligent householders 6*d.* per sledge, and present them at sessions.[22] By 1698 each gate had a scavenger, who carried the dirt dumped there to nearby villages, where it was used to manure the fields.[23] But dirt was

[16] Hants RO, W/B1/6, fo. 15.

[17] MCB 23, fo. 259. See M. Pelling, 'Health and Sanitation to 1750', in *Norwich since 1550*, 136–7.

[18] MCB 26, fo. 69; FAB 8, fos. 128–9; Pelling, in *Norwich since 1550*, 126–31.

[19] BRO, JQS/PR/1, St Mary's, 20 Oct. 1662 and 12 Oct. 1664, Temple, 12 Oct. 1665; JQS/C/1, 2nd pagination, pp. 43, 52, 77. For keeping pigs, see Cambs RO, Cambridge Corporation MS II.10 (Order Book, 1686), pp. 34–5; East, 92, 96, 99; BRB 6, pp. 174, 190. For the misdeeds of butchers, see Hants RO, W/D3/86, fos. 23, 57, D3/93a, D3/104; East, 95, 100.

[20] Gloucs RO, GBR B3/3, p. 722.

[21] N. Brett James, *The Growth of Stuart London* (London, 1935), 436–7.

[22] BRB 6, pp. 357, 398–9.   [23] Ibid. 424.

still dumped secretly at the gates, in ditches and sewers, and even in Holy Trinity churchyard.[24] In 1722 the bench ordered that, if householders failed to clean the streets, any alderman could appoint a constable and a scavenger to do it for them, charging them in proportion to the amount of dirt removed.[25] In view of the increase in the town's trade and population, it is unlikely that the streets became cleaner in this period.

Norwich tried repeatedly to establish scavengers, but the assembly and mayor's court continued to remind householders that it was their responsibility to sweep the streets and cart away the muck.[26] Having resolved to appoint scavengers in 1664, 1678, and 1685, the assembly decided in 1686 to appoint a surveyor in each great ward, who was to fine householders who failed to cart their muck away.[27] For the corporation, responsibility for street cleaning lay with householders; the corporation's task was to ensure that they were properly supervised and informed of what they had to do. The surveyors failed to do this satisfactorily and others were appointed to perform the same tasks.[28] In 1711 and 1719 the assembly appointed a scavenger for each great ward, but (like the surveyors) they were to see that householders kept the streets clean, not clean them themselves.[29] The Norwich quarter sessions records show occasional prosecutions for failing to repair the streets, but not for failing to clean them.[30] Similarly, Bristol corporation experimented repeatedly with entrusting street cleansing and rubbish removal to a scavenger or scavengers, paid for by rates, and repeatedly shifted the burden back to householders, so the two sets of duties —those of the householders and those of the scavengers—continued, uneasily, side by side. Scavengers were repeatedly accused of negligence.[31] Attempts to shift responsibility to the parishes were no more successful. In 1673 the common council ordered that there should be a scavenger for each parish, paid for by a rate. The order was extended in 1686 and reissued several times thereafter.[32] But some inhabitants refused to pay the rate and some parishes

---

[24] BRB 6, pp. 473, 693, 694.   [25] Ibid. 709.

[26] MCB 23, fos. 215, 279, MCB 24, fos. 21, 87, 113, 221, MCB 25, fos. 36, 192; FAB 8, fo. 81.

[27] FAB 6, fos. 260, 275, FAB 8, fos. 64, 118, 119, 128–9; MCB 25, fo. 206.

[28] MCB 25, fos. 226, 329, MCB 26, fos. 57, 69; FAB 8, fos. 170, 180, 190, 212, 227; NCR, Case 20a/17, 18 Jan. 1707.

[29] FAB 9, fos. 28, 77; MCB 27, fo. 66.

[30] After a great storm in 1715 the chamberlain, not the inhabitants, was ordered to clean up: NCR, Case 20a/18, 30 Apr. 1715.

[31] BRO, JQS/PR/1, St Mary's, 20 Oct. 1662, Trinity, 11 Oct. 1664, St Ewin's and St Stephen's, 12 Oct. 1664, Temple, 12 Oct. 1665, pp. 12, 30, 39, 12 Jan. 1681, 04417/3, fo. 28; JQS/M/5, fo. 56.

[32] BRO, 04264/6, p. 276, 04264/7, fo. 235.

persistently failed to appoint a scavenger.³³ In despair, in 1677 quarter sessions reverted to the principle that cleansing was the responsibility of householders, which they tried to enforce with the threat of a £10 fine.³⁴ In 1694 the common council reverted to the idea of a general scavenger, but complaints continued.³⁵ The Act of Parliament of 1700 reaffirmed the responsibilities of householders and churchwardens to clean the streets twice a week; the parishes were to pay scavengers to carry dirt away.³⁶ Some parishes seem to have taken their responsibilities seriously. In 1708 St Stephen's and St Nicholas, the parishes that included the Marsh, were given permission to build a wharf where dirt and ashes could be stored until they could be carried downriver by lighters; two years later the mayor and aldermen were again asked to find a suitable place.³⁷ However, in 1722 the inhabitants of Queen Square complained of the state of the waste ground behind their houses and the mayor reported that there was no convenient place in the two parishes to dump dung and waste.³⁸ With the common council unwilling to spend more than a pittance on cleaning, it is unlikely that the state of the streets improved at all. An Act of Parliament of 1715 empowered city corporations to levy a rate of up to 6*d.* in the pound towards the cost of a scavenger, but none of our towns seems to have done so.³⁹

Other towns fared little better. In Portsmouth householders were supposed to sweep up the dirt and scavengers to carry it away, but the scavengers were often accused of negligence and at times there was no scavenger—and the streets were filthy.⁴⁰ At Oxford both city and university claimed jurisdiction over the streets. In 1672 the university and city justices agreed to appoint a common scavenger, with the colleges and the city ratepayers providing the money. In practice, however, the responsibility for cleansing the streets normally fell to the city. The freemen were expected to clean the streets before their houses, twice a week, and pile the dirt up ready for the scavenger to carry away.⁴¹ The relative paucity of orders about cleansing the streets suggest that it was done as well as the council expected, which may not be saying very much. However, Fiennes thought the streets very clean.⁴² At Winchester, householders were expected to sweep the streets and leave the dirt (including that from inside

---

³³ BRO, JQS/M/5, fos. 85, 87–8, JQS/C/1, 9 Jan. 1677, pp. 125, 129, 2nd pagination, pp. 3, 13, 18, 04264/7, fo. 244.
³⁴ BRO, JQS/M/5, fo. 137.   ³⁵ BRO, 04264/8, p. 105, JQS/C/1, p. 49.
³⁶ BRO, 04264/8, fo. 187; Latimer, i. 491.   ³⁷ BRO, 04264/9, pp. 159, 254.
³⁸ Ibid. 623.   ³⁹ Jones and Falkus, 'Urban Improvement', 136.
⁴⁰ East, 67, 72, 74, 95, 99–101, 103–4, 172, 195, 728.
⁴¹ *OCA*, iii. 54, 137.   ⁴² Fiennes, 32.

their houses) to be collected by scavengers. If they failed to do this, they could be fined one shilling.[43] A succession of scavengers were appointed, paying rents as low as 6*d.* a year in return for which they were able to dispose of the dung to farmers and market gardeners.[44] A rate was imposed for the scavenger; although many refused to pay, by the 1690s it was bringing in about £20 a year.[45] Despite the scavenger's potential profits, there were frequent complaints of negligence on his part,[46] and on the part of householders.[47]

If most towns made some effort to keep the streets paved and clean, some did little or nothing to have them lit. Many towns had a 9 p.m. curfew and little social life in the evenings.[48] At Leicester the first lamps were set up in 1768–70.[49] At Winchester, the only orders to hang out lights came on the occasion of royal visits, in 1683 and 1705.[50] At Oxford the council continued to rely on a by-law of 1614, which required householders to set out lanterns and candles between 6 and 9 p.m. in the winter months, on pain of a fine; many neglected or refused to do so.[51] The Act of 1700 reiterating Bristol householders' obligation to pave and clean the streets, also required those paying 2*d.* or more per week in poor rate to set out lanterns from dusk to midnight between Michaelmas and Lady Day, on pain of a fine. If parishes decided to levy a rate instead for the maintenance of lights, they were empowered to do so.[52] Some parishes chose to set up fewer and more powerful lights (presumably oil lamps), but some became negligent with time.[53] At Hull, since 1621 wealthier householders had been required to put lanterns at their doors in the winter and this obligation was extended in 1672.[54] There was, however, an increasing awareness that lanterns and candles did not provide enough light and in 1713 the corporation purchased a suitable number of oil lamps. As the cost was too great to be borne by individuals, the aldermen were to solicit subscriptions.[55] These did not

[43] Hants RO, W/B1/6, fos. 24–5.
[44] Hants RO, W/F2/5, fo. 193, W/B1/6, fo. 154, B1/8, fo. 2, B1/9, fos. 16, 68, B2/5, 15 Apr. 1707, F2/6, fos. 231–2.
[45] Hants RO, W/D3/1, fos. 12, 15, 20–1, 80–2, 106, 115, 119.
[46] Hants RO, W/B1/5, fos. 156–7, W/D3/78, D3/85, fos. 29, 64, D3/95, fo. 36.
[47] Hants RO, W/D3/86, fo. 20. For other towns, see Borsay, *Urban Renaissance*, 69–71.
[48] Ellis, *Georgian Town*, 89–90, 101.
[49] Greaves, *Corporation*, 27; Simmons, *Leicester*, 122.
[50] Hants RO, W/B1/6, fo. 154, B1/7, fo. 219.   [51] *OCA*, ii. 333, iii. 195–6, 251.
[52] BRO, 04417/2, 22 Dec. 1660, 04264/8, fo. 181; Latimer, i. 301–2, 492. See also Jones and Falkus, 'Urban Improvement', 134–5.
[53] Latimer, ii. 37–8, 82.
[54] Gillett and MacMahon, *Hull,* 204; BRB 6, pp. 451–2, 457, 458.
[55] BRB 6, pp. 625, 641, 665.

bring in enough, so the corporation made up the deficit of ten to fifteen pounds a year. A lighting rate for the town was introduced in 1762.[56]

Norwich, too, became aware that candles and lanterns could not light the streets satisfactorily and, anyway, many failed to put them out.[57] In London there was increasing use of oil-burning lamps, but these were much too expensive for individual householders and provided more light than was normally needed. By 1694 London householders were contracting with lighting companies to fulfil their obligations.[58] In 1700 a clause in the Norwich Waterworks Act empowered the corporation to appoint an undertaker to set up lamps as directed by the mayor's court. Citizens were invited to subscribe towards the cost, through a voluntary parish rate; those who did not wish to do so were to hang out lanterns, as before. In addition, all householders were to pay a rate towards the lights provided by the city—probably the first compulsory lighting rate. The citizens' reaction was hostile; some of the new lamps were broken.[59] After complaints to quarter sessions in 1699, many people were exempted from paying the rate or had their assessments reduced. As these complaints antedated the Act, it seems that the corporation introduced the rate on its own authority and then secured the authority of Parliament when it met with opposition.[60] The mayor's court complained in 1708 and 1711 that the Act was much neglected.[61] A clause added to the Norwich Workhouse Act of 1712 empowered the aldermen of each ward to assess how many lamps would be needed and again citizens were to be invited to subscribe towards them. Those who refused were to set up lanterns, on pain of a two shilling fine.[62] However, the private enterprise element threatened to get out of control, as unauthorized undertakers set up lamps and tried to charge for them. The mayor's court stressed that only those who subscribed to the city scheme would be exempt from providing lights themselves.[63] In 1715 it was clear that the subscriptions

[56] BRB 6, pp. 650, 665, 676; Gillett and MacMahon, *Hull*, 204.

[57] NCR, Case 12c/2. No. 496.

[58] M. Falkus, 'Lighting the Dark Ages of English Economic History: Town Streets before the Industrial Revolution', in D. C. Coleman and A. H. John (eds.), *Trade, Government and Economy in Pre-industrial England* (London, 1976), 254–7. Oil lamps in Norwich cost 17s. each in 1716: MCB 27, fo. 242.

[59] MCB 26, fos. 94, 96, 118, 139; Falkus, 'Dark Ages', 257; Jones and Falkus, 'Urban Improvement', 134–5; Blomefield, *Norfolk*, iii. 427. On other towns, see Falkus, 'Dark Ages', 257–62; Borsay, *Urban Renaissance*, 72–4.

[60] NCR, Case 20a/16, 22 Apr. 1699: sixty-six people secured exemptions or reductions; there were only eight such cases between 1701 and 1706.

[61] MCB 26, fos. 272, 274, MCB 27, fo. 63.

[62] MCB 27, fos. 94, 99, 103, 104, 128.   [63] Ibid. 108, 140–1.

were not bringing in enough, so the existing lighting rate, to meet the cost of lights on public buildings, was increased.[64] The dual system continued, with some opting to set out their own lights and other subscribing to the city scheme. A few were fined for not setting up lights, or challenged the level at which they were rated, and occasionally lamps were broken, but overt opposition to the scheme seems to have diminished.[65] While the citizens of Norwich may well have thought that street lighting was desirable, they did not wish to set up lanterns, or pay others to provide oil lamps. Although the scheme was rooted in the by-laws, reinforced by two Acts of Parliament, some fought it all the way.

Norwich corporation enjoyed greater success in its efforts to improve the water supply, which in 1660 consisted primarily of wells; water was also conveyed from the river to cisterns in the city, from which it was piped to the homes of a few wealthy citizens.[66] Here there was no question of individual obligations imposed by by-laws, although parishes could be ordered to repair their wells.[67] New wells and pumps were added, the use of which was restricted to those with shops in the fish market or paying a rent to the city.[68] In 1698 discussions began with undertakers, who were to supply new cisterns; the undertakers paid a rent to the city and charged consumers for their water.[69] The experience of other towns was similar. Since the reign of James I, water had been pumped into Hull, presumably using a horse-driven engine, to a limited number of paying customers.[70] The bench ordered the setting up of additional pumps and in 1700 bought one-third of the shares in the water company, for around £370.[71] A committee found many faults in the water house and engines; the horses were inadequate and the pipes were faulty.[72] The purchase gave the corporation some control over the delivery of water and yielded an annual profit, which by 1711–12 had reached £42.[73] Leicester, too, already had a conduit in the market place; there was a water house, where the water was pumped (by horses?) into pipes to serve the town once a day. There were also a number of wells, with pumps or wheels to draw up the water, which were the responsibility of the wards, and were supposedly supervised by pump or well reeves.[74] Some wells were decrepit or

[64] MCB 27, fos. 210, 211, 214, 231–2.
[65] Ibid. 246, 250; *Norwich Gazette*, 11–18 Nov. 1710.
[66] Pelling, in *Norwich since 1550*, 131–6.   [67] FAB 6, fo. 258.
[68] FAB 8, fos. 85, 117, 118; MCB 25, fos. 100, 218, MCB 26, fo. 117.
[69] MCB 26, fo. 49*; FAB 8, fo. 226, FAB 9, fos. 11, 20; NRO, MS 453, 'A Description', under 1697.
[70] Gillett and MacMahon, *Hull*, 111; Jackson, *Hull*, 314.   [71] BRB 6, pp. 148, 158, 465–6.
[72] Ibid. 431, 435, 438, 440.   [73] Ibid. 527, 555, 627.
[74] LHP 32A, no. 157; *RBL*, vii, p. xxxiii; Fiennes, 163; Greaves, *Corporation*, 31–2.

dangerous, others were allegedly filled in by private individuals.[75] The corporation accepted responsibility for the conduit, which was 'handsomely' rebuilt in 1709; it also contributed towards the cost of a cistern, to increase the amount of water that could be stored at the conduit. But there was no attempt to reform the provision of water until 1749–50.[76] Oxford was another town that improved its water supply; work started in 1695 on a new water engine capable of conveying water to all parts of the city.[77] Celia Fiennes, as she toured England in the 1690s, noted a number of towns with piped water. At Beverley it was drawn up by pulleys and weights; at Derby there was a water engine; at Shrewsbury, the water was currently drawn up by horses, but it was intended to make a water engine, using the flow of the river.[78] Worcester already had such an engine, but also used horses to pump water, and water was sold in leather bags.[79]

One exception to the general improvement of water supplies was Bristol.[80] In 1660, apart from wells, the city had only a conduit supplying pipes on the quay and Back with water from a spring. There are frequent references to removing dead cats from the pipes, a problem not resolved until the council built a conduit house at the spring in 1679. There were also complaints that the woman who kept the pipe on the quay disposed of the water as she pleased; the pipe was sometimes broken and unusable.[81] The initiative for improving the supply came from undertakers. The common council haggled at length about financial terms and ordered its MPs to oppose a bill to establish a water company. The bill passed nevertheless. Water from the Avon was pumped into a reservoir and fed by gravity into the city in elm pipes. Customers paid £2 per house per year. Meanwhile, the city continued to pipe water from Jacob's Well to College Green for those prepared to pay for it.[82] The council seems to have had as little as possible to do with the water company and continued its own supply alongside the company's.[83]

---

[75] *RBL*, vii. 55, 74–5, 87.

[76] Ibid. v. 48, 58–9; LHP 38, no. 222; Fiennes, 163; Greaves, *Corporation*, 31–2.

[77] *OCA*, iii. 250–1; Wood, iii. 485; *HMC le Fleming*, 335.

[78] Fiennes, 86, 169–70, 227; McInnes, 'Leisure Town', 72–3. Other towns mentioned as having piped water or a conduit were Coventry, Newcastle, Durham, Exeter, and Plymouth: Fiennes, 113, 209–10, 215, 247–8, 252.

[79] *HMC Portland*, ii. 291.

[80] Portsmouth seems to have been supplied only by pumps and water carriers: East, 13, 17, 83, 172.

[81] Latimer, i. 289–90, 396; BRO, JQS/PR/1, St Stephen's and St Ewin's, 9 Oct. 1666, JQS/M/4, fo. 151, JQS/M/5, fos. 47, 58.

[82] BRO, 04264/8, pp. 110, 115, 117, 119, 124, 143–4; Latimer, i. 468–9.

[83] Latimer, ii. 17, 82–3, 237.

Most town governments took some responsibility for providing the basic necessities of civilized living, but their approach was generally unimaginative, based on the traditional responsibility of individual householders to keep the streets paved, clean, and lit, and for disposal of sewage and rubbish. This is what the citizens expected, but they were not prepared to put in the necessary work, or to pay others to do it for them. Only in street lighting did new technology, in the form of oil lamps, make a different approach possible. There was also some response to new technology in the means used to combat fire: alongside the traditional requirement that certain citizens keep leather buckets and fire hooks, towns began to acquire fire engines, and replace them with newer models.[84] One apparent exception was Portsmouth, which had greater need than most. There were large stores of pitch and tar, gunpowder was carried through the streets in open carts, and the townspeople had a habit of 'anointing' rats with turpentine and setting light to them.[85] In perhaps the most important area of innovation, the supply of water, the initiative generally came from undertakers but, with the exception of Bristol, most corporations embraced their proposals and Hull acquired a share in the company. As town corporations proved more willing to embrace new approaches when dealing with the poor, it must be assumed that townspeople were reasonably satisfied with the way they looked after the streets. They might complain about dirt, broken paving, and the dangers of ill-lit streets. But they were not prepared to pay more or put in more effort to improve the situation.

II. SOCIAL AND MORAL ORDER

Much discussion of social policy before the Restoration centres on 'Puritan' morality, and how far it drove 'parish elites' to discipline the unruly and ungodly poor.[86] This view emphasizes the social at the expense of the sacred,[87] and, by focusing on the exercise of authority, inevitably identifies Puritans as the more powerful members of the community. It can be refined by adding a spiritual

---

[84] BRO, 04264/6, pp. 149, 185–8, 04264/9, pp. 3, 438–9, 467–8; Latimer, ii. 53–4; BRB 6, pp. 351, 547, 556, 569, 646, 649, 651, 657, 664; *RBL*, iv. 556, v. 94; LHB 5, fo. 18.

[85] Portsmouth RO, CE 1/8, fo. 42; East, 91, 93, 94.

[86] K. Wrightson. *English Society 1580–1680*, new edn. (London, 2003), 173–81; K. Wrightson and D. Levine, *Poverty and Piety in an English Village: Terling, 1525–1700* (Oxford, 1995), 133–41, 175–83.

[87] M. Spufford, 'Puritanism and Social Control?', in A. J. Fletcher and J. Stevenson (eds.), *Order and Disorder in Early Modern England* (Cambridge, 1985), 43.

dimension: fighting sin could ward off the wrath of God.[88] In analysing social policy, one could try to distinguish between order and moral improvement, purely practical concerns and those driven by religion, but this is easier said than done. Unproductive vagrants and illegitimate children placed a burden on the poor rate and had been condemned in the thirteenth century as well as the sixteenth.[89] Punishment of drunkenness or gambling, and attempts to suppress stage plays, might stem from moral distaste or a belief that people were spending money that they could not afford and being tempted away from their work. The prohibition of travelling, working, drinking, or playing games on the sabbath could reflect fear of provoking God, or the knowledge that temptations to self-indulgence were greatest on the day people did not work.

None of the elements of post-Reformation social policy was wholly new or exclusively 'Puritan'. There had been attempts to suppress church ales, and wrestling, dancing, and gaming on Sunday, in the thirteenth century.[90] Humanist programmes of social reform were directed against similar ills, and used similar methods, to those of Elizabeth's reign. Moral improvement and the material good of the community went together: setting the poor on work was designed to inculcate habits of hard work and thrift.[91] Much of the social policy of godly towns was acceptable to Archbishop Laud.[92] In the 1640s and 1650s, Puritans tried to reform their fellow citizens, with limited success. Lacking widespread public support, even the major generals achieved relatively little.[93] At the Restoration, some aspects of urban social policy were generally accepted, such as preventing those with no visible means of support from becoming 'chargeable' to the poor rate. As Puritans lost power in towns, one might expect distinctively 'Puritan' concerns, such as rigorous sabbath observance, to become much less prominent: Paul Slack claimed that 'zeal had little place in Restoration towns', so he said little about urban social policy.[94] However, it might be asked whether 'Puritans' really did lose power in towns. After the purges following the Corporation Act, partial conformists, Dissenting sympathizers, and even

---

[88] Seen brilliantly in D. Underdown, *Fire from Heaven: Life in an English Town in the Seventeenth Century* (London, 1992). See also P. Slack, 'Poverty and Politics in Salisbury, 1597–1666', in Clark and Slack (eds.), *Crisis and Order in English Towns*, ch. 5.

[89] Spufford, 'Puritanism and Social Control?', 51–7.   [90] Ibid. 50–1.

[91] P. Slack, *From Reformation to Improvement: Public Welfare in Early Modern England* (Oxford, 1999), 9–17, 29–36, 48–9.

[92] Ibid. 43–4.

[93] Ibid. 50–1; C. Durston, *Cromwell's Major Generals* (Manchester, 2001), ch. 8 and *passim*; C. Durston 'Puritan Rule and the Failure of Cultural Revolution, 1645–60', in C. Durston and J. Eyles (eds.), *The Culture of English Puritanism, 1560–1700* (Basingstoke, 1996), ch. 7.

[94] Slack, *Reformation to Improvement*, 51 and *passim*.

Dissenters soon returned to municipal office.[95] Besides, no major element of earlier policy was exclusively Puritan; many Tories and High Anglicans also wished to make the feckless poor into useful citizens.[96] In Norwich the leading advocate of a workhouse in the 1660s was Lord Henry Howard, a Catholic.[97] From the 1690s movements to promote moral reformation, corporations of the poor, and workhouses involved people from the whole religious spectrum. Within the Church, the Society for the Propagation of Christian Knowledge emphasized the link between labour discipline and piety.[98]

Writers in the Puritan, Nonconformist tradition tend to claim for their forebears a monopoly of moral fervour, and depict the Church of England as concerned more with conformity than with combating sin. But the Restoration Anglican clergy preached endlessly on the dangers of scepticism and libertinism, urging their flocks to lead good Christian lives.[99] The Cavalier House of Commons, which passed many laws against Dissent, condemned sabbath-breaking and profane swearing; the bishops tried to keep morris dancers out of the churches.[100] Under Charles II the aldermen of Norwich practised a broad churchmanship, attending church regularly, usually without taking communion, and making little effort to persecute Dissenters. Under Anne, the majority were High Church Tories, deeply committed to the Church's liturgy and rituals.[101] 'Toryism to the height' was the 'prevailing humour' in the city.[102] Yet the corporation's social policy remained much the same, except that it tried to use its power over the poor for partisan and denominational ends. The vision underlying this social policy was Christian and traditional. The labouring poor needed to work hard to make ends meet. Fathers should accept their responsibilities, live frugally, avoid the temptations of idleness and the alehouse, and maintain discipline over their families. Wives and children should submit willingly to this discipline, because women and the young were more

[95] See Gauci, *Yarmouth*, 73–4, 103–4; Hurwich, ' "Fanatick Town" ', 16, 19–26.
[96] Slack, *Reformation to Improvement*, 104–6; Barry, 'Popular Culture', 75–6; J. Barry, 'Bristol as a Reformation City', in N. Tyacke (ed.), *Britain's Long Reformation* (London, 1998), *passim*; M. E. Fissell, 'Charity Universal? Institutions and Moral Reform in Eighteenth-Century Bristol', in *Stilling*, 121–3. See also N. Key and J. P. Ward, ' "Divided into Parties": Exclusion Crisis Origins in Monmouth', *EHR* cxv (2000), 1162.
[97] MCB 24, fo. 46.
[98] Slack, *Reformation to Improvement*, 103–9, 12–14, 124; T. Hitchcock, 'Paupers and Preachers: The SPCK and the Parochial Workhouse Movement', in *Stilling*, 149, 152–3.
[99] J. Spurr, *The Restoration Church of England, 1646–89* (New Haven, 1991), chs. 5–6.
[100] R. Hutton, *The Rise and Fall of Merry England* (Oxford, 1994), 232–3.
[101] Note references to kneeling on 'dosses', which became worn out: MCB 26, fos. 160, 219, 254, 261, 278, MCB 27, fo. 41.
[102] NRO, DCN 115/1, p. 224.

likely to err. Single women should find a husband or master to take care of, and answer for, them. As fallen humankind could not resist temptation unaided, the city fathers intervened to save people from themselves, punishing lapses and removing temptation, by restricting stage plays, closing disorderly ale-houses, and keeping the sabbath holy. Not all could be reduced to keeping the peace and lowering the poor rate. Plays not only tempted the unwary to waste time and money, they were also allegedly often obscene. Boys playing in the streets during Sunday services were neither neglecting their work nor wasting their money, but they were an affront to God.[103] The moral vision of the Norwich mayor's court clearly enjoyed the support of many respectable citizens, as shown by grand jury presentments and informations against dis-orderly alehouses; how far the corporation's desire to ban smoking in the streets was shared by the citizens is unknown.[104] The enforcement of this moral vision helped to legitimize the authority of the city's rulers in the eyes of the 'better sort' in the city.

At the heart of the treatment of the poor lay a distinction between the deserving and undeserving, enshrined in the poor law statutes of 1598 and 1601. The deserving were poor through no fault of their own—the old, the sick, children, and men unable to find enough work in difficult times to support their families. The undeserving were vagrants and the 'loose, idle, and disorderly', unable to support themselves because of their moral inadequacy. These could be sent by a single JP to the house of correction, where they were whipped and put to hard labour; fathers who failed to support their families were made to work and part of their income was paid to their wives and children. Children who disobeyed and abused their parents might also be sent there.[105] This punishment was intended to make the idle and irresponsible see the need to support themselves and their families. Vagrants could be sent back to their home parish and flogged in every parish en route. In fact, in Norwich far fewer people were punished as vagrants after 1660 than under James I. There and at Bristol most of those punished had been caught begging or pilfering; the magistrates sometimes also punished pedlars and fortune tellers.[106] One reason

---

[103] Barry, 'Reformation City', 271–2; Fissell, in *Stilling*, 123, 128.

[104] FAB 8, fo. 43, MCB 24, fo. 275, MCB 25, fo. 7.

[105] MCB 24, fo. 99, MCB 25, fo. 255; *VCH City of York*, 228. Legislation laid down more and more specific offences for which people could be committed, but many were still punished for defects of character: Innes, 'Prisons for the Poor', 85–8 and *passim*.

[106] Pound, *Tudor and Stuart Norwich*, 111; BRO, 04417/1, fo. 40, 04417/2, 16 June 1661, 04417/3, fos. 50, 57, JQS/M/4, fos. 78, 104, 109, JQS/M/5, fos. 30, 45. (In only two of these cases is there no reference to begging or pilfering.)

for the fall in the number of vagrants was the Act of Settlement of 1662. This extended the assumption that each parish was responsible for its own poor by establishing a procedure for deciding the parish where each person was 'settled'. Migrant or seasonal workers were granted certificates showing where they were legally settled, so that they would not be treated as vagrants. Hitherto, deciding whether someone was a vagrant or legitimately seeking work had depended on the magistrates' impression of their moral worth; now there was the objective criterion of the certificate.[107] The Act also made it more difficult for people to find settlement in a new parish, by laying down stringent conditions, including finding sureties that they would not become a burden on the poor rate.[108] The authorities watched out for lodgers, whom poor people took into their homes in order to make a little money: if they remained undetected long enough, they would be able to claim settlement.[109] They were particularly suspicious of unemployed single women, 'living at their own hand', who were told to 'get themselves a service'—find a master or employer—or leave town.[110] The authorities also tried to prohibit begging. In Norwich the poor were traditionally allowed to beg in the period before Christmas. The mayor's court prohibited this in some years, and ordered collections for the poor in the churches, but these brought in so little that it reluctantly allowed the poor to resume begging.[111] Begging continued to be tolerated, especially in assize week, well into the eighteenth century.[112]

The Act of Settlement reduced the element of moral judgement in the treatment of the poor. It was reduced further by an Act of 1697, which said that a person could be removed only if they became chargeable.[113] The creation of objective procedures for deciding who was legally settled created a sense that relief was an entitlement, rather than something which could be granted or denied by the parish officers. Many poor people, sharing that sense, negotiated with the officers about what was due to them.[114] The closer supervision of

[107] P. Clark, 'Migration in England, 1660–1730', *P & P* 83 (1979), 72–4, 83–90; Slack, *Poverty and Policy*, 194–5; G. Taylor, *The Problem of Poverty 1660–1834* (London, 1969), 27–8.

[108] MCB 24, fos. 174, 333; P. Styles, *Studies in Seventeenth-Century West Midlands History* (Kineton, 1978), 184–9.

[109] BRB 6, fo. 258. One woman in Bristol was said to be harbouring forty-six lodgers: BRO, JQS/PR/1, St Nicholas, 12 Oct. 1665.

[110] MCB 24, fo. 154; BRO, 04417/3, fos. 24, 27, 202, JQS/M/4, fo. 87; BCL, B6578, no. 43. Those described as living at their own hand were usually women, but see NCR, Case 20a/13, 31 Aug. 1668. Many single women *were* able to support themselves: Ellis, *Georgian Town*, 58–60.

[111] MCB 23, fo. 270 (bis), MCB 24, fos. 54–5, 160, 226–8.

[112] Kilmartin, 'Popular Rejoicing', 277–8.   [113] Styles, *Studies*, 189–93.

[114] Ellis, *Georgian Town*, 107–8.

parish officers by the magistrates, to whom those denied relief could appeal, tended in the same direction, and the amount raised by the poor rates increased substantially in the second half of the seventeenth century.[115] But elements of moral judgement remained and magistrates and officials were careful not to give too much. Detailed lists were drawn up of those receiving 'collection', including the value of their property and the income of each family member; all members of the family had to appear in person when the money was paid out.[116] Eager to prevent the poor from wasting their dole money, the Norwich mayor's court ordered in 1679 that all in receipt of poor relief should wear a conspicuous badge on their sleeves and that any pauper who was found in an alehouse, or who failed to wear their badge, would forfeit their right to relief. In 1697 an Act of Parliament required badging nationwide.[117] When a woman was given an old bed, the parish officers were told to take care that she did not sell it.[118] In 1700, noting that many who received relief spent Sunday idly and dissolutely, the mayor's court ordered that doles should be paid out in church.[119]

Apart from punishing the idle and dissolute, the poor laws encouraged setting the able-bodied poor on work, by providing them with work materials, in the home or a workhouse. Pauper children were apprenticed, but in general town authorities found paying doles easier than providing work or materials, especially as the goods produced would compete with others produced in the town.[120] From the 1690s, faced with difficult economic conditions and a rising poor rate, some towns secured Acts of Parliament enabling them to set up corporations of the poor, consisting of elected guardians. These were to receive the rates collected in the parishes and could arrest vagrants and idle and disorderly people, and bring the unemployed poor off the streets into the work-house, where they could earn their keep and be subjected to work discipline.[121] Those too old or infirm to work should work as much as they could and obey the workhouse rules.[122] (Those admitted to almshouses and hospitals were

---

[115] Slack, *Poverty and Policy*, 173–80 (especially 175), 190–2; Styles, *Studies*, 193–204.

[116] MCB 23, fo. 203, MCB 25, fos. 264, 290, MCB 26, fos. 59, 226, MCB 27, fo. 9.

[117] MCB 25, fos. 44–5, 56, NCR, Case 20a/17, 20 July 1706; *Norwich Gazette*, 3–10 Sept. 1709.

[118] MCB 25, fo. 54. Salisbury had tried to get round this problem by issuing tokens to be spent on basic foods (including beer) and fuel: Slack, 'Poverty and Politics in Salisbury', 183.

[119] MCB 26, fo. 95. See also Slack, 'Poverty and Politics in Salisbury', 185.

[120] For one example of providing materials, see MCB 25, fo. 255. Setting the poor on work was one of the original purposes of Bridewells: Innes, 'Prisons for the Poor', 52–3.

[121] FAB 9, fo. 411; Blomefield, *Norfolk*, iii. 432–5; BL, Lansdowne MS 891, fo. 199.

[122] J. Cary, *An Account of the Proceedings of the Corporation of Bristol* (London, 1700), 16–17, 19–20; E. E. Butcher, *Bristol Corporation of the Poor, 1696–1898*, BRS, iii (1932), 72.

also punished for indiscipline.[123]) Workhouse regulations formalized the work ethic at the heart of the poor laws. The aim was moral improvement as well as reducing the poor rate; many who promoted workhouses were active in Societies for the Reformation of Manners.[124]

Bristol secured the necessary Act in 1696, Hull in 1698, and Norwich in 1712. Leicester tried unsuccessfully to secure an Act. When it failed, the initiative passed to the parishes: St Mary's erected a workhouse in 1714 and St Martin's took the first steps towards doing so in 1721.[125] Leicester also 'invested' in lottery tickets, with the intention that any winnings should go to the poor.[126] Portsmouth had included provision for a workhouse in its abortive street paving bill of 1674. It already had a small poor-house, but many refused to pay towards it, saying it was illegal and that, anyway, it was too small. The town does not seem to have tried again.[127] Maidstone acquired a workhouse, a gift from a wealthy brewer, in 1720. Over the door it announced that it was to 'subject the poor to a better discipline of life'—and to reduce the poor rate (which it did).[128] In Hull, where there was little unemployment, the workhouse became mainly a school for pauper children and a home for those too old or frail to work. The able-bodied workshy were sent to the house of correction.[129] In Bristol and Norwich, costs spiralled.[130] Bristol had a large transient population and attracted many beggars and allegedly dubious characters, especially during fairs.[131] Norwich's textile industry suffered a slump in the 1710s; many weavers got badly into debt and ran away, leaving their families dependent on poor relief.[132] Contrary to the hopes of the promoters, at Bristol and elsewhere, the new schemes did not bring an end to outdoor relief, and those who received it were not subject to the discipline imposed in the workhouse.[133] It proved

---

[123] MCB 24, fos., 314, 316, 384, MCB 28, fo. 97. For the punishment of undisciplined boys, see MCB 24, fos. 225, 226, 276, MCB 25, fos. 307, 308, 333. See also BRO, 04264/7, fo. 201.

[124] *Proposals of the Better Maintaining and Employing the Poor of . . . Bristol* (Bristol, 1696). There are two printed papers with the same title: BL 816.m.15 (54 and 55). See also Cary, *An Account*, 1–7.

[125] *RBL*, v. 39, 53–4; Greaves, *Corporation*, 42, 44–5.   [126] *RBL*, v. 27; LHP 38, no. 218.

[127] *CJ*, ix. 301; Portsmouth RO, CE 1/8, fos. 29–30.

[128] P. Clark and L. Murfin, *The History of Maidstone* (Stroud, 1995), 93.

[129] Jackson, *Hull*, 320–3, 324.

[130] NRO, MS 79, pp. 188, 199–201; BRO, 04264/9, pp. 217, 248, 256, 284, 326.

[131] *Post Boy*, 19–22 Feb, 1698; Latimer, i. 462; Butcher, *Corporation*, 62–3, 77; C. Brent, *Persuasions to a Public Spirit* (1704), 1–2. There were also many beggars at Winchester, no doubt attracted by the affluent visitors. Some had permission to beg from the mayor and JPs: Hants RO, W/D3/1, fo. 149.

[132] FAB 9, fo. 86; BL, Add MS 61649, fos. 202–3.

[133] BRB 6, pp. 166, 338, 346, 458, 463, 618, 665. Critics of the Bristol corporation of the poor claimed that discipline in the workhouse was non-existent: *Some Considerations Offered to the Citizens of Bristol* (1711), 3.

difficult to sell the goods produced there and the provision for educating children was said to be inadequate.[134] Parish officers resented losing power over the poor and did not always obey the guardians.[135] Last but not least, the management of both the workhouses and charities dealing with the poor fell victim to political and religious differences.[136] Despite their problems, the workhouses gradually became established, their costs stabilized or fell, and they achieved at least some of their objectives. In 1727 it was said that begging had been eliminated in Bristol.[137]

Town magistrates assumed responsibility for punishing moral lapses, irrespective of whether they involved cost to the ratepayer or breaches of the peace. Mothers of bastards, but also women accused of 'incontinency', were sent to the house of correction; the men involved were required to give sureties for good behaviour.[138] At Portsmouth an adulterous woman and a widow who had a bastard child were sent to gaol; the widow was also whipped.[139] Some fathers of bastards were gaoled until they agreed to marry the mother, or provide for the child.[140] Women accused of prostitution, or keeping brothels, were punished; their customers were not.[141] In Bristol, whores or 'incontinent' women were carted through the city.[142] Couples taken *in flagrante* were ordered by the magistrates to ride on a horse, back to back, with the man facing the tail; sometimes the man rode alone.[143] Evidence of popular shame punishments is sparse, but there is a reference to a 'riding' in Norwich in 1670.[144] Magistrates saw women as inherently more sinful than men, but also as less responsible for their actions; husbands, kin, or friends, usually male, were asked to undertake for their good behaviour.[145] Norwich women by no means lived up to the model of submission and docility advanced by men. Some showed considerable sexual independence or beat and abused their husbands. There were frequent instances of scolding, in which the victims of verbal and

[134] Butcher, *Corporation*, 6–8, 53, 58, 69–72, 74, 76, 78, 80. For complaints that producing goods in workhouses threw others out of work, see Slack, *Reformation to Improvement*, 119–22.
[135] Butcher, *Corporation*, 4–5; Latimer, i. 480–1; *Some Considerations*, 4 and *passim*.
[136] See below, Ch. 13.
[137] NRO, MS 79, pp. 199–201; Fissell, in *Stilling*, 138; P. T. Marcy, 'Eighteenth-Century Views of Bristol', in McGrath (ed.), *Bristol in the Eighteenth Century*, 30.
[138] MCB 24, fo. 105, MCB 25, fos. 71, 94, 112; NCR, Case 20a/16, 18 Jan. 1696.
[139] *PSP*, 16, 133.   [140] NCR, Case 20a/15, 7 Oct. 1673, 17 Apr. 1674.
[141] MCB 23, fo. 251, MCB 24, fos. 61, 313, MCB 25, fo. 19; NCR, Case 20a/16, 15 July 1695.
[142] BRO, 04417/2, 17 May 1665, 2 Aug. 1666, 25 May 1667, 04417/3, fos. 19, 44.
[143] BRO, 04417/2, 22 May 1666, 25 May 1667, 04417/3, fos. 19, 22.
[144] MCB 24, fo. 135.   [145] MCB 24, fo. 70, MCB 25, fos. 97, 137.

physical attack were as often women as men.[146] The normal punishment for scolds, in the 1660s and 1670s, was to be ducked in the cucking stool, and perhaps also put in the cage.[147] After the early 1670s there were few cases of scolding; most ended with an apology or the women was sent to the house of correction.[148] Canterbury had a cucking stool, in the fish market, in 1682; the city was said to be 'much troubled' with scolds and brawlers.[149] Portsmouth had a cage, pillory, stocks, and cucking stool; the cage was still in use in 1721.[150] At Oxford a cage was set up in 1677, apparently for the first time, and moved in 1714.[151] In 1707 Hull sessions ordered that a cucking stool be set up; it is unclear whether the town had one before this.[152] Dorchester continued to punish scolds and other moral offenders, but far fewer than in the early seventeenth century.[153] A woman sentenced to be ducked at Warwick, in 1697, asked for a milder punishment. She was led through every street with a scold's bridle on her head, with a tinkling bell on top, and a bit in her mouth, with a paper explaining that she was a scold. Her equally turbulent husband was whipped.[154]

In using shame punishments to punish fornicators and scolds, the magistrates were upholding traditional Christian moral teaching. They were also concerned to save the more vulnerable members of society, the young, women, and the poor, from temptation. There were repeated complaints that there were far too many alehouses and that many of them were disorderly, allowing (or encouraging) drunkenness, gambling, and sexual misconduct. There were periodic attempts to close the more disorderly houses,[155] but they all foundered in the face of the brewers' determination to sell beer and the fact that many people liked their alehouses disorderly (even if their respectable neighbours did

---

[146] NCR, Case 20a/13, 1 Apr. 1667, Case 12b/1, unlabelled bundle, informations of Thomas Pitcher and others and Mr Robert Game, 1 and 2 Dec. 1690, Case 12b/2, information of Mary Dye, 21 Apr. 1707.

[147] MCB 24, fos. 70, 144; BRO, 04417/2, 14 Oct. 1660, 9 July 1664, 19 June and 1 Sept. 1666, 04417/3, fos. 15, 47, 56, 86, 101. The Bristol records refer only to ducking.

[148] MCB 24, fo. 322, MCB 25, fos. 39, 75, 91. The mayor and aldermen's order books for Bristol, in which punishments for scolding are recorded, come to an end in 1674, so it is impossible to tell whether they continued after that date. The Norwich cage continued to be used: NRO, DCN 115/2, p. 139.

[149] Canterbury RO, Burghmote Minute Book 5, fo. 212, Book 6, fo. 189.

[150] East, 63, 66, 69, 452, 455.

[151] Wood, ii. 371; *OCA*, iii. 251, iv. 87. Winchester, too, had a cage and a ducking stool: Hants. RO, W/D3/80, W/D3/85, fo. 29.

[152] BRB 6, pp. 572, 573.   [153] Underdown, *Fire from Heaven*, 248–9, 262–3.

[154] *Post Boy*, 10–13 July 1697.

[155] MCB 24, fos. 36, 78, 99, 142, MCB 25, fo. 180; NCR, Case 20a/19, 20 Apr. 1720. See also East, 90.

not). The brewers were said to be all-powerful in Norwich[156] and magistrates who tried to suppress alehouses were accused of reducing the crown's excise revenue.[157] As for the customers, there were numerous complaints of loose women and drunken brawls, and of customers being encouraged to run up large bills and to gamble.[158] The assembly tried to reduce the damage done by alehouses by ordering that they should close by 10 p.m.[159]

Temptation also came in the form of stage plays, interludes, and shows of all kinds—puppets, exotic animals, human freaks, acrobats. Among the most spectacular were medicine shows in which a 'mountebank' (often a qualified physician or surgeon) set up a large stage. His servants—one had sixteen—used music, tumblers, and rope dancers to attract a crowd and then sold medicines and carried out surgical operations on stage.[160] Some mountebanks performed a useful service, treating ailments which the local practitioners could not.[161] Norwich mayor's court condemned some of their 'drolls' as obscene, but still allowed them to return. It was consistently hostile to stage plays, which were sometime obscene and always encouraged people to waste time and money; but the players and the owners of most of the other shows—and the lottery sellers—had licences from the master of the revels, so the mayor had no legal pretext to deny them permission to perform, unless there were fears of serious disorder.[162] Charles II allowed the mayor to limit the amount of time the players could remain in the city. He could also impose conditions as to the hours at which they performed and require them to make payments to the poor; lottery sellers were asked not to admit servants or 'indigent persons'.[163] The players also had powerful patrons, notably the dukes of Norfolk; their visits became more frequent and they stayed for longer, with an ever-wider repertoire. The court's order of 1710 that there were to be no stage plays, comedies, or other shows without its permission was a futile gesture.[164] In 1723–4 one company performed for two months and another for four.[165]

---

[156] 'Reflections on the Present State of Norwich', *London Post*, 14 May 1705; Defoe, *Letters*, 85.

[157] Prideaux, 120–1; Browne, *Works*, ed. Keynes, iv. 203.

[158] NCR, Case 12b/1, bundle labelled 1690–9, informations of William Gibson and Elizabeth Hall, 13 Mar. 1691, Case 12b, information of James Combe, 20 June 1706, Case 20a/18, 9 Oct. 1714, 11 Apr. 1719.

[159] FAB 8, fo. 221.

[160] J. Miller, 'Back to Normal? Government and Society in Restoration Norwich', in D. Wilson (ed.), *The Restoration of Charles II: Public Order, Theatre and Dance*, Early Dance Circle (Cambridge, 2002), 6.

[161] MCB 24, fo. 384; Browne, *Works*, ed. Keynes, iv. 113–14.

[162] MCB 25, fo. 244, MCB 26, fo. 57*.   [163] MCB 24, fo. 221.

[164] MCB 27, fo. 17; Miller, 'Back to Normal?', *passim*.

[165] S. Rosenfeld, *Strolling Players and Drama in the Provinces 1660–1765* (Cambridge, 1939), 53.

In Bristol plays and interludes were performed at fairs.[166] In 1698 the magistrates cracked down on idle, disorderly people at the fairs, especially those who haunted the 'music houses', threatening to punish them as vagrants.[167] In 1699 players were forbidden to perform and from 1700, at the request of the local Society for the Reformation of Manners, the mayor banned plays, music houses, lotteries, and gaming houses at the fair; in 1702 the Society persuaded the mayor to ban plays, interludes, and puppets.[168] The Society rarely met after 1703, but the campaign against the stage was taken up by the common council. In 1704, apparently following the opening of a theatre, it urged the mayor not to allow players into the city. A grand jury alleged that plays led to 'profaneness, lewdness, murders, debauching and ruining youth of both sexes, infusing principles of idleness and extravagancy'. In cities with many nobles and gentry, their 'estates and leisure made such extravagancies more tolerable'. But Bristol was a working city and such distractions could not be allowed.[169] Plays continued outside the city and the players opened a theatre in 1706; it was closed by the magistrates, after pressure from the grand jury and the clergy. The players returned from time to time, never without vocal opposition. Another theatre opened in 1726.[170]

While Norwich's rulers were unable to prevent more and more plays being performed, those of Bristol took a firmer line from the late 1690s, first at the fairs and then in refusing to have a theatre in the city. Elsewhere, there are no references to players in Hull and the first post-Restoration mention in Leicester came when the mayor was forbidden to allow them to use the town hall, in 1722.[171] Winchester, eager to attract gentry custom, occasional received strolling players, but they were forbidden to perform in 1715, presumably because of a fear of disorder.[172] At Oxford there were frequent stage plays and shows. The mace bearers and sergeants often let out the upper hall to rope dancers and other performers; the council forbade this as 'dishonourable'

---

[166] Latimer, i. 336, 348–9, ii. 28; BRO, JQS/C/1, second pagination, p. 42.

[167] *Post Boy*, 19–22 Feb., 30 July–2 Aug. 1698; *Post Man*, 30 July–2 Aug. 1698; BRO, 04264/9, p. 191.

[168] Latimer, i. 462; *Ref and Revival*, 21–2, 38.

[169] Latimer, ii. 26; BRO, 04264/9, p. 43; *Flying Post*, 26–8 Dec. 1704; *Ref and Revival*, 3–6, 49–51, 55 (quotations from 50, 51).

[170] BRO, 04264/9, pp. 104, 213; *Ref and Revival*, 52–4 and 54 n. 105; Latimer, ii. 60–2. Borsay, *Urban Renaissance*, 329–331, gives only two provincial theatres that opened before 1722: one at Bath, 1705, and the one opened at Bristol in 1706, which did not stay open long. For the Bath theatre, see Rosenfeld, *Strolling Players*, 169–70.

[171] *RBL*, v. 94.

[172] Rosen, 'Winchester in Transition', 180; Hants RO, W/B2/6, 6 May 1715.

in 1678, but the practice soon resumed.[173] Stage plays were revived soon after the Restoration, along with maypoles, May games, and morris dances, allegedly to spite the Puritans. In May 1660 the (Puritan) vice-chancellor came to saw the maypole down, but was driven away by the people.[174] The revival of maypoles was a nationwide phenomenon.[175] In April 1661 a maypole 41 yards high was set up in the Strand, in London; 'in the balcony that was made about one storey high were wine, music, and under it a knot of morris dancers, the worst that ever were'.[176] Young people went into the fields on May Day, to dance with the country people. The maypole was finally taken down in 1717.[177] The civic authorities disapproved of rough sports, such as tethering cocks to the ground and throwing heavy sticks at them. In Bristol in 1660 the mayor forbade throwing at cocks and tossing dogs on Shrove Tuesday, so the apprentices tossed bitches and cats and threw at geese and hens; when a sheriff tried to drive them away, they broke his head.[178] The authorities in Norwich banned throwing at cocks (except on Shrove Monday and Tuesday, traditional days of licensed misrule) in 1716, 1720, and 1723.[179] The mayor of Portsmouth forbade throwing at cocks, just before Shrove Tuesday in 1721, saying that it was 'barbarous', but also that it could lead to riots and quarrels.[180] The fashion for maypoles waned soon after 1660, but for some reason there was a rash of them in Oxford in 1693.[181]

Most towns made at least some show of forbidding work and recreation on Sundays. In Restoration Oxford the clergy were accused of tolerating or promoting Sunday sports.[182] Barbers were forbidden to work on Sundays and the vice chancellor ordered that coffee houses should close, but the order did not apply after Sunday prayers. In 1700 a man was gaoled by the vice chancellor for a quarrel after he reproved a man for mowing on a Sunday; the commitment was eventually declared unlawful.[183] In Bristol the city fathers were much more diligent. Between 1695 and 1728 there were several convictions each month

---

[173] Wood, i. 322, 356, 405–6, ii. 165, iii. 59, 191; *OCA*, iii. 39, 294, 311.

[174] Wood, i. 314, 317, 360.

[175] Underdown, *Revel, Riot and Rebellion*, 271–5; Latimer, i. 293–4; Hutton, *Merry England*, 223.

[176] T. Rugg, *Diurnal, 1659–61*, ed. W. L. Sachse, Camden Society (1961), 175–6; Hutton, *Merry England*, 225–6.

[177] Schellinks, 84; *Weekly Journal or British Gazetteer*, 15 Apr. 1721.

[178] Schellinks, 73; BCL, B10166, 'A Catalogue', B10163, 'A Copy of a Manuscript in Parchment'; Bodl, MS Gough Somerset 2, p. 80.

[179] MCB 27, fo. 216, MCB 28, fos. 16, 139; NCR, Case 12c/2, no. 205.   [180] East, 717.

[181] Wood, iii. 421.   [182] Ibid. i. 356.   [183] Ibid. ii. 280, 396, 463; Luttrell, iv. 644.

for profane swearing.[184] Grand jury presentments linked swearing with profanation of the sabbath; behaviour which was offensive at any time was doubly
so on Sunday, and risked provoking the wrath of God.[185] The vigorous line
taken against stage plays from the 1690s could be said to reflect the dominance
of Whigs and Dissenters in the corporation, but grand jury presentments
of 1682 and 1685, which condemned billiard tables, disorderly riding in the
Marsh, and tippling and playing in service time, also called for firmer action
against Dissenters.[186] In Winchester strict orders for Sunday observance in
December 1714 coincided with the Whigs regaining control over the body
of freemen.[187] At Yarmouth in the 1720s the corporation ensured that the
Lord's Day was properly observed and gave no encouragement to plays or
gambling.[188] In 1663 the Norwich mayor's court ordered that the city gates
should be shut all day on Sunday; no travellers (other than doctors) could
pass in or out, without the mayor's permission.[189] In 1689 the court issued an
order against trading, idle sports, and the 'loathsome sin' of drunkenness on
Sundays.[190] In 1707, when Tories dominated the corporation, the first article
in a list drawn up by sessions to be read to constables asked if anyone indulged
in unlawful sports or games on Sundays.[191] The problems of keeping Sunday
holy were set out by the grand jury in 1697. Great crowds of disorderly people
dishonoured God by swearing and playing idle games; others lost time and
money at ninepins. Far too many people spent time in the alehouses, 'both
before, in and after service and sermon, by which we mean not such as are civil
and sober, whose circumstances will allow them a refreshment, but such whose
poverty bespeaks better husbandry', who risked ruining their families and
becoming dependent on the poor rate.[192] It would be difficult to find a better
example of the intermingling of moral, religious, and economic considerations
in the management of the poor.

[184] BRO, JQS/C/1, end of volume.
[185] BRO, JQS/M/4, fos. 125, 150, JQS/C/1, second pagination, p. 38; *Flying Post*, 17–19 Sept.
1696. See also J. Spurr, 'Virtue, Religion and Government: The Anglican uses of Providence', in *Pol
of Rel*, ch. 2; J. Spurr, 'The Church, the Societies and the Moral Revolution of 1688', in Walsh et al.,
129–30.
[186] BRO, JQS/C/1, pp. 89, 112, 120–1.
[187] Hants RO, W/D3/1, fos. 159–60. For the Whigs gaining control see: Hants RO, W/B1/8,
fos. 156–9, 164–5, W/B2/6, 21 Jan. 1715.
[188] Defoe, *Tour*, i. 69.   [189] MCB 23, fo. 201.
[190] MCB 25, fos. 280–1, 288.   [191] NCR, Case 20a/17, 18 Jan. 1707.
[192] NCR, Case 12c, unnumbered, dated 17 Apr. 1697. See also East, 90.

III. LAW AND ORDER

With police resources so flimsy, to maintain order town authorities had to rely on the law. Larger towns had a range of courts, most handling both civil and criminal business. At Norwich, the assizes met only once a year, so more business was handled by quarter sessions, which usually sat for a period of weeks.[193] They dealt with criminal cases and matters relating to the public peace and good, such as alehouse licensing and street maintenance. The court was concerned to maintain its authority and dignity. Officers and counsel were expected to attend and wear gowns, but not all did.[194] Some jurymen and witnesses left the court without permission, came in drunk, or were abusive.[195] There were frequent complaints of the negligence of ward inquests and grand juries, without whose information the court could not act.

The punishments imposed at sessions varied. Fines were common, for failures of duty, market offences, and minor interpersonal violence. In cases of violence, the court sometimes preferred compensation to punishment.[196] In cases of insults, especially to those in authority, the fine or other punishment was often remitted or reduced in return for a public apology. Ellen Sadler apologized to 'Madame Helwys' for throwing chickens at her in the market square; she was let off with a 5s. fine.[197] Offenders often petitioned, successfully, for a lower fine. In 1662 the assembly appointed a committee to compound with offenders.[198] Most punishments for property offences were physical—hanging, branding, whipping, the pillory, and the stocks. Most involved public shame, as a warning to others. Those who were branded—usually on the hand, but from 1699 to 1706 on the cheek—literally carried their criminal record with them. Each ward had a set of stocks. Constables and magistrates could use them to punish those who were drunk or otherwise disorderly (including 'notorious wenches').[199] There was only one pillory, in the market place, where

---

[193] The quarter sessions records survive, in NRO; the assize records for this period, which should be in TNA, do not.

[194] NCR, Case 20a/13, 1 Apr. 1667, Case 20a/17, 14 July 1705.

[195] NCR, Case 20a/15, 10 Dec. 1684, Case 20a/16, 9 Oct. 1691, Case 20a/17, 29 Apr. 1704.

[196] NCR, Case 20a/17, 21 Apr., 17 July 1705.

[197] MCB 26, fo. 5; NCR, Case 20a/16, 11 Oct. 1695. The lady in question was probably the wife of Alderman Nicholas Helwys.

[198] FAB 6, fo. 237.

[199] MCB 25, fo. 183; J. M. Beattie, *Crime and the Courts in England 1660–1800* (Oxford, 1986), 491.

offenders (such as cheats) would stand on market day, when they risked considerable harm.[200] Whipping was an essential part of punishment. In 1666, when plague was rife, a set of stocks and a whipping post were sent to the pest house, to discipline the infected poor.[201] Whipping could be imposed for minor thefts, as when two boys stole apples from Alderman Cockey's orchard, or for refusing to pay fines.[202] The whipping post was in the market place; both men and women were stripped to the waist and beaten until their back was bloody. From the 1680s the court adapted the punishment to fit the crime. A thief was whipped from where he stole the goods to where he tried to sell them.[203] Some were whipped at the post, others at the cart's tail as it moved slowly around the market place, and others, yet more visibly, on the cart. Some were to be given a specified number of lashes under each shop or inn sign.[204]

A final form of punishment was imprisonment. Long custodial sentences were rare, but those accused of serious offences, or deemed a threat to the public peace, could be gaoled until they could be tried. These were not necessarily numerous: sometimes at Leicester there was nobody in gaol awaiting trial.[205] Those who refused the oath of allegiance could be gaoled for as long as they continued their refusal; the Quakers suffered heavily for this. Others who suffered were those too poor or friendless to pay fines or find sureties, and debtors. Even before the establishment of a court of conscience, which dealt with cases of debt, the mayor's court tried to mediate between debtors and their creditors, and secure their release from gaol.[206] Miscreants could also be imprisoned in the house of correction. Originally intended to provide a short sharp shock for the 'loose, idle, and disorderly', it also became a place of incarceration for those convicted of felony and petty larceny. But many who were acquitted were also sent there, to remain, hard at work, until further order from the court.[207]

Historians of the criminal law often stress the discretion exercised at each stage of the process, from the decision to prosecute to the decision whether to carry out the death sentence.[208] Juries decided whether a killing was murder or

[200] NCR, Case 20a/16, 13 July 1694, 7 Oct. 1699, Case 20a/17, 6 Oct. 1711, 3 May 1712, Case 20a/34, 16 Jan. 1691.

[201] MCB 24, fo. 12.   [202] Ibid. 232, 287.   [203] NCR, Case 20a/15, 14 Jan. 1687.

[204] NCR, Case 20a/18, 15 Jan., 30 Apr. 1715. See also Beattie, *Crime and the Courts*, 461–4.

[205] LHP 30, nos. 133, 256, LHP 32B, no. 443.

[206] MCB 24, fo. 373, MCB 25, fos. 17, 38.

[207] NCR, Case 20a/13, 23 Mar. and 22 May 1662, 23 Apr. 1664, Case 20a/16, 6 Oct. 1693.

[208] See for example Beattie, *Crime and the Courts*; Sharpe, *Crime in Early Modern England*.

manslaughter and valued stolen goods; if the value was less than one shilling (12*d.*) the accused could be found guilty only of petty larceny, as opposed to grand larceny, which potentially carried the death penalty. In Norwich, as elsewhere, accused persons were found guilty of stealing goods to the value of 11*d.*[209] (At Leicester, thieves were found guilty to the value of 10*d.*, although in one case the goods had been valued at 5*s.*[210]) The use of discretion was heavily coloured by perceptions of the moral worth of the accuser and accused, and the nature of the crime—how serious it was, and how premeditated. The power to send people to the house of correction made it possible to punish those who could not be convicted of a crime, but were still seen as deserving chastisement.[211] In Norwich, as elsewhere, those sentenced to hang for property offences were usually convicted of robbery, horse stealing, burglary, or pickpocketing, rather than simple theft.[212] The court's normal practice was that those who stole goods valued at less than 10*s.* should not be hanged, but it hanged a woman pickpocket who stole goods valued at 9*s.*; others who stole goods to a much higher value were only branded, presumably having successfully pleaded benefit of clergy.[213] The element of premeditation, and the invasion of the person, made pickpocketing appear heinous. Sometimes those convicted proposed an alternative sentence, such as transportation or military service.[214] More often it was the court who imposed additional punishments on convicted felons, or punished those who had been acquitted. The most extreme case was John Blancher, alias Browne. He was sentenced to death for murder in 1667, but escaped hanging because of a 'defect of law'. He was also charged with escaping from gaol and perjury. He remained in gaol; people came to him for legal advice, although he was only a journeyman shoemaker. Every sessions there was an order to keep him in custody, the last being in January 1684; he had been in gaol for almost seventeen years.[215]

[209] NCR, Case 20a/13, 16 Aug. 1669, Case 20a/15, 28 Apr. 1679, Case 20a/18, 4 May 1717, Case 20a/20, 19 Jan. 1723.

[210] *RBL*, vii. 33, 38, 39, 52.

[211] An Act of 1706 allowed judges to sentence convicted felons who had been allowed benefit of clergy to the house of correction for between six months and two years: Beattie, *Crime and the Courts*, 493; Innes, 'Prisons for the Poor', 88–90.

[212] For pickpockets, see Case 20a/13, 15 Aug. 1670, 20a/15, 7 Apr. 1673, 9 July 1677. For horse stealing, Case 20a/15, 14 Jan. 1678.

[213] NCR, Case 20a/15, 7 Apr. 1673, 14 Apr. 1674, 19 Apr. 1680, 11 Apr. 1681 (goods valued at £17 16*s.*); Beattie, *Crime and the Courts*, 142, 144.

[214] NCR, Case 20a/13, 13 Mar. and 3 July 1665, 7 Jan. 1668, 24 Jan. 1670.

[215] *CSPD 1668–9*, 424, 425–6; NCR, Case 20a/13, 23 July and 23 Sept. 1667, 13 Jan. 1673, Case 20a/15, 14 Jan. 1684.

This was a unique case, but many who were acquitted were not discharged. Some were held until they could be sent back to their home parish, but the court regarded others as bad characters, including a suspected highwayman (and confessed gamester) who was to be released only when he gave substantial sureties for good behaviour.[216] Those acquitted on serious charges, such as witchcraft or pickpocketing, or as accessories, were similarly required to find sureties.[217] A woman acquitted of murder and a man suspected of being a confederate of pickpockets were sent to the house of correction until further order.[218] Such use of discretion enabled the magistrates to counter the inadequacies and eccentricities of jurors, in the interests, as they understood them, of justice and the public peace.

IV. ECONOMIC ORDER

Towns showed a similar concern for order and control in the economic sphere. Corporations tried to protect the interests of both producers and consumers, the former by trying to ensure that the profits of manufacture and retail were enjoyed only by freemen, the latter by maintaining standards of workmanship and fair dealing. These regulations assumed that there was a finite volume of trade, so that one man's excessive profit was another's unjust loss. In an age of rapid economic growth and incipient consumerism, such regulations might seem doomed to fail in the face of market forces, but urban rulers still tried to enforce them.[219] They were strongly supported by many manufacturers and traders, and faced vehement opposition from others. Corporations were hampered by the fact that many of these regulations depended on by-laws of the town and its various companies, rather than Acts of Parliament. In 1698 the assembly at Norwich was advised that it lacked the legal power to compel citizens to take up the freedom.[220]

Traditionally, only freemen could practise trades, employ apprentices or journeymen, or sell retail, and many towns tried to prevent 'foreigners' (people from outside the town) and non-freemen from doing so.[221] The Norwich

---

[216] NCR, Case 20a/13, 14 Jan. 1670.

[217] NCR, Case 20a/15, 17 Apr. 1671, 25 Oct. 1675, 8 Jan. 1677.

[218] NCR, Case 20a/13, 15 Aug. 1670, Case 20a/16, 19 July 1700.

[219] *CUHB*, ii. 546.   [220] FAB 8, fo. 220.

[221] *CSPD 1672–3*, 577 (Penrith), *1679–80*, 279–80 (Wootton Bassett), *1691–2*, 114–15 (Tiverton), *1699–1700*, 178, 229 (Wilton); CKS, Md/ACm 1/3, fo. 153 (Maidstone); DAM fos. 238–40 (Dover); C. H. Cooper, *Annals of Cambridge*, 4 vols. (Cambridge, 1842–52), iii. 514; *VCH City of York*, 215–17.

assembly repeatedly ordered that those who traded in open shops without being free should be sued, but also took counsel's advice as to how best to proceed. Among the options considered were an Act of Parliament or a new charter, but in the end the assembly passed a new by-law. It cited the charter of Edward IV, which empowered the corporation to make good any defect in its powers, provided the change was in the interests of king and subjects and agreeable to good faith and reason—criteria which could admit of more than one interpretation. It ordered that no unfree person was to carry on any retail trade, on pain of a fine of £2.[222] The by-law proved ineffective: between 1678 and 1703 the assembly presented a series of bills to Parliament, but none passed; the Commons disliked bills that imposed undue restrictions on trade. In 1710 the assembly passed another by-law, which repeated much of the last and raised the fine to £3.[223] The assembly still tried to force traders to take up their freedom and sued some who refused, but to little effect. Other towns experienced similar difficulties. Oxford corporation tried to enforce its by-laws against non-freemen opening shops and trading in the city, adding a new by-law in 1707 covering a range of trades, from grocers to milliners.[224] It allowed the companies to use the city by-laws against foreigners and non-freemen.[225] But problems of enforcement remained. These stemmed partly from the difficulty of identifying which shops belonged to non-freemen,[226] and partly from the cumbersome procedures of prosecution and distraint, exacerbated by uncertainty about the legal status of the by-laws.[227] In 1665 the council decided to petition the king to prevent strangers encroaching on the trade of the freemen, to no effect.[228] At Leicester the companies sought to prevent 'strangers' from purchasing the freedom to practise the more overcrowded trades, and they and the corporation tried to prevent those who were free to practise one trade from practising another.[229] As usual, their efforts were hampered by uncertainty about the legal status of the by-laws, compounded by the ingenuity of lawyers: when a barber was sued for unfree trading in 1709, counsel were retained on both sides.[230]

Some corporations, faced with the difficulty of preventing unfree trading, made the best of a bad job. At Winchester the corporation allowed non-freemen

---

[222] FAB 6, fo. 262, FAB 8, fos. 25, 33, 39, 48–9; MCB 24, fo. 227. For the charter of Edward IV, see FAB 9, fos. 20–1.

[223] FAB 9, fos. 20–1.   [224] *OCA*, iii. 233, 235, 240, 244, iv. 47.

[225] Ibid. iii. 225, 240, iv. 91, 127.   [226] Ibid. ii. 334–5, 342, iii. 175, iv. 22.

[227] Ibid. ii. 333–4, iii. 253, iv. 101.   [228] Ibid. ii. 344.

[229] *RBL*, iv. 520–1, v. 9–10, vii, p. xxix; LHP 29B, nos. 931–2; Greaves, *Corporation*, 48–54.

[230] LHP 35, no. 34; *RBL*, v. 47, 59–60, vii. 64; Greaves, *Corporation*, 51–2.

to practise trades which were not widely used in the city.[231] From at least 1663 the mayor and aldermen were empowered to allow foreigners, or those who had not served an apprenticeship, to compound—to open shop windows in return for an annual fine of up to £5; it was claimed that the power to do this was 'very ancient'.[232] (Maidstone began to allow non-freemen to compound in 1671.[233]) Although a few paid fines of £4 19s., the vast majority who compounded paid between 6d. and 3s. 4d.[234] It seems that the fines ceased to be levied after about 1675, although some incomers were required to pay a one-off fine before starting to trade.[235] In 1713 it was debated whether to prosecute nine men and five women for using their trades, or give them the chance to compound. As at Leicester, some were qualified to practise one trade, but used another; the assembly asked counsel if it could require them to enter into bonds to practise only one trade. Such bonds, for £100, began to be demanded; they were common in Bristol.[236] The corporation was not sure of the legal force of the 'ancient usages' under which it claimed the right to deny foreigners, and those who had not served apprenticeships, the right to trade. To this end, it petitioned the Commons in 1714 for leave to bring in a bill to prevent the unqualified from trading.[237] Predictably, the move came to nothing.

Bristol as a major port, dependent on overseas trade, wished to attract foreign merchants, but to ensure that Bristolians enjoyed as large a share as possible of the profits of their trade. (It should be remembered that 'foreigners' included inhabitants of Bristol's 'out-parishes'.[238]) To prevent foreigners from trading freely with the citizens, they were required to store and sell their goods in the Backhall; there were strict by-laws against them selling to other foreigners or to citizens (except in the Backhall), and against freemen 'colouring' the goods of foreigners and passing them off as their own. However, both foreigners and citizens proved adept at flouting these regulations.[239] There were complaints of

---

[231] Hants RO, W/B1/7, fos. 57, 227 (pewterer and watch-maker). See also BRO, 04264/6, p. 56, 04264/8, fo. 121 (organ maker and printer; the printer was made free just after the lapsing of the Licensing Act in 1695; see also BL, Add MS 5540, fo. 78).

[232] Hants RO, W/B1/6, fo. 6.   [233] CKS, Md/ACm 1/3, fos. 178, 188, 208, 249, 251.

[234] Hants RO, W/B1/6, fos. 20–1, 41–2, 70–1, 98. See also East, 175; Reed, 'Economic Structure and Change in Ipswich', in Clark (ed.), *Country Towns*, 122–3.

[235] Rosen, 'Winchester in Transition', 176. The last set of annual fines was in 1675 (W/B1/6, fo. 98) but a tallow chandler had been given permission to trade in 1674 on giving spoons to the value of £6 (ibid., fo. 98).

[236] Hants RO, W/B2/5, 22 Sept. 1713. For bonds, see W/B1/8, fos. 144, 168–9, B2/5, 16 Apr. 1714, B2/6, 4 Mar. 1715.

[237] Hants RO, W/B1/8, fo. 136.   [238] Latimer, ii. 20–2.

[239] BRO, 04264/6, pp. 138, 144–6, 154–5, 204–5, 04264/9, pp. 132–3, 433, JQS/M/4, fo. 151.

negligence and incompetence in the management of the Backhall.[240] Although goods sold by foreigners to foreigners were supposed to be confiscated and sold for the benefit of the city, they were often allowed to buy them back cheaply.[241] A few freemen were disfranchised for 'colouring' foreigners' goods, but they were usually reinstated after paying a fine.[242] Attempts to stop non-freemen from selling retail were as unsuccessful in Bristol as they were elsewhere.

In most significant towns, the freemen were grouped in companies, according to their trades. Each company was governed by by-laws, approved by the corporation and assize judges. They were supposed to hold regular assemblies, which elected officers responsible for enforcing the by-laws and suing errant members, often assisted by the corporation. Although the guild system was in decline in London, in many provincial towns it remained vigorous and enjoyed the full backing of the corporation and many citizens. New companies were formed, new by-laws were approved, assemblies met, and officers were appointed; these endeavoured to enforce the by-laws relating to quality of workmanship, unfree trading, apprenticeship, and the employment of 'foreigners' as journeymen.[243] The companies attempted to uphold traditional values, including quality of workmanship, fair dealing, and Christian charity; apprenticeship was seen as a moral as well as technical training.[244] At Norwich, freemen were fined for failing to appear at assemblies,[245] employing 'foreigners,'[246] setting journeymen on work without leave,[247] or refusing to co-operate with officers searching for defective goods.[248] The companies' juries reported meat that was unfit to eat, substandard carpentry, and inadequately tanned leather; some of those involved were prosecuted and fined.[249] At Hull, a woman was fined £6, following a complaint from the coopers' company that she sold inferior wooden wares; following a plea from her father, she was given five months to sell the confiscated items, on promising not to sell 'insufficient wares' in future.[250] In Leicester, in 1662, the corporation granted the petition of the cordwainers to re-establish the leather hall, where leather could be checked for quality and

---

[240] BRO, 04264/9, pp. 126–9, 276.   [241] BRO, JQS/M/5, fo. 82.
[242] BRO, 04264/6, pp. 170, 172, 181.
[243] For new by-laws between 1695 and 1720, see FAB 8, fos. 196, 215, 255, FAB 9, fo. 79. For new companies in Winchester, and attempts to regulate trades, see Hants RO, W/B1/6, fos. 3, 109–14, W/B1/7, fo. 57; Rosen, 'Winchester in Transition', 176. See also *VCH City of York*, 169–70, 218.
[244] C. Brooks, 'Apprenticeship, Social Mobility and the Middling Sort', in Barry and Brooks (eds.), *The Middling Sort of People*, 75–7.
[245] MCB 24, fos. 146, 224.   [246] MCB 25, fo. 124, MCB 26, fo. 146.
[247] MCB 24, fo. 385.   [248] Ibid. 190, 202, MCB 25, fo. 104.
[249] MCB MCB 24, fo. 276, MCB 25, fos. 203, 225, MCB 26, fos. 75, 76.
[250] BRB 6, p. 169.

sealed; however, the hall had been abandoned by 1701.[251] At Southampton the guild system was decaying in the early eighteenth century and non-freemen claimed a right to open shops. Nevertheless, in 1747 the corporation, encouraged by legal advice, tried to revive the ban on unfree trading. Its efforts provoked violence and petered out after some failed prosecutions.[252]

Despite all the efforts to make the regulatory system work, often it did not. Officers were accused of compounding with offenders or ignoring offences altogether.[253] At Norwich there was a divergence of interest between masters and journeymen: the former were often glad to employ 'foreigners', especially if they would work for lower wages.[254] In 1700, after a dispute between the master carpenters and their journeymen, the mayor's court ordered that the masters should not employ foreigners if there were qualified journeymen available.[255] There was also opposition to searches for defective goods. In 1700 Arnold Wallowing and his man threw four officers of the Worsted Weavers' Company out of his warehouse, injuring them and tearing their clothes.[256] There were deep divisions within the company. In 1703 a worsted weaver dispersed a libel attacking the company.[257] In 1705 the weavers' hall was broken into and the books were burned, after which no more cloths were sealed in the city.[258] The above would suggest that the disgruntled weavers' main complaint was against the company's system of quality control, but the company also investigated whether those practising the trade were qualified according to the by-laws[259] and tried to prohibit all weaving between 15 August and 15 September. In this they were enforcing an Act of Parliament of 1662, which incorporated the company, but in the fraught and competitive conditions of Anne's reign, many weavers felt impatient at such restrictions.[260] The Colchester weavers also wanted to end the tradition of a month-long break, but the privy council saw no reason for change.[261]

---

[251] *RBL*, iv. 482, 515, v. 39; LHP 34, no. 58.   [252] Patterson, *Southampton*, 23–5, 35–6.

[253] MCB 24, fo. 97, MCB 25, fo. 96.   [254] MCB 24, fos. 340, 341, MCB 25, fo. 96.

[255] MCB 26, fo. 81.

[256] NCR, Case 12b/2, bundle labelled 1700–10, informations of Bartholomew Medhouse and Richard Atthill, 6 Nov. 1700, Thomas Mott and William Fella, 26 Nov. 1700. See also MCB 24, fo. 287; NCR, Case 12b/2, information of John Money and others, 24 Feb. 1707, Case 20a/18, 19 Jan. 1717.

[257] NCR, Case 12c/2, unnumbered, under 10 Apr. 1703.

[258] NRO MS 79, p. 250; Blomefield, *Norfolk*, iii. 432.

[259] *Norwich Gazette*, 16–23 Oct. 1708.

[260] Ibid. 31 July–7 Aug. 1708, 16–23 Aug. 1709; BL, Add MS 61649, fo. 203. For the Act, see *SR*, v. 370–4; Beloff, *Public Order*, 82.

[261] PC 2/85, pp. 205–6.

A similar tension between traditional regulations and a commercial economy can be seen in the markets. Norwich corporation ordered that all goods that should properly be sold in the market should be sold there, and nowhere else. It was in the interests of public health that meat should be sold only in the designated shambles.[262] Concentrating trading in the market made it easier to guard against false weights and measures (and to collect market dues). The corporation's normal instinct was to restrict and reduce the number of traders. Unsure of its legal authority to prohibit unauthorized traders, the assembly resolved to allow no new stalls.[263] It enforced restrictions on who could buy what and when; by-laws laid down that certain goods could be bought and sold only between certain hours and forestalling and regrating were prohibited. The prices of several products were fixed by the mayor, assembly, or sessions: tallow and candles, salt, and, above all, wheat for the bakers. In the assize of bread, the mayor decreed the size of a penny and two-penny loaf.[264] Although the price of food fell in the later seventeenth century, and the corporation ceased to buy grain for the poor in the late 1660s, it continued into the 1720s fixing prices and combating forestalling and regrating.[265] In this, it had the occasional backing of the central government, but only when prices were exceptionally high. Only in years of real dearth, such as 1699 and 1709, did Parliament impose a ban on exports, for a limited period. There were also proclamations to enforce the laws against forestalling and regrating and orders to tighten up the licensing of grain dealers.[266]

The city's efforts did not go unopposed because its legal authority to regulate the market depended on by-laws. There were doubts about the legality of the assize of bread and the regulation of corn buying. The mayor and assembly continued to issue orders, but also made a variety of legal enquiries.[267] Often these orders came in response to grand jury presentments.[268] By 1721 there were signs that the old system of trading in the open market and in shops was breaking down. There were complaints of carriers taking 'unlawful' goods to London at dead of night,[269] of hawkers in the market, and of 'lumberers,

---

[262] For a similar concern at Oxford, see *OCA*, iii. 195, 261.
[263] FAB 6, fos. 238, 245, FAB 8, fos. 69, 116.   [264] MCB 27, fo. 238, MCB 28, fo. 84.
[265] MCB 28, fos. 27, 29, 67, 84. The corporation had begun to run down its corn stock in the 1640s: Slack, *Poverty and Policy*, 147. From the 1660s money bequeathed to the corn stock was loaned out at interest and the proceeds paid to the poor.
[266] PC 2/82, pp. 445–9; Outhwaite, 'Dearth and Government Intervention', 389–92, 397; Beloff, *Public Order*, 57–60, 69–70; Stevenson, *Popular Disturbances*, 123–4, 133–5.
[267] MCB 26, fo. 52 (bis), MCB 27, fos. 132, 133, 136; FAB 9, fo. 54.
[268] NCR, 12c/2, nos. 491, 496, 516.   [269] NCR, Case 20a/17, 13 July 1703.

breakers, pettifoggers, etc', 'no trade corporate', who underhand bought goods of all sorts, possibly stolen.[270] In 1717 the assembly issued an order against selling goods on waste ground. By 1737 many stalls in and around the market sold clothing and small wares.[271] In 1722 shopkeepers complained of women hawking from door to door, selling earthenware and buying old clothing. They claimed that they did not take money, but bartered to get clothes;[272] given the crisis in the textile industry, this could have been true. But even where there was no crisis in manufacturing, more and more trading was taking place away from the market. In 1691 Winchester corporation condemned transactions in alehouses, private houses, and the street, and private sales of corn outside the market.[273] This was a general trend: there was simply too much trade for the markets to handle.[274] Similarly, at Oxford, the council tried to ban hucksters, pedlars, and petty chapmen from the city; they sold small wares, such as glass and cutlery, and were seen as competing unfairly with the resident freemen shopkeepers.[275] At Bristol the bakers complained that hucksters bought up bread which they sold to poor people in the out-parishes at inflated prices; they encouraged their customers to buy on credit and then insisted that they buy only from them. Quarter sessions issued an order against selling bread to hucksters and alehouse keepers, who sold it to their customers.[276] There were several attempts to legislate against pedlars and hawkers. They had their defenders, who argued that they provided ribbons, gloves, and small items for people who found it difficult to get to shops. But most borough MPs opposed them, claiming that many were Scots or travelling thieves.[277]

Under the twin pressures of an increasingly commercial economy and the desperate poverty of many clothworking families, the old system of market-based trading and regulation was coming under severe strain by 1722, but corporations continued to try to enforce it. In this they had the support of many, but by no means all, citizens, who also endorsed the moral order, or moral

---

[270] MCB 26, fo. 256; NCR, Case 12c/2, endorsed (5).

[271] FAB 9, fo. 62; NRO, MS 79, p. 139.   [272] MCB 28, fo. 130.

[273] Hants RO, W/B1/7, fos. 57–8.   [274] McInnes, *English Town*, 14.

[275] *OCA*, ii. 332, iii. 123, 138, 231, 252. For a much earlier attempt to prevent stalls selling small wares at Norwich, see FAB 6, fo. 238. In 1685 there were complaints of women in Bristol selling stockings and yarn in the market and the High Street: BRO, JQS/C/1, pp. 112, 118. Portsmouth tried to keep out pedlars and petty chapmen: *PSP*, 47, 77, 79–80, 82.

[276] BRO, JQS/M/4, fo. 180. It was alleged that many hucksters also went in for forestalling and regrating.

[277] Norths, iii. 182; M636/30, John Verney to Sir Ralph Verney, 29 Mar. 1677. For the hostility of the city of Rochester to pedlars, see *CSPD 1691–2*, 34. See also Spufford, *Figures in the Landscape*, ch. 9.

economy, on which it rested. In much the same way, the magistrates' policy towards the poor, alcohol, and sexual morality showed a striking continuity with the past. Social policy was much the same under the high Anglicans of Anne's reign as it had been under the Puritans of the 1630s. Anglicans as well as Dissenters adhered to an enduring ideal of behaviour that emphasized hard work, thrift, sobriety, and ordered, patriarchal family life; political and religious conflict gave an added incentive to regulate the lives of, and indoctrinate, the poor. The fact that the authorities actively upheld such an ideal must have done much to legitimize their government in the eyes of their respectable fellow citizens. By punishing the deviant, the loose, idle, and disorderly, they reaffirmed the values by which the majority lived, or at least claimed to live, and helped maintain a degree of cohesion and order within the community.

4

Legitimizing Authority:
Dignity, Conviviality, and Celebration

This chapter addresses two questions. First, how did civic rulers legitimize their
rule and secure obedience? Second, why were men prepared to take on civic
office, which cost them time and money? The first question was addressed
in the previous chapter, but more can be said. For the second, the last chapter
offered one reason why they served—civic duty—and eliminated another:
town governments at this time were not conspicuous for corruption, not
least because many corporations were poor. One could add that corporation
membership offered opportunities for networking and business contacts. This
chapter considers three overlapping aspects of civic life which shed light on
both questions. It shows how all three were designed to enhance the civic rulers'
standing in the eyes of the townspeople, and offered some recompense for
their service, in the form of status, pageantry, and admission to 'exclusive' social
circles, together with good food and drink and good fellowship.[1] But once the
civic rulers left the confines of the council chamber and went into the streets,
there was always a danger that the ceremonies in which they were supposed
to have the starring role might be subverted or taken over, especially in times
of fierce political division.

I. DIGNITY

The need for dignity, and decorum, started inside the council chamber. Most
corporations had rules for the conduct of meetings. Members were supposed
to appear promptly, wearing gowns. No one was to leave before the meeting

---

[1] Few historians discuss this point, but see Gauci, *Yarmouth*, 32–5; J. R. Davis, 'Colchester
1600–62: Politics, Religion and Office-Holding in an English Provincial Town', Ph.D. thesis
(Brandeis University, 1981), 538–9.

ended, without the mayor's permission. The mayor decided the order in which members spoke; they should stand up to speak and no more than one person should speak at once.[2] No member was to reveal to any non-member any information about their proceedings. This cannot have been enforced on all occasions, as non-members were sometimes allowed in, particularly for elections.[3] Fines were laid down for breaches of these rules. Some rules were peculiar to particular towns. Norwich mayor's court ordered that there should be no smoking at its meetings, but the fact that the order was repeated several times suggests that it was not fully obeyed.[4] Dignity was also required in the corporation's public appearances. Queenborough, Kent, might be 'miserable' and 'decayed', but the mayor had the mace carried before him in great state as he went to church.[5] In most towns, the aldermen were expected to accompany the mayor to church on Sundays and other solemn occasions, wearing their gowns. Once there, they were seated in a prominent place and expected to be treated with respect. Often, the procession would be led by the civic mace or sword and it was expected that these would be treated with respect by the clergy.[6]

In most towns, the aldermen and common council wore different gowns, making clear to spectators the differing degrees of dignity and seniority; the mayor, and sometimes the sheriffs, sergeants, and mace bearers, would wear distinctive dress. At Maidstone the common councillors' gowns were black and 'as near as may be of one and the same fashion'. They differed from the gowns of jurats (aldermen) in that they were plain, with a knot of black ribbons on the right shoulder.[7] Members of Gloucester corporation were to wear 'cloth or partlet' gowns made in the 'gravest and seemliest manner'.[8] A gown was an expensive item. When Samuel Newton became an alderman of Cambridge, he

---

[2] The orders for Cambridge corporation were fairly typical: Cambs RO, Corporation MS II 10 (Order Book, 1686), pp. 1–2. See also Davis, 'Colchester', 500–3; Kirby, 'Restoration Leeds', 136–40.

[3] Beds RO, Bedford Borough Minutes, Book 2, pp. 194–5; CKS, Md/ACm 1/3, fo. 134; *VCH City of York*, 240–1. See also the painting of the election of an alderman at Oxford in 1688 by van Heemskerk, now in Oxford city museum: a number of non-members are present, including a woman selling oranges.

[4] MCB 25, fo. 224, MCB 26, fos. 85, 223, MCB 28, fo. 59. The Bristol Merchant Venturers made an order against smoking at meetings in 1722: McGrath, *Venturers*, 110.

[5] Defoe, *Tour*, i. 110.

[6] For a case where they were not, see LHB 3, p. 890; *RBL*, iv. 548; LHP 34, no. 138; for the dispute at Bristol in the 1670s, see below Ch. 9. Leeds lacked a tradition of civic ceremonial, so had to invent one: Kirby, 'Restoration Leeds', 141.

[7] CKS, Md/ACm 1/3, fo. 191; Barry, 'Popular Culture', 72.

[8] Gloucs RO, GBR B3/3, pp. 755, 765–8.

bought a scarlet gown from an alderman's widow and had a common councillor's gown converted into an alderman's black gown. Together with a saddle, footcloth, and other 'riding furniture', the gowns cost him over £13.[9] In some towns, the aldermen wore scarlet on all formal occasions, in others on specific days— typically, when the mayor was elected and sworn, 5 November, Christmas Day, New Year's Day, Easter Day, and Whit Sunday, and on sessions days.[10] Fines were imposed for non-appearance or not wearing a gown, but many failed to appear for the annual election of the mayor at Oxford: the council complained that 'the mayor having so few or no attendants on such a public day the reputation of the city is impaired'.[11] Royal visits brought elaborate instructions concerning dress and accoutrements for the horses. At Oxford anybody who was improperly dressed, or who failed to appear, could be fined £10.[12]

The regulations for the corporations' private business and public appearances reflected aspirations rather than reality. Orders about attendance and wearing gowns were repeated over and over again. It was noted at Sandwich that fines for not wearing gowns were usually paid, fines for non-attendance usually not.[13] Fines were remitted on promises to attend in future, or because too many were piling up; corporations could not afford to be too rigorous. At Norwich in 1681 the assembly ordered: 'if not all do pay, the money paid by some shall be repaid.'[14] It was better to keep a full complement of more or less adequate members, rather than alienate those who were willing to serve, but not very diligent; if meetings became inquorate, the corporation could not function. (Refusals to serve were taken much more seriously.) Several towns petitioned for new charters in which the size of the corporation would be reduced, on the grounds that they were having difficulty maintaining a quorum.[15] In 1683 the king was advised against removing three aldermen of Coventry 'here being so small choice'.[16] The quorum on Oxford's council fell from 67 in 1660 to a low of 41 under Anne, in a council which numbered between 80 and 100.[17] The largest numbers of absentees were 45, in 1660, and 41 in 1696.[18] The

[9] Newton, *Diary*, 29.

[10] BRB 4, p. 397, BRB 5, p. 12, BRB 6, p. 54. BL, Lansdowne MS 891, fos. 56–7 adds 29 May. For the Leicester scarlet days, see *RBL*, iv. 513–14, 524. For Portsmouth, East, 9–11.

[11] *OCA*, iii. 57.   [12] Ibid. ii. 284–5, 310–11.   [13] EKRO, Sa/AC 8, fo. 181.

[14] FAB 8, fos. 91–2. Only 5 aldermen had appeared out of 24 and 24 common councilmen out of 60.

[15] *CSPD 1673–5*, 295 (Salisbury), *1690–1*, 199 (Saffron Walden); PC 2/79, pp. 252, 308 (Great Yarmouth), PC 2/86, p. 47 (Pontefract).

[16] BL Add MS 41805, fo. 52.   [17] *OCA*, ii. 272, iii. 291, iv. 41.

[18] Ibid. ii. 273, iii. 269.

sergeants proved unable to collect the fines, despite threats of dismissal, or having the money deducted from their salaries.[19] At Norwich, some meetings were abandoned as inquorate. On one occasion the mayor urged that absentees should be fined, but the assembly asked that they should be forgiven; after all, it was market day.[20] Once at Southampton only the mayor turned up.[21] Rules designed to ensure seemly behaviour proved no more effective. In 1674 a burgess of Portsmouth said he would never wear his gown under the current mayor. He was disfranchised, along with an alderman who queried the aldermen's right to disfranchise him, and another burgess who said he would never wear his gown again.[22] Details of quarrels within the corporation, and of unseemly behaviour, occasionally appear even in the sanitized official records.[23] There were quarrels about precedence, especially at Bristol, and at Hull the corporation repeatedly decreed who was to sit in the first pew in church, to prevent an unseemly scramble.[24]

II. CONVIVIALITY

Eating and drinking were an important part of civic life. Business meetings often ended with a visit to a tavern and major days in the civic year were marked by feasts, 'the end of which said feasting was as well for upholding the honour and esteem of this city [Winchester] as also for the maintaining and preserving of love and unity among the citizens and rejoicing one with the other'.[25] 'Honour and esteem' came partly from the corporation parading through the streets in their gowns, partly from entertaining distinguished guests. Although Leicester corporation generally tried to keep down the cost of entertainment,[26] it was prepared to be more lavish if it had important guests. In 1719, on the anniversary of George I's coronation, the corporation was to provide ale, but

---

[19] Ibid. iv. 77, 114.   [20] FAB 8, fo. 197.   [21] Patterson, *Southampton*, 21.

[22] East, 176–7; *PSP*, 165. Of the three, only the alderman, Thomas Hancock, was a member of the corporation. He must have been reinstated because he later twice served as mayor: East, 316.

[23] FAB 8, fo. 106; MCB 25, fo. 150; EKRO, Sa/AC 8, fos. 152–3. For the quarrels within Bristol corporation, see below, Ch. 9.

[24] BRB 5, p. 192, BRB 6, pp. 622, 676. The churchwardens were not to allow anyone else to sit in the aldermen's seats: BRB 5, p. 612.

[25] Hants RO, W/B1/6, fo. 26. The Bristol Merchant Venturers offered dinners after meetings to encourage attendance: McGrath, *Venturers*, 43. For the conviviality of the 'companies' at Newbury, see *HMC Portland*, ii. 285–6.

[26] LHP 31, nos. 383, 553, LHP 32B, no. 300, LHP 33B, no. 326, LHB 5, fo. 99.

the mayor could send for wine if any 'person of distinction' appeared.[27] All members were required to attend, to show their unity and to pay due respect to their guests. Fines were imposed for failing to attend or to wear the appropriate gown. At dinners, members were normally expected to pay for their meal (a shilling a head). If they did not attend, they were fined the same amount, double for aldermen, so they did not save money by staying away.[28] Ale, pipes, and tobacco were provided and, increasingly, wine as well.[29] Some aristocratic guests repaid the favour. From the early eighteenth century there was often a venison feast, in August, for which venison was donated by local landowners, including the town's MPs.[30]

As for eating and drinking fostering 'love and unity', it was natural that men who came together to work should wish to relax together afterwards. At Bristol, committees repaired to the tavern after every meeting, often consuming two gallons of sherry.[31] At Cambridge, Newton's diary is full of references to taking sugar cakes, wine, and feasts (for example, after the annual audit).[32] Sometimes the mayor and corporation went fishing, taking bread, cheese, and wine. They took the mace with them and were accompanied by 'doctors' from the university. They also took the mace when they went to Barnwell, where they picnicked on gammon and prunes.[33] Such conviviality clearly mattered to Newton, who also commented on the hospitality provided at funerals.[34] Commensality helped foster a sense of camaraderie, as well as good relations with the neighbours—particularly, in the case of Cambridge, the university; relations between town and gown were notably better in Cambridge than in Oxford.[35] This camaraderie was valued. After a period of factionalism, the assembly at Norwich referred wistfully to losing 'the comfort of converse, hospitality and good neighbourhood among us'.[36] Many towns made a considerable financial effort to hold feasts. In the early 1660s the little Hampshire borough of Lymington allowed the mayor £3 (out of an annual income of

[27] *RBL*, v. 83. See also LHB 5, fos. 142, 160.	[28] LHP 32B, no. 424.

[29] The provision of wine became more common under George I, perhaps a mark of the town's growing prosperity: *RBL*, v. 71–2, 92; LHB 4, fo. 128, LHB 5, fos. 18, 132.

[30] *RBL*, v. 38; *HMC Rutland*, ii. 167; LHP 39, fo. 217; LHB 4, fos. 36, 52, 149. It does not seem to have been held every year; presumably it depended on the gift of venison, although in some years no donor is recorded.

[31] Latimer, ii. 31–2. See also Davies, 'Colchester', 500–2, 538–9; Gauci, *Yarmouth*, 32–5.

[32] Newton, *Diary*, 2–3, 10–11, 13, 23.	[33] Ibid. 11, 27.	[34] Ibid. 5–6, 8–9, 26.

[35] Ibid. 33, 35–7, 52; Cooper, *Annals of Cambridge*, iii. 578. See also A. Shephard, 'Contesting Communities? "Town" and "Gown" in Cambridge, *c*.1560–1640', in Shephard and Withington (eds.), *Communities in Early Modern England*, ch. 12. For Oxford, see below, Ch. 5.

[36] FAB 8, fo. 107.

under £20) to hold a feast; cash-strapped Dover made its mayor a similar allowance in 1679.[37] In the early eighteenth century Southampton corporation was in chronic financial difficulties, but continued to entertain itself lavishly, until forced into severe retrenchment in 1720.[38] At Maidstone the town paid the whole charge for guests at the sessions dinners, and half the charges of freemen and freeholders.[39]

The Maidstone sessions dinner was unusually inclusive. At Oxford, newly elected councillors were expected to entertain the council, to wine and sweet-meats, and the commons, presumably to beer. In 1676 fines of between £4 and £20 were imposed for failing to provide this, which diminished the honour of the city.[40] When financial stringency compelled the council to substitute cash payments for these entertainments, the duty to entertain the commons continued. The council also laid down rules of conduct on these occasions, but councillors passed wine to their friends, who crowded around.[41] Many civic feasts, however, were exclusive to the corporation, and selected guests. Often members, as at Leicester, had to pay for themselves.[42] Newton noted one occa-sion when the mayor invited aldermen's wives to accompany their husbands (only about half came); on another only the mayor's wife was present.[43] At Leicester the common hall resolved in 1671 that all members of the corpora-tion should bring their wives to the 29 May dinner; all members had to pay, whether they attended or not. This does not seem to have happened again.[44] There is also a reference in 1684 to a 'merry day', when the mayoress bought wine at the Angel for members of the corporation and their wives.[45] The wives of aldermen were invited to the guild day feast at Norwich.[46]

It has been argued that in an uncertain and competitive business world, the urban middling sort needed a sense of cohesion and fellowship. This could be achieved through guilds or companies, or the vestry, or through clubs, which often had an intellectual or philanthropic purpose. They provided good company, in which men met as equals, on neutral ground. A similar purpose seems to have

[37] Hants RO, 27M74/DBC 2, fos. 62, 63; BL, Add MS 28037, fo. 22.
[38] Patterson, *Southampton*, 21–3, 27.   [39] CKS, Md/ACm 1/3, fo. 197.
[40] *OCA*, iii. 90. At York, on the day the new lord mayor was sworn, the citizens were invited to drink his health: *VCH City of York*, 238.
[41] Wood, i. 399; *OCA*, iv. 11.   [42] MCB 23, fo. 145; FAB 6, fo. 288, FAB 8, fo. 55.
[43] Newton, *Diary*, 38, 30–1.   [44] *RBL*, iv. 454.
[45] R. W. Greaves, 'The Earl of Huntingdon and the Leicester Charter of 1684', *HLQ* xv (1952), 377.
[46] B. Mackrell, 'Account of the Company of St George', *Norf Arch* iii (1852), 361. Wives of Bristol Merchant Venturers were invited to the charter day feast, but only from 1722: McGrath, *Venturers*, 112.

been served by the Company of St George, at Norwich.[47] Its main function was to organize the guild day feast. It was headed by the 'alderman of the feast', always the previous year's mayor, and a council, the twelve, elected annually. Its membership was much wider than the corporation and consisted of 'the livery'. Each year the twelve drew up a list of freemen, who were 'elected' to the livery at the meetings for the election of common councillors. Before 1705 these nominations were never challenged.[48] The liverymen paid 2s. 6d. each year towards the feast and were expected to wait on the mayor to church, in their gowns, on pain of a fine.[49] After eight years they became liable to be elected one of the four feast-makers. This could cost as much as £30 and some preferred to pay a substantial fine rather than serve. The company also imposed fines for breaches of its orders.[50]

At first sight, election to the livery would seem to have brought only burdens, but it had its compensations. Meetings of the twelve (and its committees) and of the feast-makers were convivial. More important, membership of the company gave access to the guild day feast, the most important event of the civic year, and socially exclusive. Members of the company mixed with the civic elite and dignitaries from the county. The feast transcended religious and political divisions, emphasizing common membership of the civic body. It continued throughout the 1640s and 1650s. When in 1649 Parliament declared disfranchised all citizens who had petitioned in favour of a mayor whom Parliament had disqualified from office, the company resolved unanimously that the petitioners should remain members of the company.[51] Similarly, under Charles II the feast-makers included Dissenters as well as Anglicans.[52] In 1695 two Independents, Bartholomew Balderstone and John Fenn, were admitted to the livery.[53]

The first signs of political division came in 1686, when the company ordered that an inscription under a statue of St George should be obliterated, together with a list of names in the kitchen; instead there was to be a simple statement that the kitchen had been paved by order of the company.[54] Unity and amity seem to have been restored, but ended in 1705 when the company

[47] J. Barry, ' "Bourgeois Collectivism?" Urban Association and the Middling Sort', in Barry and Brooks (eds.), *The Middling Sort of People*, ch. 3; Borsay, 'Introduction', in Borsay (ed.), *Eighteenth-Century Town*, 12–13.

[48] Mackrell, 'Company', 344; SGCR, pp. 255, 287, 558.   [49] SGCR, pp. 269, 276, 477.

[50] Mackrell, 'Company', 361–2; SGCR, *passim*.   [51] SGCR, p. 224.

[52] Ibid. 281, 282, 288, 299, 497. John Barnham, John Leverington, and William Dade can all be identified as Dissenters.

[53] Ibid. 479. For membership of the Independent congregation, see NCR, Case 13c/4, 13 July 1689. For non-political, essentially convivial mock corporations in the eighteenth century, see P. Langford, *Public Life and the Propertied Englishman, 1689–1798* (Oxford, 1991), 218–19.

[54] SGCR, p. 422. It seems likely that the dragon was described as standing for sedition or schism.

took the side of the Tory mayor, who refused to accept the election of a Whig alderman; the company thanked the mayor for preserving the honour of the city and company.[55] Suddenly opposition appeared to electing freemen into the livery. In 1706 the company was reduced to declaring its nominees for that ward elected, whether the freemen had endorsed them or not.[56] In 1706 some aldermen were excluded from the mayor's table at the feast, which may or may not have been an accident: there was a problem with gatecrashers, which suggests that the feast itself remained popular.[57] There were complaints that the twelve spent large sums of company money on drink: in 1704 and 1706 tavern bills totalled more than £15.[58] In 1706 the company contributed £10 towards an organ for St Peter Mancroft, which would not have pleased Low Churchmen and Dissenters.[59] The company's appeal faded as it became more partisan; from 1714, the artillery company provided an alternative centre of sociability for Whigs.[60] Once the Whigs gained control of the corporation, the company's tone became more conciliatory.[61] In 1726 one of the sheriffs questioned the company's right to demand money and won much support among magistrates and citizens. He demanded that the company hand over its assets, and its responsibility for the guild day feast and procession, to the city. The company complied and in 1732 it ceased to exist.[62] Once it had ceased to be non-partisan, it alienated the Whigs and was accused of being 'tyrannical'. In its last years, it 'occasioned much rancour and uneasiness every annual election of common councilmen, whereby the conquerors always put the vanquished on to the livery, thereby delivering them over to the mercy of St George'.[63] Once election to the livery was seen as a punishment, it could no longer foster 'love and unity' among the citizens.

III. CELEBRATION

Most towns had a cycle of celebration, partly civic, partly national. The most important civic celebration was usually the swearing and inauguration of the new mayor. When authority was transferred it was fragile; it was necessary to

---

[55] Ibid. 560. [56] Ibid. 558, 572–3; Kilmartin, 'Popular Rejoicing', 305–8.
[57] SGCR, pp. 586, 595; *Norwich Gazette*, 31 May–7 June 1707, 4–11 June 1709; MCB 27, fo. 118.
[58] Mackrell, 'Company', 364–5; SGCR, pp. 546–7, 579. [59] SGCR, p. 576
[60] Branford, 'Powers of Association', 187–91. [61] SGCR, pp. 700, 711. See also ibid. 680.
[62] Mackrell, 'Company', 366–74; Kilmartin, 'Popular Rejoicing', 308–13.
[63] Mackrell, 'Company', 374. In 1681 the company was accused of exercising arbitrary power: SGCR, p. 395.

emphasize the authority of the mayor and corporation, and to involve as many townspeople as possible, in a public expression of civic unity.[64] Coventry's Godiva procession was a statement of civic identity and independence, with extensive participation.[65] Another occasion which symbolized civic unity was riding the bounds of the city, which in Oxford was done by boat, and was usually followed by a dinner. Three days were commemorated nationwide following Acts of Parliament: a fast on 30 January, for Charles I's execution; Charles II's birthday and 'restoration' on 29 May; and 5 November. Other royal anniversaries were added, notably the coronation, which in the case of Charles II, James II, and Anne was on St George's Day, 23 April. In later reigns new royal birthdays, accession days, and coronation days were added and sometimes these continued to be celebrated in succeeding reigns: William III's birthday was commemorated under Anne, Anne's under George I, when the birthdays of the prince and princess of Wales were also celebrated. There were also additional days of rejoicing, for military victories or the conclusion of peace. Often there were two: a fairly spontaneous celebration when the victory or peace was announced, then a more carefully prepared official day of thanksgiving. The format was generally much the same. The day began with the ringing of bells. The corporation would go in procession to and from church, in their gowns, often accompanied by musicians. They would hear a suitable sermon and retire to dinner in the town hall. Later guns would be fired, sometimes accompanied by volleys from the militia or garrison. In the evening there would be bonfires, loyal healths, and, from the reign of James II, people put lighted candles in their windows. This started because James's government forbade the lighting of bonfires on 5 November.[66] The fashion for illuminations seems to have reached Oxford in 1691; the practice of breaking the windows of those who did not put up candles is first mentioned, in London, on 4 and 5 November 1691 (the 4th was the king's birthday).[67]

The aims of such celebrations were, first, to enhance the corporation's standing in the eyes of the people, as central actors in a drama and providers of spectacle and largesse; and, second, to affirm civic pride and unity. The people were welcome as spectators and, in a limited sense, as participants, but

[64] Borsay, ' "All the Town's a Stage" ', 230, 239–40.
[65] Kilmartin, 'Popular Rejoicing', 334–52.
[66] Morrice MS P, pp. 492, 654–5; Delapryme, *Diary*, 10; *HMC 6th Report*, 473; *HMC Downshire*, i. 276. Morrice first mentioned illuminations in 1685, Delapryme in 1686. Evelyn noted them for the first time in 1691 (*Diary*, v. 72), as did Luttrell, ii. 208.
[67] Wood, iii. 377, 406; FHL, MfS 8, pp. 2, 152.

maintaining those limits, encouraging participation while maintaining distance, could be difficult. Processions can be fun. They can also be intimidating, triumphalist shows of strength. For civic rulers, people were welcome to decorate their houses, to strew the streets with greenery, to dress up in their best clothes, to cheer, and to drink loyal healths; and they enjoyed doing so. Once involved, they might seek to celebrate in their own way. This was not disruptive if there was a broad consensus about the purpose of the celebration. It could become so if one group tried to appropriate it for a different purpose, as when high Tories and Jacobites celebrated Charles II's birthday with oak leaves and white roses as a deliberate snub to George I. The civic and national authorities needed to involve the populace in celebrations: a good turnout would show that they had its support.[68] New days of celebration were added as towns vied to show their loyalty. But some celebrations were bitterly contested and, under George I, the military often took over, with soldiers providing most of the participants (apart from the corporation—or the 'loyal' part of it), and ordinary people mere spectators. The celebrations were reported in the newspapers by the supporters of the dominant party, with obvious propagandist intent: often the senders of letters had to pay to have them printed.[69] Some reports highlighted the town's loyalty or attractions: an account of the welcome given to a nobleman in Barnstaple referred to the town's fair and clean streets and buildings.[70]

One elaborate annual civic celebration was guild day in Norwich, when the new mayor was sworn. On 'guild eve' people whitewashed their houses and hung cloths, pictures, garlands, and streamers. The street where the 'new-elect' lived was decorated especially elaborately, with the colours of the various companies. The streets and the cathedral were strewn with greenery and a long streamer hung from the cathedral spire.[71] Guild day began with the new-elect entertaining the aldermen and the livery of St George's Company to wine, followed by a substantial 'breakfast' at the old mayor's house. Some time after noon, the company repaired to the guildhall where the procession to the cathedral began. The old mayor, new-elect, sheriffs, and aldermen rode on horseback, wearing their gowns and foot-cloths. They were accompanied by the common council and livery, on foot. The procession was led by whifflers, who cleared the way with their swords; two standard bearers wore red silk

---

[68] Barry, 'Popular Culture', 72–3; Borsay, ' "All the Town's a Stage" ', *passim.*
[69] A writer from Atherston asked if his letter could be printed gratis, as it was the editor's home town: *Post Boy,* 26–8 May 1713.
[70] *Post Boy* 10–13 Oct. 1713.
[71] Fiennes, 149; MCB 23, fo. 247; NRO, MS 78, pp. 116–17, MS 79, p. 241.

coats and hats and they and the whifflers wore red and white taffeta scarves. They were accompanied by trumpeters and the city waits. Guns were fired and church bells rang. There were also 'dick-fools', in painted canvas coats and red and yellow caps, embellished with small bells and cats' tails. They were popular among 'the children and the mobility', but for many the star of the show was Snap, a man inside a wickerwork dragon, which flapped its wings and moved its jaws.[72] Throughout the afternoon there were pageants, plays, and shows, like the London lord mayor's show 'in little'.[73] In the evening there was the feast, where the best of the city's paintings were on show, and the day concluded with bonfires and repeated firing of guns.

Guild day was a highlight of the civic year and many gentry families came to enjoy the spectacle and join in the fun. But such celebrations had their dangers. Firing cannon—particularly the 'great guns'—could be risky. In 1668 inhabitants of Tombland complained that their houses had been shaken and damaged; in 1675 the guns damaged the windows of the grand jury chamber in the county hall.[74] In May 1660 the mayor's court worried that public joy at the proclamation of the king might spill over into Sunday and pollute the sabbath.[75] There was also the danger that popular exuberance might get out of hand. After the proclamation of the peace in 1697 the mayor's court warned against throwing fireworks, squibs, or serpents on 4 or 5 November. The order was repeated after the thanksgiving for the peace of Utrecht, which came just before guild day. There was another order against throwing fireworks in 1715. There were complaints that, on the day that the peace was proclaimed, many people had cut down branches or trees belonging to others.[76]

Despite such problems, for the citizens of Norwich guild day was one of the highlights of the year and they put a lot of effort into decorating their houses. Sometimes the decorative garlands also included silver: at Ampthill in 1713 some were said to contain plate worth £1,000.[77] At times the festive mood could grip the whole town for days at a time. The peace of Ryswick of 1697 was welcomed across the political spectrum and celebrations were generally free of partisanship. At Bruton, Somerset, when the peace was proclaimed the trained bands fired volleys, the people drank the king's health, and hogsheads

---

[72] This account is based on Mackrell, 'Company', 360–4; D. H. Kennett, 'Mayor-Making at Norwich, 1706', *Norf Arch* xxxv (1971), 271–3; E. Breitenbach, 'Guild Days in Norwich', *Quarterly Journal of the Library of Congress*, xxix (1972), 2–13. For similar celebrations at the mayor's inauguration at Coventry, see Kilmartin, 'Popular Rejoicing', 89–92.
[73] Fiennes, 149.   [74] MCB 24, fos. 92, 319.   [75] MCB 23, fo. 120.
[76] MCB 26, fo. 37, MCB 27, fos. 120–1, 195.   [77] *Post Boy*, 2–4 June 1713.

of beer were set at the cross and the town hall, for all comers. The following evening the women and girls of one street, dressed in white, marched through the streets with drums and music, with candles in their hands and colours inscribed in gold 'God bless king William'. Over the next few days the women and girls from other streets also marched through the town, holding candles and wearing laurel wreaths.[78] When the official thanksgiving day came, they had had longer to prepare. A thousand people from the countryside came to watch as 200 women and girls, in companies of fifty, marched through the town. Each was headed by a woman captain, with a rich sash, periwig, and hat. The colours of each company were richly embroidered. They marched to trumpets, drums, hautbois, and violins; the gentlemen of town and county formed a guard and waited on them. In the evening they marched again with lighted candles and the day ended with bonfires and fireworks.[79]

Such accounts of collective celebration could be multiplied many times.[80] When Halstead in Essex celebrated the peace of Utrecht 'all persons were employed in forming something to adorn and add to the glory and ornament of this wished for day'.[81] Leicester corporation normally showed little enthusiasm for celebration, but made an exception for the peace of Utrecht. The chamberlains were ordered to buy 100 yards of white ribbon for cockades for the corporation, its officers, and the town clergy.[82] After the sermon a procession passed through the town, featuring gardeners, with crowns and garlands of greens, fruit, and flowers; 100 framework knitters with sashes of white yarn; wool-combers, including 80 in white woollen caps of their own invention, and 300 with cockades of blue and white wool in their hats, in the shape of a cinquefoil, the town emblem; and a pageant, drawn by six horses, showing all the processes of cloth- and stocking-making. Then followed the waits and the corporation, preceded by the great mace; all wore white ribbons in their hats with 'pax', a crown, and 'AR' in gold; they were followed by drummers, other mace bearers, and several hundred gentlemen on horseback, all with white gloves and cockades. The conduit ran with port and the nobles and gentlemen gave the corporation six fat bucks. The corporation entertained at dinner 300 gentlemen and 700 tradesmen. Several sheep and lambs were roasted in the streets and food was sent to the prisons and hospitals. The houses

---

[78] Ibid. 16–18 Nov. 1697   [79] Ibid. 9–11 Dec. 1697.

[80] There was a similar procession at Chard on the news of the peace: *Flying Post*, 18–20 Nov. 1697. There were many processions to celebrate Anne's coronation (for which there had been more time to prepare): *Post Man*, 9–12, 21–3 May 1702; *Post Boy*, 28–30 Apr., 30 Apr.–2 May 1702.

[81] *Post Boy*, 23–6 May 1713.   [82] *RBL*, v. 66.

were adorned with greenery, flowers, and plate. The evening concluded with bells, bonfires, illuminations, and fireworks.[83]

Some celebrations took on the characteristics of a bucolic street party. Tents and bowers were set up for people to dine in the street.[84] After a military victory in 1705, the company at Tunbridge Wells lit a large bonfire above the town, drank healths, and huzza'ed, with music and cannon. Barrels of beer were provided near the fire for the common people. The company then returned to the walks, which were illuminated.[85] There were similar celebrations of the anniversary of George I's accession. In 1718 there was a marvellous outdoor supper for the nobles and gentry and a ball that lasted until morning. The costs were met by subscriptions from the company; many country people flocked to see the rejoicings.[86] But perhaps the most charming al fresco celebration was at Dursley in Gloucestershire in May 1660. The day after the men had celebrated the king's imminent return, the maids of the town got on to the scaffold, built to hold 200 people on the previous day. They issued an 'order' that anybody who prevented their daughter or maidservant from participating in their 'solemnity' was to forfeit a shilling. Two to three hundred young women came to the scaffold. They mounted a guard to stop any men coming in and spent some time dancing and cheering the king. They then formed themselves into a band, with a captain, lieutenant, and ensign, and marched (each carrying a green beech bough) with drums and trumpets to a nearby hill, where they drank the king's health on their knees. They marched back to the scaffold and continued their jollity until midnight. Next day the young men formed themselves into a 'militia' and had their day of rejoicing.[87]

From the above it is clear that, while some celebrations were carefully organized, ordinary townsmen and women could organize celebrations of their own, which entered into the spirit of the occasion. However, the joy and good humour shown by the young women of Bruton or Dursley could be offset by partisan animosities. Nobody was likely to complain in Shrewsbury in 1696, when an effigy of Louis XIV was arraigned, convicted of many crimes, and burned.[88] In several towns 23 April 1661, coronation day, and 29 May,

[83] *Post Boy*, 16–18 July 1713. The processions in Peterborough, Coventry, and Devizes also celebrated the cloth industry: *Post Boy*, 30 May–2 June, 27–30 June, 14–16 July 1713.

[84] *Post Man*, 28–30 Apr., 5–7 May 1702.   [85] Ibid. 19–21 July 1705.

[86] *Weekly Journal with Fresh Advices*, 6 Aug. 1715; *Post Man*, 3–6 Aug. 1717, 2–5 Aug. 1718.

[87] *Mercurius Publicus*, 24–31 May 1660 (the report calls the town 'Pursley', but other place names make it clear that it is Dursley). For equally spontaneous celebrations at Salisbury on the news that the seven bishops had been released from the Tower, see BRO, 07831, June 1688.

[88] *Flying Post*, 21–3 Apr. 1696.

the anniversary of the king's return, were marked by burning effigies associated with the previous regimes: Hugh Peter at Bury St Edmunds, Cromwell at Halesworth, Cambridge, Oundle, Wycombe, and York, Bradshaw (president of the high court of justice which tried Charles I) at York, Argyle at Sherborne, and an anonymous Covenanter at Exeter. The embarrassment caused to those who had supported Parliament and the Protectorate was heightened in many places by the burning of the Covenant. At York Cromwell, Bradshaw, the Covenant, and the arms of the Commonwealth were burned in front of the door of a leading figure in the city's government in the 1650s.[89] In 1689 arbours were set up in the streets of Stamford as people prepared to celebrate the coronation; the town was said to resemble a wood, with green booths and boughs and 'April' maypoles. But the mayor, said to be a Jacobite, sent for the militia and used the town fire engine to disperse the people. One man was shot and an alderman who remonstrated was knocked down and threatened.[90]

The celebration of the peace of Utrecht at Leicester had its partisan element too. The peace was fiercely opposed by the Whigs and a newspaper report remarked that there was not a single Dissenter in the corporation.[91] Some celebrations featured maypoles, likely to offend Dissenters.[92] There were, it is true, some towns where the peace of Utrecht, and the accession of George I, were celebrated by all, irrespective of party.[93] But often elements of partisanship crept in, especially in healths. In celebrating the peace of Utrecht at Tamworth, they drank to the 'honest members' of the corporation; elsewhere there were numerous toasts to the ministry and to Dr Sacheverell.[94] At Devizes the revellers were affronted by a gang of Whigs.[95] In the next reign, Whig newspapers routinely reported that it was only the loyal and the military who celebrated royal anniversaries. On the first anniversary of George I's coronation, the corporation of Hertford did not appear, so it was left to the king's friends and the soldiers to mark the day. On a thanksgiving day in

---

[89] *Kingdom's Intelligencer*, 29 Apr.–6 May, 3–10, 10–17 June 1661, *Mercurius Publicus*, 25 Apr.–2 May 1661.

[90] BL, Egerton MS 3337, fo. 3; Carte MS 228, fos. 75–6; *CSPD 1689–90*, 61.

[91] *Post Boy*, 16–18 July 1713.

[92] Ibid. 19–21, 23–6 May, 2–4 June, 16–18 , 23–5 July 1713.

[93] *Post Boy*, 8–11 Aug. 1713; *Flying Post*, 12–14, 14–17 Aug. 1714, 22–4 Aug. 1717. (The *Flying Post* was a Whig paper, so would naturally wish to suggest that the regime had almost universal support.)

[94] *Post Boy*, 12–14, 21–3 May, 2–4, 23–5 June, 14–16 July 1713.

[95] Ibid. 14–16 July 1713.

1716 the 'honest gentlemen' of the corporation attended the mayor to church; they included only three aldermen.[96] On the king's birthday in 1716, loyal gentlemen in Liverpool wore cockades in their hats, to distinguish themselves, and this became common.[97]

Civic celebrations, traditionally intended to demonstrate unity, were now routinely used to emphasize division. This could happen even to purely civic celebrations. Every year the mayor of Oxford 'rode' the franchises, or bounds, by boat, accompanied by drums and the waits, and preceded by colours and the city mace. Members of the corporation were encouraged to accompany the mayor and to dine with him (at their own expense).[98] From 1672 there were complaints that certain freemen were throwing water at members of the corporation, or pushing their way into the mayor's boat; the council ordered that such misbehaviour should cease. In 1680 the duke of Buckingham took part; his august presence prevented any misbehaviour, but the complaints continued.[99] The disorders reached a peak in 1696, when there was more than horseplay. The city was embroiled in a dispute over the election of a town clerk. The Whigs, under the patronage of Lord Wharton, supported Job Slatford; the Tories' patron was the earl of Abingdon. The 1695 mayoral election was hotly contested; after their candidate won, the Whigs rampaged around the town, abusing Tories and breaking their windows.[100] When the mayor 'rode' the bounds, a group of men stopped his boat, demanding money. They then stopped the chamberlains' boat and threatened to throw one of them in the river unless he paid Slatford all the money that he claimed was due to him. The men were disguised, had blacked their faces, and were extremely abusive, insulting Abingdon to his face.[101] What was intended to be a dignified civic occasion had turned into a show of public—and partisan—defiance, leaving the corporation and the earl humiliated. Even Norwich's guild day fell victim to party politics. In 1715 the Tory new-elect, Peter Attlesey, decorated his house with pictures of Queen Anne and Dr Sacheverell on one side of the door, and William III and Oliver Cromwell on the other.[102] In such circumstances, any claim that this was an occasion for civic unity could be no more than a pious fiction.

---

[96] *Flying Post*, 20–2 Oct. 1715, 12–14 June 1716.
[97] Ibid. 9–12, 12–14, 14–16 June 1716.   [98] *OCA*, ii. 264, 284.
[99] Ibid. iii. 56, 126–7, 221, 288; Wood, ii. 493.
[100] *HMC le Fleming*, 338; Wood, iii. 489.   [101] *OCA*, iii. 264–5.
[102] BL, Add MS 38507, fo. 133.

5

Getting on with the Neighbours

In governing towns, corporations had to contend with others whose power and jurisdiction might impinge on, or clash with, their own. Within the town, these included cathedrals, the universities, and the armed forces. Outside, they sometimes clashed with county magistrates, but there was also the less formal power of great landowners, capable of doing both good and harm. Each of these might hinder civic government, but they also brought benefits, in the form of custom, hospitality, and influence in the national corridors of power, and so needed to be handled carefully.

I. CATHEDRALS

Cathedrals were often architectural gems, a source of civic pride, and attractive to visitors.[1] They provided significant employment and custom, especially if they also had a school. The cathedral clergy, lawyers, and administrators were educated, cultivated people, who mixed easily with visiting gentry and the civic elite.[2] Finally, the cathedral provided an impressive setting for civic ceremonial; the mayor and aldermen normally attended the cathedral on a Sunday, with full civic regalia, and were seated in a prominent place. But alongside these advantages were drawbacks. The cathedral clergy might mix socially with the civic elite, but they had a strong sense of their own identity as priests, which, together with their university education, rendered them (in their eyes) superior to tradesmen. This was stated most brutally by Bishop Guy Carleton of Bristol, who described the city's aldermen, most of whom were merchants

---

[1] One cathedral with which visitors were unimpressed was that of Bristol: Fiennes, 237; Defoe, *Tour*, ii. 38. Schellinks, 102–3 described St Mary Redcliffe as 'glorious' but did not discuss the cathedral.

[2] Fiennes, 47; Defoe, *Tour*, i. 186; Rosen, 'Winchester in Transition', 177–8. See also Defoe, *Tour*, i. 188–9, ii. 80, for other cathedrals.

(and several were knights), as 'coopers and heel-makers' or 'a bumpkin pack of peddling mechanics'.[3]

While showing solidarity when dealing with the town, cathedral clergy often quarrelled among themselves. Many were difficult individuals, made more irritable by drink. Humphrey Prideaux, a canon and then dean of Norwich, had the misfortune to be regarded as a Whig by a mainly Tory cathedral chapter.[4] He was scathing about his colleagues. Of John Moore, bishop from 1691 to 1707, he wrote that he plundered all that he could from his bishopric, failing to mention Moore's learning or his library, which later became the nucleus of that of Cambridge university.[5] Prideaux's predecessor as dean, Henry Fairfax, had led the opposition of the fellows of Magdalen College, Oxford, to James II, for which he claimed he deserved a bishopric. Denied this, he determined to spend most of his £300 a year on claret and tobacco. The inscription he ordered for his tomb stressed his kinship with Sir Thomas Fairfax and mentioned the battle of Naseby.[6] Prideaux feared the city's Tory 'rabble' would tear the tomb down if it was unveiled in its present state; he persuaded the late dean's executors to remove the most offensive elements.[7]

If the bishop and dean were bad, in Prideaux's eyes the minor canons and lesser officials of the cathedral were worse. One of the lay clerks said that there was no such thing as heaven or hell and made sexual advances to a choirboy; another was obstreperous and rude, but was tolerated because of his fine counter-tenor voice.[8] In 1702 a minor canon, John Stukeley, was expelled after numerous cases of indecent exposure. Some 'hot-headed' men in the city wished to petition the privy council to have him reinstated; Prideaux shuddered to think of such obscene behaviour being discussed before the queen.[9] Another minor canon was frequently admonished for drunkenness, for which he was eventually removed; he also conducted illegal marriages and was sent to gaol for debt.[10] Two more minor canons were dismissed for adultery with a wagoner's wife and for getting a maidservant pregnant.[11] But the greatest

[3] Coventry MS 7, fos. 94, 98–9; *CSPD 1677–8*, 320, 351–4, 382–3; Tanner MS 129, fo. 138.

[4] He was probably a moderate Tory, like his patron the earl of Nottingham: he would not abjure James II, to whom he had sworn allegiance; he thought William was 'lawfully' king, because he had been declared to be so by Parliament, but not 'rightfully'. He concluded that it was best not to probe into these matters too deeply: Prideaux, 157–8; *CSPD 1702–3*, 237.

[5] NRO, DCN 115/2, pp. 136–8, 198–9; Evelyn, *Diary*, v. 235.

[6] Prideaux, 150–1, 157, 159, 161, 164, 222; Tanner MS 134, fo. 94.

[7] NRO, DCN 115/1, p. 224, MS 78, pp. 37–8.

[8] NRO, DCN 115/2, pp. 40–2, 44–5, 148–9.

[9] *CSPD 1702–3*, 237; Tanner MS 134, fos. 1–2, 51, 113–14.

[10] NRO, DCN 115/2, pp. 186–8, 322, 334, 337.   [11] Ibid. 9, 27–32, 37.

scandal involved Searles, the chapter clerk, taken with a whore in a bawdy house. Alderman Gardiner was inclined to discharge him, which would imply that he was innocent, but Prideaux argued against doing so: the story was all over the city and the woman had been put in the cage as 'Searles's whore'. He added that he had already reprimanded Searles for the scandal and for drunkenness. He concluded: 'This shows the mischief that follows from the town elections and our people interposing in it, for hereby they being all engaged, either on the one side or the other, if any falls under censure . . . the whole party takes the alarm and interposeth in the case and we have the trouble of their impertinence.'[12] Searles was far from penitent. He continued to drink heavily, denied that the dean had any jurisdiction over him, and appealed to the bishop. Eventually, he was persuaded to resign and given a job as a porter.[13]

One major source of contention was the claim of many chapters that the cathedral and close were exempt from the jurisdiction of the city magistrates. Such exemptions may have been of some economic advantage to the cathedral and its staff (especially if they did not have to pay the city poor rate), but they were preserved primarily to maintain the power and prestige of the Church as an institution. Many cathedral clergy thought it their duty to pass on to their successors the age-old rights of the Church, which they defended tenaciously, especially as some had been lost during the Interregnum.[14] Even city governments which broadly supported the Church, as Norwich's did under Anne, were annoyed that cathedral closes were a haven for those evading city bylaws, noticeably those requiring that those who practised trades and sold retail should be freemen. In 1701 Prideaux protested to the aldermen that a bill in Parliament against unfree trading contained a clause that it extended to the close. Alderman Blofield, Tory MP for the city, received his complaint courteously, and promised that in future the corporation would inform the dean of any such proposals; the bill did not pass.[15] In 1703 Blofield informed the dean that the corporation wished to bring in a bill against unfree weavers and combers practising their trades in the city or the close; he argued that if it did not extend to the close, it would be ineffective. Prideaux insisted that the close should be excluded from the bill and got his way.[16] The bill did not pass and no more such bills were introduced; the corporation was reduced to asking the dean politely not to allow shops or warehouses in the close.[17]

---

[12] Ibid. 139–41 (quotation from 141).   [13] Ibid. 156–61.
[14] BL, Harl MS 7377, fos. 29–30.   [15] NRO, DCN 115/1, pp. 142–3, 148.
[16] Ibid. 243–8.   [17] FAB 9, fo. 27; MCB 27, fo. 132.

From Prideaux's account of these disputes, one gets the impression that the aldermen approached the dean with caution, knowing how he would react to any perceived threat to the cathedral's rights.[18] The two bishops who served at Norwich for most of Charles II's reign, Reynolds and Sparrow, were careful to remain on good terms with the corporation. Both at Exeter and at Norwich, Sparrow persuaded the corporation to attend the cathedral regularly.[19] Others were less tactful. Bishop Guy Carleton, having picked a series of fights with Bristol corporation, moved to Chichester, where he became embroiled in a very public row with his chancellor.[20] He alienated the city by refusing to pay towards the poor rate; his predecessors had paid voluntarily, but he declared that he did not wish to prejudice the rights of his successors. He was besieged in his house by townspeople who, when they could not get in, carried off horses and cattle worth considerably more than he had refused to pay.[21] A year later, as he tried to have the laws enforced against Dissenters, his enemies tried to make him pay extra for the poor rate. Again he refused, shots were fired and windows broken, and two of his horses were killed. The bishop's coachman, acting as an informer, was fatally injured trying to disperse a conventicle.[22] The duke of Monmouth's visits to Chichester only added to the animosity between the bishop and the citizens. But the bishop had the last word. When a new charter was issued for Chichester, Carleton had a clause added that the cathedral close was part of the county, outside the jurisdiction of the city.[23]

Even more bitterly contested were disputes about the corporation's attendance at the cathedral. In 1664 the canons allocated to the archdeacons the seats in York minster where the lord mayor, recorder, and aldermen formerly sat. Later, it was reported that the lord mayor and aldermen were having a large pew built for them in one of the city churches.[24] The dispute was apparently not resolved until 1684.[25] Meanwhile, the corporation of Gloucester withdrew

---

[18] For a rather less polite response from certain aldermen, see NRO, DCN 115/1, pp. 186–7.

[19] Bodl, MS Add c. 308, fo. 232; MCB 25, fos. 30, 71, 102, 107; Tanner MS 39, fo. 117.

[20] L. McNulty, 'Priests, Church Courts and People: The Politics of the Parish in England, 1660–1713', Ph.D. thesis (London, 2005), 90–2.

[21] *Currant Intelligence*, 12–16 July 1681; *Impartial Protestant Mercury*, 28 June–1 July, 1–7 July 1681. One of the churchwardens who signed a petition against the bishop was Richard Farrington, a great enemy of Carleton, who was later accused of abetting the killing of his coachman: *HMC House of Lords 1678–88*, 164; *Domestic Intelligence, or News from Both City and Country*, 26–30 Oct. 1682.

[22] *Loyal Protestant*, 12 and 15 Aug., 10 Oct. 1682.

[23] *CSPD 1684–5*, 199, *1686–7*, no. 1170.

[24] *CSPD 1663–4*, 447–8, 466–7, 501, *1667*, 291, 511; D. Scott, 'Politics, Dissent and Quakerism in York, 1640–1700', D.Phil. thesis (York, 1990), 301–3.

[25] T. Comber, *Autobiography and Letters*, ed. C. E. Whiting, 2 vols., Surtees Society clvi–clvii (1946–7), i. 14–15.

from the cathedral and prepared to sue the dean and chapter in a dispute concerning the corporation pew.[26]

There were also disputes about the manner in which the mayor and aldermen entered the cathedral. The mayor was the chief magistrate of the city, but the cathedral was the bishop's domain. At Norwich, on guild day, the new mayor knocked nine times on the cathedral gate, requesting admission, making it clear that he had no jurisdiction over the cathedral and entered it only with the bishop's permission.[27] There were long-running disputes about carrying the city sword into the cathedral at Bristol and Exeter.[28] It should not be assumed, however, that relations between city and cathedral were invariably bad. In Winchester, they were generally good, and no other Restoration bishop seems to have possessed Carleton's exceptional talent for making enemies. Many understood, like Sparrow, that they could achieve more by maintaining the corporation's goodwill and cultivating the magistrates. Some were timid men, or sought to avoid trouble as they tried to secure a better bishopric. Conversely, many members of corporations, while conforming to the Church of England, disliked being ordered around by uppity priests. With the advent of partisan politics, the potential for conflict, in cities with Whiggish corporations, was considerable; Whig clerics could be equally at odds with Tory corporations.

II. THE UNIVERSITIES

The position of the two universities in their towns was unique. Some towns contained autonomous bodies which exercised authority within particular areas—cathedral closes, dockyards—and so limited the power of the town corporation. But the universities claimed to exercise over the whole city powers which were normally exercised by the corporation. Two chartered bodies, the university and the city, claimed authority over the same geographical area and the same group of people, although the university also possessed uncontested authority over its own academic staff, students, and servants, and those of the colleges. The authority of both university and city rested on a mixture of charters and custom, and there were inevitably clashes of demarcation. In Cambridge these were generally contained. The numbers and spending power of the students gave the university great leverage in its dealings with the town,

---

[26] Gloucs RO, GBR B3/3, pp. 866–7.   [27] Kennett, 'Mayor Making in Norwich', 272.
[28] See below, Ch. 9; *HMC City of Exeter*, 338.

but Cambridge found it prudent to maintain good relations.[29] In Oxford the university asserted its rights and claims to precedence with the tenacity of the most determined cathedral chapter. Because its rights were not legally unquestionable, in 1689–90 and 1692–3 it sought to have its charters confirmed by Act of Parliament. This was opposed, successfully, by the city, but some in the university feared that too close an examination of its charters might expose irregularities, and were not sorry to see these moves fail.[30] The situation reverted to one of uncertainty, in which both parties tried to exploit the prevailing political circumstances.

The university's exercise of authority in the town was based partly on the claim that it was the superior body, and partly on its duty to ensure the welfare of the young men entrusted to its charge. It could subject citizens to considerable pressure, using the power it claimed to 'discommon' citizens who infringed its rights, barring them from trading with the university, which for many would ruin their business.[31] The university's control over the night watch enabled it to maintain a curfew and keep the students from the dangers associated with staying up, and drinking, late, but the university claimed that the curfew applied also to townspeople.[32] The vice chancellor claimed the right to license alehouses, to prevent the opening of establishments unsuitable for students, although in 1681 it was alleged that alehouses denied licences by the mayor had been licensed by the vice chancellor.[33] The rationale for the university's claim of the right to control the markets, the licensing of certain trades, and the management of the streets and paving was less obvious. The claim that its members and employees, and tradesmen licensed by the university, were exempt from burdensome city offices, and city rates, rested on their alleged need to devote all their time to the university. In 1690, however, the Court of Common Pleas decided that to matriculate as a member of the university, in order to avoid office, was unlawful.[34] To enforce its claims the university had its own officers, notably the proctors who patrolled the streets at night, its own

[29] Defoe, *Tour*, i. 86; Shephard, 'Contesting Communities?', in Shephard and Withington (eds.), *Communities in Early Modern England*, ch. 12.

[30] *OCA*, iii. 216, 219, 226, 239; Wood, iii. 322; BL, Add MS 36707, fos. 115, 117–18, 123; *HUO*, iv. 119.

[31] *HUO*, iv. 111–13, 119.

[32] *HMC Finch*, i. 443–4; *HUO*, iv. 125–6. This was also true at Cambridge: Defoe, *Tour*, i. 86–7. If Anthony Wood and Defoe are to be believed, Cambridge was more successful in maintaining good order among its students.

[33] Prideaux, 107. By the end of the seventeenth century the university was granting fewer licences than before: *HUO*, iv. 131.

[34] *HUO*, iv. 127–31; Wood, iii. 311, 323–4; Morrice MS R, p. 106; BL, Add MS 36707, fo. 73.

justices of the peace, and its own court, presided over by the vice chancellor, which exercised jurisdiction over townspeople in cases falling within the university's sphere of authority.[35] At times, the university justices acted as if they were subject to the county rather than the city.[36] Normally the magistrates of university and city worked together, in the city sessions. At times of tension, it became a matter of which had the greater number of justices, to outvote the other.[37]

The university claimed authority in areas normally dealt with by corporations, above all the night watch: the mayor was responsible for maintaining order, but did not control the means of enforcing it. This frustration was compounded by the arrogance with which the university often addressed the city. The city was required to pay the university 63*d.* each year on St Scholastica's Day, 10 February, to commemorate a massacre of sixty-three students by citizens. The mayor and sixty-two of his brethren were also expected to swear to respect all the privileges of the university. In general the corporation's tone towards the university was restrained and conciliatory, reminding the university that the corporation had privileges too. The governors of the university, by contrast, asserted their claims with the certainty of men who believed that they were obliged to maintain centuries-old privileges. They also, as men of learning and, often, gentle birth, looked down on the citizens as mere tradesmen.[38]

This was made very clear in a dispute about precedence when Queen Anne visited the city in 1702, when relations between the university and the predominantly Tory corporation were generally good. The university claimed the right to ride first on such occasions, but had been forced to give place to 'a promiscuous crowd of mechanics'.[39] There were great disorders; the corporation blamed a few troublemakers and argued that the main problem had been the size of the crowds.[40] The university proceeded to 'discommon' four of the corporation and demanded that the city pass an Act stating unequivocally that the university had precedence over the city in all public processions.[41] The city responded that nothing had been proved against any of the four. However, it wished to avoid a public quarrel and asked its high steward, the earl of

[35] When Parliament met at Oxford in 1665 the university's guards were deemed too weak to keep order: Bodl, MS Add c. 303, fo. 124.

[36] *OCA*, iv. 6–7.

[37] Prideaux, 102–3, 109; *CSPD 1680–1*, 646–7. In Cambridge the university and town worked together better: Cooper, *Annals of Cambridge*, iii. 578; Newton, *Diary*, 4, 36–7, 60–1.

[38] *HUO*, iv. 105, 121. [39] *OCA*, iv. 293. [40] Ibid. 18, 289–91.

[41] Ibid. 291–4. Cambridge university used a similar tactic to force a brewer who had insulted the vice chancellor to apologize: Defoe, *Tour*, i. 86.

Abingdon, to mediate. A compromise appeared to have been agreed, only for the vice chancellor to announce that it would not be accepted by the university convocation, so it was up to the city to accept the university's terms: as he put it, where there were two corporations, one had to be superior.[42] The university delegates drew up a 'recognition', to be subscribed by the corporation, that the university was the more honourable body and so should have precedence during royal visits; the corporation was also to apologize for not having observed this customary order.[43]

The city responded that this would enable the university to blame the city for any disorder. To agree would be against the members' oaths to uphold the city's rights. However, it resolved to behave respectfully, informing the vice chancellor that once the 'discommoned' four had been reinstated, the city would give all reasonable satisfaction.[44] The vice chancellor and delegates demanded that the corporation subscribe the 'recognition'. When it did not, they declared that the mayor and seven others should be 'discommoned'.[45] The corporation claimed that it was ready to give all reasonable satisfaction, but the delegates ignored all views but their own, and punished members of the corporation without due cause. The delegates replied that the house's response was false, scandalous, and insolent, seeking to advance the corporation to parity with the university. It resolved to 'discommon' all the 'trading part' of the common council, except for those who subscribed the 'recognition' within ten days. Very few did so, and negotiations resumed, culminating in an agreement.[46] More than a year of acrimony ended in something very like the status quo ante.

In this dispute, the corporation's demeanour had been courteous and respectful, if occasionally exasperated. At other times, it was less deferential, but it was always torn between resentment of the university's claims, and awareness of the economic and social benefits that it brought to the city and the harm it could do by withdrawing its custom.[47] The university also had powerful friends, with many of its alumni active and influential at court and in Parliament, so the city sought powerful friends of its own. At the Restoration, the university looked to its friends to help it regain the power it had lost during the Interregnum. In October 1660 it demanded that the mayor and corporation should swear to respect the university's privileges. The mayor demurred, remarking that the custom had not been observed for some years. The upshot was a peremptory

---

[42] *OCA*, iv. 18–19, 294–6.   [43] Ibid. 296–7.   [44] Ibid. 19–20, 295, 297–8.
[45] Ibib. 299–301. The dispute made the national press: *Post Boy*, 15–17 Oct. 1702.
[46] *OCA*, iv. 24, 28–9, 305–7.   [47] Prideaux, 83–4.

insistence that the mayor and his colleagues make the oath; the university began to send out the night watch. It secured an order from the privy council that the corporation should swear to respect the university's privileges, pay the oblation on St Scholastica's Day and stop interfering with the night watch. Some points, such as licensing and government of the streets and markets, were to be left to the law, but in general the corporation should acknowledge those privileges enjoyed by the university before 1640.[48] The corporation agreed to comply, and continued to swear the oath and pay the 63*d.* until 1681. It also ordered the recorder to draw up a petition asking how far the mayor could lawfully act at night to preserve the peace, without infringing the council's order.[49]

The 1660s saw a series of lawsuits in which the townsmen generally came off better than the university.[50] In April 1668 the vice chancellor demanded an unequivocal recognition of the university's right to impose fines for breaking its curfew. In September there were complaints that the city had elected as mayor John Lambe, who had been put out by the Corporation Act commissioners in 1662. The privy council forbade the election of men not qualified under the Act. Lambe remained as mayor, but the order may have dissuaded the corporation from bringing back others who had been removed.[51] In 1669 the corporation responded to the university's choosing the duke of Ormond as its chancellor by electing Ormond's arch-enemy, the duke of Buckingham, as its high steward.[52] In 1678 the university's right to impose fines for night-walking was challenged in the courts. The corporation minutes referred to the 'slavery' of being 'imprisoned' in their homes after 9 p.m. The case was vigorously promoted by Buckingham, who employed his own counsel and was present in court: the court told the city and university to compromise.[53] The mayor was accused of quartering soldiers on those privileged by the university and the soldiers patrolled the streets at night, rather than the university officers.[54]

The Exclusion Crisis added a party political element to the divisions between town and gown. The city seemed to go out of its way to offend and embarrass the university. In January 1681 Alderman William Wright, one of the town's MPs, called for an end to the oath and oblation on St Scholastica's

[48] *OCA*, ii. 275–6; *CSPD 1660–1*, 548–9; Wood, i. 372–5.
[49] *OCA*, ii. 282–3; *CSPD 1661–2*, 14; Wood, i. 376.
[50] *OCA*, ii. 338, 346, iii. 6, 11; Wood, ii. 125.
[51] *OCA*, ii. 294, iii. 307–8; *CSPD 1668–9*, 589, 611.
[52] *OCA*, ii. 31; *HMC le Fleming*, 66. Cambridge university elected Buckingham as its chancellor in 1671 and removed him, at the king's command, in 1674: *CSPD 1671*, 223, 228–9, *1673–5*, 305.
[53] Wood, ii. 248–9, 270, 390, 403, 421; *OCA*, ii. 106–7, 109, 311; *HMC Ormond*, iv. 166.
[54] *CSPD 1678*, 183–4; Wood, ii. 408, 426.

Day; the house resolved to petition the council and Parliament against this 'slavery'. The mayor appeared as usual, but only about twenty townsmen came with him; he resisted pressure to take over control of the night watch.[55] In the 1681 parliamentary election there were cries of 'damn the university, damn the clergy'.[56] Fears of a challenge to the city's charter, compounded by a dispute about its choice of town clerk, led to the full number of corporation members appearing on St Scholastica's Day in 1682.[57] It took James II's assault on the Church of England to bring the city and university together, as they united in common hostility to the Catholics installed in the university.[58] Thereafter, as the corporation became increasingly Tory, relations generally remained good, with the exception of the flare-up in 1702–3. However, the corporation was quick to spot any threat to what it saw as its rights.[59]

III. THE ARMY

At the Restoration, the English people were weary of military rule. In November 1660 Andrew Marvell wrote to the corporation of Hull that he was sure that they would be willing to pay handsomely to be 'ungarrisoned'.[60] The Convention handed back to the king the executive role that had been assumed by the Long Parliament, but it insisted on paying off almost all of the New Model Army, leaving the king unable to fulfil his offer, in the Declaration of Breda, of taking it into his employment. The Cavalier Parliament refused to acknowledge the need for a 'standing army', but accepted that the king needed 'guards and garrisons', to guard against foreign attack and domestic rebellion. In the 1660s and early 1680s, the king and his old Cavalier, or Tory, supporters feared revolt by the 'disaffected'. It took time, at the Restoration, to re-establish the militia after twenty years of neglect. It was supplemented at times by volunteers, raised by members of the nobility or gentry or of corporations, which enjoyed a shadowy existence alongside regular troops and the militia.[61] Regular troops tended to be concentrated in the London conurbation, although keeping order in the City itself was left to the trained bands, supplemented

---

[55] *OCA*, ii. 134; Wood, ii. 465, 498, 512, 517; *Loyal Protestant*, 9 Mar. 1681; *True and Serious Intelligence*, 24 Feb.–3 Mar. 1681.

[56] *Loyal Protestant*, 9 Mar. 1681.   [57] Wood, iii. 4.

[58] Ellis, i. 375, ii. 102; Luttrell, i. 421.   [59] *OCA*, iv. 120–1.   [60] Marvell, ii. 2.

[61] *Kingdom's Intelligencer*, 14–21 and 21–28 Jan., 4–11 Feb. 1661; *CSPD 1664–5*, 366, *1665–6*, 497, 508; Wood, iii. 145; *London Mercury*, 15 Dec. 1688; *Flying Post*, 1–3 Dec. 1715; Miller, *After the Civil Wars*, 169–71.

by the Honourable Artillery Company. In the provinces, the first priority was defending the coast, and more particularly major ports and naval bases like Hull and Portsmouth. In January 1661 the king decided to disband inland garrisons, mainly to save money: as he could not afford substantial garrisons, he saw fortified towns as more of a threat than an asset, and in 1662 he ordered that the fortifications of several towns—Taunton, Gloucester, Northampton, Coventry, and Shrewsbury—should be demolished.

Charles's policy was to have fewer and stronger garrisons. The citadels at Hull, Plymouth, and Portsmouth were repeatedly strengthened. After the Second Dutch War, he ordered an extensive programme of strengthening coastal fortifications. Some coastal fortifications were demolished, because they were decrepit or in a town regarded as disaffected.[62] Some inland garrisons continued. A small garrison was re-established at Ludlow, to safeguard the militia money and the plate and jewels belonging to the president of Wales.[63] Chepstow remained the personal garrison of the marquis of Worcester, later first duke of Beaufort. An order in 1680 that it should be suppressed, along with garrisons at Chester and Scarborough, in order to save money, was subsequently reversed.[64] In the fraught climate of the early 1680s there were calls to strengthen inland garrisons. Even before Monmouth's visit in late August 1682, there were complaints that Chester was full of disaffected people and that the castle should either be better garrisoned or demolished; the king also needed a garrison at Shrewsbury.[65] Also in 1682 a Yorkshire gentleman urged that the garrison at York, currently only thirty men, should be strengthened and that a strong citadel should be constructed.[66] Coastal towns naturally felt vulnerable in wartime: the Dutch made several raids in 1667 and the French burned Teignmouth in 1690.[67] The corporation of Dover asked the king in 1661 to install a substantial garrison and in 1667 to strengthen its fortifications; on the latter occasion it resolved, despite its shaky finances, to meet the cost itself, if the king did not.[68] In 1707, again at the request of the corporation, the government moved two companies there from Canterbury.[69] The local gentry pressed the king in 1678 to continue the fort at Bridlington,

---

[62] *CSPD 1667*, 517; PC 2/57, fo. 24.   [63] *CSPD 1664–5*, 347, 363.

[64] *CSPD 1661–2*, 490, *1663–4*, 359; PC 2/68, p. 343.

[65] John Rylands Library, Legh of Lyme Correspondence, Sir John Chicheley to Richard Legh, 13 Dec. 1681; *CSPD 1682*, 342–3.

[66] WYAL, MX/R 18/124, 20/14.   [67] S. Baxter, *William III* (London, 1966), 268.

[68] *CSPD 1660–1*, 582; DAM, fos. 230, 237.

[69] BL, Add MS 61652, fos. 27–8. For similar requests from Yarmouth, Aldeburgh, and Dunwich, see ibid. 48, 82.

which they saw as essential for the security of the surrounding countryside.[70] During the wars of 1689–1713 coastal towns continually petitioned for guns, powder, and ammunition to defend themselves against the French.[71] In 1689, with the army in disarray, the mayor of Dover asked for some militia units to be quartered there. Hull, unusually without a garrison, mobilized its own militia, as it had in similar circumstances in 1667.[72]

Apart from defending towns against attack, soldiers could be a source of profit. As there were no barracks outside London before the 1680s, and not many thereafter, most soldiers had to lodge with civilians. The keepers of inns and alehouses were required, as a condition of their licences, to provide lodging gratis; if they could not accommodate all the soldiers, they were pay for their lodging in private houses. Private householders could not, under an Act of 1679, be forced to receive soldiers against their will, but many (especially in Hull and Portsmouth) were happy to do so and received 8*d.* a week for a bed (often a share of a bed), laundry, fire, and small beer. For many poor families, lodging soldiers provided a significant addition to their income and, in Hull, the corporation preferred to quarter soldiers in private houses; the garrison was so large that it would impose an unbearable burden on public houses if the soldiers were all quartered there. Many alehouse keepers were poor and had little lodging other than what they needed for their families.[73] Even if the soldiers were lodged gratis in public houses, they still paid for their food and drink, so brought money into the town. They were welcome so long as they paid promptly for their lodging and subsistence and were under effective discipline. In general, the monarch and the officers did their best to meet both these expectations. Until the first Mutiny Act in 1689, there was no statutory basis for punishing mutiny and desertion. Officers needed the goodwill of the civil magistrate. At Norwich in 1667 and 1678 the magistrates sent soldiers to the house of correction and to gaol for desertion.[74] The king was very conscious that undisciplined soldiers could provoke disorder and lead to angry questions in Parliament.[75]

---

[70] WYAL, MX/R 12/44.

[71] *HMC Finch*, ii. 493; *CSPD 1694–5*, 140, *1700–2*, 443, 508–9, 517, *1702–3*, 419, 420, 422, 433–4, 439.

[72] *CSPD 1689–90*, 67; BRB 5, pp. 95, 96, BRB 6, p. 244. Normally Hull relied on the garrison to maintain order.

[73] J. Childs, *The Army, James II and the Glorious Revolution* (Manchester, 1980), 85–6; BRL 1242, 1506.

[74] MCB 24, fo. 37, 25, fo. 38.

[75] See L. G. Schwoerer, *No Standing Armies! The Anti-army Ideology in Seventeenth-Century England* (Baltimore, 1974).

Town rulers had good reason to remain on good terms with the military. They too feared disorder, and reprimand from 'above' if things got out of hand. In garrison towns, the civic rulers made a point of inviting the officers to civic functions and often elected the governor or deputy governor to Parliament. Andrew Marvell did not always get on with his fellow-member for Hull, Lieutenant Colonel Anthony Gilby, but acknowledged that he tried hard to serve the town.[76] Similarly, governors and their deputies often made a real effort to cultivate the magistrates' goodwill. Sir John Reresby, when he became governor of York, took care to show 'good humour and civility' when entertained by the citizens.[77] He was therefore embarrassed by a fracas between some of his soldiers and the townsmen of Doncaster, as his loyalty was divided between his men and his 'neighbours'.[78]

One illustration of the concern of the military establishment to avoid giving offence came in 1668, after a Lieutenant Wise had insulted the mayor of Hull. The town complained to Lord General Albemarle, the town's high steward. Although one of the bench's friends at court warned it not to overreact to the alleged insult, Albemarle ordered Wise to apologize to the (now former) mayor—even though the lieutenant was his cousin. The duke of York, whose officer Wise was, declared that he would not tolerate indiscipline among his officers. Small wonder that the bench was advised to respond graciously to any apology, but Wise ran away, rather than apologise.[79] This concern to maintain the goodwill of civilians was typical of Charles II's regime. In 1672 a troop of horse under Colonel Stradling threatened the magistrates of Huntingdon, broke open doors, and took what they wanted, saying that the town was a nest of rebels and that Cromwell had been born there. Stradling was cashiered and the council ordered that he should be tried at the assizes. An account of the council's action appeared in the *Gazette*, to show the king's disapproval of such conduct.[80] Most of the more serious complaints came in wartime (in 1666–7 and 1672) and some involved Scots regiments.[81] One major problem in 1672 was lack of ready money to pay for the soldiers' quarters; there were fewer

[76] Marvell, ii. 39.

[77] Reresby, 281–2. One product of this concern to establish good relations came early in 1685, when the lord mayor gaoled a citizen for insulting a soldier: *CSPD 1685*, no. 10.

[78] Reresby, 339–40, 342.

[79] Marvell, ii. 77–82, 145–6; BRL 780, 791a.

[80] *CSPD 1672*, 415–16, 449–50, 550; PC 2/63, pp. 294–5. See also *CSPD 1665–6*, 350, *1679–80*, 144–5; *Protestant (Domestic) Intelligence*, 3 Feb. 1680.

[81] *CSPD 1666–7*, 210, *1667*, 522. For the Scots, see *CSPD 1671–2*, 461, *1672*, 265, 509, 555. At least some Scots officers tried hard to maintain discipline: *CSPD 1672*, 511–12.

complaints of misconduct in 1673, after the Commons had voted the king money for the war. It was alleged that some complaints were unfounded. In 1668 accusations of illegal and arbitrary conduct by Sir Philip Musgrave, governor of Carlisle, were dismissed as the product of the malice of one alderman.[82] There were also towns where the troops were reported to have been well received and to have behaved well.[83]

Although the high command in London and town magistrates might wish to maintain good relations between soldiers and civilians, certain aspects of army culture made this problematic. Although they lodged among towns-people, soldiers saw themselves as set apart, governed by a distinct set of rules and with a strong sense of solidarity; in 1692 the execution of a soldier con-victed of murder was delayed until his regiment had left town.[84] An attack on one of their number was resisted and avenged by his colleagues. Small quarrels escalated into a confrontation, or battle, between soldiers and civilians, which led to injuries or even death.[85] The townsmen did not always get the worst of it, especially if soldiers were reluctant to fire on civilians or had only powder, but no bullet, with which to do so.[86] Officers were likely to be carried away in the heat of the moment. In a quarrel between the mayor of Gloucester and the major commanding the troops, the major ordered his men to fire, one of the captains ordered them not to. The men obeyed the captain, who was promptly placed under arrest by the major.[87] Sometimes, the provocation came from the townsmen, especially if they released soldiers who had been recruited against their will, or imprisoned for military offences.[88] In May 1717 the people of Newbury complained bitterly of the conduct of the dragoons quartered there, but then interceded for two men who were due to be shot for desertion.[89] An additional problem was that soldiers were recruited from among those seen as the least useful members of society. Under Anne, householders, farmers, and those with a steady job were exempt and the recruiters targeted those seen as loose, idle, and disorderly; for some, a spell in the army was seen as a dose of wholesome discipline, to encourage them to change their ways.[90]

Although a sense of solidarity and of alienation, or even contempt, towards civilians was always a part of the military mindset, it was normally held in

[82] Carte MS 60, fo. 663 (misdated 1665?); *CSPD 1668–9*, 30–1, 68. See also *CSPD 1672*, 265.
[83] *CSPD 1672–3*, 32, 141.   [84] *CSPD 1691–2*, 372.   [85] Luttrell, iii. 63, 78, 114.
[86] Reresby, 339; M636/31, Edmund to John Verney, 15 Apr. 1678.
[87] *HMC Portland*, vii. 215.   [88] *CSPD 1695*, 3, *1696*, 1; PC 2/76, p. 475.
[89] *Weekly Journal or Saturday's Post*, 25 May 1717.
[90] *HMC Portland*, viii. 169, 189; *HMC Cowper*, iii. 56.

check by the need to secure co-operation from the civil magistrates and fear of a reprimand from 'above'. There were, however, times when such constraints became much weaker and soldiers behaved more brutally towards civilians. Soldiers and their political masters regarded much of the civilian population as disaffected and so deserving punishment, especially in the wake of Monmouth's rebellion in 1685 and the Jacobite rebellion of 1715. James II believed that towns like Bristol and Taunton deserved a little rough treatment because of the sympathy they had shown for Monmouth and individual officers took it upon themselves to punish magistrates and citizens for 'disloyalty'. But James also sought to tip the balance of authority between military and civilians; military governors demanded that mayors hand over the keys to the town gates.[91] Although he was concerned to maintain discipline and to ensure that regiments paid for their quarters, officers maltreated civilians and failed to pay what was due, confident that the king would always believe their version of events rather than that of the townspeople.[92] Similarly, under George I officers could be confident that complaints from towns identified as 'Jacobite' would be dismissed.[93] The bad habits acquired under James continued for a while under William III, especially among units which had fought in Ireland or Flanders.[94] This was despite the fact that, from the outset, William's regime ordered that soldiers should be punished for violence against civilians and handed back the keys of town gates to mayors.[95] The deputy governor of Hull had the deputy postmaster tied neck and heels for refusing to hand over a packet to him.[96] In general, William's government was careful to punish military indiscipline.[97] The difficulties it faced were highlighted in a much-reported dispute at Coventry. Alderman Nathaniel Harryman discharged a soldier who had been

[91] Morrice MS P, p. 639; Tanner MS 29, fo. 116; BRO, JQS/M/6, fo. 242. The practice of demanding the keys began late in Charles II's reign, when there were signs of a more military tone in government circles: *HMC Ormond*, vii. 229; NLI, MS 2440, pp. 129–30.

[92] See the case of the officer who had the mayor of Scarborough tossed in a blanket: *HMC Downshire*, i. 301; Ellis, ii. 212–13, 225–6.

[93] See *The Several Papers . . . Relating to the Riots at Oxford* (1717). The depositions suggesting that the fault lay with the soldiers rather than the citizens are much fuller and more persuasive than those suggesting the contrary, but the Lords showed no hesitation in accepting the soldiers' version of events.

[94] J. Childs, *The British Army of William III* (Manchester, 1987), 90–1, 95; *HMC Dartmouth*, i. 242, 244; East, 190–3; *English Currant*, 21–6 Dec. 1688.

[95] *CSPD 1689–90*, 10, 52.

[96] BL, Egerton MS 3337, fo. 55; *CJ*, x. 265. For other incidents see BL, Egerton 3337, fos. 76, 86; *HMC Finch*, ii. 251.

[97] Carte MS 76, fo. 704; *CSPD 1689–90*, 52, 57, *1690–1*, 246–7, 269, *1695*, 52; PC 2/73, p. 511, 2/76, pp. 147, 150, 180.

imprisoned for a breach of discipline, with a certificate saying that he had been imprisoned because he had demanded his pay. Captain Aubrey Porter ordered two soldiers to beat the alderman (who was over 70). The privy council heard both parties and decided that both were at fault. Harryman was reprimanded for meddling with military matters and Porter was suspended, for not showing due respect for the civil magistrate.[98]

Under William III the most frequent complaint was that the soldiers lacked money to pay for their quarters. Successive Mutiny Acts made provision for this, but securing payment was a real problem.[99] In Hull the situation was made worse by the Mutiny Act of 1690, which fixed the subsistence for foot soldiers at 4*d.* a day; previously, rates had been negotiated locally, or fixed by the magistrates, and in Hull they had normally been double that. There were loud complaints when officers insisted on having their men quartered in public houses, and fed, for 4*d.* a day, but the law was on their side. The public house keepers complained to the Commons, but secured no redress.[100] The corporation began to advance money for the troops' subsistence and ended up writing off arrears.[101] In 1696, with coin in short supply, the bench effectively maintained the troops, with scant hope of reimbursement, because the alternative was the threat of free quarter.[102] The barracks were unable to accommodate soldiers, because they had no beds; even after the end of the war, they hoped 'soon' to get the much-reduced garrison into barracks.[103] The bench complained of the 'insolencies' of the officers; many keepers of public houses abandoned their trade rather than plunge further into debt. Caught between a cashless soldiery and a restless citizenry—'we border very near unto a mutiny'—the bench had little option but to borrow more money.[104] Not until July 1698, nine months after the peace, did the treasury order that all arrears due to corporations should be paid.[105] The same pattern can be found elsewhere. In Plymouth the garrison was moved out of the citadel and quartered in public houses, shifting the cost of maintenance from the crown to the townsmen.[106] In Norwich, not normally a garrison town, the mayor's court began issuing

---

[98] *CSPD 1694–5*, 506; Carte MS 239, fos. 25, 37; Luttrell, iii. 502; PC 2/76, pp. 150, 163; *Flying Post* and *Post Boy*, 23–5 July 1695.

[99] PC 2/74, p. 424; *CSPD 1692*, 232.

[100] Childs, *Army of William III*, 92, 96; BRL 1145; *CJ*, x. 629, xi. 309, 467.

[101] Childs, *Army of William III*, 92; BRL 1149; BL Egerton MS 3337, fo. 141; BRB 6, pp. 337, 350, 365.

[102] Childs, *Army of William III*, 96–8; BRB 6, pp. 391, 393; BRL 1163a.

[103] BRL 1172, 1515.   [104] BRL 1163a, 1515.   [105] BRL 1175.

[106] *Flying Post*, 13–16, 16–18 June 1696.

orders for soldiers to be allowed extra credit in July 1696, and such orders continued at frequent intervals until after the end of the war.[107] In general, corporations did their best. The earl of Portland found that the people paid the soldiers' subsistence regularly, and the little Cornish town of Penryn took in soldiers for whom there was no room at Falmouth or Pendennis, even though the officer in charge had no authority to demand quarters in the town.[108]

Complaints about the burden of quartering soldiers continued in Anne's reign, when the armies raised were even larger and the troops were dispersed in a wide range of towns, often quite small, such as Masham and Yarm in Yorkshire, and Newton and Garstang in Lancashire. (On the other hand, many large towns, and indeed large areas of the country, were at times exempt: in January 1712 all the regiments were quartered in the north, the Midlands, Somerset, and the London area.)[109] The increased size of the army meant that there were still conflicts about enlisting soldiers. In 1704 there was a dispute between soldiers and townsmen at Meriden, Warwickshire, in which several were injured on both sides. The officer in charge refused to hand over a man who he claimed was a deserter; the man's landlord told the officer that if he did not do so he would raise the country and pursue him from place to place. The officer submitted and the magistrates committed him to gaol.[110] In 1705 a magistrate tried to enlist John Leach of Pembroke, but he fled into the town and the people resisted all attempts by the constable to seize him.[111] But in general, there seem to have been fewer clashes about recruiting than under William, either because people were getting used to the army, or because discipline (and the regularity of pay) had improved, or because the recruiters targeted the loose, idle, and disorderly.

The quartering of soldiers in towns created a potential conflict between two groups of men subject to different authorities and different laws or regulations. As Marvell told Hull corporation in 1668: 'It were a happy thing if there could be such a line drawn betwixt you and the soldiery, as you might keep both your own way, without molesting one another.'[112] There were complaints about the potentially arbitrary implications of the articles of war, especially those issued in 1672, which were seen as a blueprint for absolutism; the lord keeper resigned rather than affix the great seal to them. But even these stated that soldiers should

---

[107] MCB 26, fos. 15, 16, 17*, 18, 19, 30, 40. The court also made provision for sick soldiers: ibid. 28, 32.

[108] *CSPD 1696*, 311, 200.   [109] NLI, MS 2474, p. 487.

[110] *HMC Bath*, i. 59–60; *HMC Portland*, viii. 123–4.

[111] *HMC Portland*, viii. 169.   [112] Marvell, ii. 78.

be subject to the civil magistrate in civil affairs.[113] Nevertheless there were offences which could be seen as breaches of both common law and military discipline, and officers sometimes felt that they should be able to deal with their men in their own way. At times, when they and the government saw much of the civilian population as disaffected, they were almost a law unto themselves, but the government was generally wary of provoking Parliament, which was suspicious of the army and wary of military rule. By the 1720s its fears were probably anachronistic: as Defoe wrote, 'our sovereigns have ceased to encourage the soldiery to insult the civil magistrates'.[114] In garrison towns, with a citadel and barracks, there was an area at least partly outside the magistrates' jurisdiction, but these were few and saw the garrison as (in the case of Hull) 'rather an advantage than a burden'.[115] Similarly, the royal dockyards had to be partly closed off, to prevent unauthorized entry and pilfering, and to be governed partly by their own rules. Very occasionally this led to conflict. In 1697 the magistrates of Portsmouth broke open the dockyard gates, which they found locked against them on their annual perambulation of the bounds of the town. The privy council reprimanded the magistrates for breaking open the gates, but refrained from punishing them because of their constant loyalty to the government. It also reprimanded the navy commissioner for locking the gates, and urged the magistrates and dockyard officers to live together like good neighbours—which they normally did.[116] Elsewhere, troops were generally quartered in relatively small numbers among the civilian population. This proximity could make for friction, but it prevented the soldiers from becoming a caste apart—which is why James II made a point of moving regiments around, so that they did not become too familiar with civilians. Normally, however, soldiers and civilians lived together without too much serious conflict.

IV. THE LANDED ELITE

The relationship between towns and major landowners was reciprocal and complex. Many towns depended at least in part on their markets, shops, and leisure facilities attracting affluent and socially prestigious customers, whose presence would in turn attract others. Winchester, with little industry, depended mainly on distribution and retailing, helped by its importance as an

---

[113] Miller, *After the Civil Wars*, 27.   [114] Defoe, *Tour*, i. 138.   [115] BRL 1242.
[116] *CSPD 1697*, 169, 170–1; *Flying Post*, 14–16 June 1697; PC 2/77, p. 29.

administrative, legal, and ecclesiastical centre. The facilities it provided grew apace. In 1662 there was said to be insufficient accommodation for the bishop's retinue; by 1686 there were over 300 beds and stabling for over 1,000 horses.[117] For a brief period it was also a royal city: Charles II built a palace there in 1683–5, which (unfortunately for the city) was not used by his successors.[118] Leicester was also a county capital, and a major marketing and distribution centre, but it proved far less attractive to the county nobility and gentry. Norwich was an important industrial city, but was also eager to attract aristocratic custom, at times of county business, for major events in the civic year, and over the Christmas period. Towns also needed powerful friends and patrons, men with significant influence in the county (above all, the lord lieutenant) and at the centre, at Whitehall and in Parliament.[119] Some bestowed the office of high steward on such men. Picking an influential patron was a tricky business: a turn of the political wheel could leave a town with a patron who was no longer of any political use. Only in 1672 did Reading corporation ask Bulstrode Whitelocke, Cromwell's lord chancellor, to resign as its steward, remarking, 'as your circumstances are, it may not be so proper for yourself to appear for us'. He duly resigned.[120] Hull was well served by Lord Bellasis, its governor, in the 1660s, and made him high steward in 1670, but, as a Catholic, he could do nothing for the town after the passing of the Test Act in 1673, and he resigned. He was replaced, as governor and high steward, by Monmouth, the king's illegitimate son. In 1683, having fallen from favour, Monmouth told the town that he could no longer do it any useful service, and advised it to choose another high steward.[121] The duke of Buckingham, however, ignored letters from York suggesting that he should resign, so the city chose the young duke of Richmond, son of the duchess of Portsmouth, hoping that his mother would protect the city against the king's displeasure.[122]

In return for the service that they could do for the towns, great aristocrats expected the townsmen to show the courtesy and deference due to their rank. When they visited, they would be met some way outside the gates by the

---

[117] Schellinks, 138; Rosen, 'Winchester in Transition', 172–3.

[118] In 1694 William III visited the palace with Sir Christopher Wren, with a view to resuming building work, but nothing was done: Luttrell, iii. 280.

[119] For an earlier period, see C. F. Patterson, *Urban Patronage in Early Modern England, 1580–1640* (Stanford, 1999).

[120] *HMC Leeds etc.*, 218; B. Whitelocke, *Diary*, ed. R. Spalding (Oxford, 1990), 794–5. There is no suggestion in the diary that he had done anything for the town since 1660.

[121] BRB 6, p. 55.

[122] WYAL MX/R, 21/26–7; BL Althorp MS C18, fo. 59; Carte MS 216, fo. 319.

corporation, on horseback and in their gowns, and they would be entertained with every mark of respect. In 1703 Leicester corporation decreed that the new lord lieutenant of the county, the earl of Denbigh, should be given a 'handsome treat', 'fit for an earl'. Denbigh's coat of arms was set up, alongside those of other landed families, at the Gainsborough, where most civic festivities were held.[123] Aristocrats also expected some say in the disposal of parliamentary seats, for their sons, clients, or nominees. And they expected obedience. As agents of the king, their credit at court depended in part on securing compliance with his will. One way of expressing that compliance was through loyal addresses, which added to the reputation of the peer who procured them (and frequently also introduced those who presented them—often the town's MPs). They could be published in the *Gazette* or the newspapers, to show popular support for royal policy and dislike of the conduct of the crown's enemies. Sometimes towns could not be brought to present such addresses at all; at others they were couched in terms which the peer thought lukewarm or unacceptable. But the discord they aroused was nothing to that which arose when peers were charged with procuring the surrender of charters in the 1680s. Charters gave towns their existence as corporations. They had derived that existence from the crown, and knew that they had usually infringed some condition of the grant, which a compliant judiciary could decide rendered the charter forfeit. They feared, or claimed to fear, that to surrender the charter would jeopardize corporation property. They also argued, probably sincerely, that having sworn to uphold the town's privileges, surrender could be construed a breach of their oaths. In securing the surrenders, the peers were trying to procure a benefit for the crown far more tangible that the loyallest of addresses. For that reason, corporation members needed a great deal of persuading, cajoling, or worse.

From the towns' point of view, peers holding major county or national offices were best placed to serve them. Under Hull's charter of 1661, the high steward was to be a privy councillor. Norwich, a large but poor city, badly needed a friend at court at the Restoration. The county was destitute of well-established peers, so the city looked to the Honourable Henry Howard, *de facto* head of the Howard clan, which had held the dukedom of Norfolk until the execution of the fourth duke in 1572. In 1660 Parliament revived the dukedom, ostensibly for Henry's elder brother, incarcerated at Padua as a lunatic, but really for Henry, the 'deputy duke'.[124] In 1660 the corporation asked Howard to join in presenting a gift to the king and in 1661 it consulted

[123] *RBL*, v. 42, 46.   [124] Marvell, ii. 6, 7; *HMC 6th Report*, 369.

him about seeking a new charter.[125] When news arrived of the revival of the dukedom, the city rang the bells, and in 1664 the corporation obediently chose Thomas Corie, one of Howard's men of business, as its town clerk.[126] Howard was rich and extravagant. He spent £30,000 refurbishing the Duke's Palace in Norwich and in 1663 he spent Christmas there, entertaining lavishly until March.[127] When the king visited Norwich in 1671, Howard kept open house for a week, bringing the necessary furniture down from Yorkshire.[128] As a Catholic, he was ineligible for office, but he remained very influential in Norfolk, even after the Test Act: Lord Yarmouth, who became lord lieutenant in 1676, regarded Howard's support as one of his greatest assets in establishing his power in the county.[129] Howard's influence collapsed with the Popish Plot—ironically, just after he had succeeded to the dukedom. He remarked sadly in 1679 that if he tried to use the electoral influence that he had had in 1661 (when he virtually nominated four MPs) it would prove counter-productive.[130]

The influence wielded by Howard, despite his religion, showed that high office was not essential, if a patron had sufficient wealth and a distinguished enough lineage. Nevertheless, office undoubtedly helped. Henry Somerset, who became third marquis of Worcester in 1667, and first duke of Beaufort in 1682, also came of a distinguished and very wealthy Catholic family. Unlike Howard he had no qualms about converting to Protestantism and made his peace with Cromwell. He set out to build a regional power-base, not in the family's traditional sphere of influence in South Wales (he was the first head of the family who did not speak Welsh), but in the Welsh Marches and Monmouthshire (regarded as part of England). His influence rested partly on great wealth, but also on an extensive range of offices, especially military offices: he became lord lieutenant of Gloucestershire, Herefordshire, Monmouthshire, and all of Wales (of which he was lord president). It was said even in 1666 that he could bring into the field 5,000 foot and the best regiment of horse in England.[131] By contrast he held no major central government office and became a privy

---

[125] FAB 6, fos. 213, 219.

[126] MCB 23, fos. 138*–139; T. Corie, *Correspondence*, ed. R. H. Hill, NRS xxvii (1956), 10. A letter was addressed to Corie at Howard's London residence, Arundel House: MCB 24, fo. 165.

[127] E. A. Kent, 'The Houses of the Dukes of Norfolk in Norwich', *Norf Arch* xxiv (1932), 84–5; Sir T. Browne, *Works*, ed. T. Wilkin, 4 vols. (London, 1836), i. 44–5.

[128] Corie, *Correspondence*, 32–5.

[129] *HMC 6th Report*, 377–8, 380; BL Add MSS 36988, fos. 117, 119, 41656, fo. 54.

[130] *HP 1660–90*, i. 323, 332, 394–5; Badminton, FmE 4/4/1.

[131] *CSPD 1665–6*, 556. He became lord president of Wales, and lord lieutenant of all the Welsh counties, in 1672.

counsellor only in 1672. He was renowned for the great state in which he lived and had an immensely high opinion of himself. He and his wife lived in almost medieval state, with a household of 200; the neighbouring gentry would plant or prune their trees to 'humour his vistos'.[132] His wife was as proud as he was. In 1674, when the duchess of Portsmouth tried to pull rank on her, the marchioness remarked that titles gained by prostitution never made much impression on persons of good sense.[133]

Worcester initially had few dealings with towns and probably had a haughty disdain for townsmen. Although he accumulated a string of stewardships and recorderships from 1682, the only urban offices he held before then were the high stewardship of Gloucester (from 1661) and the lord lieutenancy of Bristol —a logical extension of his lieutenancy of Gloucestershire—from 1673.[134] His only recorded activity at Gloucester before 1671 was as a member of the Corporation Act commission, which removed many members of Gloucester corporation, even though they had subscribed the oaths and declaration, on the grounds that they were 'disaffected'.[135] Early in 1672 Worcester was named to a small committee to draw up a list of men fit to be named as corporation members in a new charter for the city; his suggestions were mostly rejected.[136] His first foray into Bristol's internal affairs was even less successful: in 1676, his nominee for election as town clerk did not even make the shortlist. From 1680 he began to build up his power in the city through the newly formed artillery company, of which his son was captain. In September 1682 Worcester ostentatiously mustered the militia on the day for electing the mayor and sheriffs.[137] When the time came to press the corporation to vote to surrender the charter, Beaufort left the grubby business of canvassing aldermen and councillors to others, so that he would suffer no loss of face if their machinations failed. But there was no doubt that he was now the directing force in the city's affairs. He played a significant part (at Whitehall) in shaping the new charter and when the bishop died it was remarked that no decision could be

---

[132] *Norths*, i. 170–3.

[133] CPA, 114, fo. 119 (newsletter dated 16 Aug. 1674 NS); *HMC Portland*, iii. 346. The best study of the duke is M. McClain, *Beaufort: The Duke and his Duchess* (New Haven, 2001).

[134] Gloucs RO, GBR B3/3, p. 168; *HP 1660–90*, iii. 454.

[135] Halliday, *Body*, 357. In March 1663 he urged his fellow commissioners to undertake a second review of the corporation, saying it was better to err on the side of safety (by removing too many rather than too few): R. Austin, 'The City of Gloucester and the Regulation of Corporations, 1662–3', *Transactions of the Bristol and Gloucestershire Archaeological Society*, lviii (1936), 265–7. He also over-saw the destruction of Gloucester's fortifications in 1662.

[136] See below, Ch. 7.   [137] *CSPD 1682*, 392.

made about his successor until Beaufort came to town.[138] In 1685 his nominees were chosen in a parliamentary election.[139]

Bristol was an unusually independent and truculent city, but the fact that it could defy as powerful a man as Beaufort shows why lesser men were more tentative in the way they managed corporations. Robert Paston, first earl of Yarmouth, came of an ancient family but was beset by financial problems. The major goal of his political life was to find some way of escaping from debt and, as alchemy proved slow to yield results, the most probable source of relief was the king. But the king's bounty had to be earned and in 1676 Yarmouth found himself appointed lord lieutenant of Norfolk, with instructions to lead the newly emerged 'church party' in the county.[140] At the end of 1677 he was also drawn into the affairs of Norwich, when one of the city's MPs died. Yarmouth put forward his son, Lord Paston, and, although he was elected, Yarmouth was infuriated by the opposition that he had faced. He set out to remove those aldermen he regarded as 'fanatics' or 'disaffected', but received only limited backing from the king. In 1682 he had a new chance to win royal favour, by persuading Norwich corporation to set an example to others by surrendering its charter. But the aldermen were far from willing and he had to come to Norwich in person to push through the surrender. Unfortunately for Yarmouth, any kudos he may have gained from the surrender was tarnished by the delay of several months in securing it and bitter infighting among the local Tories over the terms of the new charter. His financial problems remained as intractable as ever.[141]

Attempts by peers to persuade corporations to surrender their charters were concentrated in the 1680s. Far more pervasive, and ongoing, were the efforts of peers and gentlemen to influence parliamentary elections.[142] Five-sixths of the members for England and Wales sat for boroughs, ranging in size from London down to towns that had decayed or even disappeared since they had been granted representation, such as Gatton and Old Sarum.[143] Many had no charter or corporation; these included manorial boroughs, whose 'officers' were appointed by the lord of the manor. This does not necessarily mean that

---

[138] BRO, 04264/7, fos. 191, 194–5, 208; Tanner MS 32, fo. 37.

[139] *HP 1660–90*, i. 239. [140] Miller, *After the Civil Wars*, 230–2.

[141] Miller, 'Containing Division', 1046–7. For other peers and the surrender of charters, see ch. 8.

[142] What follows is based in large part on the comprehensive and authoritative account of elections by David Hayton in *HP 1690–1715*, i. 36–261.

[143] Ibid. ii. 577, 690.

they were in the 'pocket' of the lord, although some were. Towns exhibited a complete spectrum of electoral behaviour, from supine acceptance of patrons' nominations to defiant independence. In general the larger towns, and those with charters and corporations, were more independent, but this was by no means always the case. One would have expected the little unincorporated Wiltshire town of Wilton to be dominated by the earl of Pembroke, whose great mansion, Wilton House, was close to the town. In fact, he found it difficult to control the town's representation and was often opposed by the local clothiers.[144] Much depended on local configurations of power—how many aristocratic and other interests were competing for the town's seats—and the franchise. Parliamentary franchises were almost infinitely various and some changed over time, but they can be divided into four basic types.[145] First, in many towns the right to vote was restricted to the corporation, which meant that changes in membership altered the electorate. Second, there were towns where the franchise was vested in the freemen. This could mean those who were free to practise a trade and to sell retail, having completed an apprenticeship or acquired the freedom by inheritance or purchase. But many towns also appointed many honorary freemen from outside, often specifically for electoral purposes, and these could outvote the resident freemen.[146] In Winchester these honorary freemen were members of the 'guild merchant' and were distinct from those who were qualified to practise a trade; it was the former who had the right to vote in elections and in the choice of new freemen. Peers who were members of the guild merchant voted in parliamentary elections.[147] Such considerations led some towns to try to restrict the franchise to resident freemen. The third type of town was that where the franchise was attached to a particular piece of property, often known as a burgage; electoral influence could be acquired by buying up burgages, but also by 'splitting' them and creating additional voters.[148] Finally, there were those where the franchise extended to all house-holders, though this was often qualified by including only those who were resident or who contributed to the poor rate or other local taxes.

It will be seen that there was scope for a wide range of electoral behaviour. The influence of corporations—where they existed—varied greatly, as did the opportunities for voters to show their independence. Small electorates often

---

[144] *HP* 1690–1715, ii. 696–9.

[145] My categorization is cruder than that used by Hayton in his much fuller study.

[146] See the notorious example of Hertford: *HP 1690–1715*, ii. 282–92.

[147] Hants RO, W/B1/5, fo. 159, B1/6, fos. 5–6, B1/7, fos. 61, 67, B2/5, 8 Dec. 1705.

[148] See for example Castle Rising, Norfolk: *HP 1690–1715*, ii. 412–14; see also ibid. i. 96–100.

increased the voters' individual bargaining power; voters generally welcomed contests, which meant that they would be entertained lavishly by the candidates and offered all sort of inducements—most often cash, but sometimes corn or coal.[149] Thus, while there were boroughs where a single patron could nominate to one or even both seats, there were far more where the voters or corporation could play off two or more interests against each other. When they did so, they expected not only material benefits for themselves or the town—contributions to charities or new civic buildings, addition to the town's plate —but also to be wooed and treated with respect: at election times, normal expectations of deference could be suspended or even inverted. The situation was complicated by a growing number of rich merchants or financiers from London seeking seats: the clothiers around Wilton encouraged Londoners to seek an interest in the town, to counter that of the earl of Pembroke.

Electoral considerations also led peers and gentlemen to seek municipal office. Usually they sought the relatively honorific posts of steward or recorder (with the deputy recorder to undertake the necessary legal work), which gave them some influence in the town; this arrangement suited the town, as well, if it gave the corporation a friend at court and in Parliament. As elections became more frequent and regular from 1695, there was a strong incentive to secure a friendly returning officer. In manorial towns, the lord of the manor nominated the appropriate officers, but in corporate towns the key figure was the mayor. In 1708—an election year—Lord Wharton served as mayor of Appleby; the duke of Bolton's son was mayor of Lymington, Hampshire, in 1701–3, 1724, and 1728.[150] Competing aristocratic interests could cause problems for towns—they did not want to alienate a powerful neighbour—but also offered opportunities. Leicester (the only parliamentary borough in the county) had to contend with competing noble interests; perhaps fortunately for the corporation, success ultimately depended, not on aristocratic recommendations, but on 'the suffrages of the unstable vulgar'.[151] On the other hand, some towns were virtually the private property of a peer. In 1682 the earl of Bedford strongly opposed the incorporation of Tavistock, of which he was the 'proprietor', but, as he was a leading Whig, his objections, although heard, were overruled. After 1689 the Russell interest was the strongest in the borough, but by no

---

[149] Ibid. 107–10.
[150] Ibid. 101, v. 190. In 1667 the earl of Derby was mayor of Liverpool: J. A. Picton, *Liverpool Municipal Records* (Liverpool, 1863), 244.
[151] *HP 1690–1715*, ii. 351–2; *HMC Cowper*, ii. 408.

means overwhelming: the dukes of Bedford could usually nominate to one seat, occasionally two, but sometimes none.[152]

After 1689 electoral interests fought[153] for seats, usually without any interposition by the central government. Earlier, such intervention was more common. In 1670 Lord Cornbury, son of the disgraced earl of Clarendon, protested against a new charter for Christchurch, Hampshire. This installed a set of capital burgesses, most of whom were of the rank of gentleman and above, headed by Lord Ashley, currently high in the king's favour. Cornbury claimed that this charter infringed his privileges as lord of the manor, but he also must have resented Ashley's attempt to take over his electoral interest in the town. After a hearing before the privy council, the king ordered a *scire facias* against the charter, an action to revoke a patent that should not have been granted.[154] The outcome of this action is unclear, but, whatever it was, Cornbury, now second earl of Clarendon, retained his electoral influence. In 1679 he reminded the corporation that it had promised to choose whoever he recommended, but assured them that his nominees were good 'patriots'. They were returned unopposed, but in 1681 Clarendon got his way only after a vigorous contest.[155] After 1689, despite a challenge from the formidable dukes of Bolton, Clarendon continued to control both seats and there was only one contest between 1695 and 1713.[156] Such control was rare, and it should be remembered that, even where there was no contest, there was sometimes considerable preliminary skirmishing, which ended with one or more competitors deciding not to proceed to a poll.

Parliamentary elections show the complexity of relations between town corporations, townspeople, and the landed elite. Peers and gentlemen had the wealth, power, and influence to help, or possibly harm, the town. They could help cash-strapped corporations repair or replace civic buildings; they supported local charities; their presence at civic events added to the corporation's prestige;

---

[152] *HMC Somerset etc.*, 108; PC 2/69, pp. 267–9; Luttrell, i. 211; SP 44/66, pp. 79–81; *HP 1690–1715*, i. 198, ii. 152–4. He also sought a caveat against a new incorporation in 1688: *CSPD 1687–9*, no. 1931.

[153] For the use of military terminology, see *HP 1690–1715*, i. 186–7.

[154] Christchurch Civic Offices, MS D57; SP 44/25, fos. 173–5; PC 2/62, p. 326; Halliday, *Body*, 199.

[155] Christchurch Civic Offices, volume of 'Letters' on elections etc., p. 49; *HP 1660–90*, i. 247–8; *CSPD 1680–1*, 165. The charter was certainly granted (Halliday, *Body*, 351) and there is a copy of it in Christchurch Civic Offices, MS D57; if it was revoked, the town must have reverted to its previous charter, as no new one was issued in this period.

[156] *HP 1690–1715*, ii. 233–4.

they accepted civic offices and promoted the town's interests at the centre. They could also, if displeased, promote the interests of the town's rivals, or have quarter sessions, the assizes, or militia musters moved elsewhere. Although peers in general were not supposed to vote, and non-resident gentry might not be qualified to vote in towns, they might appear on election day with large entourages and try to influence proceedings. And most towns, except for the largest and most independent, elected members of the landed gentry as their MPs, rather than townsmen. But if the balance of social and political power was weighted against the town in normal circumstances, this was often not the case in the run-up to a general election. The town had something—seats in the Commons—which these aristocrats wanted, and wanted badly. This strengthened the bargaining and negotiating position of the corporation and the townsmen, and they knew it. Whatever sorts of pressure and whatever dirty tricks candidates and returning officers might use, MPs, even for the smallest towns, had to be elected, and voters normally were expected to make their choice with a modicum of freedom: there came a level above which force and fraud were unacceptable. This gave the voters—many of them poor—a rare opportunity to enjoy hospitality and respect from their 'betters', and in some cases to make money. But it also gave them a chance to make political choices, defying both powerful aristocrats and the civic elite in the pursuit of political and religious principle. Candidates knew this, and campaigned on their and their opponents' record in Parliament, and on issues. Not the least important effect of frequent elections—in the Exclusion Crisis and after 1689 —was to divide urban populations along partisan and denominational lines. Townspeople were already aware of the issues of the day; elections brought them closer to home and gave voters a chance to move from debate to action, to try to influence national politics.

6

Religion

I. CHURCH AND DISSENT: HIGH CHURCH AND LOW CHURCH

Discussions of religion in this period normally centre on the relationship between Church and Dissent, and assume that this relationship changed radically after the Toleration Act of 1689. This approach projects backwards Victorian conflicts between church and chapel and focuses on persecution: with the Toleration Act England moved from 'the great persecution' to 'the plain called ease'.[1] The early 1680s undoubtedly saw the most intense persecution of religious dissidents in seventeenth-century England. The Act of Uniformity of 1662 was designed to drive Puritan ministers out of the Church; the Five Mile Act sought to exclude them from corporate towns, by requiring them to take an oath not to attempt to change the government in Church or state. The first Conventicle Act imposed heavy penalties for attending unauthorized religious meetings, culminating in banishment for a third offence. The second, passed in 1670, gave informers a third of all fines levied, including £5 on constables, and £100 on magistrates, who failed to enforce the law; this enabled informers to compel reluctant magistrates to persecute Dissenters and was condemned as 'the quintessence of arbitrary malice'.[2] However, neither Act was as severe as that of 1593 against separatists, which prescribed penalties, if they refused to recant, including imprisonment for life; this was sometimes used against Dissenters under Charles II.[3] Nor were they nearly as severe as the laws against Catholics, which forbade a wide range of Catholic practices, including possession of rosary beads. Protestant Dissenters were free to worship

---

[1] G. R. Cragg, *Puritanism in the Period of the Great Persecution, 1660–1688* (Cambridge, 1957); M. Watts, *The Dissenters from the Reformation to the French Revolution* (Oxford, 1978), ch. 4.

[2] Marvell, ii. 314.

[3] G. W. Prothero, *Statutes and Constitutional Documents, 1558–1625*, 4th edn. (Oxford, 1913), 89–92; Miller, *After the Civil Wars*, 183, 282; *Currant Intelligence*, 17–21, 21–4 Nov. 1681.

privately in small groups, Catholics were not. The severity of the penalties (and widespread dislike of informers) meant that for much of Charles II's reign the laws were enforced little, if at all.[4] Sometimes it was unclear which laws were in force. Also, for much of the reign Dissenters claimed that the king did not want the laws to be enforced, and the mixed signals he sent out suggested that they might be right; magistrates were reluctant to act too diligently, for fear of being reprimanded.[5] Charles was torn between the fear that Dissenters might meet too openly and in too great numbers, and the fear that too much severity might goad them into revolt. Underlying both fears was a belief that Dissenters were far more numerous than they really were. That belief was dispelled in part by the Compton census of 1676, but Charles still preferred to avoid undue severity, especially when faced with the difficult Parliaments of 1679–81. Only after the Oxford Parliament, and especially after the Rye House Plot, did he throw his weight (almost) unequivocally behind persecution.[6]

Much of the emphasis on persecution comes from Nonconformist historians, who prefer to dwell on the suffering of their forebears at the hands of the Church, rather than on the periods, and places, where the laws were enforced little, if at all. Of the seven towns considered in detail in this book, only Bristol saw repeated severe persecution. Some denominations were persecuted more severely than others, notably the Quakers. This may in part be an illusion, created by their meticulous collection of details of sufferings, but their uncompromising insistence on meeting publicly forced even reluctant magistrates to take action against them.[7] Others, faced with persecution, met secretly, gave over meeting, or attended their parish churches.

The focus on persecution encourages a more fundamental misconception: that England was divided between two monolithic entities, 'Church' and 'Dissent'. The Church of England had always been a broad church, with an ambivalent theology and ecclesiology: the Thirty-Nine Articles 'were a statement of what the Church held to be true doctrine, but they were not a confession of faith'.[8] Restoration divines sought to create a theology which reconnected behaviour

[4] The same was true of the laws against Catholics: J. Miller, *Popery and Politics in England, 1660–88* (Cambridge, 1973), ch. 3.

[5] D. Granville, *Remains*, ed. G. Ornsby, Surtees Society xxxvii, xlvii (1861, 1867), ii. 13; *CSPD 1679–80*, 45–6, *1681*, 479.

[6] See Miller, *After the Civil Wars*, chs. 9–13.

[7] Miller, ' "A Suffering People" ', *passim*; J. Miller, 'The English Quakers and Authority, 1660–85', *Anglophonia*, xvii (2005), 243–51.

[8] Spurr, *Restoration Church*, 109; see also ibid. 328–30. Also E. Duffy, 'England's Long Reformation', in N. Tyacke (ed.), *England's Long Reformation* (London, 1998).

and salvation, through an emphasis on 'holy living', but without sliding into Catholic teaching on the efficacy of good works.[9] Others argued for an ecclesiology which stressed the importance of episcopacy as the mark of a true church, while at the same time firmly upholding the royal supremacy.[10] In 1715 Wigan corporation expressed the hope that episcopacy would be extended to the Reformed churches abroad, to unite the Christian world.[11] Both of these tendencies marked a departure from the Puritan tradition, based on predestination (in which the actions of the believer could contribute nothing to salvation), and a hope that the English Church would become more like the Calvinist churches in Scotland and on the continent. But these new views never became universal, and those who challenged them were normally left unmolested, except in the early 1680s. Moreover, they contained elements quite acceptable to many in the Puritan tradition, notably a rigorous approach to personal morality, and a firm belief in the importance of the national Church. Many clergymen and laymen in the Puritan tradition remained within the national Church. The Act of Uniformity drove out a minority of the parish clergy, but four-fifths of the incumbents in livings at the end of 1662 had served in the 1650s, in a Church without bishops or Common Prayer. Unlike the clergy, the Puritan laity were not required to declare their 'unfeigned assent and consent' to everything in the Prayer Book, or to renounce the Covenant, unless they wanted to qualify for public office. They were simply required to attend their parish church and to take communion once a year, stipulations originally intended to force Catholics into conformity—and which were laxly enforced. What they did in their homes, or small private meetings, was their own affair. Many attended both their parish churches and Nonconformist conventicles, and served as churchwardens.[12] Celia Fiennes, in her travels, normally attended Dissenting meeting houses, but was quite prepared to go to church instead, and praised sermons she heard there.[13]

These 'partial conformists', later known as occasional conformists, ensured that the boundary between 'Church' and 'Dissent' was vague and permeable, especially for the laity. It should have been more distinct for the clergy: either they agreed to conform, or they did not. But there was much common ground between those who made the subscriptions required by the Act of Uniformity

[9] Spurr, *Restoration Church*, ch. 6.   [10] Ibid. ch. 3.   [11] *HMC Kenyon*, 459–60.
[12] J. D. Ramsbottom, 'Presbyterians and "Partial Conformity" in the Restoration Church', *JEH* xliii (1992), 249–70; Tanner MS 36, fo. 196.
[13] Fiennes, 101, 146.

and those who refused, often after considerable soul-searching. Ralph Josselin subscribed: he had a large family, but also he wished to save his parishioners from an inadequate minister. He rarely received communion and hardly ever wore a surplice.[14] Philip Henry refused to subscribe, because he could not in conscience use 'corrupt' ceremonies. He attended his parish church and longed to receive communion, but could not: 'for myself, I am not free to kneel, but dare not condemn those that are.'[15] His ideal remained a fully reformed national Church, preaching the pure gospel of Christ, with no 'popish' cere-monies, in which ministers were not under the tyranny of 'prelates'. Driven out of the Church, he condemned separatism: the Independents 'unchurch the nation . . . pluck up the hedge of parish order . . . throw the ministry common and allow persons to preach who are unordained'.[16] Richard Baxter, too, felt closer to 'sober conformable men' than to Independents. He continued to hope that, one day, a godly prince would complete England's Reformation, creating a Puritan national Church, with godly preaching and parish discipline. He was to be disappointed, not least by a younger generation of Presbyterian preachers, who recognized that the national Church was not going to change and formed separate congregations.[17]

The creation of separatist 'gathered churches' in the 1640s and 1650s left deep and painful fissures in English Puritanism. Baxter divided other denominations into tolerable (Presbyterians, Independents, and perhaps 'honest Anabaptists') and intolerable ('Quakers, Seekers, Ranters and infidels').[18] The Quakers in Norwich thought that Presbyterians were more hostile than conformists.[19] The chronicler of the Baptist church in Broadmead, Bristol, thought that Quakers were 'heretics', 'of damnable principles', but described the Presbyterians as 'our friends'.[20] During the persecution of the 1670s, Presbyterians, Independents, and Baptists consulted regularly on how to respond; they did not include the Quakers, or the General (non-Calvinist) Baptist congregation in the city.[21]

---

[14] R. Josselin, *Diary*, ed. A. Macfarlane (Oxford, 1976), 516; Spurr, *Restoration Church*, 188–9.

[15] P. Henry, *Diaries and Letters*, ed. M. H. Lee (London, 1882), 99, 134 (quoted), 177–9.

[16] Ibid. 184–5, 277 (quoted).

[17] W. M. Lamont, *Richard Baxter and the Millennium* (London, 1979); Miller, *After the Civil Wars*, 143–4.

[18] *Reliquiae Baxterianae*, ed. M. Sylvester (London, 1696), ii. 437; R. Baxter, *Calendar of the Correspondence of Richard Baxter*, ed. N. Keeble and G. F. Nuttall, 2 vols. (Oxford, 1991), ii. 73, 92.

[19] A. J. Eddington, *The First Fifty Years of Quakerism in Norwich* (London, 1932), 77–8.

[20] *Church of Christ*, 133, 137.

[21] Ibid. 146–7. For a brief dismissive reference to Baptists 'somewhat of the free-will point', see ibid. 145.

When their minister was imprisoned, the Presbyterians planned to stop meeting: 'their principle was not to hear a man not bred up at the university and not ordained.' The others persuaded them to meet, to pray, read chapters from Scripture, and sing psalms; they jointly published a justification of their conduct. When one of the Independent ministers died in gaol, his funeral procession 'was accompanied with all sort of professors (except Quakers)'.[22]

Such formal co-operation among denominations was unusual; informal collaboration was not. Presbyterians and Independents sometimes formed common meetings and joined to appoint the minister.[23] After 1690 there were local unions between the two: that in London was over by 1695 but the Devon union lasted until the mid eighteenth century.[24] More unusual was the willingness of the General Baptists at Frome in 1719 to allow Quakers to use their meeting house.[25] The General Baptists were, like the Quakers, outside the Calvinist mainstream of Puritanism. Others were less tolerant. In 1701, at Sleaford, the renegade Quaker Francis Bugg 'proved', at a conference, that the Quakers blasphemed and profaned Scripture; the magistrates ordered that their books should be burned.[26] In 1735 Quakers in Exeter resolved not to meet on the day the bounds of the city's parishes were beaten, 'Friends having been generally abused in coming to meetings that day'.[27] But long before this the major division within English Protestantism was not that between Church and Dissent. True, much of the language used in arguments suggested that it was: men were frequently accused, by their opponents, of being 'fanatics' or 'disaffected', but that did not mean that they were Dissenters.[28] Celia Fiennes remarked that Coventry was 'esteemed' a 'fanatic town', because the majority of the corporation were 'sober men'—which could mean moderate conformists as well as Dissenters.[29] Committed members of Dissenting meetings were not

---

[22] *Church of Christ*, 149–50; *Some Reasons Briefly Suggested which have Prevailed with the Dissenters in Bristol to Continue their Open Meetings* (1675).

[23] Corie, *Correspondence*, 21; G. Gould (ed.), *Open Communion and the Baptists of Norwich* (Norwich, 1860), pp. xxvii–xxxi; J. Browne, *History of Congregationalism in Norfolk and Suffolk* (London, 1877), 259–60, 280; S. W. Carruthers, 'Norfolk Presbyterians in the Seventeenth Century', *Norf Arch* xxx (1952), 99: Wake MS 325, pp. 1–6.

[24] Watts, *The Dissenters*, 289–97; A. Brockett, *Nonconformity in Exeter 1650–1875* (Manchester, 1962), 64–8.

[25] W. Alexander, *Life of Thomas Story*, 2 vols. (York, 1832), ii. 208.

[26] *English Post*, 10–12 Sept. 1701.   [27] Brockett, *Nonconformity in Exeter*, 111.

[28] As J. T. Evans does, when considering the aldermen of Norwich: Evans, *Norwich*, 257. See M. Mullett, 'Conflict, Politics and Elections in Lancaster, 1660–88', *Northern History*, xix (1983), 63, 69.

[29] Fiennes, 113. The Tories on Coventry corporation routinely referred to their opponents as Dissenters: Hurwich, ' "Fanatick Town" ', 40 n. 48.

very numerous. The Compton census of 1676 suggested that fewer than 5 per cent of the population 'wholly absented themselves' from church. This would not have included partial conformists, and the census was designed to show that the Dissenters were less numerous than many thought.[30] But the Evans list, an internal estimate of numbers between 1715 and 1718 (plus figures from the Quaker records), puts Dissenters at a little over 6 per cent of the population. Presbyterians—the spiritual descendants of the 'church puritans' of the reigns of Elizabeth and James I—made up just over half, which shows how few were the true separatists. As the surveys were designed to show the numerical strength of Dissent, the figures are unlikely to have been an underestimate.[31] Moreover, these figures were collected a generation after the Toleration Act, after a period in which Dissenting numbers were said to have increased, as 'partial conformists' were free to worship as Dissenters.[32] Some returns made considerable claims for the Dissenters' electoral significance; it is likely that the influence of Dissenting merchants, employers, and members of corporations was more significant than the Dissenting vote as such.[33] Even so, in terms of numbers or influence, Dissenters were a minority in the Whig party, and would have been politically insignificant without the very many Whigs who conformed to the Church.

The battle to decide the nature of the Church of England was intensified by the new strains of theology and ecclesiology developed by the clergy. Often these were linked to a form of worship which appealed to the senses (through music, ritual, and the visual arts) as well as to the intellect, and which placed a greater emphasis on the authority of the clergy, as preachers (through more systematic catechism) and as priests (through more frequent communion). This trend was first labelled 'High Church' in 1677.[34] Changes to the form of worship were more visible to the ordinary parishioner than theoretical writings, and could generate considerable tension within the parish. In addition, faced first with a king who could not be relied on to defend the Church, and then with the vigorous political attacks on the clergy in the Exclusion Crisis, the High Church clergy played an increasingly active role in politics, through the pulpit and the press, and in elections. Together with their stress on their spiritual authority, this led to denunciations of 'priestcraft', of overweening

[30] Whiteman, pp. xxiv–xxxi, lxxvi–lxxxii.
[31] Watts, *The Dissenters*, 267–89 (overall figures on 270).
[32] D. Wykes, in *Parliament and Dissent* (special issue of *Parliamentary History*, 2005), 14–15.
[33] DWL, MS 38.4, pp. 31, 48–9, 102; *HP 1690–1715*, i. 207–11.
[34] M. Goldie, 'Danby, the Bishops and the Whigs', in *Pol of Rel*, 81 n. 22.

clerical power, and accusations of crypto-popery, or worse, which were no more accurate than claims that their 'moderate' or 'sober' opponents were 'fanatics', or Dissenters.[35]

The points at issue between High Church and Low Church included the old issues of theology, worship, and the role of the clergy, together with the treatment of Dissent. To High Churchmen, Dissenters were guilty of rebellion and regicide, and still wished to overthrow the monarchy. The Conventicle Acts rested on the premiss that their meetings used religion as a cover for plotting against the state, and needed to be suppressed. For the High Church clergy, Dissenters were misled by pride of conscience into error; they needed to be saved from themselves by the wholesome censures of the Church. To arguments of 'liberty of conscience' they opposed the need for a 'counselled conscience'—and that counsel had to come from the clergy.[36] Low Churchmen responded that the High Church persecuted harmless, sober people because they would not submit to their authority, or follow their crypto-popish rituals. Dissenters stayed away from church because they found no edification there. The High Churchmen damaged Protestant unity, by persecuting fellow Protestants and distancing the Church of England from the continental Protestant churches.[37]

The High Churchmen responded that the best way to achieve Protestant unity was by bringing Dissenters into obedience to the Church; while agreeing that the papists were the common enemy, the more immediate threat to the unity of Protestantism came from Dissent. For some, the issue was not one of Dissent, but of schism. Presbyterians and other Dissenters had divided the once united national Church, and Low Churchmen wished to perpetuate that division, either by allowing toleration to Dissenters, or by diluting the worship of the Church in order to accommodate those Dissenters who wished to come in. By the 1680s, some divines saw toleration as a lesser evil than comprehension, allowing divergent forms of worship within the Church.[38]

[35] Goldie, in *Pol of Rel*; M. Goldie, 'Priestcraft and the Birth of Whiggism', in N. Phillipson and Q. Skinner (eds.), *Political Discourse in Early Modern England* (Cambridge, 1993), ch. 10; J. A. I. Champion, *The Pillars of Priestcraft Shaken: The Church of England and its Enemies, 1660–1730* (Cambridge, 1992).

[36] M. Goldie, 'The Theory of Religious Intolerance in Restoration England', in O. P. Grell, J. I. Israel, and N. Tyacke (eds.), *From Persecution to Toleration: The Glorious Revolution in England* (Oxford, 1991), ch. 13.

[37] See the analysis (using the terms Tories and Whigs) in A. F. W. Papillon, *Memoirs of Thomas Papillon* (Reading, 1887), 374–6.

[38] J. Spurr, 'Schism and the Restoration Church', *JEH* xli (1990), 408–24; J. Spurr, 'The Church of England, Comprehension and the Toleration Act of 1689', *EHR* civ (1989), 941–6.

Persecution could end the schism by bringing most Dissenters within the Church. Some recognized that there was no hope of reclaiming the Quakers,[39] but accepted that they were harmless, if eccentric. Several bishops showed kindness towards them.[40] Tory magistrates gave them certificates stating that they were peaceable subjects, while continuing to persecute Presbyterians. Judge Jeffreys had Quakers released from prison. At Launceston assizes, he took a brief swipe against those who refused oaths, then launched into a diatribe against Presbyterians and occasional conformists.[41] By the 1710s, High Churchmen saw the Low Churchmen and occasional conformists as the main enemy, along with the Presbyterians, and their hostility was reciprocated. At Chichester in 1711 the Low Church dean and chapter suspended the cathedral organist for refusing to drink to the confusion of Sacheverell or the pious memory of William III.[42] In the attacks on meeting houses in the summer of 1715, almost all of those destroyed belonged to the Presbyterians. The 'loyal mob' of Shrewsbury issued a 'proclamation' to Independents, Baptists, and Quakers, that if they allowed 'that damnable faction called Presbyterians' to join their meetings, their meeting houses would suffer the same fate.[43] There remained a sense that, while the other denominations were separatists, Presbyterians were guilty of the greater sin of schism, and that they harboured dreams of taking over the national Church, as they had in Scotland. There was also a sense that they were responsible for the rebellion and regicide of the 1640s.[44]

II. THE FORTUNES OF THE CHURCH

Most older towns had more parish churches than they needed, creating the problem of a numerous, underpaid body of clergy. It was difficult, if not impossible, to collect tithes in towns, so parish ministers were dependent on

---

[39] Between 1674 and 1678 Bishop Carleton, in Bristol, persecuted Presbyterians, Independents, and Baptists, whom he called 'schismatics', but left the Quakers alone: Coventry MS 7, fo. 43; below, Ch. 9.

[40] R. Davies, *An Account of the Convincement of Richard Davies* (London, 1771), 172–81, 202–9; R. Hawkins, *A Brief Account of the Life and Death of . . . Gilbert Latey* (London, 1707), 106–10; FHL, MfS 2, pp. 80, 98, 139. However, the bishop of Gloucester was reduced to apoplectic rage by their refusal to remove their hats and at being addressed as 'thou', FHL, MfS 1, fo. 174.

[41] Besse, i. 724; FHL, ORS 3, no. 370, ORS 4, no. 398.

[42] *Norwich Gazette*, 29 Sept.–6 Oct. 1711.

[43] *Weekly Journal with Fresh Advices, Supplement*, 3 Aug. 1715.

[44] Clarendon MS 77, fo. 236.

parish endowments, controlled by the vestry, together with payments from individual benefactors, the parishioners at large, or the corporation. In some towns, as in Bristol, many incumbents were chosen by the parishioners and approved by the corporation.[45] This could lead to bitter disputes over the choice of minister.[46] It also meant that the clergy were dependent on their parishioners or the corporation in a way that did not normally happen in the countryside. Added to this problem of clerical poverty and dependence was the damage to many churches in the civil wars and subsequent changes to the parish structure. Exeter cathedral had been partitioned and used by two congregations. The mayor and chamber had secured an Act of Parliament to divide it and reduce the city's seventeen parishes to four. Some of the freemen alleged in 1660 that the corporation had sold off the remaining churches, with a stipulation that they should not be used for worship, and removed the plate and bells. A committee of the House of Lords brokered an agreement between the inhabitants and aldermen whereby eleven churches should be repaired at the parishioners' expense, all church plate should be returned, and the partition should be removed from the cathedral. The mayor and aldermen challenged many of the freemen's claims; they claimed that only five churches could accommodate a congregation large enough to maintain a preaching minister, and feared that removing the partition might do serious structural damage. They added that if the two congregations worshipping in the cathedral were expelled, there was nowhere else for them to go.[47] The partition was eventually removed, but reverting to the old parochial system restored the problem of clerical poverty. In 1666 the bishop complained that the stipends attached to all of the city's churches added together would hardly be enough to pay for one good minister.[48] In 1718 the bishop's successor claimed to have found a solution to the problem. He intended to present each of the better ministers to a second, rural parish as these fell vacant. This was the only way to save the clergy from dependence on 'disaffected' (Tory) parishioners; it was not given to every priest 'to persevere in principles that starve him'.[49]

Not all towns had a superabundance of small parishes. Portsmouth had a single parish church, which was far too small for the townspeople, let alone the

[45] Barry, 'Reformation City', 269–70; J. Barry, 'The Parish in Civic Life: Bristol and its Churches, 1640–1750', in S. Wright (ed.), *Parish, Church and People* (London, 1988), 153–5.
[46] Tanner MS 36, fos. 62, 72; *CSPD 1676–7*, 211–12.
[47] *HMC 7th Report*, 117, 136; *LJ*, xi. 122, 151–2. See I. Roy, 'The English Republic, 1649–60: The View from the Town Hall', in H. G. Koenigsberger (ed.), *Republiken und Republikanismus im Europa dem frühen Neuzeit* (Munich, 1988).
[48] Bodl, Add. MS c.305, fo. 175.   [49] BL, Add MS 61612, fos. 99–100.

garrison.[50] Yarmouth, for most of this period, had only one church; Halifax parish was 12 miles across, with one church and twelve or thirteen chapels.[51] Hull had two large, fine churches, Holy Trinity and St Mary's. In 1661 the town secured an Act of Parliament to make Holy Trinity, technically a chapel of the parish of Hessle, a parish in its own right; the Act confirmed the bench's right to choose the vicar and laid down that he should receive a salary of £100 a year. The mayor and burgesses traditionally appointed and paid for the readers (or lecturers) and assistant readers in both churches.[52] The Act did not resolve the problems of paying the town's clergy. The salary of the vicar of Holy Trinity was always in arrears. The money was to be raised, at 8*d.* in the pound, on lands valued at just over £3,000, but many were reluctant to pay and making them do so was a cumbersome process. In 1712 six years' arrears from a group of butchers brought in 42 shillings.[53] In the 1690s the bench advanced a series of loans to the vicar, because part of his salary was in arrears.[54] Only in the 1710s did complaints about arrears of salary die away. These difficulties were not due to lack of goodwill: the corporation was on good terms with Robert Banks, vicar from 1689 to 1715.[55]

At the other extreme was Norwich, with thirty-four parishes. An undated letter claimed that only thirteen had any settled maintenance, ranging from £2 to £28 a year and totalling £144. As a result the clergy were 'enslaved' to 'the extravagant humour of the populace'; if the people did not like the services their minister provided, they withdrew their contributions. If any felt themselves over-rated for the church or poor, they deducted the money from their contribution to the minister. The clergy could manage only by holding two or three livings, which meant that each parish was inadequately served.[56] The corporation tried to alleviate the problem. It decided to seek an Act of Parliament to unite parishes and to allow a rate to be levied for the ministers' maintenance, as at Hull.[57] (A similar bill for Southampton was rejected by the Commons in 1668, on the grounds that it would lay a charge on the people. Hull corporation had had to secure the consent of those who were to contribute to the minister's maintenance before the bill for Holy Trinity could

[50] BL, Add MS 61612, fo. 175; Bodl, North MS b2, fo. 41.

[51] Defoe, *Tour*, i. 68, ii. 197–8.

[52] Gillett and MacMahon, *Hull*, 190; BL, Lansdowne MS 890, fo. 297.

[53] BRB 6, pp. 363, 618.   [54] Ibid. 383, 400, 426, 483, 492.

[55] In 1697 the bench contributed £10 towards the cost of beautifying one of the dining rooms in the vicarage: BRB 6, 415.

[56] Tanner MS 137, fo. 30. (A reference to 'James I' suggests that the letter dates from 1685 or later.)

[57] FAB 8, fos. 48, 57. These patrons could include the crown, bishops, or other senior ecclesiastics, or Oxbridge colleges.

go through.[58]) A draft bill was ready for submission in 1678, but (according to the bishop) it was not presented, thanks to the 'froward' mayor. Undeterred, and encouraged by the bishop, the assembly prepared another bill, but its chances of success disappeared as Parliament became preoccupied with the Popish Plot.[59] There were no more attempts to solve the problem of maintenance on a city-wide basis, but the corporation tried to improve the remuneration of individuals.[60] In 1718 quarter sessions ordered that the clergy should no longer be required to pay the poor rate.[61]

The examples of Hull and Norwich suggest that the corporations were by no means hostile to the parish clergy or the Church. Leicester paid £30 a year for Sunday afternoon lectures at St Martin's,[62] and £10 a year to successive vicars of St Mary's and one vicar of St Margaret's; it also helped the parishioners of St Mary's to purchase a house for the vicar.[63] The mayor and corporation of King's Lynn complained of the failure to provide sufficient services in church and chapel.[64] Evidence of the exact nature of corporations' churchmanship is hard to find. At the Restoration many ordered that Common Prayer should be used, well before the passing of the Act of Uniformity: Dover and Maidstone in 1660,[65] Southampton, Norwich, and Hull in 1661.[66] Several towns stopped paying for lectures, alleged by Royalists to have been used by Puritan preachers to stir up the people against Charles I. These included such 'disaffected' (or godly) towns as Gloucester and Coventry.[67] In Oxford lectures ceased in the university

[58] *HMC 8th Report,* 103; Marvell, ii. 24–6. The dire poverty of Southampton's churches continued: BL, Add MS 61612, fos. 143–4.

[59] Tanner MS 39, fo. 64, MS 37, fo. 29; MCB 25, fo. 29; FAB 8, fo. 69. For more opposition to the bill, see Tanner MS 40, fo. 79, MS 137, fo. 29.

[60] FAB 6, fo. 227, FAB 8, fos. 75, 94.   [61] NCR, Case 20a/18, 19 July 1718.

[62] LHP 32A, no. 221; *RBL,* v. 21–5. Bristol corporation also paid for lectures: Barry, 'Parish in Civic Life', 154.

[63] LHP 30, no. 91, LHP 33B, nos. 249, 252; *RBL,* iv. 550–1, 555; Bodl, Willis MS 85, fo. 45. It also, together with the parishioners, helped a vicar of St Mary's to pay his debts: LHP 32B, nos. 353–4, LHP 33B, no. 155; *RBL,* iv. 532–3. The corporation hoped that a bill to augment vicarages might improve the financial condition of the clergy, but found that it did not apply to urban livings: LHP 34, nos. 72, 75. Yarmouth corporation provided a substantial house for the curate: Gauci, *Yarmouth,* 248.

[64] BL, Harl MS 7377, fo. 27.

[65] DAM, fo. 209; *Kingdom's Intelligencer,* 31 Dec. 1660–7 Jan. 1661. (For Dover, see also *Mercurius Publicus,* 9–16 Jan. 1662.)

[66] Southampton RO, SC 2/1/8, fo. 177; FAB 6, fo. 221; MCB 23, fo. 148; Browne, *Works,* ed. Keynes, iv. 8, 10; BRB 4, pp. 402, 405.

[67] Gloucs RO, GBR/B3, p. 214; Coventry RO, Acc 2/3, p. 84; G. Burnet, *Supplement to the History of his own Time,* ed. H. C. Foxcroft (Oxford, 1902), 71; S. A. Strong, *A Catalogue of Letters and Other Historical Documents at Welbeck* (London, 1903), 188; Roy, 'View from the Town Hall', 232–3.

church, St Mary's, but continued in the corporation's church, St Martin's, paid for in part by contributions from all the members. In 1702 it ordered that no member who had not paid his preachers' money should be allowed to vote or attend civic entertainments.[68] Late in 1662 Leicester corporation revived an Elizabethan order that at least one member of each family should attend Wednesday and Friday lectures.[69] The corporation and clergy had earlier had a reputation for Puritanism. Churches were seen as preaching houses and there was little enthusiasm for spending money on the church fabric.[70] At the Restoration the old stone font was restored in St Martin's and the parish bought a copy of the revised Book of Common Prayer. St Mary's was using a surplice by 1663, but still had a traditional communion table.[71]

Hull corporation, too, had a tradition of moderate church puritanism, with frequent sermons, daily prayers, and an emphasis on godly behaviour. At the insistence of the military and central government, and against the wishes of the corporation and parishioners, Holy Trinity had been partitioned, with Presbyterian worship in one half and Independent in the other.[72] At the Restoration the partition was removed and parochial worship resumed. York corporation had encouraged godly preaching in the parish churches in the 1650s and tried to avoid persecuting Dissenters under Charles II. In 1667 the common council called for more rigorous observance of the Lord's Day. It seems likely that the views of Norwich, Bristol, Oxford, and other corporations were similar.[73] The mayor and aldermen of Norwich began in 1661 to attend services in the cathedral, which they had ceased to do in 1642, after a dispute with the bishop; the corporation of Exeter could not be persuaded to attend the cathedral until 1671.[74] In 1678 the Norwich mayor's court agreed that those who wished to do so should receive communion once a month. In June 1680 the mayor said that he hoped that his brethren would join him in receiving the sacrament; in November 1681 the court ordered that they should all do so.[75]

---

[68] Wood, i. 357; *OCA*, ii. 301, iii. 287, iv. 11.
[69] Simmons, *Leicester*, 63; *RBL*, iv. 481–2; LHP 31, no. 310.
[70] Simmons, *Leicester*, 63, 79–81.
[71] J. Nichols, *History and Antiquities of Leicestershire*, 4 vols. (London, 1793–1815), i. 581; J. R. Abney (ed.), *The Vestry Books and Accounts of the Churchwardens of St Mary's Leicester, 1652–1729* (Leicester, 1912), 24–5, 36.
[72] *VCH East Riding*, i. 107–9; Gillett and MacMahon, *Hull*, 177–8; BL, Lansdowne MS 890, fos. 208–9.
[73] *VCH City of York*, 203–5; Withington, 'Views from the Bridge', 132–3; Scott, 'York', 305–8.
[74] FAB 6, fo. 221; MCB 23, fo. 148; Bodl, Add MS c.308, fo, 232.
[75] MCB 25, fos. 30, 71, 102, 107; Tanner MS 39, fo. 117, MS 36, fo. 114.

Assiduous attendance at the cathedral might seem a politic gesture, as Lord Yarmouth had cast doubts on the aldermen's loyalty, but the mayor and his brethren were becoming more committed Churchmen.[76] Liturgical preferences were changing in many towns. St Peter Mancroft, Norwich, acquired an organ in 1707, Ashbourne, Derbyshire, in 1710; Nottingham already had one in 1675.[77] An organ, paid for by public subscription, was installed in Portsmouth church in 1718.[78] At Hull, Celia Fiennes remarked in 1698 that the altar in Holy Trinity was set table-wise in the middle of the chancel; she made no mention of rails.[79] In about 1711 a new altar, with an altarpiece depicting the Last Supper, was set up at the east end of the church, and railed off. Meanwhile, a subscription for an organ raised about £600.[80] Bristol corporation made repeated gifts to parishes to beautify their churches; the pace of improvement grew in the early eighteenth century, with several acquiring organs. One leading proponent of church music in the city was a Whig clergyman, Arthur Bedford, prominent in the Society for the Reformation of Manners.[81] At Leicester, in 1686–7 St Mary's acquired an altar, with stone steps and rails.[82] St Martin's must have had an organ before 1696, when there was an order to remove it, but it stayed; in 1716 £70 was spent on repairing it. The church also acquired an altar in 1719, at a cost of £40.[83] The vicar from 1699 was Samuel Carte, a High Tory, who had a running battle with John Jackson, who preached anti-Trinitarian sermons in St Martin's; the corporation supported Carte.[84] Oxford corporation gave money for repairing and beautifying St Martin's and recasting and hanging the bells. It also provided a new pulpit and appropriate hoods for the lecturers.[85] Once-Puritan Dorchester provided rails for the communion table in 1686.[86]

The restoration of the old liturgy, and moves towards High Church modes of worship, were not uncontested. The mayor of Reading and the vicar of Faversham opposed the reintroduction of Common Prayer, although it is

[76] MCB 25, fos. 191, 195, 205, MCB 26, fos. 160, 219, 254, 261, 278, MCB 27, fo. 41; FAB 8, fo. 130.

[77] NRO, MS 453, 'A Description', 8 June 1707; *HMC Cowper*, iii. 98; *HMC Portland*, ii. 309.

[78] *Weekly Journal or Saturday's Post*, 2 Aug. 1718.

[79] Fiennes, 89. She also found the altar table-wise in the chancel in the main church at Taunton and in one of Plymouth's two churches: ibid. 244, 252.

[80] Gent, *Annales Regioduni Hullini*, 21, 31; Gillett and MacMahon, *Hull*, 208–9.

[81] J. Barry, 'Cultural Patronage and the Anglican Crisis', in Walsh et al., ch. 8.

[82] Abney, *Vestry Books of St Mary's*, 104–5.

[83] Nichols, *History of Leicestershire*, i. 583–5.

[84] Simmons, *Leicester*, 106–7; Greaves, *Corporation*, 95–6.

[85] *OCA*, ii. 301, iii. 89, 285, iv. 45, 84.

[86] Underdown, *Fire from Heaven*, 258–9, 261. It is not clear whether the table was placed altar-wise.

significant that the latter was denounced by the corporation.[87] In May 1662 the burgesses of Beverley elected a 'disaffected' minister and refused to admit one who was properly licensed. At Coventry the ministers of both churches were said to be 'disaffected' but the mayor and aldermen (knowing that the king had ordered the demolition of the walls) ordered them to use Common Prayer.[88] (On the other hand at Taunton, it was said that many Presbyterians came to church on St Bartholomew's Day, 1662; the town was under virtual military occupation.[89]) There were also reports of outrages against the Prayer Book, surplices, and the like.[90]

More common were disputes between priests and parishioners. In rural areas many centred on tithes and property rights, but these were rarely an issue in the towns.[91] Puritans who wished to remain in the Church hoped to adapt the prescribed forms of worship to suit their preferences. Sometimes they were encouraged by their minister,[92] or reached an accommodation. In the 1660s some ejected ministers were invited to preach in church by the incumbent.[93] Often laypeople came willingly to the sermon, but were reluctant to receive communion. Many urban magistrates came to church because it was a duty of office, and a social obligation, or because the law required it. They took communion if they had to: customs officers in Great Yarmouth allegedly said, 'it is a madness to lose an office for a bit of bread and a cup of wine'.[94] But sometimes there was bitter conflict. Occasionally vacant churches or chapels were taken over and used for 'conventicles'.[95] More often there were struggles about the form of worship in the parish church, in which parishioners fought their parson through the church courts, which showed how important the parish church and its worship were to them.[96] At Tewkesbury churchwardens

[87] *CSPD 1661–2*, 116, 287.   [88] *CSPD 1661–2*, 379; Clarendon MS 77, fo. 236.

[89] *Mercurius Publicus*, 21–8 Aug. 1662.

[90] Carte MS 222, fos. 4–5, 34; HMC *le Fleming*, 29; *CSPD 1663–4*, 277, 553–4, 556.

[91] D. Spaeth, *The Church in an Age of Danger: Parsons and Parishioners 1660–1740* (Cambridge, 2000), ch. 6.

[92] The minister of Lyme was said to preach wearing his surplice and then ring the bell to summon the Nonconformists; he then preached again without it: Tanner MS 35, fo. 39.

[93] Spurr, *Restoration Church*, 204–9; Miller, *After the Civil Wars*, 142 and sources there cited.

[94] *CSPD 1676–7*, 232. See also Gauci, *Yarmouth*, 88–91; Miller, *After the Civil Wars*, 138–41; Barry, 'Parish in Civic Life', 156–7, 171.

[95] See the cases of churches at Ipswich and Sudbury in 1669–70: Bodl, MS Add c.308, fo. 130; LPL 674, fo. 24; *CSPD 1670*, 287, 303. For attempts by Dissenters to take over chapels under James II, see *CSPD 1687–9*, nos. 176, 318, 430, 995, 1123; T. Cartwright, *Diary*, ed. J. Hunter, Camden Society (1843), 77.

[96] McNulty, 'Priests, Church Courts and People', 40–6, 117, and *passim*; Spaeth, *Age of Danger*, *passim*; Barry, 'Parish in Civic Life', 156–7, 171.

prosecuted Nonconformists for offences other than going to conventicles, hoping to keep them within the parish community.[97] Parishioners in the Puritan tradition often sought office as churchwardens, or used the vestry, in order to put pressure on the vicar to adapt the form of service. At Berwick the church-wardens were said to keep a second register, in which to enter those who were irregularly baptized. This led to disputes about the form of vestry and the selection of churchwardens: were the latter agents of the hierarchy or champions of the parishioners?[98]

Ministers at odds with their people felt isolated and persecuted, and a few suffered violence, but sometimes it could be seen as their own fault. Many believed that they were obliged to follow the canons of the Church and expected the laity to submit to their authority.[99] St Clement's, Sandwich, was traditionally used for town elections; townsmen placed wine and tobacco on the communion table. In 1683 the minister appealed to the king to order that the elections be held elsewhere, because he feared the desecration of his brand-new altar. In 1716 the vicar fell out with the churchwardens; he wanted to spend money on repairing and beautifying the church, they wished it to go on wages and other parish expenses.[100] Some parsons' behaviour was bound to provoke hostility. Thomas Godwyn, vicar of St Philip and Jacob in Bristol, was fervently Royalist, rigidly Anglican, and irascible. When a man's family wished to bury him without the Prayer Book burial service, Godwyn insisted on reading it and was indignant when relatives snatched the book and struck him. On another occasion, he was reading the evening service when about fifty boys made a 'hideous' noise outside. When the sexton and clerk tried to disperse them, they were driven back by stones. When the service ended, most of the boys left, but a few were still playing in the churchyard; one dropped his trousers and affronted Godwyn, who (he said) was 'compelled' to kick and cane the boy. His grandmother complained to the mayor, Sir John Knight I; he and four other aldermen committed Godwyn to gaol. Knight was at that time the main promoter of the persecution of Dissent and two of the other

[97] D. Beaver, *Parish Communities and Religious Conflict in the Vale of Gloucester, 1590–1690* (Cambridge, Mass., 1998), 226, 267–72, 278–81. For a determinedly non-conforming parish minister, see ibid. 264, 281–99.

[98] McNulty, 'Priests, Church Courts and People', 119–23, 160–70, 180–4 and *passim*. For Berwick, see *CSPD 1683–4*, 254–5.

[99] McNulty, 'Priests, Church Courts and People', 23, 164–5; Spaeth, *Age of Danger*, 9–10, 16–19, 52–3, 56–7, 202.

[100] *CSPD 1683–4*, 88, 106; Wake MS 284, fo. 305.

aldermen, Hickes and Lawford, assisted him, but Knight had no time for over-weening parsons. Godwyn dismissed them as 'a company of noddies'.[101] He was to endure years of lawsuits at the hands of his parishioners.

There was a similar story of persecution at Portsmouth. At Easter 1703, the vicar of the parish church, William Ward, tried to nominate one of the churchwardens, claiming he had a right to do so. He was violently opposed; two wardens elected (as usual) by the parishioners were sworn and the same happened in 1704.[102] Ward seems to have been a difficult man. When the governor's chaplain sought to preach afternoons as well as mornings, Ward opposed him. He may have feared that he would lose some of his congregation, but the chaplain and others claimed that many people could not get into the parish church, or hear the service.[103] Ward had been a chaplain to the strongly Whig earl of Tankerville, which would suggest that he was a Whig.[104] Over the next few years, the annual elections of parish officers became partisan contests, in which the Tories came to side with Ward. In 1709, the Whigs were success-ful and from July Ward was prosecuted in several courts on a variety of charges. The vestry agreed in September 1709 to reimburse the churchwardens for any money they spent in these lawsuits. Each time Ward was exonerated, but his costs were heavy and his stipend modest, and the only occasion on which a judge ruled that he should have damages a 'moderate' jury awarded only £20, even though the judge sent them back to reconsider. Sometimes the church-wardens would not allow Ward to use the church plate, so he was reduced to administering communion in glasses. In 1711 the Tories, in the best-attended vestry meeting in living memory, outvoted the Whigs in the election of parish officers by over a hundred votes, but Ward's troubles continued and he was due to have a trial at Winchester assizes in March 1713.[105]

It would be wrong to suggest that such conflict was the norm: indeed, Ward's travails made the national press. There was much evidence of healthy parochial life in many towns. Both parishioners and corporations contributed to the beautifying and improvement of churches. New churches, funded in large part by public subscription, were built in growing towns like Birmingham,

[101] T. Godwyn, *Phanatical Tenderness* (1684), 3, 6–9.
[102] East, 672. For Ward's first name, see his admission as a burgess: East, 375.
[103] Bodl, North MS b2, fos. 24, 41.   [104] BL, Add MS 33283, fo. 158.
[105] *Post Boy*, 5–7 Apr. 1711, 19–21 Mar. 1713; Bodl, North MS d1, fo. 212. For a great contest between High and Low Churchmen over the election of a parish clerk at Shrewsbury, see *Weekly Journal or Saturday's Post*, 7 Dec. 1717.

Liverpool, and Sheffield.[106] For an illustration of the condition of the Church at this period, let us consider Leicester, which contained six parishes, but only five churches, St Leonard's having been destroyed during the civil wars. Three of the six parishes had salaries of £8 a year or less, and a fourth less than £15.[107] And yet returns made to William Wake, bishop of Lincoln, between 1706 and 1715, supplemented by comments made by Carte, show active worship and lay piety. St Nicholas lacked a minister of its own between 1660 and 1714, and one of its aisles had been pulled down as ruinous in 1697, but, thanks to a grant of £10 a year from the corporation in 1714, and contributions from parishioners and Queen Anne's Bounty, it acquired a minister and had sermons every Sunday instead of once a month.[108] All Saints', too, thanks to the corporation and parishioners, had its own curate and two sermons every Sunday rather than one a fortnight.[109] St Martin's already had two sets of lectures, one of them paid for by the corporation. In this, the largest of the town's churches (it is now the cathedral), divine service was said twice a day, and there were also weekday services (though not every day) in St Margaret's and All Saints'.[110] Most parishes had, or were planning to introduce, monthly communion, although some incumbents were disappointed at the number who received.[111] Four of the five also catechized, but none did so every week and most said that it was difficult to get parishioners to send their children and servants.[112] The returns from Canterbury in 1716 give a similar picture. In one parish the incumbent tried to introduce weekly sermons, but the inhabitants asked for only one service a fortnight. However, another minister, who served two churches, preached 'in a catechetical way' and the churches were 'much thronged'.[113] All the evidence suggests a considerable affection for the Church and its services: it is striking how many loyal addresses in the summer of 1710, after the Sacheverell trial, referred to the Church as

[106]   *HMC Portland*, v. 135; *HMC Dartmouth*, i. 320; *CSPD 1703–4*, 380; PC 2/86, p. 265; *Post Man*, 20–2 July 1704; *Weekly Journal or Saturday's Post*, 26 Nov. 1720; Defoe, *Tour*, i. 68, ii. 68–9, 258, 262. For a new chapel at the much smaller town of Deal, see LPL, MS 2686, fo. 69. For moves to build a church at Brigg, see Delapryme, *Diary*, 122, 142–4. For the church at Birmingham, see Borsay, *Urban Renaissance*, 76.

[107]   Wake MS 325, pp. 1–6.

[108]   Wake MS 278, St Nicholas, 1712, MS 325, p. 6; *RBL*, v. 76; Bodl, Willis MS 85, fo. 48.

[109]   Wake MS 325, p. 1, MS 278, All Saints, 1715; Bodl, Willis MS 85, fo. 48.

[110]   Wake MS 325, pp. [4], MS 278, St Margaret, 1715, All Saints, 1715.

[111]   Wake MS 325, pp. 1, 3, [4], 5, 6, MS 278, St Margaret, 1715, St Mary, 1712, St Martin, 1715, All Saints, 1715.

[112]   Wake MS 325, pp. 3, [4], 5, MS 278, St Martin, 1715, St Margaret, 1715, All Saints, 1715.

[113]   Wake MS 284, fos. 64, 60. The minister of Cranbrook also preached catechetical sermons (ibid. 105)—a series of sermons each focusing on a particular point, as in a catechism. A second sermon, or 'catechetical lecture', could be given in place of catechism: Spurr, *Restoration Church*, 355.

holy and 'apostolic' (or 'apostolical').[114] Sometimes, popular enthusiasm was reduced by the attitude of the clergy. In the diocese of Salisbury, the growing use of singing, and choirs, attracted many people to church, until the authorities resolved to suppress them; they also refused requests to have psalms sung at funerals.[115] If this was indeed 'an age of danger' for the Church, its clergy were partly responsible.

III. THE CHANGING FACE OF DISSENT

In the 1640s the separatist 'gathered churches' were denounced by conventional Puritans as a cancer, eating away at the very being of ordered Christianity. Many set the spirit above the Word and proclaimed that ordinary men, with the spirit within them, were better qualified to preach than university-trained clergymen. By withdrawing from the national church they made it impossible to maintain orthodox doctrine and undermined the establishment of parish-based moral discipline. The Quakers elevated the spirit still further above the Word. Through it, Christ spoke directly to the individual believer, enabling him, or her, to overcome the sinfulness within. Quakers also abandoned any semblance of a structured service or designated preachers: anyone could speak, man or woman, when the spirit moved them. Friends *had* to meet when the spirit required it and could not disperse until the spirit moved them to. If it moved them to preach in market places, to confront ministers in their churches, or to go naked as a sign, they had to do so. By contrast, they had no more respect for worldly authority than for other things of the world—fine clothes and food or other creature comforts. If magistrates commanded something contrary to their duty to God, they could not obey. They could not promise not to meet, or enter into recognizances to be of good behaviour, because that would suggest that they had done something wrong. They would not remove their hats before magistrates, or use the respectful 'you' form, because such deference was due only to God. They would not swear oaths, partly because the Bible told them to 'Swear not at all', but more fundamentally because they did not need the sanction of an oath to make them keep their word.[116]

---

[114] *Collection*, 14 (Taunton), 25 (St Albans), 26 (Brecon), 27 (Canterbury), 35 (Stamford), 41 (Totnes); *Post Boy*, 15–17 June (Hertford), 1–4 July (Cardigan), 6–8 July 1710 (New Windsor). The term 'apostolic' was used to mean that it taught the faith delivered by the apostles, not that it was founded by an apostle: Spurr, *Restoration Church*, 108–9.

[115] Spaeth, *Age of Danger*, 188–94, 200, 225–7, 230–49.

[116] See W. C. Braithwaite, *The Beginnings of Quakerism* (York, 1974); Davies, *Quakers*.

It seemed to many that Quaker teachings would lead to religious and social anarchy, but they did not. This was due partly to Fox stamping his authority on the movement, but more because of the internalized discipline of individual Quakers: they kept their word, and lived good Christian lives. It took time for this to become apparent. As Quaker numbers grew, Presbyterians and Independents came together to counter this perceived menace. The Baptists, too, concentrated on holding on to what they had rather than trying to win converts. The great hopes among the godly of the early 1640s had by 1660 subsided into disillusionment and recrimination. Whatever radical impetus they once had had long since dissipated.

At the Restoration, the Presbyterians were unapologetic about their record. They had had no part in the regicide and claimed that they had made a crucial contribution to the Restoration. They had some reason to expect that they would be accommodated within a restored national Church. The other denominations pinned their hopes on the king's statement in the Declaration of Breda, of April 1660, that he intended 'a liberty to tender consciences'. However, this liberty was to be granted by Parliament and it was to apply only to such as 'do not disturb the peace of the kingdom'.[117] The Independents and Baptists were therefore at pains to assure the king that they were peaceable and law-abiding.

And so did the Quakers. Unlike the Independents and Baptists they had had no part in the regicide, but many, including Fox, had actively opposed the Restoration. Starting with the Peace Testimony of January 1661 they repackaged themselves as peaceable and harmless; the movement became pacifist: eschewing carnal weapons, it would use only the weapons of the spirit. An increasingly elaborate central organization was set up, to regulate behaviour and publications, and to lobby in the corridors of power, doing all they could to alleviate their hardships without compromising their fundamental duty to God.[118] To a substantial extent, it worked. Their stubborn insistence on meeting publicly brought heavy persecution, but in many places their determination wore out their persecutors.[119] Many magistrates and even judges and bishops came to accept that they were indeed harmless—more so than the Presbyterians and partial conformists. Much of the popular animus against

[117] Browning, *Docts*, 58.
[118] W. C. Braithwaite, *The Second Period of Quakerism* (York, 1979); C. L. Leachman, 'From an "Unruly Sect" to a Society of "Strict Unity": The Development of Quakerism in England, 1650–89', Ph.D. thesis (University College London, 1997); Miller, 'Quakers and Authority', 247–50.
[119] Miller, 'Containing Division', 1037–40.

them died away. They were included in the Toleration Act, with a proviso allowing them to affirm, rather than swear, allegiance. After 1689 there was still occasional friction between Quakers and their neighbours, especially over their refusal to observe days of public thanksgiving (or Christmas). There were also complaints at their avoiding chargeable offices (although some did take them on, if they could avoid swearing) and their refusal to pay militia rates.[120] But by 1700 they were much more integrated into the wider society around them than they had been in 1660. They paid a price for their lost dynamism: Quaker numbers, which had continued to rise in the 1660s and 1670s, began to decline in the 1690s. Other denominations, too, were concerned with keeping hold of their existing members rather than seeking new ones. The Baptists and Independents stagnated and became introverted. Only the Presbyterians retained an element of dynamism and took the first steps towards metamorphosing into Unitarians.

IV. PERSECUTION AND TOLERATION

Most magistrates in most towns under Charles II at least seemed to conform to the Church. Some were far from eager to receive communion, even though they were required to do so by law in order to qualify for office, and many were reluctant to renounce the Covenant; some—we cannot tell how many—avoided doing either. The corporation of Norwich included several members whose loyalties were divided between Church and conventicle.[121] The corporation seems to have seen no incompatibility between seeking to improve the maintenance of the city's clergy and allowing Dissenting meetings to use civic buildings, when it was legal to do so: in 1672 the assembly agreed to lease parts of the city granary to a Presbyterian and an Independent meeting. The magistrates made little effort to harass Dissenters before 1681, although a few meetings came to light when searching for arms during security scares. Before the persecution of the early 1680s, the mayor's court politely asked the various Dissenting preachers in the city, and the Quaker leaders, if they would refrain from meeting.[122] The persecution that ensued fell far more heavily on

[120] Miller, ' "A Suffering People" ', 101–3; Davies, *Quakers*, 204–5; W. Stephenson, 'The Social Integration of Post-Restoration Dissenters', in M. Spufford (ed.), *The World of Rural Dissenters, 1520–1725* (Cambridge, 1995), 369–70.

[121] Miller, 'Containing Division', 1026–7.   [122] Ibid, 1029–31.

the Quakers than on others, partly because they insisted on meeting publicly and partly because their open defiance of orders to disperse infuriated the magistrates. Even then there were some modes of proceeding against them— for example, using the recusancy laws—which were little used.[123]

The pattern of limited, and reluctant, persecution can be found elsewhere. At York Quakers were left alone after 1670 and suffered their most severe persecution in 1659–60.[124] A Quaker was appointed as chamberlain at York in 1669 and Quakers were admitted to the freedom at Lancaster; they do not seem to have been asked to take the usual oaths.[125] There is very little evidence of conflict or persecution at Winchester. In 1677–8 the corporation began belatedly, and seemingly reluctantly, to investigate complaints of a conventicle in the house of Edward Hooker.[126] At Leicester Robert Atton was removed from the common council in 1671 for not coming to church and other mis-demeanours.[127] There was a newspaper report in 1682 that meetings had been disturbed and names taken.[128] In 1683 the corporation was advised that it would be legal to break down doors to distrain on convicted conventiclers; it is not known what use it made of it.[129] Quaker records show that a few Leicester Quakers were fined late in 1684, after the notorious informer John Smith arrived in the town, but the persecution did not last long.[130] After 1689 the corporation showed no evidence of hostility to Dissent, admitting Quakers to the freedom as early as 1691, allowing them to affirm, rather than swear.[131] Bristol followed suit in 1697, Norwich not until 1722.[132]

Hull's civic leaders valued the preaching of the Word more than the liturgy. The tomb in Holy Trinity of William Ramsden, MP, refers to him dying 'in the true faith of Christ' and 'waiting the morning of the Resurrection'. Such men were unwilling to persecute Dissenters within the same broad Puritan and Calvinist tradition. The small Quaker community in 1661–2 suffered

---

[123] Miller, 'Containing Division', 1032.   [124] Scott, 'York', 49–55, 103.
[125] Ibid. 308; Mullett, 'Conflict in Lancaster', 73. Quakers were also admitted to a number of London livery companies, from at least the 1670s: S. N. Dixon, 'Quaker Communities in London, 1667–1714', Ph.D. thesis (London, 2005), 212–21.
[126] A. Coleby, *Central Government and the Localities: Hampshire 1649–89* (Cambridge, 1987), 138.
[127] *RBL*, iv. 522.   [128] *Loyal Impartial Mercury*, 27–30 June 1682.
[129] *RBL*, iv. 557.   [130] Besse, i. 344, 345–6.
[131] *RBL*, v. 11, 15, vii. 85; LHP 37, nos. 59–60, LHP 38, nos. 224–5, LHP 39, fos. 33–4, 91–2.
[132] BRO, 04264/8, fos. 143, 155–6; FAB 9, p. 98. In 1692 John Gurney of Norwich, who had completed a seven-year apprenticeship, was, at the request of the officers of the Cordwainers' Company, allowed to practise his trade, but he was 'not to have any further privilege of his freedom until he take his oath': MCB 24, fo. 293.

sustained persecution at the hands of some officers of the garrison. In 1665 several were arrested and gaoled for meeting.[133] But thereafter the Quaker sufferings records contain virtually no references to persecution in Hull. As for other Dissenters, it seems that the boundaries between conformity and nonconformity were blurred. Those who signed the petition to make Richard Kitson lecturer at Holy Trinity included several later identified as Nonconformists or Nonconformist sympathizers.[134] In May 1670 a Nonconformist preacher got into the pulpit at Holy Trinity, after the vicar had left to conduct a burial. Many had remained in church after the service, presumably because they knew what was going to happen. Alderman Crowle and Captain Bennett had the preacher removed and soldiers from the garrison prevented any serious disorder.[135] Crowle was abused by several of his brethren and he and his wife were insulted in the street.[136] The king's cabinet council was alarmed that the civic authorities ignored conventicles. Gilby, the deputy governor, was ordered to report on those who failed to do their duty.[137] It was reported that both magistrates and Dissenters were awaiting the outcome of the trial of strength in London between the Dissenters and the authorities. So long as they hoped that their brethren would triumph, the Dissenters remained defiant. When it became apparent that they would not, there were fewer meetings, and these were less public and less well attended. By the end of the year the town was quiet.[138]

The events of 1670 showed the conflicting pressures on the aldermen, as they were torn between reluctance to antagonize their fellow townsmen and fear of being complained of 'above'.[139] As a port and a garrison town, Hull needed the crown's goodwill, but after a show of compliance in 1670 the bench seems to have made no effort to act against meetings until the arrival of the earl of Plymouth, as governor, in 1682. He complained that he heard that two conventicles met in the town. The bench sent for the preachers, Astley and Charles, together with some of their leading 'hearers', and admonished them not to meet.[140] A constable informed against Charles for preaching;

[133] Besse, ii. 107–8, 110–11.

[134] Whitaker, *Bowl Alley Lane Chapel*, 39–40. For a similar story from Dorchester, see Underdown, *Fire from Heaven*, 242.

[135] *CSPD 1670*, 233, 289.   [136] Ibid. 249, 267.

[137] Ibid. 240, 249, 289; SP 104/176, fo. 241.

[138] *CSPD 1670*, 267, 309, 366, 454–5, 477, 566. For the struggle in London, see Miller, *After the Civil Wars*, 208–9.

[139] The corporation was warned of the danger of such complaints: BRL 801, 807.

[140] Whitaker, *Bowl Alley Lane Chapel*, 56; BRB 6, p. 40; BL Add MS 8936, fo. 121.

he was condemned to six months in gaol under the Five Mile Act and later left the town; Astley had already gone. Charles sent handwritten sermons to his congregation, but meetings in the town ceased.[141] Some aldermen were unhappy at this state of affairs. Humphrey Duncalfe told Plymouth that he found the Dissenters pious, peaceable, and loyal; he added that he was old and would soon meet his Maker, and wanted no part in persecution. Thomas Johnson was accused of refusing to act against conventicles.[142] But despite the reluctance of some of the aldermen, conventiclers were convicted and fined and distraints made on those who failed to pay their fines. Several leading Dissenters were fined £20 a month for recusancy.[143]

The experience of Hull shows why it was harder to get the laws enforced in towns than in the countryside.[144] As Ormond wrote, of Bristol, in 1676: 'the unconformable are many of them rich and are so interwoven in partnerships, alliances and other interests with the conformable that much zeal for their conversion is not to be expected.'[145] A Yarmouth coffee-seller and self-appointed spokesman for the 'loyal' party agreed: the laws against Dissent could easily be enforced 'in the country, where the gentry live and the people have a dependence on them and not they upon the people, but in corporations it will never be carried through by the magistrates or inhabitants their livelihood consisting altogether in trade and this depending one upon another'.[146] When the mayor of Taunton closed the meeting houses in 1683 the townspeople boycotted his shop and he had to abandon his business.[147] In 1670 the magistrates of Hertford were rewarded for their atypical level of diligence by being awarded the king's third of conventicle fines.[148] The difficulty of enforcing the laws against Dissent in corporate towns was the major reason for the assault on their charters in 1682–5: magistrates who had been chosen by the townsmen, and lived in close proximity to them, would inevitably be more likely to respond to their neighbours than to a distant central government, unless that government

[141] Whitaker, *Bowl Alley Lane Chapel*, 58, 61, 66.   [142] Ibid. 57; BRB 6, p. 42.

[143] BRB 6, pp. 44, 46, 84, 116, 166, 193, 309; Whitaker, *Bowl Alley Lane Chapel*, 62.

[144] See also Glines, 'Colchester', 279–80; Hurwich, ' "Fanatick Town" ', 18; M. Mullett, ' "Deprived of our Former Places": The Internal Politics of Bedford, 1660–88', *Publications of the Bedfordshire Historical Society*, lix (1980), 34.

[145] V & A, Forster MS 426/1, fo. 95 (copy in Carte MS 70, fo. 447). See also *CSPD 1683–4*, 254–5.

[146] *CSP 1675–6*, 1; Gauci, *Yarmouth*, 73. See similar comments from Dover and Chester: *CSPD 1665–6*, 225, *1666–7*, 12. See also Hurwich, ' "Fanatick Town" ', 20–3.

[147] *CSPD July–Sept. 1683*, 251, 358. See also *CSPD 1680–1*, 695–6.

[148] *CSPD 1664–5*, 138 (undated, but presumably belonging to 1670), *1670*, 352.

had ways of putting pressure on them.[149] Constables, much poorer men, living even closer to their neighbours, were even more reluctant to act.[150]

Persecution under the Restoration was confined mainly to the early 1660s, 1670, and 1681–6. The Toleration Act of 1689 ended the persecution of Protestants in England, with the exception of those who denied the Trinity and those who refused to swear allegiance to William and Mary. Many new meeting houses were opened: the houses and preachers were supposed to be registered at quarter sessions, but not all were.[151] Anglican clergymen and magistrates were very wary of what they still saw as the Dissenters' sinister and subversive designs: the Toleration Act specified that they had to meet with doors unlocked. They responded nervously to signs that Dissenters were creating clandestine organizations,[152] and angrily to reports of preachers attacking Common Prayer[153] or trying to take over Anglican chapels.[154] But there were also signs of peaceful coexistence between Church and Dissent. In Dorset the lower clergy were moderate and Dissenters suffered no ill treatment. At Dorchester Anglicans and Dissenters did not allow their religious differences to divide them and the parson took tea with the Dissenting minister 'with civility and good neighbourhood'.[155] Much the same was true at Bideford and at Bridgwater the meeting house had a designated place for the mayor and aldermen, some of whom attended.[156] At Tunbridge Wells, that most 'polite' of towns, both the Anglican minister and the Dissenting preacher were paid out of the funds collected by 'the company'.[157]

---

[149] For example, Lord Windsor at Worcester (BL, Althorp MS C1, Windsor to Halifax, 13 July 1682); the bishop at Exeter (Tanner MS 37, fo. 17); and a letter from the king to the mayor of Berwick who had allegedly refused 'haughtily' to enforce the laws (Coventry MS 6, fos. 117, 188; BL, Add MS 15643, fo. 15).

[150] See the case of the constable of Whitby, who, in a town with no charter or magistrates, was the chief law enforcement officer: *CSPD 1670*, 295–6, 418; PC 2/63, fo. 31.

[151] Wake MS 284, fos. 104, 309; *HMC Kenyon*, 290.

[152] Bodl, MS Rawl Letters 51, fos. 158–9.

[153] *Post Boy*, 3–6 Sept. 1698, 30 Mar.–1 Apr. 1699, 23–6 Sept. 1710.

[154] *HMC Kenyon*, 245–6, 262, 289, 290, 417–18; *HMC Portland*, iii. 507. (These reports mostly come from Lancashire, where chapels were particularly numerous.)

[155] Defoe, *Letters*, 94–5; Defoe, *Tour*, i. 210.

[156] Defoe, *Tour*, i. 260, 270.   [157] Fiennes, 132–3.

7

From Restoration to Exclusion

Charles II's government intervened actively in the affairs of towns in two short periods—just after the Restoration and in 1682–5. On each occasion his main concern was to ensure that members of corporations could be relied on to suppress disaffection. In 1661 the government planned to do this by issuing new charters, giving the crown more extensive powers of intervention. This policy was abandoned when the House of Commons offered an alternative approach. The Corporation Act laid down political and religious tests which members of corporations had to take before they could be admitted to office, and provided for the appointment of commissioners to impose them. The Act achieved what the crown wanted in a manner acceptable to Parliament, and the king abandoned his plan to change the terms of charters. Many new charters were issued in 1661–4, but most confirmed the towns' existing privileges. Between 1664 and 1678, the king's relations with Parliament were often turbulent, but this was not generally reflected in the internal politics of towns, until three general elections in 1679–81 brought national political issues to the fore and forced electors to make choices. Between 1664 and 1678 the government devoted little attention to urban affairs, with the exception of a few 'factious' towns, two of which are discussed below. The elections and other events of 1679–81 showed that in many towns the Corporation Act had failed to prevent the admission to office of many who were politically obnoxious to the government and who could not be relied on to enforce the laws against religious dissent, which the government identified with political disaffection. The final section of the chapter shows how the failure of the Corporation Act forced the government to consider other means of establishing control over town magistracies, which are considered in the next chapter.

I. THE RESTORATION

In many towns the proclamation and return of the king were greeted with rejoicing, maypoles, and morris dancing, by most of the people, but with trepidation on the part of the civic rulers. Many had opposed Charles I in the civil wars and, after the purges of the 1640s and 1650s, feared that this latest turn of the political wheel would mean their expulsion from office—or worse. Local Royalists were quick to make accusations of disaffection and to call for the readmission of 'loyal' men. Some towns had to play down their Parliamentarian past. The king had been with his father when he had been rebuffed at Hull in 1642, so the aldermen tried hard to persuade him of the town's loyalty. On 8 May 1660 they ordered that the Commonwealth's arms should be taken down and the king's set up and proclaimed the king with drums, bells, and guns.[1] On 8 June the bench drew up an address to the king, which combined expressions of loyalty with a moral message acceptable to church puritans. It referred to the 'sad spectacle' of Charles and his father standing outside the walls. Such rudeness and inhumanity had been the work, not of the townspeople, but of the military. Now, under a forgiving king, the town looked forward to a golden age of mutual love between king and people. Trade was increasing, magistracy and ministry were encouraged, vice and profaneness discountenanced. The 'insects procreated out of the corruption of religion' had been knocked back into the nastiness from which they had sprung.[2]

Gloucester had a similarly difficult task, after surviving a long Royalist siege. It was more than a year before the arms of the duke of Gloucester and his brother, the duke of York, which had been defaced during the wars, were repaired and set up again, below an inscription 'a city assaulted by man and saved by God', which was removed only in 1671.[3] A fulsomely loyal address abhorred the cruel murder of Charles I and compared his son's restoration to the sun emerging from behind dark clouds. Both towns needed powerful protectors. Hull approached George Monck, the architect of the Restoration, and now duke of Albemarle and lord general; he agreed to become its lord steward.[4] Gloucester chose less fortunately, electing the king's youngest brother, the duke

---

[1] BRB 4, pp. 304, 306.   [2] Ibid. 309; Tickell, *Hull,* 517.
[3] Gloucs RO, GBR B3/3, p. 195; *CSPD 1671,* 420. For Gloucester's civil war record, see Roy, 'View from the Town Hall', 218–19.
[4] BRL 655; BRB 4, p. 386.

of Gloucester, as its high steward; he died before the end of the year.[5] So the city approached Lord Herbert of Raglan, later marquis of Worcester and duke of Beaufort, who was to become a significant figure in the region. Other gestures were directed at the king: like many other towns, Gloucester handed back to the crown the fee-farm rents which it had (it claimed) been forced to purchase by the 'threatening violence' of the times.[6]

If corporations felt vulnerable, so did the king. He placed little trust in professions of loyalty and was conscious that he lacked military power and money. He decided to raise additional regiments and to offset some of the cost by disbanding inland garrisons. Excluding Windsor and Chepstow, which continued, there were only three—Shrewsbury, Ludlow, and York, with a combined complement of a little over 300 men.[7] Some coastal garrisons were also to be reduced in size, including Dover and Deal.[8] These reductions were not welcomed by the towns concerned: the lord lieutenant of Shropshire remarked of Shrewsbury and Ludlow, 'they are very well content to be safe, but not to pay for it'. The inhabitants of Dover petitioned the king not to reduce the garrison, remarking that in 'the late times' the castle had been seized by a small party of Parliamentarians.[9] The king, fearful of disaffection, may have thought that small inland garrisons, which were all that he could afford, were of limited value and possibly dangerous, especially in towns, whose fortifications made them potent threats in the event of another civil war. His anxieties grew in the summer of 1662; the Act of Uniformity was about to come into force, the commissioners appointed under the Corporation Act were beginning their work, and the militia was still not fully operational. In June he ordered that the fortifications of five towns should be demolished, remarking that this was cheaper than installing garrisons.[10]

These were not the first fortifications to be demolished since the Restoration,[11] but they were all substantial towns with a record of strong Parliamentarianism

   [5] Gloucs RO, GBR B3/3, pp. 134, 137–9; *CSPD 1660–1*, 66. Dorchester chose the duke of Richmond: Underdown, *Fire from Heaven*, 233.

   [6] Gloucs RO, GBR B3/3, pp. 137–9, 168.

   [7] *HMC 5th Report*, 150, 202; BL, Egerton MS 2542, fos. 432–3. For Chepstow, see *CSPD 1663–4*, 359; McClain, *Beaufort*, 86–8, 131–5, and *Passim*.

   [8] *CSPD 1660–1*, 485–6, 491. However, the king ordered that the garrison at Portsmouth should be increased: ibid. 500.

   [9] H. Owen and J. B. Blakeway, *History of Shrewsbury*, 2 vols. (London, 1825), i. 480; *CSPD 1660–1*, 582.

   [10] *CSPV 1661–4*, 169–70, 180; *CSPD 1661–2*, 423–4.

   [11] *CSPD 1660–1*, 316, 488. At Worcester the king ordered that the walls and gates should be repaired: Worcs RO, X496.5, Chamber Order Book 1650–78, fo. 42.

(except Shrewsbury). Like Gloucester, Taunton had survived a Royalist siege and celebrated the anniversary of its deliverance as late as 1683. Coventry had a reputation as a strongly Puritan town, as did Northampton.[12] The demolition of Taunton's walls was ordered following reports from the deputy lieutenants and magistrates of Somerset of plans for insurrection. A Dutch visitor found the town undergoing a virtual military occupation, presumably involving local volunteers, as the militia had not yet been fully settled; he claimed that there were 1,000 cavalry in the town, looking for rebels.[13] The work went on slowly: in October, the castle still had not been demolished.[14] Elsewhere work proceeded more quickly, despite doubts from leading Royalists, such as Ormond (concerning Coventry) and Herbert of Raglan (Gloucester), whether demolition was really necessary.[15] The townspeople were resentful, seeing the walls and gates as symbols of their privileges and autonomy. In county towns the castle was often used for county business.[16] At Shrewsbury a small garrison was installed, ostensibly for the security of the castle.[17] At Northampton, the earl of Westmorland brought four troops of militia horse, and some volunteers, to the town and presented his orders. He allowed the corporation a little time to put their 'foul' heads together, but knew that they had little option but to submit to the king's command. He offered the townsmen the stone in return for their meeting the cost of labour, but found them so 'slack' that he brought in several hundred labourers from the county, who had virtually completed the work by the end of July.[18] At Coventry the work was allegedly completed in three days and nights, by 500 men, at a cost of £500. One local annalist blamed the mayor for the demolition, as he had made the city 'obnoxious' to the king; the earl of Northampton, who supervised the work, did not think that the inhabitants were generally disaffected or discontented.[19] Herbert estimated

[12] Although Shrewsbury had been in Royalist hands for most of the civil war, a substantial part of the corporation was removed in 1662; the grounds for their removal are unclear: Halliday, *Body*, 359.

[13] *CSPD 1661–2*, 434, 455; Carte MS 47, fos. 336, 340; Schellinks, 110–11. Two deputy lieutenants had asked for orders to move part of the militia into the town, adding that they had already installed two companies of foot in the castle: *CSPD 1661–2*, 434, 455; Carte MS 47, fo. 340. Two months later the king was displeased that the Somerset militia still had not been settled: *CSPD 1661–2*, 511. The presence of the soldiers no doubt explains a rare demonstration of obedience in the town, when the mayor and corporation sat bareheaded in the church while Common Prayer was read: *Mercurius Publicus*, 21–8 Aug. 1662.

[14] *CSPD 1661–2*, 505, 511.

[15] T. H. Lister, *Life and Administration of Clarendon*, 3 vols. (London, 1837–8), iii. 208.

[16] The king recognized this at Northampton: *CSPD 1661–2*, 434.

[17] *CSPD 1661–2*, 421.   [18] Clarendon MS 77, fo. 66a; *CSPD 1661–2*, 447.

[19] Coventry RO, Acc 535, fo. 26. (Others put the cost at £600 or more: *CSPD 1661–2*, 462, 477.) Coventry RO, Acc 2/3, p. 84; Clarendon MS 77, fo. 236 (partly in *CCSP*, v. 254–5).

that the cost of demolishing the fortifications at Gloucester would be £1,200; here, too, the stone was to be used for the benefit of the city.[20]

It is questionable whether the demolition of the fortifications reduced the danger of rebellion, but the king and his ministers regarded it as necessary, whatever the doubts of leading men in the provinces; the Venetian resident mentioned it twice in his dispatches.[21] It was also a show of strength at a time when town corporations were being purged of 'disaffected' members. The king had initially been content to order that members of corporations take the oaths of allegiance and supremacy (which had been required by law until 1642).[22] He ordered particular towns (usually in response to petitions from Royalists) to reinstate members purged in the 1640s and 1650s, and remove those who had been elected 'illegally' in their places. Compliance was not always swift.[23] At Worcester Lord Windsor ordered in September 1660 that twelve members of the corporation be removed and ten restored, following the king's order, but nothing seems to have been done. The king sent another letter ordering the corporation to displace 'disaffected' members. It was resolved that the mayor and aldermen should draw up a reply; two members of the corporation resigned.[24] At Sandwich, in response to the king's order, the corporation dismissed ten jurats and restored two; it then proceeded to re-elect six of the ten who had been dismissed.[25] At Salisbury, the mayor wrote that the corporation consisted of well-affected persons, so had already complied with the king's wishes.[26] For much of 1661 the king lacked the confidence needed to punish those who failed to respond to his letters. The militia had not been put on a firm statutory basis and the revenue had not been settled. Charles was more likely to reprimand local officials who exceeded their powers than corporations who failed to obey him.[27]

Nevertheless, corporations knew that they were vulnerable, especially if they had received new charters since 1642. In addition, the very act of removing duly elected members and electing others in their stead could be construed as a breach of the charter, leaving them open to an action of *quo warranto*.

[20] *CSPD 1661–2*, 424, 447, 490.   [21] *CSPV 1661–4*, 169–70, 180.

[22] SP 29/23, fo. 173; *CSPD 1660–1*, 311.   [23] See below, Ch. 9.

[24] Worcs RO, X496.5, Chamber Order Book 1650–78, fos. 38, 41.

[25] EKRO, Sa/AC8, fo. 148.   [26] *CSPD 1660–1*, 552.

[27] PC 2/55, fos. 74, 89; *CSPD 1660–1*. For the misuse of the county militia in a mayoral election at Bath, see Bath RO, Corporation Book 2, pp. 266, 269–71, 275–7, 282–6; W. A. H. Schilling, 'The Central Government and the Municipal Corporations in England, 1642–63', Ph.D. thesis (Vanderbilt University, 1970), 167–70. One of those involved, Sir Thomas Bridges, had earlier called for the privy council to put in a loyal mayor: *CSPD 1660–1*, 544.

Few faced up to this as squarely as some members of the corporation of Bury St Edmunds, who claimed that, as few of the corporation (including themselves) had been legally elected, there were not enough lawful members to govern the town. They asked the king to issue a new charter, choosing such members as he thought fit.[28] Attorney General Palmer reported, in January 1661, in favour of granting the petition, adding that it was supported by some of the neighbouring peers and gentry. Nothing was done and in June Palmer expressed the opinion that the charter was void in law and that the king should grant a new one.[29] By now, the crown's law officers had come to see the power to grant charters as a key weapon in bringing towns to heel. On 7 May a warrant laid down a 'policy' to be followed when granting charters. This included the king reserving the power to nominate the first aldermen, recorders, and town clerks and future recorders and town clerks; and that the parliamentary franchise was to be confined to 'the common council'. This 'policy' was neither fully thought through nor consistently followed, but it shows that some close to the king saw new charters as a means of increasing royal control over town governments.[30]

One reason why the 'policy' was not rigidly followed can be found in the conduct of the Cavalier House of Commons. It laid down that any legislation since 1641 which had not had the royal assent was null and void. It unequivocally stated that the king had the sole right to direct the armed forces and set out to re-establish the militia after twenty years of neglect. It also began to settle a sufficient revenue on the king. But the majority of the Commons also had an agenda that differed from the king's. They disliked his conciliatory attitude towards the Parliamentarians. They wanted Charles to be a partisan king and they wanted revenge; but Charles would agree to neither. Frustrated by their failure to undermine the Act of Indemnity, they strengthened the bill that became the Act of Uniformity, making it harder for ministers in the Puritan tradition to remain within the Church.[31] And they introduced a corporation bill. This provided for the appointment of commissioners in each county to reinstate all those put out of corporations for loyalty to the crown since 1642, and to put out all who came in in their places, unless they gave such testimonies of loyalty as would satisfy the commissioners, none of whom (other than MPs) were to be members of corporations. Where there were vacancies, the corporations were to choose new men, according to their charters. According

---

[28] SP 29/22, no. 4.   [29] SP 29/28, no. 71, 29/30, no. 28.

[30] J. Miller, 'The Crown and the Borough Charters in the Reign of Charles II', *EHR* c (1985), 58–9; Schilling, 'Government and Corporations', 171–3.

[31] Miller, *After the Civil Wars*, ch. 9.

to Colonel Gilby, 'this was much contested for, but in favour to the corporations was left them as before'.[32] The Lords offered sweeping amendments, which would have forced all towns to take out new charters, given the king powers to appoint recorders and town clerks and to choose mayors from a shortlist of six, and given county JPs full power to act within the boroughs. The provisions for a purge were dropped. The Commons responded angrily that to agree to this would be a betrayal of their trust: it would destroy the towns' privileges and autonomy, and might 'have an ill influence on the free elections'. They insisted that what was needed was a purge and they got their way. The commissioners' powers were to last only until 25 March 1663.[33]

The purges under the Corporation Act were the most rigorous hitherto. The commissioners had the power to require all members of corporations to take the oaths of allegiance and supremacy, to renounce the Covenant, and make a declaration that resistance to lawful authority could never be justified. They also had to prove that they had taken communion according to the rites of the Church of England during the previous twelve months. In addition, the commissioners had the power to remove anyone who had met all these conditions if they judged him to be disaffected. They could also reinstate members who had been illegally removed and nominate others for vacant places.[34] Most sets of commissioners confined themselves to removing those who either refused the oaths and declarations or failed to appear. The proposal of the vengeful earl of Derby that the Lancashire commissioners should remove all who had been in arms against the king was rejected by his colleagues.[35] In thirty-six towns investigated by Paul Halliday, about one-third of members were removed, and of these over half had refused to renounce the Covenant. Only about a quarter were removed after having otherwise complied with the requirements of the Act; two-thirds of these came from just four towns: Gloucester (twenty-five members), Wallingford (fifteen), Reading (nine), and Beverley (six).[36] Herbert wrote, after twenty-one members had been removed at Gloucester, that many of the rest had been left in in the hope that they would show contrition for the past and behave better in future, 'in elections and other trials'. Four more were removed subsequently.[37]

    [32] BRL 659.   [33] Miller, 'Crown and Borough Charters', 59–62.
    [34] Browning, *Docts*, 375–6.   [35] *CSPD 1661–2*, 517.
    [36] Halliday, *Body*, 354–61, summary on 360. There are fifty cases where it is uncertain whether they had refused the oaths or the declaration against the Covenant. At York most of the commons were removed, but there was little obvious political or religious difference between those who were removed and their replacements: Scott, 'York', 295–8.
    [37] Austin, 'Gloucester and the Regulation of Corporations', 260–9, esp. 265–7.

Sometimes the commissioners went further. At Canterbury the oaths and declarations were tendered to over 300 freemen; 112 were removed for 'good causes and reasons . . . for the public peace and safety of the realm'. They were not to attend any public assembly or vote in any election; the same was ordered for those dismissed from the corporation.[38] One hundred and ten freemen were disfranchised at Maidstone and eighty-two at Dover.[39] At Portsmouth the commissioners removed only four aldermen, but eighty-eight burgesses (freemen), transforming the town's body of electors.[40] At Southampton the corporation disfranchised eight burgesses for misdemeanours relating to the government; three had refused the oath of allegiance in 1660.[41] The newly installed corporation of Northampton asked the privy council to order that those ejected should not be allowed to vote in a parliamentary by-election, but to no avail.[42] Similarly, at Ipswich in May 1663 the corporation and commonalty resolved that no freeman could vote in any election unless he took the oaths and renounced the Covenant. Opponents of this resolution took legal advice, which was that the Act applied only to members and officers of the corporation and should not be extended to include the freemen.[43] A series of more sweeping resolutions was passed by the Canterbury burghmote in 1665. Noting that the various companies in the city contained many who were not well affected to Church or state, who might be elected to offices in companies or the corporation, it resolved that no officer currently serving in a company was to continue in office unless he qualified fully under the Corporation Act and was approved by the burghmote. As members of one body, it declared, they should be of one mind. It also resolved that nobody was to be made free of the city unless he had taken communion in the last twelve months and had remained throughout the service.[44]

Most commissions had completed their task by the end of 1662, although a few were still active in March 1663.[45] They had met with only isolated acts of defiance, such as the refusal of six of those ejected at Sandwich to leave the hall.[46]

---

[38] Canterbury City Archives, AC5, fos. 59–62.

[39] CKS, Md/ACm 1/3, fos. 126–7; DAM fos. 213–14.

[40] East, 168–9; *HP 1660–90*, i. 253. The burgesses who were removed lost the right to trade: D. Dymond, *Portsmouth and the Fall of the Puritan Republic*, Portsmouth Papers xi (1971), 15–18. See also Styles, *Studies*, 46–7.

[41] Southampton RO, SC 2/1/8, fos. 166, 188.

[42] BL, Add MS 29551, fo. 9. The alignments in the by-election were complicated: see *HP 1660–90*, i. 339–40.

[43] *Mercurius Publicus*, 7–14 May 1663; East Suffolk RO, HD/36/2781/158. There is no mention of the vote in *HP 1660–90*, i. 403.

[44] Canterbury City Archives, Burghmote Minute Book 5, fos. 123–4.

[45] Gloucs RO, GBR, B3/3, p. 253.   [46] CKS, Sa/AC 8, fo. 162.

The king seemed well satisfied. The earlier 'policy' of using charters to reduce towns' autonomy must have seemed unnecessary now that they were in 'loyal' hands. True, there were occasional disputes about whether an individual was 'loyal',[47] and in some towns so many were removed that it was difficult to find enough suitable men to carry on the government. At Arundel all but one of the corporation refused the oaths and declaration. The earl of Northumberland persuaded two more to take them, but had to turn out thirteen and brought the militia into the town in case there was trouble.[48] At Colchester, a town deeply divided in the 1650s, the commissioners pressed the mayor to comply, knowing him to be a 'civil person'.[49] In March 1663 the privy council decided to call in the charters, by means of *quo warrantos*, of towns which were disaffected (such as Arundel and Rye) or where there were not 'persons sufficient to be made members'.[50] (However, the *quo warrantos* would have to be based on actions since the start of the Cavalier Parliament, as the Corporation Act had laid down that no charter could be made void by virtue of any act before that date.[51]) In June the king revoked the order of May 1661 that in all charters the king should name recorders and town clerks: towns were to be free to elect their own officers. As so many were now seeking new charters, he laid down procedures to expedite those which required no more than the usual alterations; these included reserving to the king the power to approve recorders and town clerks. He abandoned claims to nominate members of corporations, which must no longer have seemed necessary. A warrant of June 1663 ordered that the new charter of Coventry, regarded as a factious town, should reserve to the king the power of approving the town clerk and recorder, not that of nomination, as previously intended.[52] Only in a handful of charters issued in 1661, notably to Leeds and Hull, did the king claim such a right.[53] And at Hull the king usually nominated the person suggested by the town.

[47] See the case of the earl of Clare as recorder of Nottingham: *CSPD 1661–2*, 540, 553.

[48] PC 2/56, fo. 80; BL, Egerton MS 2538, fo. 168.

[49] *Mercurius Publicus*, 14–21 Aug. 1662. For Colchester in 1650s, see S. R. Gardiner, *History of the Commonwealth and Protectorate*, 4 vols. (London, 1903), iv. 55–77.

[50] PC 2/56, fo. 173; BL, Add MS 37820, fo. 46. At Chard all the aldermen refused the oaths, leaving only the mayor: *CSPD 1661–2*, 539.

[51] Browning, *Docts*, 375.

[52] SP 44/15, pp. 54–5. In a memorandum by Clarendon, which unfortunately does not bear a year, he writes of the problems of suppressing meetings in Coventry and of the need for commission of 'assistance' (i.e., association) to be issued to six gentlemen of the county: *CCSP*, v. 247.

[53] Halliday, *Body*, 153; Miller, 'Crown and Borough Charters', 64. The warrant for the Preston charter of March 1662 ordered that there should be a clause reserving to the king the nomination of the 'officers' of the borough, but no such clause seems to have been included: SP 44/5, pp. 93–4; Halliday, *Body*, 153–4.

II. CHURCH, DISSENT, AND THE RISE OF 'PARTY'

If the king regarded the outcome of the Corporation Act as satisfactory, the old Cavaliers were less sure. There were attempts in Parliament to extend the life of the commissions, and complaints that the Act offered a pretext for otherwise qualified men to avoid burdensome offices, but no further legislation was passed.[54] The Commons were more concerned about conspiracy and insurrection, which was the main reason for the passing of the first Conventicle Act in 1664 and the Five Mile Act in 1665. They were angered by the humiliation of the Second Dutch War and by the evidence it revealed of the corruption and incompetence of the king's court and government. They were still more angry, and perturbed, that the king showed such favour to enemies of the Church, notably the duke of Buckingham, after the fall of Clarendon. A brief and rapturous rapprochement in 1670, when the king assented to the second Conventicle Act, was followed by more confusion and disillusionment with the Declaration of Indulgence and Third Dutch War in 1672. Dissenters worshipped freely. Some corporations responded with equanimity or even enthusiasm: Norwich quickly leased city premises to Presbyterians and Independents, and sent a beadle to prevent the Quakers' meetings (not covered by the Declaration) from being disturbed.[55] Presbyterian preachers began to compete openly with the Church, enticing away erstwhile conformists.[56] Anglican ministers were inhibited from criticizing the Indulgence by fear of royal disapproval. Only in Oxford did raucous students with a very large dog disrupt meetings, leading to a severe letter from the king to the vice chancellor.[57] The cancelling of the Indulgence early in 1673 was greeted with widespread rejoicing, but the king did not withdraw the licences that he had issued to preachers and meeting places and, for two years, it remained uncertain whether or not they were still in force.[58]

The king's issuing the Indulgence less than two years after he had assented to the Conventicle Act shook the old Cavaliers' faith in him. They were if anything even more disturbed by the Dutch War and alliance with France. He had misled Parliament, and they began to consider his motives for allying with a papist absolutist king against the Protestant Dutch. The raising of an

---

[54] *CJ*, viii. 446, 517, 551, 553–4.   [55] FAB 8, fos. 28, 29; Eddington, *First Fifty Years*, 77.
[56] *Baxter Corr.*, ii. 143–4; *CSPD 1672*, 326, *1672–3*, 300.
[57] BL, Add MS 29571, fo. 151.   [58] Miller, *After the Civil Wars*, 210–11.

army to invade the Dutch Republic, which never left English soil, added to the suspicion. Was this all part of a design to overthrow Parliaments and to establish 'popery and arbitrary government'? The Indulgence, which also gave some liberty to Catholics, and increasing awareness of the conversion of the heir presumptive, the duke of York, to Catholicism, gave added credibility to these suspicions. In an effort to undo some of the damage, the new chief minister, the earl of Danby, set out to give some cohesion to the old Cavaliers, in Parliament and outside. He tried to persuade Charles to become a partisan king, but with limited success. Charles was prepared to take some action against Catholics and Dissenters, especially after the Compton Census showed how few of the latter there really were. But he was most reluctant to abandon his friendship with France and he could not conjure away his brother's Catholicism. Meanwhile, the methods Danby used to create a Cavalier, or 'court', party were denounced as divisive and designed to weaken Parliament by undermining the independence of members, through places and other rewards. Resentment of this 'corruption' led to the emergence of an oppositionist 'country' element. Ministers and peers drew up lists and one or two by-elections, notably for Norfolk in 1675, were fought on something approaching party lines.[59]

This growing partisanship initially had little impact on towns. Some were deeply divided, but their divisions can rarely be expressed in simple 'party' terms before 1678–9. At Dover there were a variety of conflicting interests: the Cinque Ports, the navy, the castle, and various mercantile and (often mutually hostile) Nonconformist elements. There were two hotly contested elections in 1673, with an admiral of uncertain political leanings opposed by a Dissenting sympathizer, who was also a victualler for the navy. Whatever other crosscurrents there may have been, the most vociferous complaints concerned the creation of over fifty new freemen to vote in the election.[60] Elsewhere, conflict can usually be ascribed to a specific, and local, cause. In Bristol, it was an exceptionally pugnacious new bishop.[61] At Oxford much can be explained by the clashes between the city and university. The election of Buckingham as high steward in 1669 may have reflected awareness of his great influence at court, but he was no friend to the Church and had been responsible for the fall of Clarendon and the dismissal of Ormond, successively chancellors of the university. The Exclusion Crisis added to the divisions in the city. In all

[59] Miller, *After the Civil Wars*, ch. 11.
[60] Kishlansky, *Parliamentary Selection*, 163–71; *HP 1660–90*, i. 493–5, iii. 468–9.
[61] Below, Ch. 9.

three elections the city returned, after vigorous contests, William Wright, the leading Whig alderman, and Brome Whorwood, who had served since 1661, and had developed into an extreme Whig. The Whig candidates enjoyed considerable support from Buckingham and from John Lord Lovelace, a significant (if financially challenged) county figure, and his formidable mother.[62] In September 1679 Robert Pauling, who had been ejected in 1663, was readmitted to the corporation and elected mayor. He walked the streets at night, arrested townsmen he found in tippling houses, refused licences for alehouses, and forbade coffee houses to open on Sundays.[63] At the end of his mayoralty, at his suggestion, the freedom was granted to 'the most noble prince' the duke of Monmouth.[64] Monmouth visited the city and was received with wild acclaim, by townsmen crying 'no York, no bishop, no clergy, no university'. The university, following the king's wishes, ignored his visit.[65] The meeting of Parliament at Oxford in March 1681 highlighted divisions in the city. When the king arrived some cried, 'Devil take the Roundheads', at which the king smiled. The students put up tables with refreshments in the streets and made all who passed drink the king's health on their knees.[66]

Norwich remained largely free of strife until a contentious by-election early in 1678 led Lord Yarmouth to seek to remove the 'disaffected' from the court of aldermen. The elections of 1679–81 added to divisions in the city.[67] Not everywhere saw such divisions. Leicester, which had had to contend with rival gentry interests struggling for supremacy in 1661 and a by-election in 1677, apparently had no contests in 1679–81, with the same two politically moderate local gentlemen elected each time.[68] Portsmouth saw only one contest, Winchester none.[69] But in the course of the Exclusion Crisis the nation became politically more polarized than at any time since the 1640s. The crisis raised again the issues of the threat from popery, the nature of the monarchy, the authority of the Church, and the consciences of Dissenters. The issues were highlighted in London, and carried into the provinces, by the practice of burning the pope in effigy, often following a procession featuring topical figures like Sir Edmund Berry Godfrey. At Lewes (where the pope is still burned on 5 November) his effigy was preceded through the streets by pictures,

[62] *HP 1660–90*, i. 359–60; Prideaux, 98.
[63] *OCA*, ii. 306, iii. 120; Wood, ii. 463; Prideaux, 80–1. Pauling had been chosen to a bailiff's place in 1676, but took it up only in 1679, in order to be elected mayor: *OCA*, iii. 93, 120.
[64] *OCA*, iii. 129. [65] *CSPD 1680–1*, 31; *HMC Ormond*, v. 449; *HMC Egmont*, ii. 99.
[66] Wood, ii. 526–7. [67] Miller, 'Containing Division', 1044–6.
[68] *HP 1660–90*, i. 296–7, 613, ii. 442. [69] *HP 1660–90*, i. 253–4, 260.

on long poles, of Jesuits, friars, devils, and (unusually) Guy Fawkes.[70] In Monmouthshire, where the opponents of the marquis of Worcester made great play of his alleged tolerance of popery, a pope was burned at Abergavenny.[71] The Tories of Salisbury responded by burning the pope, holding 'Jack Presbyter' by the hand; at Shaftesbury they burned the Rump.[72]

The crisis generated memories—and renewed fears—of civil war. In elections and in the press, in taverns and in the streets, accusations were made and names bandied.[73] Whigs and Dissenters were accused of being 'fanatics', 'disaffected', and 'rebels'. Tories, and especially Tory parsons, were accused of being favourers of popery and servile apologists for absolute monarchy. Townsmen—and especially town rulers—had to stand up and be counted: by rival candidates in elections and by rival promoters of Whig petitions (that Parliament should meet) and Tory counter-petitions (abhorring such attempts to dictate to the king). As insults flew and tempers flared, attachment to a moderate middle way, and the sort of inclusive mentality so apparent in towns like Norwich, Hull, or York,[74] became increasingly difficult to sustain. This was especially true when, as at Oxford, party bigwigs came from outside to stir up their supporters. The Whigs had the greater need for popular support. To achieve exclusion and their other goals they had to create an impression of an irresistible popular movement, in the face of which the king would have to capitulate. Their populist tactics and rhetoric added to the fear and determination of the Tories (and the king). The king kept control of the machinery of government and law, which he was to use to crush the Whigs. Meanwhile, the Tories (like the Royalists in the civil war) conquered their aversion to appealing for popular support and provided the king with the agents and information that he would need to reimpose his will in the localities.[75] In the counties, he already possessed the power to appoint and remove magistrates. In the towns, he did not, which led him to revive the policy he had briefly adopted at the Restoration—of challenging the towns' charters and so their right to choose their rulers.

[70] *Domestic Intelligence*, 14 and 18 Nov. 1679. For a pope-burning in Oxford in 1678, see Wood, ii. 422.

[71] *The Pope's Downfall at Abergavenny* (1679); P. Jenkins, 'Anti-Popery on the Welsh Marches in the Seventeenth Century', *HJ* xxiii (1980), 275–93.

[72] *Loyal Protestant*, 13 Dec. 1681, 11 Apr. 1682.

[73] For examples of this at Sandwich, see EKRO, Sa/Ac8, fos. 223, 228.

[74] Scott, 'York', 369–71 and Ch. 4, *passim*.

[75] On the processes of division in general, see Knights, *Politics and Opinion*; Harris, *Restoration*, chs. 3–4; Miller, *After the Civil Wars*, ch. 12.

III. TWO 'FACTIOUS' TOWNS

Between 1664 and 1681, the crown showed little interest in challenging charters, or intervening in the membership of corporations, with two exceptions. Gloucester survived the Restoration with its privileges and autonomy largely undiminished, despite its conspicuous opposition to the crown in the civil wars. The government's attention was drawn to the city by a dispute which began in 1670. The 'Presbyterians' on the corporation attempted to prevent Dr Henry Fowler from being elected mayor. Instead they wished to bring in William Bubb, who allegedly threatened to crush the 'royal interest'. (As Bubb was later described as 'simple' this seems improbable.) The recorder, Sir William Morton, asked the king to order that Fowler be elected. The privy council sent an order to that effect and the council complied, although five aldermen, headed by Dr Robert Fielding, petitioned against the election. The privy council saw no reason to change its position.[76] Despite this success, Fowler was pessimistic. Many of the wealthier citizens (he wrote) had been removed from the corporation, so that the common council had been filled with men of mean degree and factious principles. In an effort to stem the tide, Fowler managed to get Fielding disfranchised, for entertaining a 'foreigner' in his house and otherwise abusing the freedom. He also removed the memorial to the siege and put in its place the royal arms, with a loyal inscription in Latin.[77] The other aldermen refused to elect a replacement for Fielding. There were now only ten aldermen, and at least eleven were needed, under the charter, to elect a mayor, so the aldermen were making it impossible to proceed to an election.[78] When the day of election came, Fowler summoned the council, but while he and his allies were at a service in the cathedral, his opponents 'elected' Bubb. Amid angry words and blows, Fowler secured the mace and sword, but Bubb claimed that he was mayor, and the people paid more heed to Bubb than to Fowler.[79]

From the time that the aldermen had refused to elect a successor to Fielding, Fowler had claimed that the charter was forfeit. The king's initial response to

---

[76] *CSPD 1670*, 419, 428, 448, 455; Gloucs RO, GBR B3/3, pp. 449–50. For claims (by three different writers) that Bubb was 'simple', see *CSPD 1671*, 429, 457, 542.

[77] *CSPD 1671*, 411–12, 419–20; Gloucs RO, GBR B3/3, p. 481.

[78] *CSPD 1671*, 429, 456–7. There are no entries in the council minute book between Sept. 1671 and May 1672: Gloucs RO, GBR B3/3, pp. 484–97 are blank.

[79] *CSPD 1671*, 521–2, 531.

the 'election' of Bubb was to write to the marquis of Worcester, on 9 October, that it was his pleasure that Fowler should continue as mayor until the privy council could come to a decision. On the 31st the attorney and solicitor general told the council that the irregularities in the corporation were sufficient to make the charter forfeit. The king told the corporation that if they surrendered promptly, he would issue a good charter in which he would nominate one of them as mayor; otherwise he would proceed to a *quo warranto*. The corporation judged that it had no option but to comply.[80]

Once it was clear that there would be a new charter, several people sought to influence its content and the composition of the new corporation: the corporation was not invited to make suggestions about either. This was the first occasion since the Restoration that a corporation had surrendered all its charters, leaving the king's advisers *carte blanche* to frame a new one.[81] The dean, Vyner, complained that the magistrates had shown great hostility towards the Church and cathedral. He and Bishop Nicolson saw an opportunity to regain the cathedral precinct's former exemption from the city's jurisdiction. Vyner complained that people made too much noise near the cathedral; some citizens alleged that the clergy had helped bring about the loss of the charter, so the clergy needed to guard against their malice. He proposed that the bishop and some of the other clergy and gentlemen living in the precinct should be magistrates there, executing writs from the sheriff of the county.[82] He persuaded those citizens who had gone to solicit the new charter to include these provisions in their proposals, with the addition that the bishop, dean, and two prebends (chosen by the king) should be JPs for the city. He probably helped draw up a list of members of the corporation, with comments on their recent behaviour, marked as 'certified' by Nicolson and Morton.[83] Vyner also hoped to have John Dorney, the town clerk, removed, on the grounds that he refused to come to the cathedral, because he could not bear the organ. Dorney had been removed in 1662, but subsequently reinstated, and three of the city clergy certified that he attended church and received communion.[84] Despite Vyner's efforts, Dorney remained in post, perhaps because the king was generally reluctant to remove experienced town clerks.

---

[80] PC 2/63, pp. 95–6; *CSPD 1671*, 597.

[81] Halliday, *Body*, 182. The emphasis of Halliday's account (ibid. 178–82) differs from mine.

[82] *CSPD 1671*, 587, *1671–2*, 23.

[83] Bodl, MS Add c.303, fos. 60, 225–6. Although Vyner's name does not appear on the latter document, the correspondence in the state papers suggests that he was more actively involved in preparations for the charter than Nicolson.

[84] *CSPD 1671–2*, 2–3, 11, 32, 33.

The other significant player in these negotiations was Worcester. He had been the city's lord steward since 1661, but had hitherto played little part in its affairs, except for acting as a Corporation Act commissioner and supervising the demolition of its fortifications. There is no evidence of his involvement in the various disputes before the king's letter of 9 October, but he was nominated one of a small committee, along with Archbishop Sheldon, Lord Keeper Bridgman, and Lord Clifford, charged with drawing up a list of men fit to be included in the corporation. The king insisted that all had to be resident and to have been members of the corporation before.[85] Sheldon, Bridgman, and Clifford largely followed the list attested by Morton and Nicolson. All but two of those they recommended as aldermen and all but four of those they recommended as common councillors appeared on the agreed list.[86] Worcester's list contained four more of the existing alderman, including Anthony Arnold, identified as a leader of the opposing faction, and the recently disfranchised Fielding. It included neither of the 'persons of quality now freemen' (one of whom had recently been made an alderman) nor any of the six citizens 'fit to be inserted under submission' in the Morton–Nicolson list.[87] Worcester was displeased that his recommendations were not adopted: his followers in the city gave out that everything had been done by the archbishop and that Worcester had been outvoted.[88] Worcester managed to carry one or two changes and it was alleged that he had Bubb, originally in the agreed list, omitted by claiming (falsely) that he was dead.[89] He also managed to have John Webb (removed from the corporation in 1662) placed at the head of the list of common councillors, against the wishes of Fowler, who claimed that Webb was 'unquiet' and ambitious.[90]

[85] SP 29/302, no. 132.

[86] Bodl, MS Add c.303, fos. 58, 225–6. Another copy of the agreed list is at SP 44/34, fo. 140. The two were Bubb (of which more above) and Sir Baynham Throckmorton; the four were John Smallwood, Ferdinando Meighen, William Wood, and Isaac Comelin. Only Smallwood was already a member of the corporation.

[87] SP 29/302, no. 134; Bodl, MS Add c.303, fos. 225–6. The two 'persons of quality' were Sir Henry Norwood (already an alderman) and Henry Brett, Esq. The six were William Selwyn, Esq., Robert Halford, Matthew Bower, Giles Welsly, Cornelius Plott, and John Cromwell. For Arnold's 'opposition' stance, see *CSPD 1671*, 429, *1671–2*, 24.

[88] SP 44/34, p. 138. (Page 139 has been torn out, which suggests that there was argument over the list: the final 'majority' list appears on p. 140.) *CSPD 1671–2*, 322.

[89] SP 44/34, fo. 140; SP 29/302, no. 134; Bodl, MS Add c.303, fo. 65; *CSPD 1671–2*, 322. There is another copy of the first of these in Bodl, MS Add c.303, fo. 58. The charter is printed in S. Rudder, *New History of Gloucestershire* (Cirencester, 1778), appendix, pp. iv–xii.

[90] *CSPD 1671–2*, 444; Gloucs RO, GBR B3/3, p. 576.

This last episode is a little puzzling. Webb was not on Worcester's original list; it is probably significant in that it demonstrated Worcester's favour with the king, and forced Fowler into a public act of submission. Worcester was now lord president of Wales and a privy councillor, a major figure, who could do the city considerable good, or harm, at court.[91] His earlier interventions in the negotiations for the new charter had been clumsy. Proposing changes to the corporation more limited than Morton and the bishop judged necessary, and espousing the cause of Fielding and Arnold, were unlikely to enhance his credit at court. He may, indeed, have learned from this that supporting the church interest was politically prudent. His victory in the Webb episode, though apparently trivial, earned him several marks of respect: he was presented with a piece of plate and (after eleven years as steward) invited to become a burgess.[92] But his success was only temporary. The corporation sought the goodwill of others, including Lord Berkeley and Charles Osborne, Danby's brother.[93] Not until the Exclusion Crisis did Worcester again take an active interest in the city's affairs.

Among the 'factious' towns in England, Taunton was in a league of its own. It enjoyed a special status in the Whig Green Ribbon Club: one category of membership consisted of any inhabitant of Taunton recommended by John Trenchard.[94] It was one of the towns whose walls were demolished in 1662. Each year the townsmen commemorated 'their rebellion'—the raising of the Royalist siege on 11 May 1645. In 1668 the day was celebrated with some disorder. In 1671 the celebrations were said to last three days. The shops were shut and drums beat from early in the morning.[95] In 1676 Bishop Mew, of Bath and Wells, sent word to the constables to forbid the public celebration of 11 May, but he was sure that there was much feasting in private.[96] The town was also notorious for its large conventicles. They were said to meet behind barred doors, guarded by sentinels, some of whom were allegedly armed. When the town officers and county magistrates tried to do their duty they met violent resistance and threats to knock them down in the street. Threatening libels

---

[91] For comments on his (prospective) appointment as president of Wales, see M636/24, Sir Ralph to Edmund Verney, 25 Jan., Edmund to Sir Ralph, 29 Jan. 1672.

[92] Gloucs RO, GBR B3/3, pp. 572, 576, 591–2.   [93] Ibid. 612, 658.

[94] Magdalene College, Cambridge, Pepys Library, MS 2875, fos. 465–6.

[95] PC 2/60, p. 312; *HMC le Fleming*, 56; *CSPD 1671*, 309–10; R. Clifton, *The Last Popular Rebellion: The Western Rising of 1685* (London, 1984), 44–5.

[96] Coventry MS 7, fo. 66.

were thrown into the houses of ministers and magistrates.[97] One reason for their boldness was that for much of the time they believed they had support 'above'. In 1672 the leader of the great Presbyterian meeting, George Newton, applied for a licence to preach in the town hall; it was not granted.[98]

One reason for the disorder at Taunton was the lack of an effective government. The Corporation Act commissioners removed most members of the corporation, and failed to appoint any new ones, perhaps because they judged that there were too few loyal men in the town.[99] The corporation lapsed and the highest authority in the town consisted of the constables, assisted from time to time by the deputy lieutenants of Somerset: in June 1667 they were ordered to send a troop of horse and two companies of foot to keep order in the town.[100] Some of the local gentry, and two of the judges, supported a petition from some of the inhabitants, in 1669, that the town should again be incorporated. Recent disorders, they said, were due less to disaffection than to the lack of magistrates. The privy council received the petition warily, ordering the attorney general to include provisions that all members and officers of the corporation should be loyal and sober. He suggested that the king should reserve a power to dissolve the corporation and disfranchise any member at pleasure, although the petitioners asked that this should be only for open misbehaviour.[101] These restrictions would have been much the most stringent included in any charter since the Restoration, but the king did not proceed with it.

The idea of reincorporation was revived in 1675, promoted by Sir William Portman, one of the town's MPs, supported by Bishop Mew. They hoped to put the corporation into loyal hands, but proposals for a new charter met with considerable opposition and proceeded slowly.[102] A warrant for a new charter was drawn up in January 1676. Portman raised difficulties about reserving to the king the approval of recorders and town clerks.[103] A new proposal in February led to two new recommendations. First, the recorder and town clerk could be removed by the king. Coventry compared this to the recently adopted principle that the judges should serve 'during pleasure' rather than 'during good behaviour'. Second, the king would have the power to create freemen in

---

[97] Ibid. 66, 128, 130, 132; *CSPD 1682*, 36–7, 97–8; *Loyal Protestant*, 1 Apr. 1682.
[98] Coventry MS 7, fos. 128, 130; *CSPD 1671–2*, 446, 448, 479. Petitions for licences for civic buildings were not normally granted.
[99] *CSPD 1668–9*, 420.   [100] *CSPD 1667*, 195.
[101] *CSPD 1668–9*, 402, 420–1; SP 104/176, fo. 182.
[102] *CSPD 1675–6*, 39; BL Add MS 25124, fo. 66.
[103] BL, Add MS 25125, fo. 3; Halliday, *Body*, 183–4.

order to 'place such artificers which shall according to several proclamations come over and bring manufactures with them'. This may have represented an attempt to tackle the problems of the town's depressed cloth industry and very large numbers of poor, with whom (in the absence of a corporation) it proved unable to cope. Both clauses provoked opposition from 'very great persons' and (allegedly) many of the loyal gentry; the clause allowing the king to create freemen may have aroused fears of electoral gerrymandering. Whatever the reasons for this opposition, this proposal, too, led to nothing.[104] A warrant was drawn up, without the provision about the recorder serving during pleasure; the copy in the state papers has been crossed out.[105]

In the summer of 1677 yet another warrant for a new charter was drawn up, this time in a conventional form, with the king reserving the power to approve the recorder and town clerk. There were two innovations: the provision that the recorder was to serve during the king's pleasure was reinstated; also six JPs for the county were to serve within the corporation. There was also a clause, put in at Mew's suggestion, that the judges could expel from the corporation members convicted of serious offences.[106] Some doubted whether the new charter was intended to benefit the town. Marvell remarked acidly that Taunton had been forced to become a corporation, with Lord Rochester and Bishop Mew (an ill-assorted pair) as two of its aldermen. The new magistrates, led by the bishop, sought to suppress the conventicles and met with violent resistance.[107] The meetings continued and the magistrates' control remained tenuous. A rare success came in 1680 when a leading Whig, Thomas Dare, was fined £500 for seditious words and dismissed from the corporation; he had allegedly said that the only ways to redress evils were by petitioning or the sword. Some had feared that the witnesses against him would be too afraid to testify at Taunton.[108] Mew was pleased at his conviction, but believed that the 1677 charter had been insufficient to bring the town to order. A new charter was needed: he could see no way of reducing the town except by the sort of measures the king was usually averse to.[109]

[104] BL, Add MS 25125, fos. 4–5. For the change in judges' tenure, see Miller, *After the Civil Wars*, 225, 235–6. For the desperate economic and social conditions in Taunton, see Clifton, *Last Popular Rebellion*, 30–1.

[105] SP 44/40a, fo. 126.

[106] Ibid. 210–11; *CSPD 1677–8*, 260–1, *1679–80*, 428; Halliday, *Body*, 185.

[107] Marvell, ii. 356; Coventry MS 7, fos. 124, 128, 130, 132.

[108] *Protestant (Domestic) Intelligence*, 9 Apr. 1680; *CSPD 1679–80*, 428; Coventry MS 7, fo. 198.

[109] Coventry MS 7, fo. 204.

IV. THE FAILURE OF THE CORPORATION ACT

We have seen that some complied with the Corporation Act only reluctantly. Many of those removed by the commissioners soon returned. James Thurbarne, MP for Sandwich, had been ejected from the corporation and promptly re-elected in 1660. Ejected again in 1662, he was elected mayor in 1665 and returned as town clerk in 1667.[110] Also in 1667 the privy council heard that the last mayor of Maidstone had admitted to the corporation several who were ineligible under the Act and denied the right to vote to those admitted by the commissioners. The information came from the commissioners for regulating corporations in Kent, who continued to operate informally after their legal authority had expired.[111] In 1668, following information that one of those ejected by the commissioners at Oxford had been readmitted, the king ordered corporations to observe the Act strictly and asked whether any unqualified members had been admitted.[112] Lord lieutenants were ordered to proceed against those who had broken the law, but in Somerset the deputies showed little eagerness to do so.[113] At Cambridge Alderman Newton was willing to take the oaths and declaration, but some doubted whether they were obliged to do so.[114] Some who had no problems with the oaths were reluctant to declare that the Covenant was not binding on others, as well as themselves. Newton's account of swearing the mayor in 1668 mentions the oath of allegiance, and those of a mayor and justice, but not the declarations required by the Corporation Act.[115] In August 1678, not long after the removal of several aldermen of Norwich for not being qualified according to law, the entire corporation of Cambridge formally took the oaths and made the declaration and subscription required by the Act.[116]

The extent to which corporation members had failed to qualify under the Act was revealed in 1680. In March the privy council set up a committee for the suppression of popery, whose first action was to order the attorney general to enforce the Corporation Act.[117] Letters were sent to corporations and lord lieutenants similar to those of 1668, but this time they were followed up.[118]

---

[110] *HP 1660–90*, iii. 561.   [111] PC 2/60, p. 54.   [112] *CSPD 1667–8*, 589, 611.
[113] BRO, AC/02/23a & b.   [114] Newton, *Diary*, 34.   [115] Ibid. 33.
[116] Cambs RO, Cambridge Common Day Book 8, fo. 307; Newton, *Diary*, 77. For Norwich, see Miller, 'Containing Division', 1045; the council took extensive legal soundings before reaching a decision about the Norwich aldermen: SP 29/366, fos. 258–60.
[117] *HMC Ormond*, v. 284.
[118] PC 2/68, pp. 439–40, 455, 2/69, pp. 128, 130; Dorset RO, B7/D2/1.

At Sandwich Colonel John Strode could not find any evidence that any of the jurats had taken the oaths since 1662.[119] Many of the corporation of Dorchester were past or present Nonconformists, or had earlier refused to renounce the Covenant.[120] Some towns, pressed by local magnates, confessed to one or two omissions. The mayor, town clerk, and four aldermen of Bedford were summoned before the privy council to answer allegations that they had not observed the Act. The corporation decided that two had been chosen without having taken the sacrament as the law required; their election was annulled.[121] This did not satisfy the earl of Ailesbury, who sought more than once to have the deputy recorder dismissed as 'disaffected'; it turned out that he had been wounded in the service of Charles I.[122] Canterbury corporation also turned out three members who it found to be unqualified, while the corporation of Winchelsea admitted that none of them was legally qualified, adding that they had all received the sacrament and were ready to take the oaths and declaration.[123] It was alleged that more than half of the corporation of Hereford took the oaths and sacrament only after the council's letter arrived.[124] At York the town clerk said he could not find the roll which contained the records of oaths taken in 1671–7. At Rye, where it was said that none of the members was legally qualified, the mayor initially failed to read the letter to the corporation. When the letter was eventually read, it was resolved to reply that most were qualified, which was untrue.[125]

It is likely that in some cases this was simply a case of poor record-keeping, but it seems clear that failure to observe the Act was more widespread than most were prepared to admit. It was said that at Coventry officers were allowed to receive the sacrament after their election (not before, as the law prescribed).[126] Many who, if pressed, were prepared to take the oaths and declarations preferred neither to take them themselves nor to force them on others. This may have reflected principled dislike of the oaths and declarations, reluctance to impose on their neighbours' consciences, or pragmatic awareness that rigorous enforcement would deprive the town of some of the limited number of suitable men. The investigations of 1680 also revealed other problems with the Corporation Act. There was uncertainty as to whether those removed by

---

[119] *CSPD 1679–80*, 479.   [120] Underdown, *Fire from Heaven*, 237, 239–42.
[121] PC 2/68, p. 471; Beds RO, Bedford Borough Minute Book 2, pp. 177–9, 181–2.
[122] BL, Althorp MS C4, Sir William Coventry to Halifax, 22 Apr. 1680.
[123] *CSPD 1679–80*, 438, 487, 507–8, 514.   [124] *CSPD 1680–1*, 659.
[125] WYAL, MX/R 15/27; *CSPD 1679–80*, 479, 487–8, 526. The mayor of Coventry, after checking the records, declared that the Act had been diligently observed there: Coventry RO, A79/292. This seems improbable.
[126] Hurwich, ' "Fanatick Town" ', 23.

the commissioners in 1662 were ineligible for re-election. Many, including Secretary of State Sir Leoline Jenkins, claimed that they were,[127] but there was nothing in the Act to that effect—it said only that those admitted in future were to qualify according to the Act, which many of those ejected in 1662 had already done and were prepared to do again. Moreover, as the Kentish commissioners had appreciated in 1662, and the burghmote of Canterbury in 1665, it was a question not only of office-holding, but also the ability to vote in municipal and parliamentary elections.[128] As we have seen, in some towns those removed in 1662 were disfranchised; at Rye they were readmitted to vote in a mayoral election only in 1680.[129] In June 1680 the privy council sought legal advice on the questions of whether the Act applied to freemen and members of guilds, and whether those ejected in 1662 could qualify for readmission.[130] The response cannot have been encouraging, as the crown slowly began to move towards another approach towards town corporations, 'the seminaries of all separation in church and state'.[131]

The origin of this approach can be found in an action of *quo warranto* brought against twenty-six members of the corporation of Worcester, ostensibly by the crown, but at the behest of the local Tories.[132] The twenty-six were accused of holding office contrary to law, not having renounced the Covenant, and the aim was to use this legal procedure to purge them from the corporation. The proceedings began in 1680 and the case finally came to trial in the winter of 1682–3; the jury found against the defendants, but judgement was not entered against them.[133] Long before this, in October 1681, the mayor, encouraged by Lord Windsor, had pressed the corporation to surrender the charter. The proposal met with violent opposition, but the 'honest party', who claimed to comprise the majority, drew up an instrument of surrender which was sent to the attorney general.[134] Sir Ralph Verney remarked that the proceedings against Worcester could serve as a precedent for 'all the wicked corporations that have sent ill men to Parliament'.[135] For some reason the surrender was not

---

[127] *CSPD 1680–1*, 463.

[128] *CSPD 1679–80*, 479–80; the writer added that those who did not qualify were excused from burdensome offices.

[129] *CSPD 1679–80*, 526–8.   [130] PC 2/69, p. 25.   [131] Coventry MS 6, fo. 230.

[132] Halliday, *Body*, 201, says that the *quo warranto* was brought against twenty-six members, but it seems that it was originally brought against all members, by name; the majority confessed the fact and submitted to the king, leaving the rest to defend the case: SP 29/423, no. 97.

[133] Halliday, *Body*, 201–2; Luttrell, i. 85; FSL, V.b.302, p. 17.

[134] BL, Althorp MS C1, Windsor to Halifax, 10 and 19 Oct. 1681.

[135] M636/36, Sir Ralph to Edmund Verney, 9 Jan. 1682.

acted upon—perhaps it was not in an acceptable legal form, or the crown's legal advisers feared that, if judgement were entered against the defendants, it would 'destroy' the corporation; in fact, however, forty-six members (a clear majority) would remain.[136] In the spring of 1683 Windsor (now earl of Plymouth) still favoured the original tactic, of using the action to expel the twenty-six who were not duly qualified, so that the remainder could replace them with loyal men; the existing charter and corporation would continue. This was the option favoured by the forty-six 'loyal members of the corporation'; as one of the judges remarked, 'the reformation of the common council' was the main objective of the suit.[137] One of the king's officials, however, wrote on Plymouth's letter that it would be better to move for a final judgement, followed by a voluntary surrender of the charter. Judgement was entered in May 1683 and Plymouth was elected recorder later that month.[138] He cannot have found it easy to arrange the surrender, which was not completed until December 1684; the warrant for a new charter was issued in January 1685.[139] In an eerie rerun of the passage of the Corporation Act in 1661, a procedure to purge disaffected men from municipal office was transformed into a challenge to the towns' charters and self-government—only this time it succeeded. The action to remove twenty-six members of Worcester's corporation became part of a wider movement to challenge charters, initiated by local Tories, but increasingly driven by the crown.

[136] SP 29/423, no. 95. (The summary in *CSPD 1682*, 183–4, is misleading.)
[137] SP 29/423, no. 96.
[138] *CSPD Jan.–June 1683*, 183–4; Halliday, *Body*, 202–3; Morrice MS P, p. 366; Worcs RO, X.496.5, p. 108.
[139] Worcs RO, X.496.5, pp. 123–5; SP 44/335, pp. 424–6.

8

Campaign against the Charters, 1682–1685

I. THE MAKING OF GOVERNMENT POLICY

Normally, the central government paid little attention to provincial towns (London was quite another matter). Corporations were expected to carry on government and maintain law and order. Maintaining law and order might include enforcing the laws against nonconformity, or it might not, depending on the king's current policy. The privy council dealt with cases of office refusal or disputed elections, or requests for new charters with enhanced privileges, on the advice of the crown's law officers. The council showed a fitful concern that the Corporation Act was not properly enforced, and demanded information about riots and other disorders, but its main concern was that the towns should be quiet, and there was a preference for resolving disputes amicably.[1] However, the two general elections of 1679 showed the Whigs' electoral strength in towns. The overwhelming majority of Dissenting voters, including Quakers, supported the Whigs.[2] It was also becoming apparent that town magistrates and juries often failed to prosecute and convict Dissenters for illegal meetings. The government was concerned at reports of disorders and especially anxious about the large crowds who turned out to see Monmouth, now at odds with his father and seen by the Whigs as a rival to the duke of York.[3] The council turned its attention more systematically to the ineffectiveness of the Corporation Act in the spring of 1680 and the 'committee for corporations' became permanent.[4] It does not, however, seem to have evolved any policy for dealing with corporations, other than trying to ensure that the Corporation

---

[1] Coventry MS 83, fos. 162–3; *CSPD 1679–80*, 367–8.
[2] Miller, ' "A Suffering People" ', 89 and sources cited in n. 115.
[3] Tanner MS 38, fos. 126–7; G. Groen van Prinsterer, *Archives de la Maison Orange-Nassau*, 5 vols. (The Hague, 1858–61), v. 418, 421; *HMC le Fleming*, 170.
[4] BRB 5, p. 684.

and Conventicle Acts were enforced;[5] its determination to do so can only have been strengthened by a bill in Parliament, in January 1681, to repeal the Corporation Act.[6]

In 1681 the council took no initiative to deal with town corporations, although the king added momentum to the growth of Tory loyalism in the provinces by issuing his declaration giving reasons for dissolving the Oxford Parliament. He also gave increasingly firm orders to magistrates to enforce the laws against Dissent. Some bold individuals were already suppressing meetings in 1680; the mayor of Gloucester earned himself a rebuke from the earl of Anglesey, the only member of the council who favoured toleration for Dissent.[7] The rash of loyal addresses in response to the king's declaration must have emboldened him, as must presentments like that of the Devon grand jury, which declared that corporations were nurseries of sedition and asked that the Five Mile Act should be enforced.[8] Late in 1681 the mayor of Plymouth received increasingly insistent letters ordering him to enforce the Five Mile Act and the recusancy laws.[9] The first challenge against a charter came in London, in December; the attorney general began an action of *quo warranto*, after a Whig grand jury refused to find a true bill against the earl of Shaftesbury, who was accused of treason.[10] London, however, was a special case. There was as yet no plan to extend this policy to the provinces: in January 1682 Jenkins wrote that the king intended in future charters to reserve the right to approve town clerks and recorders, which had been the normal practice since 1661.[11]

By having recourse to the law courts, the king recognized that, as one contemporary remarked, "'tis now come to a civil war, not with the sword but [with] law and if the king cannot make the judges speak for him he will be beaten out of the field'.[12] But the king could make the judges speak for him, if he chose. After some years of political appointments he had a solidly Tory bench of judges, who could be relied upon to deliver favourable judgements,

---

[5] From December 1679, the council repeatedly ordered that the provisions of the Corporation Act should be observed in elections in London: K. H. D. Haley, *The First Earl of Shaftesbury* (Oxford, 1968), 562, 582, 619.

[6] *CJ* ix. 696, 700–1.

[7] *Smith's Currant Intelligence*, 27 Apr.–1 May 1680; *CSPD 1680–1*, 45–6.

[8] Tanner MS 36, fo. 91. See also the presentments of Bristol grand juries, below, Ch. 9.

[9] *CSPD 1680–1*, 568–9, 585, 600, 606, 626.

[10] J. Miller, *Charles II* (London, 1991), 358–9.

[11] *CSPD 1682*, 6. This provision was not always included: Miller, 'Crown and Borough Charters', 69, 73. There had been a similar order in 1675: PC 2/64, p. 467.

[12] *CSPD 1680–1*, 660.

even when the crown's case was less than convincing.[13] The case of London was important, not only because of the city's great size and political importance, but because if London proved unable to defend its charter, lesser towns would have no chance of doing so. Moreover, it would not be possible to reform other corporations until London had been brought to better order.[14]

Those advising the king seem to have had little knowledge of corporations, and their record-keeping was unimpressive. The attorney general could not find a copy of Berwick's charter and Jenkins was unaware that Taunton's charter allowed for the appointment of county gentlemen as town magistrates.[15] The secretaries of state, Jenkins and Lord Conway, and the attorney general, Sir Robert Sawyer, had taken up office only recently. None had the knowledge or experience to formulate a coherent policy, and the only document which purported to set out such a policy, drawn up by Sir Francis North, was in part a restatement of existing practice and made recommendations which were not followed.[16] All three were unsure about the legal implications of challenging charters (as the judges had been in the case of the *quo warranto* against Worcester). They were also less than confident of the government's strength and preferred to proceed cautiously, observing the spirit as well as the letter of the law. They refused to proceed on the basis of unsubstantiated allegations and allowed those accused of misconduct to defend their actions. Their preference was for reconciliation rather than confrontation. At Dover, the Tories ousted from the corporation in 1680 sought a *quo warranto*, followed by a new charter, with a corporation nominated by the king. Jenkins tried to mediate between the rival factions, and the Tories in the Kentish boroughs received no firm backing from the central government until 1683.[17] In the absence of a clear strategy, ministers reacted to local initiatives, notably the surrenders of charters which began in the spring of 1682. At Thetford the mayor, John Mendham, was involved in an unsavoury struggle with other members of the corporation. Told by Jenkins that he had no legal case and that there were no grounds for bringing it before the council, and harassed by writs, Mendham

---

[13] Jenkins had doubts about the case against London's charter: W. Wynne, *Life of Sir Leoline Jenkins*, 2 vols. (London, 1724), ii. 684–5; Halliday, *Body*, 203–11.

[14] *CSPD Jan.–June 1683*, 323; Tanner MS 36, fo. 235.

[15] *CSPD Jan.–June 1683*, 12, 266.

[16] Miller, 'Crown and Borough Charters', 76–7. R. G. Pickavance, 'The English Boroughs and the King's Government: A Study of the Tory Reaction, 1681–5', D.Phil. thesis (Oxford, 1976), 134–42; Dr Pickavance sees this document as far more of a statement of royal policy than I do.

[17] C. Lee, ' "Fanatic Magistrates": Religious and Political Conflict in Three Kent Boroughs, 1680–4', *HJ* xxxv (1992), 44–8, 54–8.

determined to surrender the charter and Jenkins helped him find a way to do so. The new charter was issued in March 1682.[18] Meanwhile, Herbert Aubrey wrote to Jenkins about securing a new charter for Hereford, giving as his reason the wish for an extra fair. Jenkins explained that a new charter could be issued only after a voluntary surrender in due form, by the magistrates and chief citizens, or after judgement on an action of *quo warranto*. Later the emphasis changed, with allegations of maladministration against the corporation; more than half the members were said not to have qualified under the Corporation Act.[19] An action of *quo warranto* was started and the 'loyal' part of the corporation agreed to a surrender. As this was not seen as good in law, the mayor obtained a new form of surrender, which was agreed by the corporation; a new charter was issued, in which the marquis of Worcester was named as the city's recorder. The charter also named the other members of the corporation, which now became predominantly Tory; the king reserved the power to approve the nomination of aldermen.[20]

The initiative for the surrenders of old charters, and the granting of new, clearly came from the local Tories; they were encouraged by a great peer (Worcester) at Hereford, but at Thetford seem to have acted on their own. In response to their requests, Jenkins and Sawyer began to work out the procedures necessary to make the surrenders good in law; the *quo warranto* against London offered an additional weapon should the corporation prove uncooperative. Only gradually did ministers come to see that new charters could be used, not only to remove Whig members, by naming the first members of the corporation, but also to give the king power to remove members whose conduct proved unsatisfactory in future, as in the Gloucester charter of 1672. The earl of Yarmouth persuaded Norwich to petition for such a clause and expressed the hope that other corporations would do the same.[21] Meanwhile, the publicity given to the surrenders and the new charters encouraged other towns and other peers to follow suit. At this stage the king was content to respond to local initiatives. He and his ministers preferred at least the appearance of a voluntary surrender, which avoided the stigma of duress and was likely to

---

[18] Halliday, *Body*, 212–14.

[19] *CSPD 1680–1*, 327–8, 659. Worcester was also active in securing new charters at Bristol, Leominster, and Malmesbury: below, Ch. 9; *CSPD 1682*, 219, *1684–5*, 151–2.

[20] *CSPD 1682*, 73, 109; SP 44/66, pp. 74–5; Halliday, *Body*, 215; Pickavance, 'English Boroughs', 157–9.

[21] BL Add MS 27448, fos. 61, 147. This was not the first suggestion of a removal clause: there was one in the Maidstone charter, issued the day before Yarmouth's letter. However, it applied only to the mayor, recorder, town clerk, and JPs; aldermen and common councillors could be removed, for misconduct, by the corporation: W. R. James, *Charters and Other Documents Relating to Maidstone* (London, 1825), 137, 149. The charter had been surrendered six months before: Luttrell, i. 181.

leave less lasting bitterness. He refrained from commanding corporations to surrender, not wishing to risk a refusal. He was not unhappy for local Tories to bring pressure to bear, or for the attorney general to bring actions of *quo warranto*. After the Rye House Plot, the tempo of confiscations quickened and it continued to accelerate during 1684.[22] By this time some of the king's servants, particularly the earl of Bath (in Devon and Cornwall) and Judge Jeffreys, were becoming notably more proactive in seeking surrenders and any pretence of voluntary surrender disappeared.[23]

II. THE PROCESS OF SURRENDER

While the king wanted at least the appearance of voluntary surrender, persuasion played a part in the process, sometimes mixed with intimidation or sharp practice. Yarmouth held out to Norwich corporation the hope of additional privileges in a new charter.[24] Sometimes the negotiations for surrender were conducted by a peer, at other times by local gentlemen or members of the corporation. At Norwich Yarmouth tried to keep out of the spotlight, relying on his agents in the city, but at last he was forced to come in person to push through the surrender.[25] At Bristol, Worcester (created duke of Beaufort late in 1682) left it to the bishop and Sir John Knight II to organize the surrender.[26] In many corporations, even moderate and loyal members were reluctant to agree to a surrender: some feared the wrath of their fellow townsmen, others believed that, having sworn to uphold the town's privileges, they could not surrender them without breaking their oaths. Some feared that surrendering might put the town's properties at risk, and there were learned arguments about the precise legal implications of surrender. Some worried that there might be a point at which government ceased in the town.[27] In many towns those who favoured surrender were a minority on the corporation or among the citizens, but not everywhere. At Norwich there was more support for surrender among the common councillors and ordinary townspeople than there was among the aldermen; the same seems to have been true in Plymouth.[28] A number of examples will show how complex and various the process of negotiation might be.

---

[22] Halliday, *Body*, 351. [23] R. North, *Examen* (London, 1740), 625–6.
[24] BL, Add MS 27448, fo. 61. [25] Miller, 'Containing Division'. 1046.
[26] See below, Ch. 9.
[27] *CSPD 1683–4*, 7; Mullett, '"Deprived of our Former Place"', 21–2.
[28] Miller, 'Containing Division', 1046; *HMC 9th Report*, part 1, 277.

At Leicester the dominant local peer, the earl of Huntingdon, had flirted with Whiggism during the Exclusion Crisis. His political rehabilitation began in 1681, when he kissed the king's hand.[29] He was made a privy councillor in 1683 and lord lieutenant in 1684, but needed to procure the surrender to demonstrate both his loyalty and his local power. Like Yarmouth at Norwich, he did not want a confrontation and could not risk a rebuff: he was well aware of the opposition to surrender within the corporation. On the other hand, the corporation knew that other towns were surrendering, and there was always the possibility of a *quo warranto*. Moreover, some county magistrates saw this as an opportunity to strengthen their jurisdiction in the town. Huntingdon's leading agent was Dr John Gery, his chaplain, who wooed and wined the members of the corporation (and their wives).[30] Assured by Gery and others that it was 'his majesty's express pleasure' that they surrender, the corporation voted 45 to 4 to surrender, but then voted 44 to 5 to delay sealing the surrender until two weeks after Michaelmas, giving time to elect and swear in a new mayor.[31] If Gery knew about this second vote, he did not tell Huntingdon until after the new mayor had been elected.[32] It is possible that the sealing of the surrender was delayed in the vain hope that the king might not insist on it after all.

On 25 September a committee was appointed to consider possible changes to the charter; it resolved to request that the parliamentary franchise be restricted to the corporation.[33] Huntingdon, too, had changes that he wished to make. He hoped to reduce the corporation by half, to twelve aldermen and twenty-four common councillors, to add some county JPs to the town magistrates, and to be appointed recorder.[34] The corporation was opposed to the first, and vehemently against involving county justices in the town's affairs, fearing that 'country gentlemen having little kindness for tradesmen may come and affront their mayor and oppose them in all they do'.[35] Huntingdon dropped the idea, and attention switched to the members of the new corporation. Gery advised him to remove relatively few, as the king would reserve the right to remove any who misbehaved in future. The issue was complicated by the fact that one of the most 'obnoxious' aldermen had married a kinswoman of Huntingdon's: it would seem unfair to leave him in and put out others, who were less 'obnoxious'.[36] In the event five aldermen were removed, three of

---

[29] Luttrell, i. 138.   [30] Greaves, 'Earl of Huntingdon', 376–8.

[31] Ibid. 377–9; LHP 35, no. 131.   [32] Greaves, 'Earl of Huntingdon', 381–3.

[33] LHB 3, p. 911; *RBL*, iv. 560.   [34] Greaves, 'Earl of Huntingdon', 384, 387–8.

[35] Ibid. 389.   [36] *RBL*, iv. 561; Greaves, 'Earl of Huntingdon', 387, 389–91.

whom had voted against surrendering the charter.[37] Huntingdon was made recorder. The common council was reduced from forty-eight to thirty-six, but the number of aldermen remained at twenty-four. The king reserved the power to remove any member of the corporation. Perhaps the most surprising provision was the confirmation of the parliamentary franchise established in 1661, with all who paid scot and lot having the right to vote.[38] Although Huntingdon had secured the surrender, it had taken a long time and the new charter was not as he would have wished.

Coventry had returned anti-court candidates in all three elections of 1679–81. At the end of 1681 the recorder died. The city's freemen wanted as his replacement Lord Brooke, son of a militant Parliamentarian, who had voted for exclusion.[39] The king refused to approve the election, but the freemen were adamant and eventually he acquiesced.[40] Brooke was thus appointed to a responsible position in a volatile city, while being out of favour at court. The city's volatility was shown in September, when Monmouth received an effusive welcome and 'the rabble' broke the windows of Nathaniel Harryman, one of the few Tory aldermen, because he refused to light a bonfire.[41] Brooke may have persuaded the corporation of its vulnerability: in February 1683 it entertained many of the county gentry to a sumptuous feast, at which healths were drunk to the royal family. The corporation ordered a portrait of the duke of York and presented a loyal address after the Rye House Plot, blaming it on the Dissenters; earlier loyal addresses had been signed only by the deputy lieutenants and freeholders.[42] The laws against Dissenters were enforced for the first, and only, time.[43]

Given Coventry's record, such gestures could not stave off the threat to its charter. In August 1683 the mayor told the council that he had been told that the king had said that if Coventry did not surrender, but stood out like London, he had a *quo warranto* ready and, if judgement was given in his favour, he would disfranchise the city. The council resolved to petition for a

[37] LHB 3, pp. 908, 921; Greaves, 'Earl of Huntingdon', 378 gives the names of four 'aldermen' who voted against, but one of them (Harris) was not an alderman.

[38] *RBL*, iv. 561, 563–79.   [39] *HP 1660–90*, ii. 438–9.

[40] *CSPD 1682*, 207, 244, 271–2, 284.

[41] 'Oates's Plot', newsletter, 28 Sept. 1682; *HMC 3rd Report*, 95; Coventry RO, Acc 2/5, fo. 53. For disorders when Monmouth visited Stafford and Chester, see *CSPD 1682*, 413, 427–8; Miller, *After the Civil Wars*, 274–5.

[42] *Loyal Protestant*, 6 Mar. 1683; *HP 1660–90*, i. 430; Coventry RO, A14(b), fo. 293; Hurwich, ' "Fanatick Town" ', 24–5.

[43] Hurwich, ' "Fanatick Town" ', 26.

new charter, as a lesser evil than having the old one confiscated: the petition complained that the city had been misrepresented. The king welcomed the offer of surrender and Brooke assured the mayor that they had taken the wisest course.[44] The decision to surrender was, however, only the beginning of a negotiation in which Brooke had the delicate task of limiting the damage to the city's autonomy and the changes to the membership of the corporation. In September he wrote that the citizens were coming to see that they had been misled by talk of the city losing its ancient rights; they now saw that the new charter would merely reduce its governors to a proper subjection to the king.[45] As the formal process of surrender followed its usual tortuous course, Brooke persuaded the king that it would be counter-productive to put 'foreigners' into the corporation and that it would be best to make as few changes as possible.[46] The warrant for the new charter contained the usual removal clause; its one novel feature was the provision that no one should be free of any company who would not take the oaths of allegiance and supremacy.[47]

One of the resident gentry complained that there were too few changes to the corporation, saying that most members had courted Monmouth when he came to the city.[48] Brooke produced a measured response, admitting that he was less confident of the citizens than he could wish, but advising the king not to take notice of things that were not exactly as he would like. Some over-zealous members of the loyal party had done more to create divisions than any on the other side. Some who might be better out of the corporation would make less trouble if left in, under 'good behaviour', as they wielded considerable influence over the 'poorer sort'. If they could be persuaded to choose honest country gentlemen instead of their previous MPs, they would do the king a great service. His main concern, therefore, was to win them over one by one, by making them see that it would be in their interest to change their ways.[49] Such arguments could easily be represented as disingenuous or 'trimming' by hard-line Tories. The privy council ordered the removal of seven members of the corporation and 'the grand jury was altered from citizens to gentlemen'.[50]

---

[44] Coventry RO, A14(b), fo. 294.   [45] BL, Add MS 41803, fo. 33.

[46] Ibid. 39, 53. Some of those put into Warwick corporation, on Brooke's recommendation, had earlier been removed for refusing the oaths: P. Styles, 'The Corporation of Warwick, 1660–1835', *Transactions of the Birmingham Archaeological Society*, lix (1938), 36.

[47] SP 44/335, pp. 68–9.   [48] BL, Add MS 41803, fos. 45–6, 50–2; *CSPD 1683–4*, 158.

[49] BL, Add MS 41803, fo. 53 (a large extract is printed in *HP 1660–90*, i. 430).

[50] Coventry RO, Acc 2/5, fo. 54; *CSPD 1684–5*, 48. See also Hurwich, ' "Fanatick Town" ', 25–6.

Huntingdon and Brooke had great personal influence within their towns. Sir John Reresby, as governor of York, had a more difficult task. He was a Yorkshireman, but hardly a major county figure, and there was a history of friction between corporation and garrison. The king had been very displeased by the city's failure to welcome his brother with due respect in 1679. He asked the attorney general whether the city's rulers 'have made any such slips as might forfeit their charter or any other way bring them under the power of the laws'.[51] The magistrates were reported to be very remiss in punishing conventicles.[52] When Reresby became governor he found the loyal party (the gentry, clergy, employees of the Church, militia officers, and soldiers) much less numerous than the 'factious' (the mayor, all but two of aldermen, and most of the common council and citizens). Many sided with the factious because otherwise their businesses would suffer. Dominant though they were within the city, the factious feared losing the charter, because they had not scrupulously observed its terms and had tolerated conventicles.[53] Reresby saw it as his task to manage the city on the king's behalf. As his income from office was important to him, he needed to maintain the king's favour, while local rivals tried to undermine him. He also wished to be respected by the citizens and gentry . He therefore tried to act as a broker between the crown and the city, so far as his personal interests allowed.

To act as a broker, Reresby needed to become familiar with the civic leaders, but some wanted nothing to do with him. He told Alderman Ramsden of the king's anger at the city's behaviour, and asked what it would offer, short of surrendering the charter, to gain the king's pardon. Ramsden acknowledged that the city had made mistakes and replied that they were ready to pass over Edward Thompson, the leading Whig alderman, whose turn it was to be lord mayor next year, if the king commanded it in writing. They would also lay aside Buckingham, the high steward, electing the duke of York in his stead, and they would choose better MPs. Reresby passed this on to Lord Halifax, one of the king's leading ministers and another Yorkshireman. He liked the idea of laying Thompson aside, but said that the king was reluctant to write unless he was certain that he would be obeyed. He also thought it would not be appropriate to have the duke of York as steward.[54] Edward Thompson was elected

---

[51] Reresby, 191; *HMC Ormond*, v. 288.   [52] WYAL, MX/R 18/93, 124.

[53] Reresby, 579–81; WYAL, MX/R 20/14. David Scott suggests that Reresby exaggerated the Whiggism of the citizens: only three were active Whigs and only two attended conventicles; but there were only two Tories. He thinks much of the partisanship on both sides came from the intervention of the county gentry: Scott, 'York', 317–22.

[54] Reresby, 283–5.

lord mayor in February; he refused to have any dealings with Reresby.[55] Faced with threats to their charter, gates, and walls, and an order from the Exchequer to collect old fee-farm rents worth thousands of pounds, the council decided to choose as their steward the young duke of Richmond, son of the duchess of Portsmouth. (They had written to Buckingham, not for the first time, asking him to resign, and had received no reply.) They hoped that their new steward's 'blessed mother' would save them from *quo warrantos*, fee-farm rents, and all other ills.[56] Portsmouth took this gesture very kindly.[57] Her acceptance of the stewardship for Richmond added to the confidence of the factious; there was no more talk of negotiation, until the Rye House Plot. The lord mayor—at the king's command—invited Reresby to dine, for the first time.[58] In November Thompson was summoned before the privy council, after a speech in which he said that someone who had had his arms seized might be as honest as the 'whiffling officers' who took them.[59] The king asked Reresby (in London) if there were sufficient grounds for a *quo warranto*. When Thompson came to London, he asked Reresby to testify that he had been diligent in investigating the Rye House Plot. Reresby agreed to do so, justified the lord mayor's conduct as far as he could, and introduced him to Halifax.[60] The privy council ordered that Thompson be prosecuted for seditious libel, but he returned to York claiming that he had come off with flying colours; he said that he had offered to be tried by the known laws of the land—'he depends much on a York jury'.[61]

Some local Tories, led by Sir Thomas Slingsby, tried to show that they were more diligent than Reresby and sent up charges against the city.[62] The long-expected *quo warranto* arrived in March 1684. Some aldermen and most of the common council wished to surrender, but most of the aldermen, and a handful of the common council, argued that they should defend the charter. As a majority of both aldermen and councillors was needed to surrender or

---

[55] Reresby, 303; WYAL, MX/R 17/36 (undated, but from April 1683).

[56] WYAL, MX/R 21/26–7; BL, Althorp MS C18, fo. 59; Carte MS 216, fo. 319: Scott, 'York', 327–8.

[57] Reresby, 301–2.   [58] Ibid. 307.

[59] WYAL, MX/R 24/13, 25/6; Morrice MS P, p. 401. For other charges against him, see *CSPD 1683–4*, 118–19.

[60] Reresby, 320–1. Thompson had complained to Jenkins about mountebanks and players, whom he saw as corrupting the youth of the city: *CSPD 1683–4*, 20. He had also tried to stop the players performing in assize week: WYAL, MX/R 21/27.

[61] PC 2/70, p. 86; WYAL, MX/R 24/21, 25/14. Thompson claimed that the charges against him were malicious and in fact nobody appeared to make them good: *CSPD 1683–4*, 103, *1684–5*, 116–17.

[62] Reresby, 329–30; WYAL, MX/R 25/7.

defend, it seemed likely that nothing would be done; if so, the case would go by default.[63] Reresby advised the corporation to surrender, but the common council urged the aldermen to petition the king to renew the charter. The aldermen believed that, if the city appeared, they could appeal to the king's justice and mercy.[64]

As the charter seemed likely to fall, Reresby and Slingsby drew up a list of citizens suitable for appointment to office, together with six gentlemen of the county to be added to the city magistrates.[65] On 29 May a commission was drawn up, like that for London, appointing a lord mayor, aldermen, and other officials to hold office during the king's pleasure.[66] Two days later the attorney general moved for judgement against the charter, which was not announced until 15 July; the commission that had been prepared earlier was now issued.[67] However, the formal seizure of the city's liberties was delayed until Jeffreys arrived. The lord mayor and aldermen 'subtly' submitted to him, offering to surrender; Jeffreys agreed to continue the city's privileges until he had discussed the matter with the king. The Slingsby party was bitterly disappointed; Reresby avoided being drawn in, 'knowing that to appear for or against the town was equally dangerous'; he thought the proceedings against the city were motivated more by private revenge (the resentment of the duke of York) than the public good.[68] In September Jeffreys wrote that the king expected corporations in the northern circuit to surrender their charters. The surrender was agreed, and referred to the attorney general, but further progress was undermined by divisions among the aldermen, some of whom wanted to keep the city's constitution as it was, while others wanted to change it. In January 1685 another *quo warranto* was launched against the charter.[69] A warrant for a new charter was drawn up in February but there were further delays because of a struggle for power between Reresby and Slingsby. The new charter was not issued until July and the special commission remained in force until then.[70]

These three cases—and there were many more—showed that there was scope for delay and negotiation, but that in time the pressure on corporations mounted and eventually most surrendered because the alternative—judgement entered on a *quo warranto*, followed by forfeiture—was worse; at least surrender left a

[63] WYAL, MX/R 24/30, 25/16, 26/18, 22; Reresby, 334; Scott, 'York', 333–7.
[64] WYAL, MX/R 26/22.   [65] Reresby, 336.   [66] SP 44/70, p. 28.
[67] *CSPD 1684–5*, 38–9, 96; *HMC Ormond*, vii. 244.   [68] Reresby, 321, 342–3.
[69] WYAL, MX/R 28/17, 28/30; *CSPD 1684–5*, 209; Reresby, 349.
[70] *CSPD 1685*, no. 88; Reresby, 363, 381, 389; *HMC House of Lords 1689–90*, 299; Halliday, *Body*, 228.

little room for bargaining. Some towns, however, showed little inclination to bargain. The corporation of Southampton, in dire financial straits, made no difficulty about surrendering the charter and its county status. It was ready to submit to any changes asked of it: its only concern was that it was too impoverished to afford the fees for a new charter. The king thought that if it surrendered its county status, all its other liberties could be restored gratis, if it really could not afford the half fees paid by other poor corporations. Jenkins was ready to waive his fees, but could not expect his clerks to do the same.[71] In December 1683 the corporation debated whether to surrender at once or wait for a *quo warranto*. It unanimously opted for the former, as that was what the king wanted, and thanked the king for his generous offer concerning the fees.[72] But no charter materialized and in July 1684 the mayor and corporation petitioned for one: Secretary Godolphin replied that the king had repeated his assurance that on surrendering the charter (in due form) and giving up county status, its privileges would be restored and its charter renewed gratis.[73] In November the mayor and his brethren waited on the king with the surrender, which was referred to the attorney general.[74] But the town did not receive a new charter until September 1688.[75]

III. THE CONTENTS OF THE NEW CHARTERS

After some uncertainty in the early charters of 1682, a fairly standard format emerged. Most contained a list of the first members of the corporation, which might, or might not, involve changes of personnel, and clauses reserving to the king the right to approve recorders and town clerks (as before) and the power to remove any member of the corporation. The main aim was to install reliable members, as the Corporation Act commissioners had done, and to ensure that reliable members would be chosen in future, which the Corporation Act had failed to do. The charters were not intended to limit the powers of the corporation and some granted new powers and privileges. Some reduced the size of the corporation, as at Leicester or Bristol; many installed leading peers or county gentlemen in civic offices (especially those of recorder and high steward), enabling county landowners to exercise power in the town. A few,

---

[71] *CSPD 1683–4*, 100, 105–7.
[72] Southampton RO, SC 1/9, fos. 46–8; *CSPD 1683–4*, 151.
[73] BL, Add MS 41803, fos. 89, 93.   [74] *CSPD 1684–5*, 205.
[75] Halliday, *Body*, 352.

as at Buckingham and Sandwich, empowered some or all of the county JPs to act within the borough.[76] The new charter for Calne, issued in April 1685, stipulated that the majority of the burgesses should be gentlemen from outside the borough.[77] Another way of achieving the same end was by a commission of association, joining outside JPs to those of the corporation, as at Berwick. In the cases of Southampton and Poole, both counties in themselves, no new charters were issued after surrender, so they came under the jurisdiction of the county JPs.[78] Poole was said to have prided itself on its 'true Protestant juries'. After it surrendered its charter, it was said that it would be impossible to find enough honest men to govern the town.[79] Some fifteen charters altered the parliamentary franchise, usually confining the vote to the corporation. At Leicester and Derby, proposals to restrict the franchise were ignored, as was a request for a wider franchise at Wallingford.[80] In several towns charters imposed new religious tests. At Sandwich the charter laid down that all those admitted as freemen had to have taken the oaths and received the sacrament 'as the Act of Parliament directs'.[81] Dover's charter required the same, adding the provision that they must have been baptized in the Church of England; any freeman who had renounced his baptism, or been rebaptized, or excommunicated, was to be ineligible to vote, unless he had been reconciled to the Church.[82] Some requests for change were more idiosyncratic. Okehampton asked for, and was granted, the power to establish a workhouse.[83] Bridgwater asked to be allowed to create an artillery company of thirty men, to enable the corporation to suppress 'the faction'. The attorney general did not think it appropriate to use the charter for this. It also asked that the bishop of Bath and Wells and Lord Stawell be empowered to remove factious members of the common council, on the complaint of the majority; the attorney general thought it better that the king should do it.[84] A petition from Wells asked that the king should reserve to himself the power to nominate the recorder and town clerk; Sawyer thought it would be sufficient for the king to nominate

---

[76] SP 44/66, pp. 320–2, 342–4; EKRO, Sa/AI 3, fo. 10.

[77] *CSPD 1685*, no. 535. At Bewdley seven out of the fifteen capital burgesses were landed gentry: Styles, *Studies*, 56–7. The new common council of Chichester included three peers, five knights, ten esquires, and two others: SP 44/70, pp. 85–6.

[78] Miller, 'Crown and Borough Charters', 81; P. Halliday, ' "A Clashing of Jurisdictions": Commissions of Association in Restoration Corporations', *HJ* xli (1998), 449–52.

[79] *CSPD July–Sept. 1683*, 431–2, *1683–4*, 10, 235–6; J. Sydenham, *History of the Town and County of Poole* (Poole, 1839), 203–8.

[80] Miller, 'Crown and Borough Charters', 82–3.   [81] EKRO, Sa/AI 3, fos. 14–15.

[82] SP 44/335, p. 137.   [83] *CSPD July–Sept. 1683*, 424, *1683–4*, 17; SP 44/66, pp. 274–5.

[84] SP 44/66, pp. 293–6; *CSPD 1683–4*, 93–4.

the first recorder, but after that to leave the choice to the corporation, with the king reserving the power of removal.[85]

The drafting of new charters gave local interests a chance to assert, or reassert, their claims to act within the borough. County landowners and JPs sought the power to sit alongside the town magistrates, as did some bishops; at Wells the bishop and his chancellor were both to be JPs.[86] Cathedral clergy sought to emancipate themselves from the town's jurisdiction. At Oxford the university saw the city's plight as offering an opportunity to extend its privileges. The city was especially vulnerable because it had chosen a town clerk, Edward Prince, in 1681, after a tumultuous election. The king had refused to approve the election, but Prince had acted anyway. The city tried to find some expedient short of surrender that would satisfy the king, but Jenkins (a former principal of Jesus College) insisted that only a full surrender would do.[87] The earl of Abingdon, who had been trying to persuade the city council to submit, now sought to sugar the pill by promising that the city would have its old liberties confirmed by a charter, and new ones added; even so, it took him several months to secure the surrender, which was accompanied by a petition for new privileges.[88] The university, led by Bishop Fell, was determined that none should be granted. Some thought the request to increase the number of alderman from five to eight was designed to increase the number of city justices, so that they would outnumber those of the university. Proposals for an annual horse fair and weekly cattle market were met with claims that this would add to the number of occasions when students might be debauched.[89] The university opposed the proposal that the parish of St Clement's should be brought within the juris-diction of the city, saying it would impose a 'heavy yoke' on the inhabitants.[90] Above all, the university wanted a proviso guaranteeing all its privileges, especially that of the night watch.[91] The bishop cited a recent riot as showing the need to entrust the night watch to the university, which deserved better of the king than the city did.[92] This was an argument which the king, and the attorney general, largely accepted.[93] Abingdon, who had promised the city new privileges, found it impossible to obtain them. He complained that the univer-sity's demands were unreasonable.[94] He managed to thwart the bishop's proposal that all those elected to office in the city should have to secure a certificate from

---

[85] SP 29/434, nos. 36I, 37.   [86] Ibid. no. 36I.   [87] BL, Stowe MS 746, fos. 71–4.
[88] *CSPD 1683–4*, 202–3.   [89] Ibid. 243, 309–11.   [90] Ibid. 203, 243, 248.
[91] *CSPD July–Sept. 1683*, 312, 381, *1683–4*, 205, 220, 309; BL, Stowe MS 746, fos. 73–4.
[92] *CSPD 1684–5*, 64–5, 67.   [93] *CSPD 1683–4*, 220, 309.
[94] Ibid. 218, *1684–5*, 12–13, 64.

the chancellor or vice chancellor that they were well affected to the government; this would have given the university a veto over elections to office.[95] The warrant for the new charter, as issued in September 1684, was for a simple confirmation, adding only the usual removal clause.[96] The university failed to secure a stronger statement of its right to the night watch and other privileges. This represented a small success for Abingdon, and the city; by July 1684 the city was ready to drop all of its other requests, if only there could be no explicit reference in the charter to the university's claim to the night watch.[97]

Not all corporations were prepared to negotiate. Bath repeatedly ignored orders to remove 'disaffected' members.[98] The corporation did not surrender the charter for another eighteen months.[99] At Nottingham, after a bitterly contested surrender, there were two rival corporations, each claiming to be legitimate.[100] William Sacheverell, a leading Whig MP, launched a legal action against the new charter, and against the mayor for surrendering the old; the only result of his efforts was that he and eighteen others were convicted of riot in 1684.[101] The most stubborn resistance came from Berwick. The corporation was threatened with a *quo warranto* in April 1681, for failing to suppress conventicles.[102] Early in 1683 the king considered issuing a commission of association, but Sawyer could not find the charter.[103] In January 1684 the king ordered a *quo warranto* and asked the duke of Newcastle, lord lieutenant of Northumberland, to ask the neighbouring gentlemen to provide evidence of infractions of the charter; by the end of February, Jenkins thought they had sufficient, consisting mainly of failures to enforce the laws against Dissent.[104] The mayor and bailiffs kept the writ secret while they took legal advice, which was that if they stood trial they would lose. When a second writ was issued, at first the corporation resolved to contest it, but in November it agreed by a narrow margin to surrender. The mayor asked the duke of Newcastle to intercede with the king on the town's behalf; he refused, because the people were

[95] *CSPD July–Sept. 1683*, 312, 381–2.   [96] SP 44/335, pp. 195–6.
[97] BL, Stowe MS 746, fo. 74; *CSPD 1684–5*, 95–6.
[98] *CSPD Jan.–June 1683*, 60, 191, 235; Bath RO, Corporation Book 1649–84, pp. 862, 868, 871, 877, 879, 886.
[99] Bath RO, Corporation Book 1649–84, p. 904; SP 44/335, pp. 370–2; Bath RO, P. R. James, 'The Charters of the City of Bath' (typescript), Part 1, pp. 178–89.
[100] Halliday, *Body*, 224–6.   [101] Morrice MS P, pp. 354–6, 367; Luttrell, i. 307, 310.
[102] *CSPD 1680–1*, 238, 239; *HMC Ormond*, vi. 34–5.
[103] *CSPD Jan.–June 1683*, 12, 355.
[104] *CSPD 1683–4*, 215, 254–5, 292. For similar charges against Ipswich corporation, see ibid. 291–2.

so disaffected.[105] In February 1685 the king issued a commission of association for the town, and no new charter was issued until September 1686.[106]

IV. CRUSHING THE WHIGS

The cases of York and Berwick show that resistance to the royal will might buy time, but it was ultimately futile. If they attempted to negotiate with the king, with or without noble mediators, corporations were in a weak position. They had almost always done something which hostile lawyers could interpret as breaching their charter. They tried to create space for manoeuvre by conciliatory gestures. Oxford council tried to avoid actions which might give grounds for challenging the charter—it did all that the university required of it on St Scholastica's Day—but the crown's law officers began to collect arguments anyway. These included infringements of regulations concerning markets and fairs; misappropriation of funds; packing juries and finding verdicts contrary to the evidence; and the city's conduct over the town clerkship.[107] The council made a special effort to welcome the duke of York when he visited the city.[108] The best corporations could hope for was damage limitation. The king already had a solidly Tory bench of judges, so could be confident of winning cases in the central law courts.[109] He appointed Tory sheriffs in the counties, who empanelled Tory juries. The only gaps in the king's control of the legal system were the boroughs, especially those which were counties in themselves.[110] Those gaps were gradually closed, as boroughs surrendered and were given new charters which did not (usually) destroy their jurisdictional privileges but, as in the counties, gave the king the power to ensure that their magistrates were 'loyal'. Until they surrendered and received their new charters, town juries could still defy the king. Edward Thompson hoped for protection from a York jury. The one Oxford rioter who pleaded not guilty was acquitted, to a great hum from the townsmen.[111]

Attempts to use the law to resist royal pressure were probably counter-productive in the long run, especially when corporations used high-profile

---

[105] *CSPD 1684–5*, 141, 212, 219, 231; BL, Add MS 41803, fo. 99. Newcastle was prepared to intercede for the 'loyal party' in the town: BL, Althorp MS C1, Newcastle to Halifax, 14 Jan. 1685.
[106] Halliday, *Body*, 237–8, 352.   [107] Prideaux, 128; Wood, iii. 4; *CSPD 1682*, 279.
[108] Bodl, MS Rawl Letters 48, fo. 37; Wood, iii. 47–8.
[109] However, refractory corporations like Rye were securing favourable verdicts from King's Bench as late as 1683: Halliday, *Body*, 132–5.
[110] Luttrell, i. 199.
[111] WYAL, MX/R 25/14; *CSPD Jan.–June 1683*, 181, *1683–4*, 303–4.

Whig lawyers, like William Williams, Sir William Jones, and Sir Francis Winnington.[112] The corporations won small tactical victories, which were often pyrrhic, because there was never any real doubt that the king would win the war. His judges could declare charters forfeit and he could then grant new charters, or not, as he chose. The courts could also be used to pursue individual Whigs. Trials for treason were always heavily weighted against the accused, as Lord Russell and Algernon Sidney found to their cost. Individual Tory peers brought actions of *scandalum magnatum* against those they claimed had defamed them. After the Rye House Plot, Tory lord lieutenants and their deputies searched the houses of Whigs, looking for arms. At Oxford the earl of Abingdon searched the houses of William Wright and Brome Whorwood. Allegedly seditious documents were found in Wright's house; he was bound to good behaviour and threatened with prosecution for possessing and publishing scandalous papers, unless he encouraged his fellow councillors to surrender their charter. This he did, but he was indicted anyway. He was allowed bail, but could not find the necessary sureties and remained in gaol. In October 1684 he wrote to Abingdon renouncing any part in the affairs of Oxford—he had resigned the post of alderman, and the freedom—and asked only that the proceedings against him should be stopped, which was done.[113]

If the Whigs found it impossible to defend themselves using the law, forcible resistance was not an alternative. The king installed Tory lord lieutenants and deputies, who could be relied on to suppress any active resistance. He also had an army of nearly 10,000 men and could call on the support of the army in Ireland, and the Scottish militia, in case of need.[114] The crown had tried to gain a near-monopoly of weapons at the Restoration, although judging by the numerous reports of guns being fired in civic celebrations it cannot have been entirely successful. The searches for arms after the Rye House Plot further reduced the number of weapons in private hands.[115] Apart from disarming the

---

[112] Prideaux, 85, 99, 104; *CSPD 1683–4*, 303–4; Halliday, *Body*, 138–9 and *passim*.

[113] *CSPD Jan.–June 1683*, 353, *July–Sept. 1683*, 161–2, 318, *1683–4*, 392, *1684–5*, 181–2, 186, 196; Morrice MS P, p. 430; Luttrell, i. 305; Wood, iii. 93–4; *OCA*, iii. 164, 167. Whorwood was also prosecuted, but died soon afterwards: *CSPD July–Sept. 1683*, 370; Wood, iii. 94. Bishop Fell argued that Wright could always be reinstated by being elected to a bailiff's or chamberlain's place: *CSPD 1684–5*, 141.

[114] C. Walton, *History of the British Standing Army 1660 to 1700* (London, 1894), 496; NUL, PwA 2080.

[115] J. Malcolm. 'Charles II and the Reconstruction of Royal Power', *HJ* xxxv (1992), 319–22. There is a list of weapons seized after the Rye House Plot in TNA, WO 55/1761. I am grateful to Peter Lefevre for this reference.

disaffected and breaking up conventicles,[116] the militia was used for carefully staged shows of force. During Beaufort's 'progress' around Wales in 1684, he mustered the militia in every town he passed through.[117] Against such over-whelming military force, occasional Whig riots were no more than futile (and counter-productive) gestures.[118]

The impossibility of contending with royal power was seen most strikingly in the Whig stronghold of Taunton. The Dissenters there remained un-molested until 1683. There were no county JPs living nearby and the provision for the king to appoint six county justices to serve in the town had fallen into disuse.[119] The initiative in enforcing the laws came from the mayor, Stephen Timewell, who on Easter Sunday, 1683, disturbed the great conventicle in the town, consisting of 2,000 people. On 11 May, the anniversary of lifting the Royalist siege, he and his brethren walked the streets. There was no disturbance until after 5 p.m., when a crowd of more than 1,000 gathered in the high street, clapping and shouting. Timewell tried in vain to arrest some of them and ordered the rest to depart; the crowd responded with blows and stones and he retreated with as much dignity as he could muster.[120] Encouraged by Bishop Mew, Lord Stawell,[121] and Jenkins, on the 29th Timewell celebrated the king's birthday with bells and a bonfire, on which he burned some of the timber from the meeting house which he had recently gutted. He and 'several' loyal townsmen, together with the county nobility and gentry, drank loyal healths, accompanied by drums and trumpets.[122] Following the Rye House Plot, Stawell and the high sheriff were ordered to search the disaffected of Taunton for arms.[123] Few weapons were found, so the mayor issued a procla-mation commanding all in the town to bring in their weapons. The loyal read-ily complied, and had their arms restored; the 'fanatics' showed great reluctance and were threatened with imprisonment if they did not obey.[124] Meanwhile,

---

[116] The Dorset deputy lieutenants broke the seats and pulpits of the meeting houses at Bridport and Lyme Regis, both corporate towns: Tanner MS 34, fo. 75.

[117] M. McClain, 'The Duke of Beaufort's Tory Progress through Wales, 1684', *Welsh History Review*, xviii (1997), 592–620; T. Dineley, *The Account of the Official Progress of the First Duke of Beaufort through Wales in 1684* (London, 1888).

[118] Wood, iii. 42–3; Halliday, *Body*, 133–5; Luttrell, i. 307, 310.

[119] *CSPD July–Sept. 1683*, 212–13, *Jan.–June 1683*, 266. It was revived in the eighteenth century: Langford, *Public Life*, 442.

[120] *CSPD Jan.–June 1683*, 212, 250, 266, 272.

[121] The lord lieutenant, the earl of Winchilsea, was not resident in the county; he was replaced by the duke of Somerset, when he came of age in the summer of 1683: ibid. 384. Stawell was one of the more active deputy lieutenants.

[122] Ibid. 266, 272, 278, 286–7.   [123] Ibid. 359.

[124] *CSPD July–Sept. 1683*, 9, 19, 75–6.

the lord keeper issued a commission of association for the town (which, given the terms of the charter, was not really necessary).[125] Timewell continued pulling down the great meeting house and tendered the oath of allegiance to all over 18; by early August about 3,000 had taken it, with only about 100 still to do so. There were no meetings, public or private, in the town, although they met in increasing numbers outside; although he was no longer mayor, Timewell continued to watch and harass them. Such achievements did not come without a cost. The townspeople boycotted his shop and he had to abandon his business.[126] Stawell asked that he should be compensated for his losses by a share of the fines levied on conventiclers and that he should be continued as a JP during the king's pleasure.[127] The Dissenters continued to meet secretly and their spirits were raised by hopes of Monmouth's being reconciled to his father, or by the prospect of a Parliament.[128] But Taunton was no longer a town where laws could be ignored with impunity. One determined individual, with the backing of the county militia and the central government, had been able to reduce a large and unruly town to obedience.

---

[125] Ibid. 226.   [126] Ibid. 130, 251, 358, 415–16, *1683–4*, 23, 229.
[127] BL, Add MS 41803, fo. 71.   [128] *CSPD 1683–4*, 229–30.

9

A Factious City:
Bristol in the Reign of Charles II

In many towns, the corrosive power of religious and political division was restrained by pressures for civic unity. Bristol, however, experienced acute political divisions and severe religious persecution. In this chapter I shall ask why this was, and suggest that a sense of civic unity sometimes prevailed. I shall also consider the extent to which conflict reflected personal, rather than ideological divisions. It is striking that several leading Bristolians shifted their ideological position in the course of the reign, while retaining a considerable capacity for hating one another. We can follow these developments because the sources are particularly rich. Frequent references to Bristol in the state papers and the press show how seriously the divisions there were taken by the government and the wider public.[1]

Several reasons could be suggested to explain why Bristol was more deeply and bitterly divided than (say) Norwich. The civil war (in which the city was taken first by the Royalists, then by the Parliamentarians) had left deep scars, as had the military presence in the 1650s. Bristol had a large Dissenting population, including many Quakers. It also had a small oligarchic corporation, in which decisions could be influenced by a few individuals changing sides. As all members served for life, the balance of power could change only slowly —unless either 'party' could purge the corporation of its enemies. Politics in a confined space, involving a small number of people, can be vicious, especially when the forces are fairly equally balanced. Consider, for example, the struggles for the votes of the thirteen burgesses of Buckingham in 1679–85,[2] or the conflicts through the ages within cathedral chapters and Oxbridge colleges. But Bristol, despite its small corporation, was a large city, with a volatile and informed population. If the corporation and vestries were closed, there was

---

[1] Another major source is the Tanner MSS (Sancroft papers).

[2] Kishlansky, *Parliamentary Selection*, 201–23; *HP 1660–90*, i. 139–41.

extensive popular participation in the running of guilds and parishes, and the parliamentary electorate was large, consisting of all the freemen. From 1681, elections were often bitterly contested and political interest was sustained by the press and newsletters, which were read and discussed in taverns and coffee houses. The government was alarmed to learn of the Whig clubs, which met at the White Hart (later moving to the Horseshoe) and the Mermaid, while Tory grand juries demanded the suppression of Kimber's coffee house.[3] The Tories had the artillery company and the Society of Loyal Young Men, which held an annual feast, to which the mayor, aldermen, and loyal gentry were invited, preceded by a sermon, All wore red ribbons in their hats, with 'rex et haeredes' embroidered in silver—Tories wore red, Whigs blue or violet.[4]

The economic and social structure of Bristol exacerbated the situation. Although manufactures were important, it was primarily a trading city. Alongside its great merchants, in the Merchant Venturers' Company, were very many small independent traders, who brought in goods from North America and the Caribbean and sent them inland and to Wales and Ireland. These trades were ruthlessly competitive and led to fierce competition within the city for storage space in the streets, on the quays, and in open spaces. Bristol's merchants acquired a reputation for being uncouth, rude, and totally dedicated to the search for profit.[5] They also drank heavily. Just about every corporation or vestry meeting ended in a tavern and the corporation's bills for wine and beer were considerable. Such socializing could maintain good relations within the corporation, but sometimes drink made men quarrelsome—especially if, like Sir Robert Cann, they drank sherry morning, noon, and night.[6]

I. THE RESTORATION

There was little evidence of division in the years immediately following the Restoration. In June 1660 a group of Royalists excluded from the corporation since 1645 demanded to be reinstated. The king responded circumspectly— Hyde remarked that the petitioners 'are impatient to have all done at once, but

---

[3] I. Chauncy, *Innocence Vindicated* (1684), 3–4; *CSPD 1680–1*, 251, *1682*, 336, *July–Sept. 1683*, 165–6, 221, 250–1, 263, 303; BRO, JQS/M/6, fos. 12–13; Barry, 'Popular Culture', 68–9.

[4] *Loyal Protestant*, 2 and 4 Nov. 1682.

[5] Marcy, 'Eighteenth-Century Views of Bristol', in McGrath (ed.), *Bristol in the Eighteenth Century*, 29–30, 36–7; Latimer, i. 338.

[6] Latimer, ii. 31–2, 41; *Norths*, ii. 197.

it must be done by degrees'. However, in September the king asked that those who had been put out of the corporation for loyalty should be reinstated, and those illegally chosen in their places should be removed.[7] One of the Royalist petitioners, Henry Creswick, had just been elected mayor. He took over six months to act on the king's letter and there were no major changes in the corporation until October 1661, following a reminder. On 30 October the aldermen removed thirty-four from the council and elected sixteen replacements; others were added soon after. Their compliance owed much to the threat of a *quo warranto* against the charter.[8] Even then, of sixteen councillors 'elected', at least nine had served in the 1650s, and, of eighteen men whose reinstatement was requested in the petition of June 1660, only eight had been admitted. The Corporation Act commissioners made few changes, partly because the corporation had already been purged, but also because the mayor, Nathaniel Cale, had persuaded the king that to be forced to admit people they had not elected would infringe the city's liberties, and that they knew best the 'temper and affections' of the citizens.[9] The commissioners nominated only two aldermen, neither of whom ever sat (one was non-resident, the other very deaf). At the end of 1662 five of the twelve aldermen in office in March 1660 were still in place, as was Robert Aldworth, town clerk since 1653, despite vigorous attempts to remove him.[10] A new charter of 1664 did little more than confirm the city's existing privileges. It did contain a clause empowering the king to approve the election of the mayor, recorder, and town clerk.[11] Faced with pressure to remove the 'disaffected', the corporation had shown solidarity and had made as few changes as it could get away with. It had also tenaciously defended its privileges, notably its right to choose its own members and officers.[12]

---

[7] SP 29/14, no. 77 and annexes I–III (Hyde's comments are in annexe III); *CSPD 1660–1*, 274; BRO, 04264/6, p. 46.

[8] *CSPD 1660–1*, 569–71, *1661–2*, 107; BRO, 04264/6, pp. 45–7, 04417/2, 30 Oct. 1661; SP 29/14, no. 77(II); R. Latham, *Bristol Charters, 1509–1899*, BRS xii (1946), 3; Schilling, 'Government and Corporations', 159–63.

[9] SP, 29/52, no. 112; Latimer, i. 310–11.

[10] BRO, 04264/6, pp. 14, 83. The five were John Gonning, Miles Jackson, Joseph Balman, Arthur Farmer, and Walter Sandy. All had served as mayors, Jackson in 1649–50, the remainder between 1654 and 1659. Balman and Sandy were present on the day the thirty-four members were removed. For Aldworth, see *CSPD 1660–1*, 249, 349, 569, *1661–2*, 148, 324–5, *1663–4*, 427–8. He had been a leading figure in the militia in the 1650s, very hostile to Quakers: *History of Parliament 1640–60*, draft entry on Robert Aldworth.

[11] Latham, *Bristol Charters*, 40–1; *CSPD 1664–5*, 150.

[12] Apart from Aldworth, it also succeeded in keeping James Powell as its chamberlain, even though Alexander Gray secured a letter from the king to be admitted to the office: BRO, 04264/6, pp. 29, 54; *CSPD 1660–1*, 603. See also BRO, 04264/6, p. 23; *CSPD 1661–2*, 314.

II. PERSECUTION AND PRECEDENCE

Religious persecution was sporadic until Sir John Knight I became mayor in October 1663.[13] His zeal to suppress Dissent may have been sharpened by rumours of plotting by Dissenters, whom he constantly represented as a threat to both crown and Church. It fell mainly on Quakers and Baptists, whom Knight presumably saw as the most disaffected; no action seems to have been taken against Presbyterians, whose views were probably close to his own.[14] The Quakers claimed that he used the allegedly dangerous state of Bristol as an argument to push through the 1664 Conventicle Act, and that his experience in Bristol lay behind the provision that the first two convictions did not require juries.[15] Knight sent the two Particular Baptist pastors and one or two of their laypeople to the common gaol, Newgate, for refusing to give bonds to be of good behaviour (in other words, to promise not to meet or teach). 'Many people of quality' were outraged. The Baptists met privately, but their meetings were frequently disrupted with violence and damage to property; the persecution continued throughout 1664 and 1665.[16]

As so often, the sufferings of the Quakers were the most severe. Under Knight's predecessor, 'men of all persuasions as to religion, well persuaded among themselves, united in civil peace'.[17] Knight had allegedly complained to the government of his predecessors' moderation; now he used force to break up meetings, treated both men and women roughly, and bent the law in order to punish them. After packed juries failed to produce the desired verdicts he dispensed with them.[18] He was actively assisted by a small group of aldermen; others joined with him because they were 'foolish' or against their will.[19] The

---

[13] Latimer, i. 322–3; Hayden, *Church of Christ*, 116–17.

[14] The concentration on the Quakers and Baptists may simply reflect the fact that they kept the best records, although the Baptist account of the persecution in the 1670s (in Hayden, *Church of Christ*) also deals with the experience of the Independents and Presbyterians. Latimer, i. 325, mentions actions against the Independents. For Knight's churchmanship, see his later clashes with Bishop Carleton and the dean and chapter; on the similarities between Presbyterians and Anglicans, see J. Barry, 'The Politics of in Restoration Bristol', in *Pol of Rel*, 168.

[15] *A Relation of the Inhumane and Barbarous Sufferings of the People Called Quakers in . . . Bristol* (1665), 80. There is no hard evidence of his promotion of the conventicle bill, but he certainly was appointed to numerous committees on religious matters: P. Seaward, *The Cavalier Parliament and the Reconstruction of the Old Regime, 1661–7* (Cambridge, 1988), 328. For the Act, see *SR*, v. 517–18: a third conviction could lead to banishment.

[16] *Church of Christ*, 117–21. [17] *Inhumane and Barbarous Sufferings*, pp. 3, 32.

[18] Ibid. 47–8, 52–3, 79–80. [19] Ibid. 77, 117.

remainder wanted nothing to do with him and, although a few of the officers of the militia, which was used to break up meetings, did so enthusiastically, most were 'moderate'.[20] His cousin John Knight (also known as John Knight of the Sugar House), a man of considerable fortune and violent passions, insisted on standing surety for some Quakers, which led to angry altercations with his namesake.[21] Sir Robert Cann and Sir Robert Yeamans visited Quakers and other Dissenters in prison.[22] Cann had been moderate towards Dissenters as mayor; his sister was a Quaker and George Bishop, a leading Quaker, had married one of his kinswomen. Yeamans had several Quaker relatives.[23]

Cann and Yeamans could prove quarrelsome and difficult. Cann had initially refused to serve when elected to the common council and in 1663–4 he and Yeamans refused to attend council meetings in their gowns, for which Yeamans was ordered to be imprisoned. Instead, he went to London to complain.[24] Their enemies claimed that Cann, Yeamans, and Mr John Knight had all been active against Charles I, but this does not seem to be true.[25] Cann was also involved in a long-standing dispute about precedence. In 1662 the mayor secured a ruling from the College of Arms that aldermen should take precedence over all common councillors, even those who were knights or baronets. In the autumn of 1663 Cann, as a baronet, claimed precedence among the aldermen over Sir Henry Creswick, a knight. The recorder, Sir Robert Atkyns, ruled that, when conducting corporation business and on official civic occasions, common councillors should give precedence to aldermen and junior members to their seniors; at other times and places, the normal rules of precedence according to social rank should apply. The common council ruled accordingly, but Cann and the recently knighted Yeamans went to London to argue their case.[26] The king confirmed the common council's order and reprimanded them for withdrawing from their public duties and countenancing disaffection. They were still arguing their case a year later—some claimed, under pressure from their wives.[27]

The king had commanded Cann, Yeamans, and Mr John Knight to submit to Mayor Knight and apologize for any disrespect they had shown him; if they did so, the king wished the mayor to receive their submission with courtesy.

[20] *Inhumane and Barbarous Sufferings*, 69–70, 83.
[21] *CSPD 1663–4*, 428, 440, 478; *Inhumane and Barbarous Sufferings*, 37–8.
[22] *CSPD 1663–4*, 478, 480, 482.
[23] *Inhumane and Barbarous Sufferings*, 72, 74, 102; Barry, in *Pol of Rel*, 185 n. 35.
[24] BRO, 04264/6, pp. 59–60, 98; *CSPD 1663–4*, 477–9.
[25] *CSPD 1663–4*, 477, 482; *HP 1660–90*, ii. 5.
[26] BRO, 04264/6, pp. 65–6, 93, 96, 99; *CSPD 1663–4*, 472, 480.
[27] *CSPD 1663–4*, 484, 493, 498, 522; BRO, 04264/6, pp. 99, 103, 125–6; Latimer, i. 315.

Mayor Knight asked Yeamans, in a common council meeting, to submit, which he did. Soon afterwards, the king severely reprimanded Mr Knight for the disrespect he had shown to Sheriff Richard Streamer.[28] In 1665 the government, worried by possible disaffection during the Dutch war, saw Bristol as ripe for rebellion. Ormond was sent to organize the militia and try to compose matters. He found the city 'divided into factions and ready to break out into tumults', but was unable to heal the rifts or even say which 'party' was well affected to the king.[29] This may explain the king's order in September that the city should choose as mayor a loyal person, from among the aldermen and not the common council. This was intended to reduce the risk of a disputed election and ensure an orderly succession.[30]

Baptist and Quaker accounts of the persecution of 1663–4 suggest that it was driven by a small number of magistrates and militia officers. Most citizens were distressed or repelled by the maltreatment of their neighbours. George Bishop, a leading Quaker, told the mayor, 'we are of the city and in the city, inhabitants thereof and interwoven are we therein'.[31] Quakers were visited in gaol by eminent citizens 'as brothers in law, uncles and partners in merchandising'.[32] After 1665 persecution died away. The next brief, but sharp, outbreak came with the implementation of the second Conventicle Act in 1670. The mayor was Yeamans, formerly seen as the Dissenters' friend, but now fearful of rebellion and of being reprimanded from 'above'. The Quaker meeting houses were shut up and guarded and they had to meet in the streets; the Baptists met in lanes and highways.[33] The persecution subsided after a manoeuvre which suggested that the rifts of 1663–4 had not healed. In September 1670 Yeamans put forward as his candidate for mayor Mr John Knight, who was duly chosen, although he was only a common councillor. Sir John Knight complained to the king. The privy council ordered that the election should not stand, citing the king's letter of 1665.[34] Nevertheless, Yeamans summoned a common council and Knight was sworn. A committee drew up a letter justifying their conduct and asserting their right to choose their mayor.[35] Yeamans and Mr Knight were summoned to London and Yeamans was sent to the Tower. When the privy council examined Knight it became clear that Sir John had written a pack of lies (including that

---

[28] BRO, 04264/6, pp. 99, 101; SP 29/92, nos. 76–7. The Quakers claimed the quarrel began when Streamer reflected on Mr Knight: *Inhumane and Barbarous Sufferings*, 38. See also ibid. 13.

[29] Latimer, i. 331–2; Carte MS 47, fo. 98.   [30] *CSPD 1664–5*, 553.

[31] Besse, i. 46.   [32] *Inhumane and Barbarous Sufferings*, 33.

[33] *CSPD 1670*, 229–30, 254, 431; SP 29/278, no. 158; *Church of Christ*, 128; Besse, i. 52–3.

[34] *CSPD 1664–5*, 553, *CSPD 1670*, 441–2, 450; BRO, 04264/6, p. 211.

[35] BRO, 04264/6, p. 214.

the mayor and most of the council were 'fanatics'); Sir John was forced to crave pardon on his knees. Yeamans returned in triumph, Sir John returned as privately as he could.[36] Sir John sought revenge by accusing Mayor Knight of breach of privilege for allegedly knocking him down in the street when acting as a magistrate. The mayor was sent for in custody and an unusually full meeting of the common council (thirty-five were present, Sir John Knight was not) drew up a statement declaring the mayor's loyalty to the crown and conformity to the Church. The Commons committee of privileges thought he was not guilty, but the House disagreed and he was committed. He too returned in triumph in April and continued to make no effort to persecute Dissenters.[37]

III. BISHOP CARLETON

The Declaration of Indulgence gave the Bristol Dissenters a period of peace, but it was not to last. In February 1672 the king made perhaps the most ill-advised episcopal appointment of his reign, when he nominated Guy Carleton as bishop of Bristol. Carleton was a staunch Royalist and High Churchman; although well into his seventies he was aggressive and irascible, totally unsuited to working with a proud corporation that was tolerant towards Dissent. He began to make his mark on his diocese soon after his arrival in September 1674 (more than two and a half years after his appointment). 'Though aged and grey', he was determined to destroy meetings and to force Dissenters to come to church. His aim, he said, was to end 'schism', which is perhaps why he left the Quakers alone—there was no hope of bringing them back within the Church. He was fortunate that the newly elected mayor, Ralph Olliffe, was one of the few aldermen very hostile to Dissent. Carleton appointed three of the clergy (including Thomas Godwyn) as informers and found a willing lieutenant in John Hellier, an attorney, who (like the mayor) was a heavy drinker with a violent temper.[38] Hellier and others began to disturb meetings and arrest

---

[36] S. Seyer, *Memoirs Topographical and Historical of Bristol and its Neighbourhood*, 2 vols. (Bristol, 1821), ii. 514 (MS copies in B10163, 'A copy of a MS in parchment', B10166 'A catalogue').

[37] *CJ*, ix. 209, 226, 228; BRO, 04264/6, p. 221; Seyer, *Memoirs*, ii. 514; *Church of Christ*, 128, 133.

[38] *Church of Christ*, 144–6; BRO, JQS/PR/1, Ward of All Saints and St Nicholas, 12 Oct. 1664; *CSPD 1672–3*, 332 (this letter clearly dates from 1674, not 1672); BL, Add MS 70130, Misc. 84 (an account of the persecution in Bristol). I am grateful to Stephen Roberts for the last reference. For his concern with 'schism', see Coventry MS 7, fo. 43; for the Quakers, see Besse, i. 53; C. Horle, *The Quakers and the English Legal System, 1660–88* (Philadelphia, 1988), 283. Prosecutions for meeting also resumed in 1673 at Exeter; most of those convicted were Presbyterians; the Quakers were left alone until 1680: Brockett, *Nonconformity in Exeter*, 39–45.

preachers; the bishop sat with the magistrates and ensured that they were convicted and that fines were collected. Some constables were reluctant to act, as were most of the magistrates, but the bishop threatened them with 'penalties and Parliament'.[39]

The Dissenters sought help 'above'. In December the duke of York secured a pardon for a number of Bristol Dissenters, mostly Presbyterians. Carleton rushed to London to justify himself.[40] On 30 January 1675 he preached what was seen as a provocative sermon. He claimed that his adversaries were behaving like their forebears in 1640–1—striking at the king through the bishops. Secretary of State Henry Coventry urged him to show gentleness towards modest, quiet Dissenters, which would justify severity against the insolent.[41] But that was not Carleton's way. He assured Coventry that he would be gentle with quiet Dissenters—but only if they abandoned their errors and conformed to the Church. His hand was strengthened by the king's proclamation of 3 February, which ordered the enforcement of the laws against conventicles and stated that the licences of 1672 had been withdrawn.[42] Carleton quickly had one of the leading Independent preachers, John Thompson, imprisoned; he died in gaol soon afterwards. Carleton sent his chaplain to bury him according to the rites of the Church of England, much to the distress of the 'fanatics' who attended the funeral.[43] The Dissenters still talked of their friends 'above'. The duke of York complained that he heard that 1,500 had been indicted under the draconian Conventicle Act of 1593. Coventry wrote that the king did not want 'so warm a persecution'.[44]

Carleton worried that the magistrates would prove less than steadfast; only fear of the £100 fine for refusing to act would make them do their duty. He complained particularly of John Knight, now an alderman, whom he called the captain of the fanatic party. The magistrates insisted that all proceedings against Dissenters should be public, hoping either to wear the bishop out or that an angry public would intimidate him. Carleton hoped that the marquis

[39] *CSPD 1672–3*, 332–3; *Church of Christ*, 146–7; Coventry MS 4, fos. 193–4; BL, Add MS 70130, Misc. 84.

[40] *CSPV 1673–5*, 324, 326, 331; Marvell, ii. 331–2; *HMC Portland*, iii. 348; *Church of Christ*, 147–8.

[41] Coventry MS 7, fo. 37, MS 83, fo. 73 (BL Add MS 25124, fo. 16).

[42] Coventry MS 7, fo. 43; Miller, *After the Civil Wars*, 220; *Church of Christ*, 148; Coventry MS 83, fo. 73 (BL, Add MS 25124, fo. 15). See letter from some Dissenters to the mayor, Coventry MS 4, fos. 193–4.

[43] Coventry MS 7, fos. 39, 43; *Church of Christ*, 148–50; *The Bristol Narrative* (1675); *A Reply to the Bristol Narrative* (1675).

[44] Coventry MS 83, fos. 84–5 (BL, Add MS 25124, fos. 33, 38).

of Worcester would appoint extra militia forces to keep the peace, but was told that the justices had all the powers they needed.[45] In March a grand jury denounced the city's Dissenters as subversive and praised the bishop (a 'faithful shepherd') for his efforts to suppress them. It was alleged that the presentment had been drafted by the bishop and Hellier, and that Carleton had packed the grand jury.[46]

The persecution continued sporadically until the summer of 1677. The Presbyterians, Independents, and Baptists consulted about how best to cope; the Presbyterians considered giving over meeting, but they were talked out of it by the others. Various stratagems were used: the preacher might be hidden by a curtain, or in a different room or building, or have a trap-door through which he could escape. The Baptists lustily sang psalms when informers or constables came, pretending that they did not hear commands to disperse.[47] Olliffe was succeeded as mayor by Cann, who made clear his continued aversion to persecution, at one point leaving for London to avoid being ordered about by Hellier. In November 1675 he invited the leading Dissenters to a feast.[48] However, Hellier and Carleton had the law on their side and the 'poor aldermen' had to obey them.[49] Their main target was the pastors, who were prosecuted under the Five Mile Act. Meetings were disrupted, but meeting houses were not closed, though on one occasion Hellier burned chairs belonging to the Presbyterian meeting.[50]

On visits to London, Carleton complained of the laxity of the magistrates and suggested drafting in gentlemen from the county as JPs. Cann claimed that this would contravene the charter.[51] An opportunity to change the tempo of law enforcement came with the death of Aldworth, the town clerk, in March 1676. Carleton sought to secure the election of a good Churchman, but the election also attracted the attention of Worcester. The post was an important

[45] Dorset RO, D124, box 233, bundle labelled 'Col. Thomas Strangways', Carleton to Strangways, 24 Feb. 1675, Strangways to Carleton, 1 Mar. 1675; Coventry MS 83, fo. 75 (BL, Add MS 25124, fo. 22). There was a rumour in August 1675 that Carleton was trying to get Worcester to send a troop of horse to suppress meetings: *Church of Christ*, 169.

[46] BCL, B7949, no. 146; *A Sober Answer to the Address of the Grand Jurors* (1675), 7, 16–17, 25, 29–30, and *passim*; *Church of Christ*, 159, 161.

[47] *Church of Christ*, 149, 151, 159–64, and *passim*; *Some Reasons Briefly Suggested which have Prevailed with the Dissenters in Bristol to Continue their Open Meetings* (1675).

[48] *Church of Christ*, 170–2, 182–3.　　　　[49] Ibid. 176.

[50] Ibid. 166. The Five Mile Act (which particularly affected those who had held parish livings—in other words Presbyterians and some Independents) had not been enforced before Carleton arrived: BL Add MS 70130, Misc. 84.

[51] Coventry MS 4, fo. 331; BCL, B11152, Col. John Romsey to Southwell, 10 July 1675.

one: most of the magistrates, it was alleged, knew little of the law and took on trust whatever the town clerk told them.[52] The king wrote recommending John Romsey, who had in turn been recommended by the lord chancellor and attorney general. Worcester had not forgiven Romsey (then a servant to the earl of Pembroke) for opposing his nominee in the Monmouthshire by-election of 1667.[53] The mayor delayed opening the king's letter and holding the election. Meanwhile Nathaniel Haggett and Worcester's candidate, Jones, both tried to persuade the king to withdraw his letter and recommend them instead.[54] Worcester told the king that Romsey was a rigid Presbyterian; Carleton also wrote warmly against him. Charles was prepared to send word that he would not insist on his recommendation, but the attorney general continued to support Romsey and the lord chancellor argued that, if the king changed his mind, his recommendations were less likely to be obeyed in future and he would miss the chance to establish a useful precedent.[55] There were five candidates, of whom three were 'put in election'. Romsey was elected; Worcester's candidate did not make the final three.[56] Some thought the king's recommending Romsey had been unfortunate; nobody would knowingly have obstructed Worcester 'in so small a thing and within part of his lieutenancy'.[57] The marquis had suffered a public humiliation; he was soon to play a much more active role in the city.

The bishop's relations with the corporation went from bad to worse. In November 1676 he complained that the mayor had gone to London to wait on the duke of York—still seen as a friend to Dissenters—and alleged that all the aldermen were disaffected to the government in Church and state.[58] He forbade laymen living in the cathedral precinct to pay poor rates to the city, urged the dean and chapter to claim exemption from the city's jurisdiction, and sought a commission of charitable uses, which he hoped to pack with his own 'creatures', to enquire into the 'arcana' of the city's government.[59] Yet another cause of contention arose in July 1677 when the bishop ordered the city's clergy to mention the bishop and clergy in their prayers before the mayor and corporation. This was, in fact, required by the canons of the Church, but it had been customary in Bristol to mention the magistrates (whom Carleton

---

[52] *CSPD 1676–7*, 31, 33, 51, 52–3; Coventry MS 4, fo. 403.
[53] Coventry MS 4, fos. 408, 416; *HP 1660–90*, i. 317–18.
[54] Coventry MS 4, fos. 409, 415; *CSPD 1676–7*, 58.
[55] Coventry MS 4, fos. 408, 415–17; Coventry MS 83, fos. 98–9 (BL, Add MS 25124, fos. 71–2).
[56] BRO, 04264/7, fo. 79.   [57] Coventry MS 4, fo. 415.   [58] Tanner MS 40, fo. 37.
[59] BRO, JQS/M/5, fos. 249, 248, 233 (in back of volume); Latimer, i. 378–9. For a similar commission for Hertford, see Knights, *Representation*, 71.

described as 'coopers and heel makers') first. The corporation demanded that the clergy continue to pray in the customary form. Carleton told them to obey him; the clergy said if they did, they would lose their maintenance. Carleton was apoplectic that 'a bumpkin pack of peddling mechanics' should expect the clergy to pray for the mayor and citizens before the highest dignitaries of the Church.[60] On 15 September, the day of the mayoral election, the corporation failed to come to the cathedral, as was customary, and instead heard a sermon in Gaunt's chapel, on the other side of College Green. When the bishop forbade preaching in the chapel, the aldermen broke open the door.[61] Meanwhile, a dispute arose when the dean and chapter rejected the corporation's demand to be allowed to process into the choir of the cathedral with the civic sword carried erect in front of the mayor.[62]

The corporation united to defend its honour. Sir John Knight I and Alderman Knight, arch-enemies whose feud (one of them said) would end only with death, agreed to oppose the bishop in whatever he did.[63] Carleton now saw Sir John as his leading opponent. He had initially seen him as an ally in the persecution of Dissenters, but in February 1675 he complained that Knight talked much and did little. However, in April 1676 Sir John wrote that if Haggett was chosen town clerk, the laws would be more disobeyed than ever, which implied a continuing hostility to Dissent.[64] In the House of Commons Knight's position had continued much as in the 1660s. In 1673 he spoke against considering the complaints of Dissenters and was one of the 'court' MPs who received a letter of summons to arrive promptly in 1675. Shaftesbury, in his list of the Commons in about 1677, initially marked Knight as 'vile', only to change his rating to 'worthy'. In May 1678 Knight urged the Commons to support the king's preparations for a war against the French, whom he clearly saw as posing a threat to England, but within a few weeks he had changed his mind and opposed raising any more money for the armed forces.[65] It would seem that his change of stance in Bristol (from persecutor to protector of Dissent) antedated his change of stance at Westminster. It seems to have owed much to personal hostility to Carleton, and a dislike of meddlesome priests, seen earlier in his punishment of Godwyn. Knight accused the bishops and clergy of trying to 'domineer' over the laity, and claimed that the canons were of no legal force,

[60] Coventry MS 7, fos. 94, 98–9; *CSPD 1677–8*, 320, 351–4, 382–3.
[61] Coventry MS 7, fos. 100, 104–5.   [62] Latimer, i. 389.
[63] Coventry MS 7, fo. 102.
[64] Dorset RO, D124, box 233, bundle labelled 'Col. T. Strangways', Carleton to Strangways, 24 Feb. 1675; *CSPD 1676–7*, 58.
[65] *HP 1660–90*, ii. 692–4.

because they had not been confirmed by Parliament. He allegedly would not allow the mayor to suppress conventicles and said he would go to church and serve God as well as the bishop did.[66] The bishop responded that good law (the canons) should never submit to bad custom, and that he would not allow the Church to be trampled underfoot by 'unworthy mechanics'.[67]

There was now a virtual schism, with one form of prayer being used in the cathedral and another in Gaunt's chapel. Carleton believed the mayor and some of the aldermen were prepared to make peace, but were prevented by Sir John.[68] The mayor, Sir Richard Crump, a future Tory, admitted privately that on the issue of the prayers the bishop was in the right.[69] Sir Robert Cann, of whom he had earlier written slightingly, was now seen by the bishop as an ally. The clergy, torn between their duty to obey their bishop and their practical need for the city's goodwill, promised to use the canonical order of prayer in future.[70] The issue of the prayers seems to have been resolved, but the question of the sword continued to rankle. By November, the corporation was coming to the cathedral to hear the sermon, but not the rest of the service, and remained in the nave.[71]

If Carleton won his battle on the order of prayer (where canon law was clearly on his side), his moves to make the cathedral and the clergy more independent of the city failed. He also lost the co-operation of the magistrates, who refused to let him sit on the bench, or question witnesses. The prosecution of Dissenters ceased.[72] Carleton remained upbeat, claiming that, if a few loyal gentlemen from the county were added to the commission of the peace, the city could be brought to conformity within three months.[73] He claimed he had said nothing to provoke the governors of the city, that he left the city in greater conformity than he had found it, and that he and the citizens parted as loving friends. Others saw him as a disaster. As early as September 1675 there were rumours that a more emollient bishop would replace him. Ormond remarked in 1676 that Bristol was in need of a prudent and vigorous clergy, to woo Dissenters by persuasion and a good example, but that such qualifications were rare among the Bristol clergy.[74] The bishop browbeat any of the clergy who questioned his commands.[75] Dissent was reported to be stronger than ever;

[66] Tanner MS 129, fos. 47, 83, 139.   [67] Ibid. 138.   [68] Ibid. 136.

[69] BRO, JQS/M/5, fo. 234.   [70] Tanner MS 129, fos. 12, 13.

[71] Tanner MS 39*, fo. 98, MS 129, fos. 17, 49, MS 35, fo. 87.

[72] Tanner MS 40, fo. 107; *CSPD 1677–8*, 425.   [73] Coventry MS 7, fo. 102.

[74] Ibid. 98; Tanner MS 129, fo. 9; *HMC 7th Report*, 465; V & A, Forster MS 426/1, fo. 95 (copy in Carte MS 70, fo. 447).

[75] *CSPD 1677–8*, 352–4.

Dr Ichabod Chauncy built a Dissenting meeting house on land leased from the corporation.[76] When one of the city's MPs died Cann was chosen in his place, with the support of the Dissenters.[77] The bishop of Bath and Wells admitted that the order to pray for the clergy before the mayor had been provocative and unwise.[78] It was a relief to all concerned when Carleton was nominated to the more lucrative, but politically less sensitive, see of Chichester, where he continued to cause mayhem.[79]

IV. TORY AND WHIG

The debacle concerning the election of the town clerk exposed Worcester's lack of influence in the city. In February 1678, as lord lieutenant, he approved a proposal to re-establish the city's artillery company and a royal warrant to that effect was drawn up in March 1679.[80] For a while Worcester was politically on the defensive, as he was accused first of protecting papists in Monmouthshire and then of complicity in the Popish Plot. Early in 1680 his son, Lord Herbert, was appointed captain and the company was raised in full by June.[81] The immediate occasion for its mobilization was a report that unnamed men had been exercising in a military manner, allegedly not discouraged by the city authorities. Aldermen Cann, Yeamans, and Olliffe, all now identifiable as Tories, reported that some sixty Dissenters had been exercising in arms and had hindered the suppression of conventicles.[82] In March 1681 a Whig newspaper alleged that the company, 'this new academy of sword and musket', created by Worcester, drilled weekly and marched through the city once a month in order to overawe the citizens. Its membership was exclusively Tory and it was 'the nursery of all public employments'—jurors, parish officials, common councillors, and MPs.[83]

---

[76] Latimer, i. 388; Chauncy, *Innocence Vindicated*, 16; *CSPD July–Sept. 1683*, 265–6. Chauncy claimed to have been a 'chief instrument' in getting Romsey chosen as town clerk: *Innocence Vindicated*, 10.

[77] Tanner MS 40, fo. 107; *CSPD 1677–8*, 426; *HP 1660–90*, i. 238.

[78] Coventry MS 7, fos. 126, 128.

[79] McNulty, 'Priests, Church Courts and People', 90–2.

[80] Latimer, i. 383; *CSPD 1679–80*, 635; BRO, 8029/11, Worcester to Mayor Lloyd, 6 Mar. 1679.

[81] BRO, 8029/11, Commission to Herbert, 1 Mar., list of those lately elected, 10 June 1680. Articles and orders of the company were drawn up in December 1679: ibid., 12 Dec.

[82] Tanner MS 37, fo. 31; *CSPD 1679–80*, 597.

[83] *Smith's Protestant Intelligence*, 4 Mar. 1681. See M de L. Landon, 'The Bristol Artillery Company and the Tory Triumph in Bristol', *Transactions of the American Philosophical Society*, cxiv (1970), 155–61.

The formation of the artillery company—and the Dissenters' military exercises —showed how divided Bristol had become. Cann and Sir John Knight were returned in both elections of 1679, but by the time Parliament met in October 1680 they had quarrelled violently. Cann was still described as moderate towards Dissenters during his mayoralty in 1675–6 and was supported by Dissenters in the by-election in February 1678. But in June Carleton thanked him for the good work he had done (nature unspecified) and by November 1679 he was enforcing the laws against Dissent, a difficult and lonely task. He was obstructed by the mayor, Joseph Creswick, the son-in-law of Sir John Knight, 'the old rat'.[84] The reasons for Cann's change of stance are uncertain—he later returned to moderation—but may have included personal animosity towards Sir John Knight I. He may have been alienated by Knight's vehement attacks on the bishop and clergy; his earlier moderation towards Dissent should not be seen, in itself, as evidence of lack of commitment to the Church.[85] He may also have seen Dissent as posing a real threat to public order. In January 1680 he complained of 'enormities' committed by Nonconformists. On 30 January a body of men paraded through several streets with an axe and trumpet. Meanwhile, Sir John Knight treated his opponents with studied and public contempt.[86] The city's divisions were reflected in grand jury presentments. In April the jury condemned those who spread false reports and promoted petitions. In August another jury condemned those who accused Mayor Creswick of being 'fanatically disposed' and traduced true sons of the Church who were moderate against Dissenters.[87] The Baptists faced renewed persecution from July, despite Creswick's manifest reluctance. However, on this occasion the disruption was short-lived.[88]

In March John Rowe, the city sword bearer, a member of the Green Ribbon Club, accused Cann of having said (in a rage) that there was no such thing as a Popish Plot. Rowe had recently been questioned by the privy council for allegedly seditious words, following information from Cann.[89] When Parliament

---

[84] BCL, B11152, Col. Romsey to Southwell, 1 Feb. 1679; Tanner MS 41, fo. 62, MS 129, fos. 13, 52, 133–4; Coventry MS 7, fo. 202; BCL, B10163, 'A Copy of a MS in Parchment', 1679. Creswick was dismissed from the lieutenancy and was not knighted.

[85] For an example of someone who managed to be both a committed Anglican and a supporter of comprehension and indulgence, see H. Horwitz, *Revolution Politicks: The Career of Daniel Finch, Second Earl of Nottingham* (Cambridge, 1968).

[86] Coventry MS 6, fos. 210, 232, MS 7, fos. 196, 202.

[87] *CSPD 1679–80*, 440–1, 619–20.   [88] *Church of Christ*, 220–3.

[89] Pepys Library, MS 2875, fo. 483; BCL, B10166, 3rd 'Calendar', 25 Mar. 1680; *Protestant (Domestic) Intelligence*, 13 Feb. 1680.

met, Rowe and Sir John Knight accused Cann and Yeamans of denying the Popish Plot. Rowe accused Cann of acting under the directions of the marquis of Worcester. Cann denied the charges, adding that no jury in Bristol would believe anything Knight said and that Rowe was a 'damned rogue'. The House resolved to expel him and to send for Yeamans (not an MP) in custody. Yeamans acknowledged his fault and asked for pardon. He was discharged.[90] Soon after, the Commons resolved to impeach the Bristol parson Richard Thompson, for allegedly saying that Presbyterians were worse than papists.[91]

When the electors gathered to choose MPs for the Oxford Parliament, Sir John Knight and the recorder, Sir Robert Atkyns, were opposed by the Tories Thomas Earle and Sir Richard Hart, the mayor. It was alleged that 400 new freemen had been created in order to vote. When Atkyns came to town he was met by 300 supporters on horseback. They were confronted at the market cross by 300 or 400 men, armed with clubs, 'in military order', many of them from the artillery company. After trading insults, they attacked Atkyns, but (according to Whig newspapers) his followers defended themselves bravely and got the better of it; many were injured. Hart attempted to have Atkyns's supporters tried for riot, but even a packed grand jury would not find a bill. To general surprise, Hart and Earle were chosen; the gap between Hart and Atkyns was only twenty-seven votes.[92] The victorious candidates were presented with an address, stressing the need to punish those who accused the king of wishing to establish arbitrary government and calumniated good churchmen as papists. The address condemned illegal punishments by fellow subjects, a clear reference to the treatment of Cann, Yeamans, and Thompson. When the MPs returned from Oxford, they were presented with another address, allegedly signed by most of the aldermen and common council and several hundred citizens. It expressed confidence that, had the Parliament sat longer, it would have vindicated them against the lies of Knight and Atkyns. It called for the enforcement of all laws against papists and fanatics, especially the Conventicle Act of 1593.[93] Bristol's Tories, on the back foot in 1679 and for much of 1680, were growing in confidence and eager for revenge.[94]

---

[90] *CJ*, ix. 642, 648, 653; Grey, vii. 384.   [91] *CJ*, ix. 693–5.

[92] BCL, B10166, 3rd 'calendar', Feb. 1681; Tanner MS 37, fo. 246; *Protestant (Domestic) Intelligence*, 11 Mar.; *Smith's Protestant Intelligence*, 7–10 Mar., 4–7 Apr. 1681.

[93] *The Bristol Address to Hart and Earle* (1681) (printed in *Loyal Protestant*, 19 Mar. 1681); *Bristol's Second Address* (1681).

[94] North, in the autumn of 1680, found more 'dawnings' of loyalty than he had expected: *Norths*, i. 157.

V. THE TORY REACTION

The years 1681–3 saw a struggle for control of the corporation and the city's legal system. On 8 March 1681 the aldermen met to choose a replacement for Alderman Sir John Lloyd, deceased. The mayor was asked to preside, but refused; so Atkyns presided, as the senior alderman present. Thomas Day was declared 'elected'. The mayor claimed that the court could not transact any business in his absence, refused to admit Day, and had Atkyns, Knight, Lawford, and Creswick indicted for conspiracy and riot.[95] In September Earle was elected mayor, after several days of eating and drinking, with the militia and artillery company very much in evidence. The outgoing mayor concluded his speech with the pious hope that they would never lack one from the loins of the royal martyr to rule over them.[96] The council summoned Atkyns to the annual gaol delivery, and to swear Hart, elected an alderman in October 1680, but pointedly refused to offer him any entertainment. On 28 September a court of aldermen had chosen Earle to replace Alderman Lloyd; those voting for him were Hart, Cann, Yeamans, Olliffe, and Crump. Knight claimed that Day had already been duly elected, but he was overruled. Now on 18 October, before the court could transact any business, the mayor moved that Atkyns should swear Hart as an alderman. A majority voted in favour, Atkyns walked out, amid much hissing and stamping, but Hart was sworn anyway—by what authority is uncertain—and the court broke up without any prisoners being tried.[97]

The Tory aldermen set out to get rid of the recorder. He was accused of failing to hold the gaol delivery, refusing to swear Hart, and 'electing' Day at an illegal meeting. Protracted legal proceedings and negotiations ended with Atkyns resigning in December 1682, by which time there had been no gaol delivery for over two years. Atkyns commented caustically that the rulers of the city had too much sail and too little ballast.[98] Sir John Churchill, solicitor to the duke of York, was elected in his place. But the Tory grip on the corporation

---

[95] *CSPD 1680–1*, 163, 250; BRO, 04624/7, fo. 146: Seyer, *Memoirs*, ii. 517–19. (The recorder had the status of an alderman.) Alderman Hickes was also present, but was not prosecuted so that he could act as a witness against the others. It was alleged that Cann would have been there, but he was ill: SP 29/422, no. 18.

[96] *CSPD 1680–1*, 681; *Impartial Protestant Mercury*, 20–3 Sept. 1681.

[97] BRO, JQS/M/5, fo. 210, 04264/7, fos. 144, 157–8 (the record says that Atkyns was present in court and Hart was sworn, but not that Atkyns swore him; however, only the recorder could legally swear an alderman); *Loyal Protestant*, 27 Oct. 1681; *Impartial Protestant Mercury*, 4–7 and 21–5 Oct. 1681; *CSPD 1682*, 563, 578; Morrice MS P, p. 343.

[98] BRO, 04264/7, fos. 159–60, 171; Seyer, *Memoirs*, ii. 519–20; *CSPD 1682*, 520.

was not secure and a new mayor had to be chosen in September 1682. The candidates were Thomas Day and Thomas Eston. Day was unacceptable to the Tories because he had voted against Hart and Earle in March 1681 and had been 'elected' an alderman the following day. There was much anxious making of lists. Of fifty-three aldermen and councillors, twenty-two were seen as being for Day and twenty-three for Eston, with five doubtful, two marked as refusing to vote, and one left blank. Six of the aldermen were for Day, four for Eston, and two (Cann and Hickes) doubtful.[99] At the assizes, a few days before the election, Sir John Knight was found guilty of assaulting Mayor Hart and he, Atkyns, Creswick, and Lawford were convicted of riot (in 'electing' Day alderman). All four were expected to vote for Day as mayor. The bishop thought that their conviction could lead to their dismissal. The king sent several private letters in favour of Eston. Worcester used less subtle methods, pressurizing waverers and ostentatiously mustering the militia. Eston was elected, along with two 'loyal' sheriffs.[100]

Another sign of Tory strength within the corporation was the renewed persecution of Dissenters. Grand juries had long called for the laws to be enforced.[101] By the end of December 1681 the Baptist and Quaker meeting houses had been shut up and their furniture and fittings destroyed. Hellier and one of the sheriffs, John Knight, the son of John Knight of the Sugar House, incited the 'boys' and the 'rabble' to do as much damage as possible. Many from both congregations were sent to the Bridewell and the gaol.[102] With the exception of the Quakers, who stubbornly assembled outside their locked meeting houses, the congregations met privately, often outside the city, pursued by Hellier and his minions. Sheriff Knight, rapidly emerging as the most extreme of the ultra-Tories, complained that Mayor Earle hampered his prosecution of Dissenters. One reason for this was that Knight committed Quakers to gaol, but had no power to do so, as he was not a magistrate. Secretary Jenkins bemoaned the inability of Knight and Earle to work together, but the king's decision to knight the sheriff added to his standing and self-confidence.[103] He saw off a petition by Quaker prisoners against conditions in Newgate, persuading the privy council

[99] BL, Add MS 5540, fos. 8–9.

[100] Tanner MS 35, fo. 87; *CSPD 1682*, 373, 382, 392; *Loyal Impartial Mercury*, 19–22 Sept. 1682.

[101] *CSPD 1679–80*, 440–1, *CSPD 1680–1*, 250; *Two Presentments of the Grand Jury in Bristol* (1681), 5–6.

[102] *Loyal Protestant*, 24 and 31 Dec. 1681, 10 Jan. 1682; *Currant Intelligence*, 13–17 Dec. 1681; *Impartial Protestant Mercury*, 20–3 and 23–7 Dec. 1681; *Church of Christ*, 227–34; Besse, i. 54.

[103] *CSPD 1682*, 94–5, 100, 113, 120, 238–9; *Impartial Protestant Mercury*, 24–8 Feb. 1682; Morrice MS P, p. 328.

that the complaints were unfounded; the mayor and six aldermen thought they were justified.[104]

As all members of the council served for life, changes could come only with death or removal for misconduct: hence the suggestion that the convictions of Sir John Knight I and his allies could lead to their dismissal, a proposal revived by Churchill in January 1683.[105] The younger Sir John argued, as early as June 1682, for a more radical approach: a *quo warranto*, followed by a new charter, in which the king could nominate the first members of the corporation and reserve the power to remove members at will.[106] This strategy was slow and required a plausible legal case. The king's preference, in London and Bristol, was for the threat of forfeiture to lead the corporation to surrender the charter. This would be simpler and quicker and would leave less lasting bitterness. In February 1683 the king agreed to issue a *quo warranto* as soon as Worcester (now duke of Beaufort) or Sir John Knight II asked for it. Knight was confident that twenty-six of the corporation would vote for surrender if the *quo warranto* was issued, with twenty-two against and five absent. The writ was issued, but the surrender was rejected by twenty-seven votes to twenty-two.[107] Beaufort blamed the lobbying and insinuations of Hart and Earle, who both voted against surrender; Earle allegedly claimed that neither the king nor Beaufort really wanted the surrender and proposed that they should petition the king to stop the *quo warranto*. As a punishment, the mayor and five alderman resolved that Earle's election had been irregular and he was removed; Eston was elected in his place. Jenkins and Bishop Gulston blamed rash and hasty counsels—in other words, Sir John Knight II had been overconfident. As a result, the loyal party had become divided and its opponents were led by former adherents

---

[104] BRO, JQS/M/6, fo. 254 (the six were Sir John Knight I, Lawford, Olliffe, Crump, Crabb, and Creswick; Lawford and Olliffe had been involved in persecuting Dissenters in the 1670s; Crump was generally seen as a Tory); Morrice MS P, p. 330; *CSPD 1682*, 134; *Impartial Protestant Mercury*, 21–4 and 24–8 Mar. 1682; *The Sad and Lamentable Cry of Oppression and Cruelty* (1682), 4; *More Sad and Lamentable News from Bristol* (1682), 3, 6.

[105] The problem was that the mayor and other aldermen were evenly divided on the question of expelling these four. Hart and Crump, normally 'good' aldermen, would not vote to expel their relatives: SP 29/422, no. 18. Churchill also proposed that Earle should be laid aside because he had been elected irregularly and for misconduct in office. This should be attempted only after the other four had been removed, because Hart and Crump would be glad to be rid of Earle: SP 29/422, no. 9.

[106] *CSPD 1682*, 239–40.

[107] *CSPD Jan.–June 1683*, 76, 95–6, 99; BRO, 04624/7, fo. 174 (list of votes, giving twenty-two for and twenty-seven against). By comparing Knight's predictions (SP 29/422, no. 127(I)) with the votes in 04264/7, fo. 174, it is clear that Knight made several mistakes: he had expected Cann to vote no and Churchill to be absent; both voted yes. The balance was tipped by Hart and four common councillors, plus another who was not on Knight's list.

who had been driven out—presumably a reference to Earle and Hart.[108] It is also likely that some Tories had scruples of conscience about surrendering.

With the failure to procure a surrender, the crown turned its attention to securing a suitable mayor for the next year. Ralph Olliffe was elected, opposed only by old Sir John Knight and Cann—strange allies—but he died hours after he was sworn. The king now entrusted the management of the corporation entirely to Beaufort, who ensured that Sir William Clutterbuck, recommended by the king, was chosen in Olliffe's place.[109] Meanwhile, the attorney general proceeded with the *quo warranto* and on 31 October the council resolved unanimously to surrender the charter.

The new charter was eventually issued in June 1684. Only one alderman was removed and nineteen members of the common council.[110] By then Sir John Knight I was dead and the victorious Tories had the luxury of falling out among themselves. There were complaints of Sir John Knight II's vanity, ambition, and indiscretion. He was disappointed by the king's failure to make him governor of the Leeward Islands. In December 1684 he asked the king to discharge him from the common council—significantly, he had not been made an alderman. The king complied with his wishes, declaring himself well satisfied with his services.[111] His last contribution to Bristol was to secure the election of Richard Thompson as dean, to the astonishment of the people of the city and against the wishes of the committee for ecclesiastical promotions.[112] But Thompson had his supporters, at court and in the city. In November 1680 a certificate testifying to his loyalty and pious life was signed by twenty-five Bristolians, including Aldermen Hickes and Crump, John Knight the younger, and John Hellier. Sixteen of the signatories were members of the artillery company.[113]

By 1684 the dominance of the Tories, and of Beaufort, seemed impregnable. In the general election of March 1685 Sir Richard Crump and Sir John Churchill, Beaufort's candidates, were opposed by the members of 1681, Hart

[108] *CSPD Jan.–June 1683*, 150–1, 160; Badminton House, FmE 2/4/28, Mayor and Aldermen to Beaufort, 29 Mar. 1683; Tanner MS 34, fo. 20.

[109] *CSPD July–Sept. 1683*, 351, 372–3, 397–8, 437, *1683–4*, 1, 3, 6, 7, 17; BRO, 04264/7, fos. 181, 184.

[110] Latham, *Bristol Charters*, 50–2. The alderman was Christopher Griffiths, whose attendance had been fitful but he had voted against the surrender and the election of Eston as mayor.

[111] *CSPD 1683–4*, 245–6, 248–9, 259–60, *1684–5*, 240–1; BCL, B1153, Petitions of Sir John Knight, *c.* July and 7 Dec. 1686; Bodl, MS Eng. Letters c.53, fo. 58; BRO, 04264/7, fo. 208.

[112] BCL, B10163, 'Annals of Bristol', June 1684; Tanner MS 32, fos. 7–8, 16, 27, 41, 46, MS 129, fos. 70, 77–8, 108, 128–9; Morrice MS P, p. 443; *HMC Ormond*, vii. 213.

[113] *The Visor Pluck't off from Richard Thompson* (1680), 4. For lists of the artillery men see *A List of Such Persons as are Lately Elected to be of the Artillery Company* (1680); BRO, 8029/11, undated list.

and Earle—not thoroughgoing enough Tories for Beaufort's liking; they conceded defeat before the poll could be completed.[114] But during the summer the mood changed. Suspicions about the city's loyalty during Monmouth's rebellion led to a garrison being stationed there; there was friction between soldiers and civilians. When Lord Chancellor Jeffreys came in September he accused the mayor, Sir William Hayman, of kidnapping and made Hayman, Cann, and Lawford give sureties to appear at the King's Bench. He also expatiated on the city's record of disloyalty and rebellion.[115] In a by-election, in November, Beaufort put forward John Romsey, the town clerk. Sir John Knight II returned from the political wilderness to stand against him, but they were both defeated by Sir Richard Hart, one of the unsuccessful Tory candidates in March, with Romsey a poor third. Beaufort was incandescent, but Sir Robert Southwell, secretary to the privy council, saw a deeper significance in the result. 'The worst is that there has been nothing of Whig and Tory in this matter, but the undervaluing the recommendation given, a sort of revenge for ill-treatment by my lord chancellor and the soldiers, and as if it were high time for Protestants of all sorts to be friends.'[116] Yet again Bristolians had shown that, however divided they might be, they retained the capacity to close ranks and assert their independence.

[114] BCL, B10163, 'Annals of Bristol', 30 Mar. 1685.

[115] BCL, B10163, 'A copy of a MS in parchment', 22 Sept. 1685, B10166, 3rd 'calendar', 23 Sept. 1685.

[116] *HP 1660–90*, i.239; NLI, MS 2443, fos. 277–8, 281 (printed in *HMC Ormond*, vii. 404); *HMC* Egmont, ii. 172; BRO, JQS/M/6, fo. 241 (this is dated 17 Nov., but this is almost certainly an error, by either the writer or the copyist; the letters from Southwell in NLI and *HMC Egmont* are dated 19 and 21 Dec.).

10

James II

I. THE KING'S AIMS

Charles II lacked grandiose ambitions, at least at home.[1] His main aim was not to go on his travels again. He intervened in the affairs of towns only when he feared that their rulers posed a threat to him. James II, by contrast, had ambitious objectives. A zealous convert, he wished to improve permanently the lot of his fellow Catholics. Under the existing laws, Catholics were not allowed to worship, even in private. They could be fined heavily for absence from their parish churches and were excluded by a series of laws, culminating in the Test Acts, from holding any office or sitting in either House of Parliament. Being a Catholic, therefore, involved the acceptance of considerable risks and hardships; Catholic landowners could not take up the role in public life available to their Protestant neighbours. For James this was simply wrong. The Catholic Church was the one true Church, tracing its authority back to Christ. The laws against Catholics were based on misapprehensions and misrepresentations: Catholics were portrayed as inherently disloyal to the Protestant crown and their religion was depicted as an ugly amalgam of superstition and deceit, designed to maintain the power of popes and priests over a deluded laity. James believed that if others enquired, with an open mind, into the true nature of Catholicism, they (like him) would become Catholics. In allowing Catholics to state their case, and in seeking to promote Catholicism, James believed that he was giving his Protestant subjects an opportunity to free themselves from generations of lies and misrepresentation; and they would realize that the English Reformation had been an act of plunder and sacrilege.[2]

---

[1] His one ambitious project was his 'grand design' of a French alliance and war against the Dutch, which had collapsed ignominiously by early 1674, leaving a legacy of bad feeling and mistrust: Miller, *Charles II.*

[2] See J. Miller, *James II* (New Haven, 2000), 57–9, 122–8, and *passim.*

If James was to improve the condition of Catholics, and encourage conversions, he needed to secure the repeal of the penal laws (which criminalized many aspects of Catholic practice) and Test Acts. He hoped at first to achieve this with the aid of the Tories. In James's eyes, loyal Churchmen and Catholics had fought together for Charles I, and were natural allies now. Soon after succeeding his brother, he summoned a Parliament. The general election produced an overwhelmingly Tory House of Commons. The new charters probably contributed less than aggressive intervention in numerous constituencies by the king and his ministers, and the demoralization of the Whigs.[3] The resultant Parliament voted James an ample revenue, including money to raise troops to suppress Monmouth's rebellion. But the Tories were loyal to Church as well as king, and made it clear that they would not remove the laws against Catholics, even if they were content that they should not be enforced. By the end of 1685 relations between king and Parliament had broken down. The king resented the Commons' refusal to do anything for the Catholics; Parliament was worried by the king's insistence on maintaining the new forces that he had raised against Monmouth and on commissioning some Catholic officers. These developments seemed sinister at a time when Louis XIV was using his army for the forcible conversion of French Protestants. James was outraged by such suspicions. Disillusioned by the Tories' failure, as he saw it, to live up to their professions of loyalty, he turned to those other victims of Anglican intolerance, the Protestant Dissenters. He had flirted with their cause in the 1670s, using his influence on behalf of the Dissenters of Bristol, but he had since come to see Dissenters and Whigs as inherently hostile to monarchy. Now he began to heed the argument that the Dissenters had been goaded into disobedience only by Anglican persecution. If the Tories would not repeal the laws against Catholics, perhaps the Dissenters might be persuaded to support the repeal of the penal laws against both Catholicism and Dissent, and the Test Acts, which required office-holders to take Anglican communion, which some Dissenters found difficult.

By the spring of 1687, James was fully committed to this new policy. He issued a Declaration of Indulgence, in which he allowed freedom of worship to all and promised to dispense all office-holders from the penalties imposed by the Test Acts, and other laws, for not taking oaths or receiving communion. This was an interim measure. He hoped that its contents would soon be

---

[3] Miller, *After the Civil Wars*, 288–90.

confirmed by Parliament, but the election of 1685 suggested that it would not
be easy to secure a House of Commons that would repeal the penal laws and
Test Acts. Catholics were a tiny minority and, until the Test Acts were repealed,
they could not sit in Parliament. Dissenters were more numerous, but still
a relatively small minority;[4] most were of comparatively humble social status
and would prove electorally insignificant, unless the king won the support
of members of the Church of England—either Tories who put obedience to
the king before loyalty to the Church, or Whigs whose eagerness to secure
toleration for Dissenters, or hatred of the High Church clergy, outweighed their
suspicion of papists in power. A canvass of JPs and deputy lieutenants made
it clear that he could not count on the support of many of the county gentry,
so his electoral preparations focused on the towns, which returned the greater
part of the Commons. The new charters issued in 1682–5 gave the king the
power to remove members of corporations. Although James acknowledged that
he did not have the power to appoint their replacements,[5] by the end of 1687
he routinely told corporations whom to elect. In 1687–8 many corporations
were purged, often repeatedly, as the king reversed the changes of 1682–5,
removing Anglicans and Tories and installing Dissenters and Whigs. In this,
much information and assistance on the ground were provided by agents who
had learned the trade of electioneering with the Exclusionist Whigs.

In his dealings with the towns, James had three main concerns. First, he
believed that they were full of disaffected people. In 1685 this meant Dissenters
and supporters of Monmouth, but by 1687 he was coming to see almost any
opposition to his plans as disaffection: he described the Seven Bishops' petition,
in 1688, as 'a standard of rebellion'.[6] In late 1688 he suspected that many of
his subjects were plotting against him and feared the underhand designs of his
Dutch nephew, William of Orange. All of this made it imperative to maintain
order and repress sedition. The law courts had an important part to play in this,
but so did the army. Secondly, James wished to ensure that both Catholics and
Dissenters worshipped freely, particularly in the larger centres of population.
Thirdly, the towns had a vital role to play in his electoral plans. I shall deal with
each topic in turn, and will conclude the chapter with a discussion of the towns'
role in the Revolution of 1688.

[4] James was aware of the findings of the Compton Census, so cannot have shared the misapprehension of Charles II, in the 1660s, that Dissenters were more numerous than Anglicans.
[5] *CSPD 1685*, no. 512.
[6] J. Gutch, *Collectanea Curiosa*, 2 vols. (Oxford, 1831), i. 338; BL Add MS 34510, fos. 81–2.

II. THE MILITARY PRESENCE

James had significant military experience and valued his army as the surest defence against the 'disaffected', whose strength he habitually exaggerated. He allowed the militia to run down, after what he saw as its spineless performance against Monmouth.[7] He was content that his soldiers should behave a little roughly towards towns, like Bristol, which were believed to have supported the rebels, but he did not want discipline to collapse, and knew that misbehaviour by soldiers would provoke resentment among civilians; the inhabitants of 'loyal' towns like Wigan should not be mistreated.[8] He ordered that all offences under common law by soldiers against civilians should be tried by the civil magistrates.[9] In practice, the government's handling of disputes between civilians and soldiers was not even-handed. Soldiers who had offended against civilians were supposed to be handed over to the civil power, but the government was quick to act against anyone who arrested a soldier without leave from his superior officer.[10] When civilians tried to sue soldiers who had slandered them, or taken their property during the rebellion, the lord chancellor argued that they should not be punished if they had acted with good intentions. When soldiers caught stealing chickens were rescued by their colleagues, the owner of the chickens was imprisoned for keeping the soldiers from their duty.[11] The king temporarily established a court martial during Monmouth's rebellion, but it was generally believed that martial law could operate only in wartime. In June 1686 a council of war proposed that soldiers should be tried only by martial law. The judges were urged to rule that desertion was an offence under common law. Four deserters were sentenced to death at the Old Bailey, but judges continued to argue that this was contrary to law.[12] In April 1687 a Shropshire grand jury twice returned a verdict of 'ignoramus' on a deserter; the judge fined the foreman £200.[13] The reluctance of some lawyers helps

[7] J. Miller, 'The Militia and the Army in the Reign of James II', *HJ* xvi (1973), 661–3. Early in 1688 there was talk of calling in the militia's weapons: *CSPD 1687–9*, no. 727.

[8] *CSPD 1685*, no. 1702.

[9] Childs, *The Army, James II and the Glorious Revolution*, 91.

[10] *CSPD 1686–7*, nos. 32, 39, 45, 1236; Childs, *The Army, James II and the Glorious Revolution*, 43–6.

[11] Morrice MS P, pp. 549, 633–4.

[12] *HMC Rutland*, ii. 209; *CSPD 1686–7*, no. 975; Morrice MS Q, pp. 97–100; BL, Add MS 34512, fos. 36–7; Sir J. Bramston, *Autobiography*, ed. Lord Braybrooke, Camden Soc. (1845), 245–6, 272–4, 306; Childs, *The Army, James II and the Glorious Revolution*, 92–4.

[13] *HMC Downshire*, i. 238; Bramston, *Autobiography*, 276.

explain the king's decision, in March 1688, to set up a standing court martial to handle all cases involving soldiers.[14] 'The intention of establishing this court was to withdraw the soldiery from the civil power.'[15]

The king aimed to increase the army's reliability by detaching it from civilian society. Regiments were not quartered in the area where they were raised and were moved frequently. They were dispersed widely around the country, but many were brought together each summer in a great camp on Hounslow Heath for much-publicized exercises.[16] The government encouraged officers and men to see themselves as a caste apart, with a special mission to punish 'disaffection' in which, if their intentions were good, they could probably act with impunity: for James a loyal heart atoned for a multitude of sins. This led to frequent clashes between soldiers and civilians. A man imprisoned in the guardhouse at Yarmouth for calling soldiers rogues was rescued by a small crowd. When soldiers rearrested him and carried him before the mayor, a crowd of 200 appeared and refused to disperse, even when an officer threatened to fire on them, believing that the soldiers had no powder or ball in their muskets. The soldiers knocked some of them down, but the people dispersed only when the officer sent for powder and shot.[17] At Exeter a lieutenant was accused of setting his men on to beat Mr Martin, a lawyer, who was alleged to have written a scandalous lampoon.[18] The officers were indignant that, when they left the city, the mayor refused to grant a certificate of their good behaviour. Bath remarked that Exeter was not a loyal city, unlike Plymouth, where the soldiers lived on good terms with the people.[19] At Maidstone an innkeeper remarked, seeing a captain lose £200 gambling, that if he could afford to lose so much he could pay him for his quarters. The captain shaved one side of the innkeeper's head and led him through the streets in a halter. The townspeople attacked the soldiers, but the mayor persuaded them to desist. When the mayor set out for London, to complain, the captain threatened him with death if he told the king anything before he had had a chance to inform him.[20] The captain hoped that the king would believe his version of events, and indeed James was always inclined to believe what he wanted to believe. He can have had little difficulty in believing a report from the Catholic mayor of Gloucester that a clash between Sir John Guise and an officer was entirely Guise's fault.[21]

[14] Childs, *The Army, James II and the Glorious Revolution*, 91–2.
[15] *HMC Leybourne Popham*, 265.
[16] Childs, *The Army, James II and the Glorious Revolution*, chs. 1, 2, and 4.
[17] BL, Add MS 41804, fo. 99.   [18] *CSPD 1686–7*, nos. 60, 156–7, 184, 193.
[19] *CSPD 1686–7*, nos. 364, 372. He had earlier written that it was the presence of the garrison which made Plymouth loyal: BL, Add MS 32095, fos. 228–9.
[20] Morrice MS Q, p. 29.   [21] Ibid. 42; BL, Add MS 41804, fo. 246.

Of the towns suffering from the military presence, Hull suffered most. In 1681 Charles II had ordered a massive enlargement of the fortifications, which put pressure on the marshy soil of the banks on the east side of the river Hull. The town and the crown had long argued about who was responsible for maintaining them; the new charter of 1685 stated that it was the town.[22] Over the next three years the corporation sold off many assets in a desperate attempt to pay for the repairs, which were said to have cost over £2,000.[23] When the town received the earl of Huntingdon's regiment in September 1685 the normally amicable relationship between town and garrison was under strain. The townspeople accused the soldiers of being aggressive, the officers accused the civic authorities of being uncooperative. There were rumours that the soldiers intended to take free quarter.[24] When the regiment was drawn up in the market square, no one came forward to offer them lodgings. Lionel Copley, the lieutenant governor, sent to the mayor to billet the men in public houses, which he did. The aldermen wanted the men moved to private houses, but Copley said that, under the king's declaration, this could be done only with the householders' consent. Copley preferred to have them in public houses, because it saved the regiment (in other words, the officers) money.[25] The bench claimed that some soldiers in private houses refused to pay for their lodgings, saying that their officers said they must be at free quarter in public houses.[26] Both appealed to the governor, the earl of Plymouth, who remarked that, if the soldiers refused to lodge in private houses, it was the fault of those who had failed to invite them. However, he was sure the dispute could be resolved.[27]

This proved difficult. The soldiers would pay nothing; the bench claimed that soldiers had paid for lodging in public houses 'often' or 'for some years'.[28] The officers ordered their men to move from private to public houses; the soldiers said that if the public house keepers would not pay for them to lodge in private houses, they would remain where they were, paying nothing.[29] One alehouse keeper, Barbara Windsor, allegedly took away the soldiers' bedding, threw their muskets into the street, and abused both officers and men. The officers asked the mayor to punish her, saying she deserved to be ducked; he said he was obliged to proceed according to law.[30]

Despite Plymouth's suspicions about the bench's attitude, he persuaded Huntingdon to agree to quarter his men in private houses.[31] The officers

---

[22] *CSPD 1684–5*, 294; BRB 6, pp. 315–16; BRL 1077.
[23] BRB 6, pp. 173, 198, 316; Hull City Archives, BRM 374.
[24] BRL 2759a, fos. 3, 30.   [25] Ibid. 2.   [26] Ibid. 1.
[27] Ibid. 1–2.   [28] Ibid. 35, 36.   [29] Ibid. 3.
[30] Ibid. 4.   [31] Ibid. 5.

responded with a set of proposals, which they claimed reflected Huntingdon's wishes.[32] These required the mayor to undertake that the public house keepers would pay for the private lodgings; he was also to advance £40 a month to each captain. The corporation found these proposals 'very hard'. Plymouth agreed; he suspected Copley of stirring up ill feeling and asked if the bench could provide evidence of this.[33] He sent a copy of a declaration by the king, about paying for quarters, adding that it was very different from the officers' proposals. He ordered the officer in charge, Major Morgan, to accept quarters in private houses, on the customary terms. He sent the letter to Morgan via the bench, so Morgan could not claim that it had miscarried.[34] Morgan agreed that the soldiers should go into private houses, but then a dispute arose about money owing since the regiment's arrival. Eventually Morgan promised to pay 8*d.* per day per soldier, from the time the regiment arrived in the town, and the mayor signed a certificate that they had discharged all debts.[35] Morgan, however, had no intention of paying. He claimed some public house keepers had been prepared to sign certificates that the soldiers owed them nothing, but that the mayor had told them not to, saying that they were entitled to 8*d.* per week per man. Morgan did not believe that the public house keepers deserved to be paid. The soldiers had been badly treated, forced to lie on the floor. Their arms were thrown into the street (presumably another reference to the doughty Barbara Windsor) and they were not allowed a fire or to have their meat dressed; the mayor ignored all complaints. The mayor had signed a certificate that they had discharged all debts, and had no pretext to ask for anything. Plymouth was inclined to agree; if the soldiers had paid for their diet, they should not have to pay more.[36] Soon after, the mayor ordered the constables to find out how many soldiers were in public houses, so they could be moved to private. The officers accused him of mustering their men. The bench was caught between the cries of the people and the soldiers' 'huffing'.[37] Plymouth suspected the townspeople wished to know the strength of the garrison, to judge whether it could drive the soldiers out. It would, he said, have been better to ask Morgan for the numbers.[38]

In September 1686 Oglethorpe's regiment replaced Huntingdon's. Again the officers demanded that their men be quartered in public houses, claiming that this was the norm everywhere else. Again they refused to pay for their lodgings. Again, Plymouth was inclined to take the bench's side, but could

[32] BRL 2759a, fo. 11.   [33] Ibid. 4, 6, 9.   [34] Ibid. 10 (the declaration is at fos. 10–11)
[35] Ibid. 11, 12.   [36] *HMC Hastings*, ii. 181–2; BRL 2759a, fo. 13.
[37] BRL 2759a, fos. 7 (quoted), 8.   [38] Ibid. 12–13.

offer little advice other than to refuse to sign any discharges until the quarters had been paid.[39] The bench's argument that the soldiers were better off in private houses cut little ice with the officers; the acting commander had orders to quarter 500 men in public houses, without paying for their lodgings. The bench reluctantly agreed to co-operate.[40] When Oglethorpe's regiment was replaced by Dunbarton's, it too demanded quarters in public houses and the situation grew worse when Cornwall's regiment arrived as well, to work on the fortifications. Copley, now very hostile to the bench, demanded quarters for over 1,200 men, far more than ever before, and numerous wives and children. Public house keepers and many shopkeepers and tradesmen were forced to take in soldiers and give them their beds, while they slept on the floor. Public house keepers, unable to accommodate all the men quartered on them, had to pay 10*d.* or 12*d.* a week to lodge them in private houses.[41]

The bench's position in relationship to the central government was ambivalent. Already bitter at having to meet the cost of repairing the banks and jetties, it deeply resented the burden imposed by the soldiers—there had never been more than one regiment in the garrison before[42]—and their arrogant behaviour, and it was very conscious of the complaints of the townspeople.[43] On the other hand, any hope of redress depended on the king, who alone could impose his will on the officers, if he chose to do so. The king ordered that normal procedures be followed, but did not follow the orders up, especially when the bench failed to come up to his expectations in other matters. Plymouth was caught between the town's resentment and the king's demands. He appreciated that the town's complaints had considerable substance, but knew that the best way to secure redress was to comply with the king in all things, which the bench was not inclined to do.

III. ANGLICANS, DISSENTERS, AND CATHOLICS

Initially there was little evidence of overt hostility to the king's religion, although there was a pope-burning at Gosport on May Day in 1685.[44] From the spring of 1686 Catholic chapels were opened in a number of towns.[45] There was little

[39] BRB 6, p. 168; BRL 2759a, fos. 15–17.
[40] BRL 1507, 2759a, fos. 16–17; BRB 6, p. 172.
[41] BRL 1506, 2759a, fos. 18–20, 22, 26.   [42] BRL 2759a, fo. 43.
[43] BRB 6, p. 194; BRL 2759a, fo. 18.   [44] *PSP*, 129.
[45] Morrice MS P, p. 532, MS Q, pp. 71, 132; *CSPD 1686–7*, nos. 1381, 1486, 1487; Luttrell, i. 396; Miller, *Popery and Politics*, 242–4.

opposition. At Coventry some apprentices allegedly planned to disrupt the mass, but were dispersed before they could do so.[46] At Oxford differences between town and gown were forgotten in common hostility to the Catholics. Masters, undergraduates, and townspeople combined to hinder access to the Catholic services in Magdalen College chapel.[47] At Bristol, before the chapel opened, Sir John Knight II found a small group of Catholics with a priest about to say mass. He arrested the priest and next day examined him at the guildhall, before a large hostile crowd. Next day an Irish Catholic challenged Knight to fight; he was disarmed by spectators.[48] 'The rabble' held a procession mocking the Virgin Mary and the host, which was dispersed by soldiers; several were injured. The king, through Beaufort, warned the mayor not to be led astray by Knight's 'pretended zeal'.[49] Knight was sent for in custody and the mayor and five aldermen were summoned before the privy council. They were discharged on their humble submission, but Knight was prosecuted under an ancient statute against going armed to church. It was said that he had a blunderbuss or musket carried before him; he said he feared assassination. He was found not guilty by a Bristol jury. Despite his acquittal, Knight remained on bail, on the pretext that he was a threat to the state.[50] Meanwhile, the priest was brought to London on a writ of *habeas corpus* and discharged.[51]

If there was little overt opposition to the Catholic chapels, they brought home to townspeople the reality of Catholicism and the threat of popery and arbitrary government; in opening the chapels, the king was breaking the law. There was more opposition to orders to elect Catholic mayors: Cambridge corporation argued successfully that the order had arrived after the election had been completed.[52] In general, townspeople showed their disaffection less by open resistance (which was likely to bring punishment) than by failing to celebrate the birth of the prince of Wales in 1688, while enthusiastically celebrating the acquittal of the Seven Bishops.[53] In Oxford, on 1 July, government agents and senior army officers lit bonfires for the official thanksgiving for the prince's birth,

[46] BL, Add MS 41803, fo. 160.   [47] Wood, iii. 253–4.
[48] BRO, JQS/M/6, fo. 236; BCL, B10163, Annals of Bristol, 25 Apr. and 1 May 1686; *HMC Portland*, iii. 396: Morrice MS P, p. 538.
[49] Latimer, i. 439; V & A, Forster MS 426/3, fo. 23; *CSPD 1686–7*, nos. 371, 486; BRO, JQS/M/6, fo. 235 (another copy, BRO, 12964/1, no. 3).
[50] *CSPD 1686–7*, nos. 561–2, 1205, 1379; Morrice MS P, pp. 544, 545, 548, 549, 655, MS Q, pp. 15–16, 18, 51; Luttrell, i. 379, 380, 389; BCL, B10163, Annals of Bristol, 9 May 1686.
[51] Luttrell, i. 377, 378; BCL, B10163, Annals of Bristol, 10 May 1686.
[52] *HMC Downshire*, i. 296; Luttrell, i. 414–15; Morrice MS Q, p. 173.
[53] *HMC le Fleming*, 211, 212; *HMC Portland*, iii. 411; Luttrell, i. 449; Scott, 'York', 356; BL Add MSS 25376, fos. 188–9, 34510, fo. 137. In Somerset, when news came of the bishops' acquittal, the prince of Wales was reportedly burned in effigy along with the pope: BL, Add MS 25376, fo. 209.

but most Protestants used the occasion to celebrate the bishops' acquittal. By the end of September the public houses were full of people 'waiting for good news'; 5 November was celebrated with the greatest enthusiasm in living memory, 'in spite to the Papists'.[54] Many Catholic chapels were destroyed in the last weeks of the year.[55]

There was less opposition to the opening of Dissenting meeting houses. The king put an end to the persecution of Dissenters in the course of 1686, on the pretext that they were certified to be peaceable.[56] He seemed particularly eager to court the Baptists, who he believed would support the repeal of the penal laws and Test Acts; he had similar hopes of the Quakers.[57] The Baptists sought to take advantage of their new-found favour. Those of Tewkesbury asked that Baptist marriages should be recognized as good in law, that they should no longer be forced to serve in person as churchwardens, and that they should be allowed to pay their tithes to their own preachers.[58] The Presbyterian Roger Morrice thought the king was unwise to place too much reliance on the Baptists, who were fewer and less influential than the Independents or Presbyterians.[59] As yet James made no open move in favour of these denominations: he may still have harboured the suspicion that they were disaffected.[60] At the time of Monmouth's rebellion he had ordered lord lieutenants to arrest all disaffected persons, especially Nonconformist ministers; at Norwich those arrested included John Collinge, the doyen of the city's Presbyterian clergy.[61] According to Morrice, when the king issued his Declaration of Indulgence, many Presbyterian and Independent ministers did not want to open large meeting houses, or to hold services at the same time as the Anglicans, but he feared that their people would force them to do so.[62] But not all were so reticent. Collinge told the Anglican clergy of Norwich that he was now 'level' with them and would remember his former persecution.[63] New meeting houses were opened in Exeter, Birmingham, and elsewhere.[64]

[54] Wood, iii. 270–2, 278, 281.

[55] The bishop of Durham had advised the king to withdraw his protection from the chapels: *CSPD 1686–7*, no. 1840 (this clearly dates from late in 1688).

[56] Morrice MS P, pp. 563, 569, 572, 576; *CSPD 1686–7*, no. 488; Wood, iii. 190.

[57] Morrice MS P, p. 611, MS Q, p. 15; *CSPD 1686–7*, nos. 1160, 1215, 1281; *HMC le Fleming*, 201.

[58] Morrice MS Q, p. 141.   [59] Morrice MS P, p. 615.

[60] His declaration of indulgence for Scotland, issued before that for England, allowed Presbyterians only a severely restricted freedom of worship.

[61] *CSPD 1685*, no. 957; B. Cozens Hardy (ed.), *Norfolk Lieutenancy Journal 1676–1701*, NRS xxx (1961), 76.

[62] Morrice MS Q, pp. 84–5; PwA 2100, 2112.   [63] Tanner MS 29, fo. 8.

[64] Brockett, *Nonconformity in Exeter*, 54, 58–9; D. L. Wykes, 'James II's Religious Indulgence of 1687 and the Early Organization of Dissent', *Midland History*, xvi (1991), 86–9.

The king was keen to drive a wedge between Dissenters and Churchmen, keeping alive memories of persecution. He issued commissions to enquire into the money levied upon Dissenters and, where it had not been disposed of lawfully, to have it repaid.[65] In April 1688 he reissued his Declaration and ordered the bishops to instruct their clergy to read it in their churches. James saw this as a shrewd move: either they would read it, and so in effect endorse it, or refuse, which would suggest they were still wedded to persecution. Seven bishops presented the king with a petition, which stated that they believed the Declaration was illegal. Much to the king's annoyance, their stance won wide support among moderate Dissenters, many of whom now believed that the price James wished them to pay for securing freedom of worship would be the advancement of popery. Particularly crucial in changing their minds was the *Letter* of Gaspar Fagel, which stated that William and Mary, the heirs presumptive, favoured the repeal of the penal laws affecting Dissenters, but not the repeal of the Test Acts.[66] Churchmen and moderate Dissenters moved closer together, as the Church's leaders made conciliatory gestures and the Dissenters worried about the motives behind the king's conversion to toleration. In Norwich corporation, Anglicans and moderate Dissenters joined in voting 39 : 8 not to admit thirty-eight Quakers to the freedom. Bristol delayed reading a similar order for six months and then deferred a decision.[67]

IV. THE CAMPAIGN TO PACK PARLIAMENT

After the king issued his Declaration, it was made clear that he expected corporations to draw up addresses thanking him and promising to elect MPs pledged to repeal the penal laws and Test Acts.[68] In the autumn of 1687 he ordered lord lieutenants to summon their deputies and JPs and ask them three questions: essentially if they supported repeal and would vote for

---

[65] Morrice MS Q, p. 231; BL, Add MS 15397, fos. 5–8; Sir J. Mackintosh, *History of the Revolution of 1688* (London, 1834), 652; M. Goldie, 'James II and the Dissenters' Revenge: The Commission of Enquiry of 1688', *HR* lxvi (1993), 53–88.

[66] PwA 2112, 2118, 2129, 2161, 2167; BL, Add MSS 34510, fo. 121, 34512, fos. 83, 118; O. Heywood, *Autobiographies, Diaries, Anecdotes and Event Books*, ed. J. Horsfall Turner, 4 vols. (Brighouse, 1882–5), iv. 124–5, 133–4. For Fagel's *Letter*, see Miller, *James II*, 177; Miller, *Popery and Politics*, 253–5.

[67] FAB 8, fos. 144–6; Eddington, *First Fifty Years*, 259–61; BRO, 04264/8, fos. 10–11, 21; Tanner MS 29, fo. 147.

[68] Cartwright, *Diary*, 58 n., 74; Miller, *James II*, 172.

candidates who did so. He had decided that the time for unmanly equivocation had passed. He allegedly told the council that he who was not for him was against him and that he intended to 'regulate' the corporations.[69] In November he appointed a committee of the privy council to remove members who were against repeal and appoint more compliant men in their places.[70] In February 1688 a second committee was appointed, consisting mainly of Dissenters; its members included Robert Brent, a Catholic, a shadowy but important figure.[71] The Dissenters, such as the Baptists William Kiffin and Nehemiah Cox, were to give the king information about their brethren in the provinces. It was said that the king paid more heed to this group than to the privy council committee.[72] The early months of 1688 saw many large-scale changes in the membership of corporations. At Norwich ten aldermen and nineteen common councillors were removed; their replacements included several prominent Dissenters, three aldermen removed in 1683, and one voted off in 1678.[73] The king used his powers under the existing charters to remove members and required the corporation to 'elect' those he named in their places. From March he began to issue charters which gave him a power to nominate members.[74]

James had decided not to put the three questions to members of corporations; one lord lieutenant, who did so, received an overwhelmingly negative response.[75] Instead he relied on putting in men who he thought would vote as he wished—moderate Dissenters or moderate conformists in religion, Whigs in politics.[76] Bishop Trelawney of Exeter hoped that the Whig gentry would now be able to break the earl of Bath's electoral stranglehold on the boroughs of Devon and Cornwall.[77] Morrice rejoiced that the changes restored those put out in 1682–5. However, he was confident that they would not do as the king wished, and he was proved right. The agents sent by the committee of regulators hoped to persuade them, but enjoyed limited success.[78] Although

[69] Morrice MS Q, p. 170.   [70] Morrice MS Q, p. 207; Luttrell, i. 420–1.

[71] J. R. Jones, 'James II's Whig Collaborators', *HJ* iii (1960), 67–8.

[72] Morrice MS Q, pp. 238, 239–239 (2); Badminton, FmE 2/4/25, letter to Mr Burgis, n.d., marked '9'(?). For their identification as Baptists (William Collins, also a Baptist, appears on one of the lists), see B. R. White, *The English Baptists of the Seventeenth Century* (Didcot, 1996).

[73] FAB 8, fo. 139. The Dissenters included Barnham, Leverington, and Deresley. Wrench and Robert and Thomas Cooke had been removed in 1683 and Wigget in 1678.

[74] *CSPD 1687–9*, no. 794.   [75] *HMC le Fleming*, 205–7; *CSPD 1687–9*, no. 523.

[76] Jones, 'James II's Whig Collaborators', 65–7.   [77] Tanner MS 28, fo. 139.

[78] Morrice MS Q, pp. 234, 238, 239(2), 239(4), 243–5; *Norths*, ii. 221–2. Goldie refers to 'the Whig winter of 1687–8' and adds that the Whigs who accepted office at this time chose not to remember the fact after the Revolution: 'Dissenters' Revenge', 55.

in many towns the king ordered successive purges of the corporation, he was coming to realize that changing the membership was not enough. He had failed to win the support of most moderate Whigs and Dissenters, and could rely on only a small and motley collection of opportunists, extremists, and men over whom he had a hold, such as Nathaniel Wade, involved in Monmouth's rebellion, who was made town clerk of Bristol.[79]

The king's election agents responded to the townsmen's lack of enthusiasm for the king's plans with irritation and impatience: one observer compared them to Cromwell's major generals.[80] William Penn allegedly remarked that, as the Tories had rigged the general election in 1685, they could not complain if others did the same now.[81] When the king reissued his Declaration, it was accompanied by a proclamation, which warned his subjects not to be misled by crafty malicious men and restated his commitment to the repeal of the penal laws and Test Acts. This, he said, would secure the peace and greatness of the nation, an objective which no honest man could oppose. He had removed many people from offices who did not share this objective, and would maintain his army and navy, or enlarge them, 'if the safety or honour of the nation require it'.[82] As one contemporary put it, the king had told them that 'he has a pretty big army and will have a bigger if occasion require, which is a great comfort to us all'.[83] In the summer of 1688 there were complaints that the military were being used to coerce civilians. Dragoons were quartered on Carlisle, forcing the city to subscribe an address.[84] However, it refused a request to make the officers of the garrison freemen so that they could vote in elections.[85] In Huntingdon officers were admitted to the corporation and soldiers were to be allowed to vote; there were rumours that this was to become a general policy.[86] James was annoyed by the moderate Dissenters' refusal to co-operate.[87] He ordered the judges to give directions that towns should elect to Parliament such members as would comply with his wishes.[88]

But the towns still seemed reluctant. As the agent at Bedford remarked, there was too much 'democracy' in the town's constitution: it was deplorable that 'the exercise of the sovereign power' should be limited by the votes of the

[79] Jones, 'James II's Whig Collaborators', 68–70.
[80] Ailesbury, i. 174–5; *CSPD 1687–9*, no. 938.   [81] PwA 2129.
[82] PC 2/72, pp. 655–8.   [83] BL, Add MS 29563, fo. 130.
[84] PwA 2161; Campana, ii. 200.   [85] *HMC le Fleming*, 207–8.
[86] BL, Add MSS 41821, fo. 156, 25376, fo. 224. However, at Berwick in October army officers refused to vote in a municipal election, saying they regarded their freedom as honorary: Morrice MS Q, p. 182.
[87] BL, Add MS 34510, fo. 121; PwA 2161.   [88] Ellis, ii. 55–6.

common people, who were fickle and irrational.[89] The electorate needed to be reduced and this could be done only by charter. By August the regulators had produced a list of thirty-one boroughs needing new charters. Sometimes the king used some act of disobedience as a pretext to declare the corporation dissolved: Norwich and Warwick had both refused to admit Quakers as freemen; Ipswich had failed to present addresses.[90] Warrants were drawn up between 28 August and 14 September to prepare new charters for almost all these towns.[91] After Norwich corporation was dissolved the new charter confined the parliamentary electorate to the aldermen and common council. More Dissenters were added; of twenty-four aldermen in place at the king's accession only one remained.[92] Leicester corporation had told the earl of Huntingdon in November 1687 that it would not present an address, or elect anyone he recommended to Parliament. In 1688, after two purges, it received a new charter, which vested the franchise in the corporation, as it had requested in 1684; the mayor and at least four aldermen were Dissenters.[93] But the Dissenters' co-operation could not be relied upon. Some of those added to Leicester corporation refused to serve.[94] Those admitted at Norwich insisted on taking the oaths and making the declarations required by law, although the king had dispensed them from taking them. The mayor and aldermen also received communion together.[95] The members installed by these new charters barely had time to take their places before the king, by a proclamation of 17 October, revoked all charters issued since 1679 and reinstated all members in place when the earlier charters were surrendered.[96]

Despite the difficulties he faced, James remained confident of success. Contemporary views varied. Some thought that if he was determined and ruthless, and made no pretence that the elections were free and fair, he might succeed.[97] The bishop of Norwich wrote that the corporations of Norfolk, except Norwich, had been so 'regulated' and 'terrified' that they might elect those nominated by the king.[98] Some of those close to the king were less

[89] Duckett, ii. 61.   [90] *CSPD 1687–9*, nos. 1427, 1449; Luttrell, i. 457, 461.

[91] *CSPD 1687–9*, between 1404 and 1481; Luttrell, i. 460.

[92] BL, Add MS 34487, fo. 25; *CSPD 1687–9*, no. 1471.

[93] BL, Add MS 25375, fo, 29; *CSPD 1687–9*, no. 1440. The aldermen were Coleman, Treene, William Walker, and Samuel Wilson: *CSPD 1686–7*, no. 1523. For the purges, see PC 2/72, pp. 616, 653, 654.

[94] *HMC Hastings*, ii. 184.

[95] FAB 8, fos. 139, 141–2; MCB 25, fos. 231–2; Tanner MS 29, fo. 135.

[96] *London Gazette*, 15–18 Oct. 1688; *CSPD 1687–9*, no. 1732. James had been reluctant to restore the old charters: BL, Add MS 15397, fos. 330–1; *CSPD 1687–9*, nos. 1655, 1711.

[97] PwA 2112, 2145, 2147.   [98] Tanner MS 28, fo. 183.

confident. His chief minister, Sunderland, failed to persuade him not to insist on the repeal of the 1673 Test Act, which debarred Catholics from office, and to concentrate on repealing that of 1678, which had removed them from Parliament.[99] In September a leading regulator, Sir John Baber, stated that there was no prospect of securing a Parliament that would repeal the Test Acts.[100] Nevertheless, on 24 August the king ordered that the writs be issued for a general election.[101] This was based less on rational calculation than a desperate ploy to regain support, in the face of a possible invasion.[102] The agents were optimistic, but the precepts for elections were allegedly sent not to mayors, but to lord lieutenants, who were to summon selected members of corporations to see if they would elect the king's nominees.[103] On 20 September James issued a declaration restating his commitment to liberty of conscience and promising to secure the Church; Catholics were to be incapable of being elected to the Commons, which implied that he hoped to readmit them to the Lords.[104] Still more revealing was the instruction to electoral agents to pretend to support those against the king's interest, which would lead voters to distrust them.[105] On 28 September the king recalled the writs because of the imminent danger of invasion.[106]

There is much evidence of opposition to the king's will and to the regulators. Wigan had succumbed to pressure from Bishop Cartwright to thank the king for the Indulgence, but it refused to subscribe an address thanking him for the regulation of the corporation and promising to choose MPs committed to repeal.[107] Of our seven towns only Portsmouth promised to elect men who would repeal the penal laws and Test Acts.[108] There was thus no need for major changes in the corporation, but there was a cull of the burgesses, who comprised the parliamentary electorate: at Michaelmas 1687 there were 156; a year later there were seventy-three.[109] Even, the normally compliant city of Winchester dug in its heels. After its surrender in 1684, no new charter had been issued, but the corporation continued to function. The king's leading electoral agent was a Catholic, Bernard Howard. In April 1688 the regulators accused the

[99] Mackintosh, *Revolution of 1688*, 662.
[100] Archives Nationales, Paris, MS K1351, no. 4, pp. 54–6.
[101] PC 2/72, p. 727; Ellis, ii. 144.
[102] CPA 166, Barrillon to Louis XIV, 2 and 6 Sept. 1688 (new style); Morrice MS Q, p. 291.
[103] Duckett, i. 102; *CSPD 1687–9*, nos. 1483–91, 1504–9; BL, Add MS 34512, fo. 100.
[104] Luttrell, i. 462; BL, Add MS 34512, fo. 101; CPA 166, Barrillon to Louis XIV, 4 Oct. 1688 (new style).
[105] Morrice MS Q, p. 295.   [106] PC 2/72, pp. 738–9.   [107] *HMC Kenyon*, 189.
[108] *HP 1660–90*, i. 253; Duckett, i. 428, 432.   [109] East, 309.

city of stubbornness in refusing to surrender its charter, blissfully unaware that it had surrendered it four years before. The corporation was turned out and replaced by commissioners, headed by Howard. A grand jury refused to endorse an abhorrence of the bishops' petition and narrowly rejected a motion to present Catholic JPs for holding office contrary to law. Howard allegedly arranged to quarter more soldiers on the city in an effort to break its resistance.[110] Winchester was on the regulators' list and a warrant was issued at the end of August for a new charter, installing Howard as recorder and restricting the franchise to the mayor, aldermen, and common council.[111]

Given its track record, Oxford could be expected to oppose the king's measures. Early in 1688 the privy council ordered the removal of two aldermen and twenty-nine other councillors. The council was ordered to elect William Wright and Robert Pauling, the two leading Whigs from the early 1680s, as aldermen, along with others, including Edward Prince, whose election as town clerk Charles II had refused to approve, and Richard Carter.[112] Pauling refused to accept the place, so the king sent a letter ordering the council to elect Carter an alderman instead. In a meeting immortalized in a painting by van Heemskerk, a majority of the council twice voted for Carter, only to be outvoted when the candidates were presented to the commons for endorsement. Twice the person chosen by the majority refused to serve, so the mayor was reduced to calling another meeting at which Carter was elected; there is no mention of any other candidate.[113] The purged corporation proved no more amenable than before. In April the king ordered a *quo warranto*, which the council resolved to oppose. In June the corporation was dissolved and a commission of eight was appointed to govern the city, including Wright and Carter.[114] A new charter arrived in September; it had been drawn up in early August and did not restrict the franchise to the corporation.[115] The mayor, Carter, and the bailiffs went to St Mary's to be sworn, but the vice chancellor refused to interrupt his dinner to swear them.[116]

---

[110] Duckett, i. 427, 431–2; Luttrell, i. 438; Ellis, ii. 108–9; Bodl, Ballard MS 12, fo. 39; *HP 1660–90*, ii. 260; Coleby, *Hampshire*, 175; Childs, *The Army, James II and the Glorious Revolution*, 111, 118. The source of the story about Howard bringing in soldiers is a dispatch from the Dutch ambassador, who was not the best informed or most unbiased of authorities: BL, Add MS 34512, fos. 77–8.

[111] *CSPD 1687–9*, no. 1407.

[112] PC 2/72, p. 579; *OCA*, iii. 196–8. William Wright junior, who was later regarded as a Whig, had been elected deputy recorder in 1687.

[113] *OCA*, iii. 198; Wood, iii. 261; *CSPD 1687–9*, no. 901.

[114] *OCA*, iii. 199–200; BL, Add MS 36707, fo. 33; PC 2/72, pp. 677–8.

[115] *CSPD 1687–9*, no. 1354.   [116] Wood, iii. 277–8.

The town subjected to the greatest pressure was Hull. In September 1687 Plymouth pressed the bench to draw up an address thanking the king for his Declaration, but, when it eventually did so, it thanked the king for his promises to uphold the Church as by law established, and concluded with a promise to prove themselves good sons of the Church and loyal subjects. Plymouth wrote that he dared not present such an address and drew up another, which included a promise to promote the election of such MPs 'as are of known loyalty and affection for your Majesty's service'.[117] However, on 1 September the bench had agreed to use its interest in the next election on behalf of Sir Willoughby Hickman and John Ramsden, the town's two representatives in 1685. The fact that it did not inform Plymouth of this until 2 November suggests that it did not expect it to please him.[118] By the time this letter arrived, Plymouth was dead. The bench cannot have been heartened by the news that Lord Langdale, a Catholic, was to be the new governor, or by the advice of Bishop Watson of St David's, emerging as the town's friend at court, to propose Lord Dover, another Catholic, as the high steward.[119] The bench hoped to persuade Sunderland, who would have been a most powerful patron, to serve as recorder. When he declined, it accepted his advice to offer it to Langdale and resolved to be courteous towards him, in the hope that he would make the garrison more civil.[120]

Langdale seemed sympathetic,[121] but he knew that the soldiers could be crucial in inducing the bench to comply with the king's electoral plans, enhancing his credit 'above'. The officers knew this too; many refused to pay for their men's lodgings in public houses. They knew that they were unlikely to face a serious reprimand, as did soldiers who ran up debts or stole from townspeople.[122] When the mayor and aldermen tried to spread the burden of quartering more equally, they were again accused of mustering soldiers, and of planning an insurrection.[123] Copley's hostility towards the town became even more apparent; he poisoned the minds of newly arrived officers, many of whom withheld the money that should have been spent on lodging their men.[124] In January the king's cabinet council decided that public houses should receive only as many men as they conveniently could, the rest going into private houses at 8*d.* a week. When the bench assessed the number of places in public houses at 300,

---

[117] BRL 2759a, fos. 20–1; Delapryme, *Hull,* 112–13, 114; M. J. Short, 'The Corporation of Hull and the Government of James II, 1687–8', *HR* lxxi (1998), 177–8. Short interprets this as a promise to choose those nominated by the king.

[118] BRB 6, p. 188; BRL 2759a, fo. 22.   [119] BRL 2759a, fo. 22.
[120] Ibid. 22–5.   [121] Ibid. 26, 27.   [122] Ibid. 29, 30–1.
[123] Ibid. 31.   [124] Ibid. 30–3, 36.

the king and council accepted the figure; the officers of Cornwall's regiment refused to pay the arrears, which the bench claimed were due, when it left town.[125] Meanwhile, there loomed the question of the bench's commitment to back Hickman and Ramsden in the next election. At the end of December it tried to persuade Watson that the two would comply with the king's wishes, 'so far as may stand with the safety of our Church and religion'.[126] Watson replied that this would not satisfy the king.[127]

After being tendered the three questions, the mayor and aldermen wrote to Langdale that they could not promise something that was not in their power, but they would try to return 'such as are truly loyal to our sovereign and his interest and have a due esteem for their country'.[128] Langdale replied that the king was obliged in honour and conscience to confirm his Declaration, and that those who failed to comply with his just desires would feel his displeasure; he named as one candidate Sir James Bradshaw, 'against whom none of you, I am sure, can make any objection'; he would inform them of the king's other nominee later.[129] The bench replied (a month later) that events depended upon God and that nothing in its last letter could give any cause to believe that it would not comply with the Declaration of Indulgence—which was not the same as supporting the election of men committed to making it permanent.[130] At this point, according to Abraham Delapryme, writing a decade after the event, the king was so angry that he ordered 1,200 soldiers to have free quarter on the inhabitants, with 'liberty to insult over them as they pleased', leading to robberies, murder, and rapes.[131] There is no evidence for this in the municipal records, which suggest that the king was still trying to resolve the problems of quartering. He ordered at the end of September that only 300 men should quarter in public houses, the remainder going to private houses at 8*d.* a week; he also ordered the payment of arrears due to the town, and repeated the order that private householders should not be forced to take in soldiers without their consent.[132] He also expressed irritation that the town refused to quarter such a garrison as he judged necessary.[133] The townspeople may well have believed

---

[125] BRL 1111, 1112, 2759a, fos. 36–7.   [126] BRL 2759a, fo. 29.

[127] Ibid. 34–5.   [128] Ibid. 38; Short, 'Hull and James II', 180.

[129] Delapryme, *Hull,* 114–15.   [130] BRL 2759a, fo. 38

[131] Delapryme, *Hull,* 115. Other copies of his 'History' omit the reference to rapes: BL Add MS 9836, fo. 129, Lansdowne MS 890, fo. 188.

[132] BRL 1509, 2759a, fo. 43; G. Davies, 'Letters on the Administration of James II's Army', *JSAHR* xxix (1951), 75; PC 2/72, pp. 731–2. Despite the king's order, there were great complaints of disorders committed by the soldiers: Luttrell, i. 459.

[133] Davies, 'Letters on James II's Army', 80.

that the men had orders to take free quarter, and it is likely that officers did not discourage their men from treating the townspeople brutally, and avoided paying what was due because they thought they could get away with it.[134] It is also possible that Delapryme interpreted references to 'free quarter' as meaning more than not paying for lodging in public houses.[135]

The king's response to the bench's stubbornness was a *quo warranto*. It was hinted that if the charter were renewed, 'His Majesty might thereby have the approval of our members to serve in Parliament'—presumably by vesting the right of election in the bench, who would be nominated by the king. The bench claimed that the right to elect members was conferred by prescription, not charter.[136] It decided that it could not fight the *quo warranto* and voted to surrender, adding in a petition that this was a mark of obedience to the king.[137] It wrote with heavy irony to its agent in London that it hoped, through the favour of 'our two great patriots', Langdale and Dover, to secure a new charter at reduced fees.[138] It was reported that, when the petition was presented, James said he would grant a new charter, although they did not deserve it. On 22 July the privy council ordered the removal of the entire corporation, but the bench met as usual until 22 September.[139] Hull was on the regulators' list and a new charter was issued, which restricted the franchise to the mayor and aldermen.[140] The bench barely had time to act before the proclamation restoring charters; the old corporation reconvened on 6 November and turned out those appointed by the last charter.[141]

M. J. Short has suggested that the town's Whigs and Dissenters might have supported repeal and might have secured the election of the king's nominees. He supports this claim by stating that there were many Dissenters in the town; even though he accepts that the claim that two-thirds of the townsmen were Presbyterians was an exaggeration, he claims that 'Anglicans were probably intrinsically the weaker party'.[142] One does not know what Short understands by 'Anglicans', but if one accepts as a working definition 'conforming members of the Church of England' the bench in place at the start of 1688 could be described as 'Anglican', insisting on caveats safeguarding the Church of England.

[134] BRL 1113, 1507, 1509, 2759a, fos. 38–43; BRB 6, p. 203.
[135] Delapryme, *Hull*, 115–16; BRL 2759a, fos. 38–40.
[136] Delapryme, *Hull*, 116; BRL 2759a, fo. 40.
[137] BRB 6, pp. 208–9; BRL 2759a, fo. 41.   [138] BRL 2759a, fo. 42
[139] PC 2/72, p. 720: BRB 6, pp. 214–16; Short, 'Hull and James II', 183–4.
[140] *CSPD 1687–9*, nos. 1427, 1495; Short, 'Hull and James II', 187.
[141] BRB 6, p. 230; Short, 'Hull and James II', 190 n. 135.
[142] Short, 'Hull and James II', 189–92 (quotation from 190).

Under Charles II, in its commitment to parish worship, and its opposition to persecution, it seems to have shared the views of the bulk of the townspeople. Evidence from elsewhere suggests that the efforts of the regulators were often counter-productive. The most trenchant criticism came from the earl of Bath. He naturally resented their intrusion into his electoral empire, but his letters made a powerful statement of the disruption they had caused. Most towns did not know their own magistrates, and some had been put in by mistake or were not duly elected. At Exeter 'the most substantial rich loyal citizens' had been turned out for no reason 'and this in such a hurry that they destroyed their charter for very haste'. The city was now 'domineered over by a packed chamber of Dissenters'; 'all the interest is in one scale and nothing but bare authority in the other'. The king's wisest course would be to reinstate the old magistrates.[143] In the unlikely event that James had managed to secure a House of Commons in which the majority was pledged to repeal, it would have been difficult to claim that it was duly elected or representative.

V. THE TOWNS AND THE REVOLUTION OF 1688–1689

The contribution of townspeople to James II's departure came, first, in riots against Catholics, which demoralized the king and destabilized his government, and second, in seizing control of towns from their garrisons; some towns were seized by regular troops (and of course William's army).[144] Attacks on Catholic chapels started in London as early as 30 September, but no serious damage was done until the end of October. In Norwich a crowd of about a thousand, mostly 'boys', gathered on 14 October; the mayor and sheriffs dispersed them and the mayor escorted the worshippers to their lodgings, which suggests that they were not numerous.[145] In late October the papal nuncio wrote that the people believed they could now 'insult' Catholic chapels with impunity.[146] At Reading on 5 November there were running battles between the garrison and a crowd of 200, who wanted to burn the pope and pull down the chapel.[147] There was a

---

[143] *CSPD 1687–9*, nos. 1564, 1651 (quoted); *HMC Dartmouth*, i. 139; BL, Add MS 41805, fos. 118–19. Some of the magistrates of Exeter were later suspended for refusing to comply with William: BL, Add MS 41805, fo. 215. For other towns where the government was seriously disrupted, see *CSPD 1687–9*, nos. 1627, 1695; Bucks RO, D135/B1/4/24: BL, Add MS 34512, fo, 152; *HMC Leeds, etc.*, 201.

[144] Exeter was the first town to be 'liberated' by William's army: BL, Add MS 41805, fos. 118–19.

[145] Miller, 'Militia and Army', 673; *CSPD 1687–9*, no. 1715.

[146] BL, Add MS 15397, fo. 370.   [147] BL, Add MS 41805, fo. 148.

wave of attacks in early December; chapels were demolished at York, Bristol, Gloucester, Worcester, Shrewsbury, Stafford, Wolverhampton, Birmingham, Lincoln, Cambridge, and Bury St Edmunds.[148] A Quaker meeting house was destroyed in Sunderland.[149] At Newcastle the gentry removed the 'trinkets' from the chapel, but did not damage the building.[150] Violent self-help against Catholics was encouraged by the (forged) 'third declaration' of the prince of Orange, which declared that if Catholics did not lay down their arms within twenty days, they were to receive no quarter.[151] After news came of James's flight, the people grew bolder. Crowds from Cambridge and Bury St Edmunds searched Lord Dover's house at Cheveley. They demolished the chapel, but were given money not to harm the house. They also seized Bishop Watson, put him on an old horse with a halter around his neck, and sent him to Cambridge, where they 'obliged' the magistrates to imprison him in the castle.[152]

When James fled on 10 December, his commander in chief ordered the soldiers to disband, but not all did so.[153] Amid confusion and disorder, Irish troops tried to find their way home, amid wild and widespread rumours that they were plundering, burning, and killing everyone in their path. In the short run, the panic distracted the crowds; towns shut their gates and watched anxiously for the Irish.[154] But the panic also sustained the sense of threat and people had got used to taking the law into their own hands. At Bury St Edmunds the crowd reassembled and began to plunder Protestants as well as Catholics, imposing 'taxes' (presumably protection money). The militia was raised, but refused to fire on the crowd and forced the colonel to declare for 'free booty'. Eventually a body of gentleman volunteers dispersed the rioters.[155] At Norwich a crowd sacked the Catholic chapel, burning the furniture and fittings. They pillaged the houses of several Catholics, but were dispersed by the city militia. The following night they assembled again, attacked several citizens' houses and threatened to attack

[148] *Universal Intelligence*, 11 Dec., *English Currant*, 12–14 Dec. 1688; *HMC le Fleming*, 226; *HMC 5th Report*, 198; *HMC 7th Report*, 419.
[149] Miller, ' "A Suffering People" ', 100–1.
[150] *Great News from Nottingham the Fifth of December 1688*.
[151] *HMC Eliot Hodgkin*, 75; Bodl, Ballard MS 45, fo. 20.
[152] *Universal Intelligence*, 15–18, 22–6 Dec., *London Courant*, 18–22 Dec., *London Mercury*, 22–4 Dec. 1688; Morrice MS Q, p. 389; Newton, *Diary*, 75. Dr Arderne, the dean of Chester, suffered a fate similar to Watson's: *Universal Intelligence*, 26–9 Dec. 1688.
[153] *HMC Dartmouth*, iii. 135; Campana, ii. 430; CPA 167, Barrillon to Louis XIV, 22 and 24 Dec. 1688 (new style).
[154] Ailesbury, i. 204–7; P. C. Vellacott, 'The Diary of a Country Gentleman in 1688', *Cambridge Historical Journal*, ii (1926), 57; Newton, *Diary*, 96–7; BL, Add MS 25377, fos. 200–1; Miller, *Popery and Politics*, 259–61.
[155] *London Courant*, 18–22 Dec., *London Mercury*, 31 Dec. 1688–3 Jan. 1689; Tanner MS 28, fo. 273.

others, including the bishop's palace and some in the cathedral close. Prideaux had the close gates shut and the inhabitants armed and repulsed the crowd, estimated at 500. The crowd then plundered and gutted the Bull Inn, whose landlord was a papist. Next day a whole regiment of the city militia was raised, many citizens armed to protect their homes, and the mayor's court ordered citizens to keep their servants and children at home. Although a large crowd gathered, it did little harm. The militia guard was reduced on the 16th and by the 19th normality had returned.[156] These disorders, much the most serious since the Restoration, were reported in a suddenly revived newspaper press and created fears of anarchy. There were reports of crowds attacking deer parks (especially the king's) and refusing to pay taxes, and rumours that, since the king had left the kingdom, all authority and law had ceased.[157]

The behaviour of the crowds was uncomfortably reminiscent of 1641–2. The militia at Norwich and the gentlemen volunteers at Bury were just about able to cope,[158] but authority seemed fragile, not least because the forces of order were either in disarray—the county militias had been neglected for three years —or deeply divided. There were two rival armies, and divisions within James's between Protestant and Catholic. At Berwick Protestant officers refused to admit a body of Catholic horse; at Lancaster all but two of the soldiers in the garrison went to church 'upon a proclamation among themselves'.[159] There were also several Catholic garrisons, creating alarm among Protestant townspeople. At Gloucester Lord Lovelace had been imprisoned by the Catholic mayor, who refused to release him without an order from Beaufort, the lord lieutenant. A young gentleman gathered a band of well-armed townsmen and seized the mayor and the castle, after a few shots fired by the sentinels. Lovelace was declared governor; the mayor resigned, to avoid being sent to prison.[160] At Chester, where the Catholic Lord Molyneux was governor, Colonel Gage's Catholic regiment had caused near-panic when it arrived, at night; the city militia at first refused to admit it. Gage's regiment found the militia and townspeople very hostile. It was said that many of the soldiers wished they were back home; most had no weapons. Although they caused no trouble, there were rumours that they planned

---

[156] Blomefield, *Norfolk*, iii. 347 (where the dates are wrongly given as 7–8 December); *Life of Humphrey Prideaux* (1748), 47–8; NCR, Case 13b/7, Lieutenancy Order Book, fo. 98; MCB 25, fo. 245.

[157] *English Currant*, 26–8 Dec., 29 Dec. 1688–2 Jan. 1689; *HMC Beaufort*, 93.

[158] At Bristol crowds attacked papists' houses and a Catholic chapel, but the aldermen drew their swords and restored order: Bodl, MS Gough Somerset 2, p. 119; BCL, B10163, Annals of Bristol, 1 Dec. 1688; Luttrell, i. 482.

[159] *Universal Intelligence*, 11 Dec. 1688; *HMC le Fleming*, 221.

[160] *English Currant*, 12–14 Dec. 1688; Morrice MS Q, p. 340.

to kill man, woman, and child. The mayor, aldermen, and the commander of one of the city militia troops secretly assembled about a thousand men, who disarmed the regiment and two Irish troops of dragoons.[161] The officers were so demoralized that they allowed the boys of the city to take what they pleased from their pockets.[162] Dover castle was also seized by a party of townspeople.[163]

In some towns, the Catholics were disarmed, or persuaded to surrender, by Protestants within the armed forces. At Carlisle Sir John Lowther claimed that he could seize control from the Catholic governor if he was allowed four troops of horse from the forces under Danby's command. He had hoped to use some of the county militia, but Christopher Musgrave and other deputy lieutenants refused to summon it, preferring to negotiate. Their patience was rewarded when the governor delivered the keys.[164] At Hull there was tension because Montgomery's regiment was predominantly Catholic; many Catholics from the countryside took refuge in the town. According to Delapryme, the Catholic soldiers swore that if hostile soldiers came they would slaughter the inhabitants. In the event there was no massacre; Copley and the Protestant officers, with the mayor and aldermen, mobilized the seamen in the port. When the mayor and aldermen went on their rounds on the night of 3 December, the seamen seized the guards. Copley and the Protestant officers disarmed their Catholic colleagues. This was followed by a brief outbreak of plunder (presumably of Catholics), but the bench quickly restored order. Copley, recently the bench's *bête noire*, and the other Protestant officers were treated to drinks in the town hall.[165]

For a while it looked as if matters would not be resolved so peacefully in the other major provincial garrison, Portsmouth. Relations between the town and the soldiers had deteriorated.[166] By 1688 there was a Catholic governor, the duke of Berwick, the king's illegitimate son, and MacElligott's Irish Catholic regiment quartered in the town. The Irish were accused of violence, even murder, against civilians, of refusing to pay for their quarters, and of robbery, even robbing the mayor.[167] Their presence antagonized the townspeople, but

[161] *HMC Kenyon*, 206, 207, 209 (the reference to 'the city' shows that the last referred to Chester, not Wigan); *CSPD 1687–9*, no. 1762; Luttrell, i. 489; *HMC 5th Report*, 358; *Universal Intelligence*, 12–15 Dec., 18–22 Dec., *English Currant*, 12–14 Dec., 29 Dec. 1688–2 Jan. 1689. Some sources refer to Molyneux's regiment but it was Gage's.

[162] *HMC le Fleming*, 228. At Carlisle the dean of Durham was robbed of money and horses, but later Musgrave had them returned: Granville, *Remains*, i. 75–6.

[163] *Universal Intelligence*, 12–15 Dec. 1688; *CSPD 1689–90*, 28; *HMC Dartmouth*, i. 228.

[164] BL, Egerton MS 3336, fos. 36–7, 48–50, 97, 99, 103–4; *HMC Dartmouth*, iii. 143; Granville, *Remains*, i. 75.

[165] Delapryme, *Hull*, 117; BRB 6, pp. 231–2; *London Mercury*, 15–18 Dec. 1688.

[166] *PSP*, 120–1.   [167] East, 190; *HMC le Fleming*, 213; *CSPD 1689–90*, 108.

also the Protestant officers and soldiers. There were running battles in the streets between Catholic and Protestant soldiers, and a pitched battle, also involving townsmen, after a shot was allegedly fired into the church. Reports said that as many as eighty were killed.[168] In September six officers were cashiered for refusing to take supernumerary Irish troops into their regiment; seven others resigned in protest and up to a hundred soldiers deserted.[169]

When William landed in the south-west, the Irish feared for their lives. The earl of Dartmouth, commander of the fleet anchored off the town, wrote that the 'poor wretches' were willing to do anything and go anywhere to save their skins.[170] Some threatened and blustered, talking of firing the town or blowing up the magazine and forts. The deputy governor, Sir Edward Scott, also a Catholic, struck and berated the mayor, calling the corporation 'rebels'; he added that if William's army came, he would cut the throats of all the corporation. Scott defended this by saying that he suspected the corporation of 'caballing' with the officers of the garrison and that it was common, in time of war, to threaten civilians to keep them to their duty—a revealing comment on the military mind under James II.[171] The mayor took refuge on the fleet, having ordered torches to be lit on the church tower if the soldiers offered any violence to the people. Meanwhile the former governor, Richard Norton, raised a thousand horse and foot and exercised them near the town. Berwick assured him that he would not allow any violence against the townspeople.[172] On 14 December, some seamen drove the soldiers out of Gosport castle and refused to hand it over to Berwick, saying they would deliver it only to Protestants. Meanwhile, Dartmouth tried to persuade Berwick to hand Southsea castle over to Captain Carter, a Protestant. He argued that Berwick would be unable to hold the castle for long, as the country would deny it provisions. Berwick hesitated, but Dartmouth moved ships into the harbour and ensured that there was a strong guard on the docks. By the 18th Carter was in possession of Southsea castle and Scott had resigned and left. The Catholic units in the garrison, aware of the danger they were in, sought to

---

[168] *HMC le Fleming*, 214–15, 218; Morrice MS Q, p. 309.

[169] Coleby, *Hampshire*, 186; BL, Add MS 34510, fos. 82–3; *HMC Leybourne-Popham*, 266–7; Ellis, ii. 167–8. James had wished to punish them more severely, but a majority of the privy council thought cashiering would be sufficient: BL, Add MS 34512, fo. 98; CPA 166, Barrillon to Louis XIV, 16, 27, and 30 Sept. 1688 (new style).

[170] *HMC Dartmouth*, i. 279–80, iii. 138.

[171] East, 190; *English Currant*, 19–21 Dec. 1688; *HMC Dartmouth*, i. 230–2, 282.

[172] *HMC Dartmouth*, i. 234; *English Currant*, 19–21 Dec. 1688.

reassure the townspeople.[173] Next day Berwick received orders from his father to hand over the town to forces sent by William. The new garrison arrived on the 21st and the Irish finally left.[174]

It might seem that in 1688 English Protestants of all sorts came together in the face of the threat from popery. However, before James finally left, on 24 December, divisions opened up between Tories and Whigs as they competed for William's favour. The declaration in which William justified his invasion had been aimed far more at the Tories than at the Whigs and had ensured that Tory opposition was minimal. But most who came over with William were Whigs, who had done much to shape William's perception of the situation in England. They argued that the Tories' first loyalty was to James, and promoted the association (a promise to support William against the papists). Many Tories believed that to subscribe this was incompatible with their oath of allegiance to James, who was still their king; Whigs claimed that this showed where the Tories' true loyalties lay.[175] In October a High Church clergyman wrote that there was 'some danger of people being known by names and parties again'. On 4 December a newsletter remarked that it was 'already a scandal to be neuter passive, as it will be a crime hereafter . . . there is no such thing as treason now'.[176] Northern Whigs criticized Musgrave's refusal to act robustly against the governor of Carlisle.[177] The earl of Derby, whose actions had been timid and equivocal, found himself ousted from his lieutenancies by the far more active Lord Delamere, who claimed that Gage's regiment had seized Chester castle, which was untrue.[178] Ominously for the Tories, the Whigs tried to divert attention from the collaboration of some of their number with James by raking up the deaths of the Whig 'martyrs' of the early 1680s and other alleged 'crimes' of the Tories. By early January 1689 Whigs were gathering information on surrenders of charters in 1682–5, claiming that those who agreed to them had betrayed their corporations.[179] When the Convention met, there would be a renewed struggle for control of the towns.

[173] *English Currant,* 19–21 Dec. 1688; *HMC Dartmouth,* i. 281–3, iii. 70.

[174] *HMC Dartmouth,* i. 237–8; *English Currant,* 21–6 Dec. 1688.

[175] J. Miller, 'Proto-Jacobitism? The Tories and the Revolution of 1688–9', in E. Cruickshanks and J. Black (eds.), *The Jacobite Challenge* (Edinburgh, 1988), 13, 17. However, at Leicester nineteen aldermen and at least sixteen common councilmen subscribed the association. The corporation was restored as it had been before the surrender in 1684, but vacancies were filled from among those added by the charter or elected in 1684–5: *RBL,* iv. 590.

[176] Bodl, Ballard MS 12, fo. 41; BL, Add MS 36707, fo. 50.

[177] BL, Egerton MS 3336, fo. 114; *HMC Dartmouth,* i. 245.

[178] *HMC Kenyon,* 207; Carte MS 40, fo. 504.

[179] Miller, 'Proto-Jacobitism?', 17; *London Mercury,* 7–10 Jan. 1689; BL, Egerton MS 3336, fo. 146.

11

After the Revolution, 1689–1699

The 1690s were deeply turbulent for many towns. William III's accession, and Louis XIV's continued support for James II, brought England into the great war raging on the continent, now also a war of the English succession. The war was fought on a massive scale, making necessary taxation far higher than under Charles II. It severely disrupted trade and industry. Bad harvests led to widespread food riots, the first since the early 1660s; the situation was made worse by the recoinage of 1696, which led to a severe shortage of coin, which particularly affected the poor. The strains of war distracted attention from the political and religious issues which had been so prominent in the 1680s. Partisan animosities did not disappear, but they were less pervasive than they had been in the 1680s, or were to be after 1700.

I. THE TOLERATION ACT

The Toleration Act of 1689 virtually ended religious persecution. Faced with James II's offers of toleration, Church leaders began to talk of the need to show due tenderness towards their 'brethren', the Dissenters.[1] In the exchanges that followed, there was talk of comprehension, allowing those repelled by the Church's ceremonies to omit them, and toleration, for those who did not want to be part of the national Church. The same issues had been raised at the Restoration, in the late 1660s, and in 1680–1. On each occasion the Church's leaders had not been able to offer enough to satisfy even the more moderate Presbyterians, many of whose brethren wanted no part of a Church they saw as irredeemably corrupt. The High Church element among the Anglican clergy wanted no concessions: diversity of practice would lead to schism. To make matters worse, the Church's leaders and their lay allies saw William as

[1] Gutch, *Collectanea Curiosa*, i. 336–7.

hostile to the Church. They were committed to making some concessions to Dissent, following their assurances under James; but they were determined to concede as little as possible. Eventually the Tories in Parliament agreed to pass the toleration bill on condition that the proposals for comprehension were effectively buried. Freedom of worship to Dissenters was the price of keeping the Church's worship pure.[2]

The Act was intended to allow Dissenters to meet freely while continuing to keep them out of office: when it was passed the Commons was debating bills to repeal the Corporation Act and remove the sacramental requirement from the Test Acts, for Protestants.[3] All the existing penal laws remained in force, but their penalties were not to apply to those complying with certain conditions. Meeting houses had to be registered, and congregations had to meet with their doors unlocked: there was still implication that meetings could be covers for sedition. Preachers had to subscribe the Thirty-Nine Articles, with the exception of those relating to ceremonies and homilies; Baptists could also omit part of the article relating to infant baptism. They also had to take the oath of allegiance and make a brief statement of Christian belief, acknowledging the Trinity and that the Scriptures were 'given by divine inspiration'; Quakers were allowed to affirm, rather than swear.[4] The only Protestants excluded were those who denied the Trinity (known as Socinians) and non-jurors—those Anglican clergy who refused to swear allegiance to William and Mary. Thus by a supreme irony, the only 'conventicles' prosecuted after 1689 were led by High Churchmen who had been expelled from the Church for not taking the oath.[5] No liberty was granted to Catholics or Jews.

The Toleration Act was designed to allow the Dissenters, a small minority, to worship unmolested. It was assumed that everyone else remained members of the Church of England, and subject to its discipline. The laws requiring church attendance were still in force; everyone had to attend either their parish church or a recognized Nonconformist meeting.[6] Enforcing church attendance had always been difficult, especially in towns with several parish churches; as urban populations grew, it became harder to monitor, and many churchwardens and constables were not prepared to report their neighbours. With people required to attend one of two (or more) places of worship, enforcement became

---

    [2] H. Horwitz, *Parliament, Policy and Politics in the Reign of William III* (Manchester, 1977), 24–6; Spurr, 'Church, Comprehension and the Toleration Act', 927–8, 945–6.
    [3] Horwitz, *Parliament, Policy and Politics*, 21–4.   [4] Browning, *Docts*, 401–3.
    [5] *HMC Finch*, iii. 396; Luttrell, ii. 354; NCR, Case 20a/18, 19 Jan. 1717.
    [6] Browning, *Docts*, 403.

impossible and some parish churches saw a severe drop in attendance, due less to defections to Dissenting meetings than to people staying at home.[7] The Anglican clergy were used to relying on the law to command the people; now they had to learn to compete.[8] The competition came not only from Dissenters but from those who questioned received Christian teaching. The 1690s saw the end of pre-publication censorship. Works appeared which were denounced by the clergy as promoting blasphemy and atheism. They rarely denied the existence of God, but pared down the essentials of Christian belief. John Locke read his Bible—or at least those books he regarded as authoritative—with great care.[9] His reading led him to jettison much of traditional theology, including belief in original sin and the Trinity; he thought that the one essential truth was that Jesus was the Messiah. He kept quiet about his reservations about the Trinity, as did Sir Isaac Newton, who wrote more about theology than he did about science. They did so because they feared prosecution, but their doubts reflected a conviction that these matters were too important to be left to the Anglican clergy, with their emphasis on the authority of the Church and its priests. Their views were received sympathetically by many, inside and outside the Church, who shared their hostility to 'priestcraft'. The more High Churchmen and Tories magnified the authority of their 'holy mother', the 'apostolic' Church of England, the more Low Churchmen and Whigs defended theological dissidents. A few were found among the clergy. The most notorious was Benjamin Hoadly, who denied the need for institutional churches, or clergy, or confessions of faith, or liturgies: all that God required was that people should be sincere in their beliefs. His views reduced High Churchmen to apoplectic rage, which led Whig politicians to praise his 'moderation' and to press for his promotion; he ended his days as bishop of Winchester.[10]

It took time for perceptions of dwindling congregations to spread, or for the trickle of heterodox literature to develop into what anxious clergymen saw as a flood. They also worried about the decline of public morals. Many

[7] Prideaux, 153–5; Spurr in Walsh et al., 130. There were some presentments and punishments for absence from church in Dorchester: Underdown, *Fire from Heaven*, 263.

[8] On the Church after 1689, see G. V. Bennett, 'Conflict in the Church', in G. Holmes (ed.), *Britain after the Glorious Revolution, 1689–1714* (London, 1969), ch. 7; G. V. Bennett, *The Tory Crisis in Church and State 1688–1730* (Oxford, 1975), ch. 1; Holmes, *Sacheverell*, ch. 2; Spaeth, *Age of Danger*.

[9] J. Champion, ' "Directions for the Profitable Reading of the Holy Scriptures": Biblical Criticism, Clerical Learning and Lay Readers, c.1650–1720', in A. Hessayon and N. Keene (eds.), *Scripture and Scholarship in Early Modern England* (Aldershot, 2006), 221–7.

[10] N. Sykes, *Church and State in England in the Eighteenth Century* (Cambridge, 1934), ch. 8.

believed that England was in the grip of a crime wave. Parliament was rocked by bribery scandals, while sharp financiers in the City made large sums in ways that were incomprehensible to many in the provinces. There were claims that drunkenness, gambling, and promiscuity were increasing—impossible to prove or disprove—and complaints of obscenity on the stage. These perceptions and complaints led to the formation of Societies for the Reformation of Manners, whose main function was to prosecute those accused of drunkenness, swearing, gambling, and prostitution, although they also encouraged the extension of religious education, through sermons and schools.[11] Initially the members included Low Church Anglicans as well as Dissenters, but the latter came to predominate. The Bristol Society opposed parish-based charity schools and refused to use the Church's liturgy.[12] The High Church clergy dissociated themselves from the Societies and then denounced them for assuming a role in maintaining moral discipline which properly belonged to the Church. Instead of the 'ancient primitive discipline of the Church', which had long protected the nation against immorality, heresy, and schism, in the Societies 'every tradesman and mechanic is to determine religious truth'.[13] Together with the failure to enforce church attendance or to suppress heterodox works, High Churchmen blamed the collapse of public morals on the weakening of the Church by the Toleration Act.

And there was more. The Act made no mention of schools. Dissenting academies offered a more modern curriculum than the grammar schools, which essentially taught Latin and Greek to prepare young men for Oxbridge. The Dissenting schools were seen as enticing the young away from the Church, which responded by setting up charity schools to teach children reading, writing, and the Anglican religion; hospitals and other charitable institutions which took in poor children became arenas of competition between Anglican and Dissenter. Finally, the Toleration Act had been intended to continue the exclusion of Dissenters from office, leaving the Test and Corporation Acts in force. But these had never effectively excluded partial conformists (and some Dissenters) from office. Evasion became more common and open; in 1697

[11] *Ref and Revival,* pp. xi–xii, 6–7.
[12] Ibid. 7–9, 45. The Revd Arthur Bedford was a leading figure in the Bristol Society.
[13] T. Isaacs, 'The Anglican Hierarchy and the Reformation of Manners, 1688–1738', *JEH* xxxiii (1982), 391–410 (quotation from 401); T. C. Curtis and W. A. Speck, 'The Societies for the Reformation of Manners: A Case Study in the Theory and Practice of Moral Reform', *Literature and History,* iii (1976), 45–64. The members of the Bristol Society were not of low social status: *Ref and Revival,* 3–4.

the lord mayor of London, who had taken Anglican communion in order to qualify, publicly attended a Presbyterian meeting, preceded by the City sword.[14] High Church clergymen condemned this profanation of the sacrament and pressed for occasional conformity to be declared illegal.

In denouncing these ills, the High Church clergy looked in vain for leadership from their bishops. Six bishops refused to swear allegiance to William and Mary and were removed. Their replacements, and other new appointments, were not active Whigs, with the exception of Gilbert Burnet at Salisbury, who venomously denounced the High Church clergy.[15] They were conscientious pastors, who concentrated on running their dioceses and teaching the people in the new conditions after the Toleration Act; they did not wish to rebuild the authority of the Church and clergy over the laity. Parliament had decreed that England was now a multi-denominational Protestant nation, in which theocratic claims from one Church, albeit the largest, had no place. The High Church clergy disagreed and pressed for the revival of convocation, the representative body of the clergy, which had effectively ceased to meet after they had abandoned the right to tax themselves in 1664.[16] William was reluctantly persuaded to recall convocation in 1701 and it met annually, alongside Parliament, until 1717; the representatives of the lower clergy, in the lower house, tried to put pressure on the bishops, in the upper. The High Church hoped to use it to resuscitate the theocratic claims of the Church, to direct the spiritual and moral lives of the people, and to guide the state: some saw it as equal to Parliament and even superior to it. Bishop Cartwright, who co-operated energetically with James II, believed that the Test Act was invalid because it had not been approved by convocation.[17] Francis Atterbury, one of the most high-flying clergy, called for convocation to establish a new system of press censorship.[18] Such extreme claims confirmed Whig and Low Church fears of priestcraft, but they won widespread support among the laity. High Church ecclesiology was backward-looking, but there were many for whom the past looked more attractive than the rapidly changing present, with high taxes, moral decay, and challenges to traditional beliefs. The High Church condemnation of the brave new world of the Whigs was to be epitomized in the person of Dr Henry Sacheverell.

---

[14] Holmes, *Sacheverell*, 39.   [15] Burnet, *Supplement*, 101–5.
[16] N. Sykes, *From Sheldon to Secker* (Cambridge, 1959), 41, 43–4.
[17] *HMC Downshire*, i. 301.
[18] Information from a seminar paper by Alex Barber. See also Bennett, *Tory Crisis*, esp. 48–50; Sykes, *Sheldon to Secker*, 46–7.

II. PARTY IN THE 1690S

In the 1690s much of politics centred on issues other than those which had emerged in the Exclusion Crisis. The rapid changes made necessary by the war—notably increased taxation and borrowing, and the growth of the army and the central administration—created new fears. Many worried that the army might be used to establish absolutism, although William had no such intention. The growth of taxation and the administration created fears of embezzlement, waste, and corruption: ministers might use places and pensions to build up a 'court party' in the Commons that would sap Parliament's independence. The Triennial Act of 1694, which required a general election every three years, was designed to prevent this. Perceptions of corruption in public life formed part of the wider concern about moral decay, heterodoxy, and vice. The ills of the court—and London—were contrasted with the integrity and fair dealing that prevailed in the 'Country'.[19] 'Country' MPs, both Tory and Whig, sought to limit the power and 'influence' of the crown—the ability of ministers to buy support with places and pensions. Fissures appeared within the Whig party. It had originally been essentially oppositionist, hostile to Danby's 'corruption', and suspicious of the misuse of power. After 1689 new Whig leaders, the Junto, were eager for power and skilled in using it. Many Whig backbenchers saw their conduct as a betrayal of Whig principles and felt they had more in common with the Tories. By the end of William's reign a significant number of Whigs had joined with the Tories, making them the natural majority party in the reign of Anne.[20]

If 'Country' issues preoccupied Parliament and the public in the 1690s, the old party issues did not go away, although their nature was changed by the Revolution. The Toleration Act changed the parameters of debate on religion. James's flight and the offer of the crown to William and Mary transformed the debate on the monarchy. In the early 1680s the Tories argued that kings ruled by divine right. They were morally obliged to rule according to law, and would have to answer to God for their conduct. Their subjects could ask, but not compel, them to change the way they ruled; they certainly could not

---

[19] D. Hayton, 'Moral Reform and Country Politics in the Late Seventeenth-Century House of Commons', *P & P* 128 (1990), 48–91; C. Brooks, 'The Country Persuasion and Political Responsibility in England in the 1690s', *Parliaments, Estates and Representation*, iv (1988), 135–46.

[20] K. G. Feiling, *History of the Tory Party, 1640–1714* (Oxford, 1924), chs. 10–12; Kenyon, *Revolution Principles*; T. Harris, *Politics under the Later Stuarts, 1660–1714* (London, 1993).

resist them—rebellion was a sin. If anyone doubted the dreadful consequences of resistance, they need look no further than the civil war and regicide. Against the Whig arguments for exclusion, the Tories argued that, in a hereditary monarchy, only God could determine the succession, and it would be unjust to condemn James in advance for what his religion might lead him to do. For Tories, trusting in the king's good sense and honour was far safer than allowing resistance. And in the early 1680s it seemed self-evident that James would support the Church as a crucial support of the monarchy.

James proved them wrong and comprehensively alienated the Tories. They did little to oppose William and some, including Danby, appeared in arms. When James fled they realized that they, the proponents of non-resistance and hereditary right, had participated in an act of resistance which led to the removal of a lawful king, transferring the crown to someone other than the immediate heir. The non-jurors acknowledged this, refused to swear allegiance to William, and lost their places in the Church. Most lay Tories accepted the new king and queen, helped by a new oath of allegiance which did not describe them as 'rightful and lawful' monarchs. They chose to see James as having abdicated and got round the problem of his son by supporting a resolution that experience showed that it was incompatible with the safety of a Protestant kingdom to be governed by a popish prince. Catholics were excluded from the crown by the Bill of Rights of 1689. The Tories adapted their commitment to hereditary right into an insistence that the crown was hereditary in the Protestant line.[21] True, the change of ruler in 1689 was irregular, with Mary succeeding while her father was alive and William being named as co-ruler, but this could be blamed on James's extraordinary behaviour and the deviation in the succession would be only temporary. It would flow back into the right line when the childless William and Mary were dead. Anne would succeed to the throne and it seemed probable that she would have an heir, ensuring an ongoing Protestant Stuart succession.

This happy prospect vanished in 1700, with the death of Anne's son, the duke of Gloucester. With no possibility that she would have any more children, the Act of Settlement vested the succession after Anne in her nearest Protestant relative—Sophia, electress of Hanover, daughter of James I's daughter Elizabeth. As Sophia died before Anne, in 1714 her son became King George I. The prospect of another foreign monarch was not appealing, but there was also a sense in which neither William nor George was seen as a proper monarch.

---

[21] H. Horwitz, '1689 (and all that)', *Parliamentary History*, vi (1987), 29–30.

Belief in the divine attributes of monarchy, shaken by the civil wars and regicide, was greatly boosted by the cult of the royal martyr. Charles II appreciated this, touching thousands of people suffering from the king's evil, scrofula. The belief that the royal touch could cure scrofula was not confined to ignorant peasants. Norwich mayor's court agreed to raise money so that sufferers could go to be touched; so did the Whiggish corporation of the poor at Bristol and the still godly corporation of Dorchester.[22] In his later years, Charles held the ceremonies in the chapel royal at Windsor, in front of a large mural of Christ healing the sick.[23] This sense of the supernatural, divine attributes of monarchy grew after 1689. Anne's reign saw an intensification of the cult of the royal martyr, helped by the publication of Clarendon's *History of the Rebellion.* The glorification of Charles I, and the monarchy, did not go unchallenged. Pamphlets and newspapers debated the rights and wrongs of the civil wars. Key republican and Whig texts were published, including the works of Algernon Sidney.[24] There were stories of the subversion of 30 January, notably by eating a calf's head. A paper in the writing of John Cary of Bristol give the words of a song to be sung at the calf's head feast on 30 January 1691, which included such lines as 'Thus our fathers did before | When the tyrant would enslave us | Chopped his calf's head off to save us.'[25] On 30 January 1706 an effigy of Charles I was reportedly paraded through the streets of Bristol and then beheaded.[26] In 1712 two flesh-tasters of Southwark (both Dissenters) were convicted of burning a calf's head. They claimed that it was unfit to be sold, but the court noted that they had delayed burning it so that they could do so on 30 January, and one said that he would roast it for Sacheverell's supper.[27]

In response to the Tory view of monarchy, the Whigs argued it was a human institution, and that kings existed for the good of their people. The crown should normally pass to the next heir, as any landed estate would, but when the safety of the people required it Parliament could override hereditary right and impose fresh limitations on the crown, as in the Bill of Rights and Act

[22] MCB 23, fo. 191, MCB 24, fos. 105, 213, 227, MCB 25, fo. 125; Butcher, *Corporation,* 83; Underdown, *Fire from Heaven,* 235.

[23] A. Keay, 'The Ceremonies of Charles II's Court', Ph.D. thesis (London, 2004).

[24] B. Worden, *Roundhead Reputations: The English Civil Wars and the Passions of Posterity* (London, 2001) chs. 1–7.

[25] BL, Add MS 5540, fo. 26; Kenyon, *Revolution Principles,* 77; Knights, *Representation,* 309, 311.

[26] *HMC Portland,* iv. 287.

[27] *Post Boy,* 2–5 Feb., 31 July–2 Aug. 1712. A story of a calf's head being eaten at Tiverton on 30 Jan. 1722 was said to be untrue: *Flying Post,* 8–10 Mar. 1722.

of Settlement.[28] More hesitantly, the Whigs also began to argue that in cases of extreme danger—such as 1688—the people could take up arms against the king; in the paper debates on the 1640s, Whigs justified the conduct of the Parliamentarians in a way few had done under Charles II. These debates found their way into the provinces through pamphlets, an extensive newspaper press, and hundreds of sermons; on 30 January Tory parsons expatiated on the divine nature of kingship. They added an emotional and ideological edge to party conflict under William III and, especially, Anne. Those who embraced the idea of the divine nature of monarchy most wholeheartedly were the Jacobites, who hoped to see James II and then his son, 'James III', on the English throne. Hardly any Tories had wanted James back in early 1689, but disenchantment with the new king created support for the Jacobite movement. For many it went little further than seditious healths and assertions that James was the true king. But there were several conspiracies in the 1690s to bring James back, and the assassination plot of 1696 threatened William's life.[29] The ultimate certainty, after 1700, of the extinction of the Protestant Stuart dynasty, and with it the old form of monarchy, added to the attraction of the 'king over the water'. This was held in check by genuine affection for Queen Anne, but as she became ill Tories had to choose between a German Protestant with a weak hereditary claim and a Catholic Stuart, whom most acknowledged was the legitimate son of a legitimate king.[30] Most Tories put Protestantism before legitimism, but not without qualms of conscience, and regrets. The Whigs, who continually accused the Tories of Jacobitism, were generally disingenuous and wrong,[31] but there was an element of shared sentiment between Tories and Jacobites, harking back to an older, simpler world and an older view of monarchy. This view was not confined to a few Oxford dons or backwoods parsons, but had a wide popular resonance. The mystique and the magic went out of the English monarchy with the accession of George I, who (like William III) chose not to touch for the king's evil. For many English people, this was a change for the worse.

For much of the 1690s the issues that divided Whig from Tory were not at the centre of politics. Resentment of the consequences of the Toleration Act

---

[28] It is a moot point how extensive the changes made by the Bill of Rights really were. For differing views, see L. G. Schwoerer, *The Declaration of Rights, 1689* (Baltimore, 1981); J. Miller, *The Glorious Revolution*, 2nd edn. (London, 1997), ch. 4.

[29] J. Garrett, *The Triumphs of Providence: The Assassination Plot, 1696* (Cambridge, 1980).

[30] Some Whigs preferred to accept his legitimacy, as that would make his exclusion depend entirely on the authority of Parliament.

[31] Colley, *In Defiance of Oligarchy*, 42–3, 115–16; Rogers, *Crowds, Culture and Politics*, 52–7.

built up only gradually. The issue of the succession, and so of the nature of monarchy, lay dormant while the duke of Gloucester was alive. Recriminations about the events of the 1680s played a prominent part in the Convention of 1689–90, but were less significant thereafter. Prominent Whigs forgot their collaboration with James II and raked up the misdeeds of the Tory reaction. When Tory ministers were in power, military or naval failures were blamed on half-heartedness or treachery. The Whigs repeatedly tried to expose the Tories' alleged disloyalty by trying to impose a new oath of allegiance which described William and Mary as 'rightful and lawful' monarchs; they also tried to force office-holders to abjure James II, denying his and his son's right to the crown. They hoped that many Tories would refuse, but most complied, knowing refusal would put more power into the Whigs' hands. The assassination plot gave the Whigs a pretext to draw up an association which described William as 'rightful and lawful' king; those who subscribed it promised 'revenge' against his enemies should the king be killed. This new association was more extensive than that of 1688, an affirmation of solidarity by all adult male Protestants, akin to the Protestation of 1641–2.[32] It was supposedly voluntary; a significant minority in each House refused to subscribe. Associations soon circulated in many counties and towns; many thousands subscribed.[33] In March William declared that he thought it appropriate that all those in his service should sub-scribe and removed from the privy council three who had refused. Parliament passed an Act requiring all office-holders and MPs to subscribe the association or face expulsion.[34]

The association, and the bill to impose it, caused deep divisions in Parlia-ment. It proved equally divisive in Norwich. In March the duke of Norfolk sent down his version, seemingly a composite of those of the two Houses.[35] It was circulating when the assembly considered the matter on 27 March. It had already heartily congratulated the king on his deliverance and promised to stand by him against all enemies, foreign and domestic.[36] It approved a text which described William as 'rightful and lawful' king, but differed from others mainly in substituting the word 'punish' for 'revenge'. According to Prideaux, the great majority of the assembly thought that to endorse 'revenge' might be seen as licensing the rabble to kill and plunder anyone it chose to call

---

[32] Miller, ' "Proto-Jacobitism?" ', 13, 17; D. Cressy, 'The Protestation Protested, 1641 and 1642', *HJ* xlv (2002), 251–79.

[33] Knights, *Representation*, 119, 123, 155–6.

[34] Horwitz, *Parliament, Policy and Politics*, 175–6.

[35] Prideaux, 165–6.   [36] FAB 8, fo. 200 (VN).

a Jacobite. It ordered that in each ward the common councilmen and parish officers should gather subscriptions from all males over 16 and note the names of any refusers. The duke of Norfolk and the city's MPs were to be asked to present a copy to the king.[37]

Sir Henry Hobart, knight of the shire and a strong Whig, denounced the assembly's wording and encouraged the Worsted Weavers' Company to draw up their own association, including the word 'revenge'. He suggested that this demonstration of zeal would improve their chances of securing an Act of Parliament prohibiting the import of Indian textiles.[38] The presentation of a rival association displeased the corporation, but it was infuriated by a report in the London Whig newspaper, the *Post Man*.[39] This claimed that the magistrates —allegedly the same as in the last reign—would not promote the association until 'honest' citizens protested. These citizens favoured the form drawn up by the Commons. The assembly considered removing the word 'rightful', as well as 'revenge', but eventually decided not to. Truly loyal citizens refused to subscribe this version; they resolved to send theirs into every parish, and were confident that it would receive four times as many subscriptions as that of the corporation. (In fact the number of names on the weavers' association was slightly larger—3,918 as against 3,124; almost every adult male in the city must have subscribed one or the other.)[40] Prideaux denounced this account as untrue, adding that the writer falsely suggested that he had influenced the assembly. Prideaux was not mentioned by name, but at one point it stated that an unnamed person had ordered the assembly to omit the word 'rightful'. The vehemence with which Prideaux denied this accusation invites suspicion.[41] Whether or not the newspaper account was inaccurate, the corporation was livid at being pilloried as less than loyal. The thanksgiving day on 16 April was celebrated with great vigour, perhaps to offset the impression created by the weavers and the *Post Man*.[42] The assembly may have considered adopting more guarded wording than it eventually approved, but the difference between the final version and that drawn up by the Commons was minimal. Besides, with several versions circulating, and subscription still notionally voluntary, many must have been unsure which was the 'official' version. It seems clear that this was a cynical Whig ploy to embarrass the Tories and perhaps force some of

[37] FAB 8, fos. 200–1 (VN); Prideaux, 167, 169.   [38] Prideaux, 167, 169.

[39] Prideaux gives the name of the newspaper as the *Post Boy*, which was strongly Tory, whereas the *Post Man* was strongly Whig. MCB 26, fo. 26 gives *Post Man*.

[40] *Post Man*, 7–9 Apr. 1696; Knights, *Representation*, 158–9.

[41] Prideaux, 170, 174.   [42] Ibid. 171.

them to resign from the corporation rather than subscribe; the association drawn up at Great Yarmouth was also criticized for not being in the exact form drawn up by the Commons.[43]

III. THE CONVENTION,
THE CORPORATIONS, AND THE LAW

In March 1689 the Commons repeatedly addressed the question of admitting Dissenters to corporations, by repealing the Corporation Act and removing the sacramental requirement from the Test Act. The Tories strongly opposed the bill to repeal the Corporation Act, not least because it would have taken the corporations back to the condition they were in at the Restoration; as one MP said, in the 1650s loyal men had been put out and another sort put in. The bill was killed by a prorogation in October.[44] In April a bill for settling corporations was brought in. James's proclamation of 17 October had restored most of the old charters, but not those where the surrender had been enrolled; in those cases, it was legally necessary to issue a new charter, restoring the old privileges and reinstating the old members. Some boroughs which had not been incorporated before had been given charters; the king undertook to annul these, restoring them to their former state. The proclamation gave a list of thirty-seven boroughs where the surrender (or judgement) had been enrolled.[45] There was thus considerable confusion about the status of charters, not to mention the legal force of the king's order. It could be argued that one way to resolve the confusion was by Act of Parliament, but it also offered a possible vehicle for ensuring Whig control of corporations. The bill was quickly read twice, but then the Commons became preoccupied with investigating the misdeeds of the Tory reaction, reversing judgements against Titus Oates and other Whig 'martyrs' and trying to exclude as many Tories as possible from the indemnity bill.[46] The bill to restore corporations was lost with the prorogation, and a new one was introduced; the Commons also returned to the question of indemnity. A bill was brought in to examine those responsible for the 'murders' of the Whig 'martyrs', issuing *quo warrantos* and taking away charters.[47] The

---

[43] BL, Add MS 28880, fo. 92.

[44] Morrice MS Q, pp. 482, 488, 496, 502, 507, 525, 592, 624; *CJ*, x. 43, 183; Horwitz, *Parliament, Policy and Politics*, 21–2.

[45] *London Gazette*, 2391, 15–18 Oct. 1688.

[46] *CJ*, x. 277; Morrice MS Q, p. 638; Horwitz, *Parliament, Policy and Politics*, 36–7.

[47] Morrice MS Q, p. 668.

House had voted months before that the *quo warrantos* and regulators had been illegal.[48] Now the Whig majority hoped to achieve the objective of the bill to repeal the Corporation Act—Whig control of the corporations—by punishing those who had gained office in 1682–5 (but not, of course, Whigs and Dissenters put in by James). The bill received its first reading on 12 November and its second on 19 December. It returned from committee on 2 January 1690. It proposed to restore all the privileges and immunities that the corporations had enjoyed in 1661, before most of Charles II's charters, but not the members, many of whom had been put out in 1662–3; instead it would restore those in place in 1675, presumably a concession to the Tories.[49] William Sacheverell, a Whig who had suffered for his opposition to Nottingham's new charter and collaborated with James II, offered a proviso. For the sake of public justice, it said, any member of a corporation who had agreed to a surrender without the consent of the majority, or solicited a *quo warranto*, should be banned from holding office for seven years. By focusing on surrenders, the proviso targeted Tories involved in the surrenders of 1682–5. Tory MPs responded by asking for similar penalties for those who had served as regulators and mayors, or put in petitions, under James. The Tory proviso was rejected and the triumphant Whigs carried a vote to delete the reference to voting a surrender without a majority of the corporation, which would make it much more sweeping; the bill was ordered to be engrossed.[50] The Whigs threatened that if the king tried to prevent the bill from passing, they 'would not finish the money bills'; William was determined, however, that it should not pass.[51]

The House debated the bill for the last time on 10 January. The Tories turned out in force and the Whigs had to resort to damage limitation. Sacheverell argued that only those who supported surrenders of their own free will, before judgement was given against London's charter, should be incapacitated; he also moved to reinstate the reference to the majority. His Whig colleagues expatiated on 'the villainies of the surrenders'; those who promoted surrenders 'abhorred Parliaments and petitions for their sitting'. This clause was intended to ensure that corporations were 'put into the hands of good and moderate men'. Sir William Williams, solicitor general under James II, asked, 'will you restore those men, who have been the worst of men, and betrayed their trust?' The solicitor general, Somers, stated that the bill would restore 'the old

[48] Ibid. 489.   [49] *CJ*, x. 284, 312–13; Morrice MS R, p. 73.
[50] *CJ*, x. 322–3; Morrice MS R, pp. 73–4; Jones, 'James II's Whig Collaborators', 69–70. The Tories had expected a move like this, in a thin House: BL Add MS 29594, fo. 185.
[51] H. C. Foxcroft, *Life and Letters of Halifax*, 2 vols. (London, 1898), ii. 243.

members of the Church of England, but not that corrupt part of the Church of England, who endeavoured to destroy the government'; if the proviso passed 'you will have better men and unspotted men in their stead'. The Tories replied that 'instead of reconciliation it [the clause] lays the foundation of perpetual division'; 'this bill is a restoring of corporations and is not a bill of pains and penalties'. They argued that the proviso fundamentally changed the character of the bill and that it had been pushed through in a thin house (a little over 200 members were present on the 2nd, at least 372 on the 10th). The House rejected Sacheverell's various attempts to salvage the proviso, and then the proviso itself, by no more than ten votes on each occasion. The bill passed and went up to the Lords.[52] It declared that all surrenders and forfeitures since 1675 were null and void and that the towns were to be restored to the condition they were in before the surrender. Those who had acted under the new charters were indemnified for their actions. The most controversial provision which remained in the bill was that the oaths and declaration required by the Corporation Act were not in future to be tendered or taken; there was no mention of the sacramental test.[53] The peers consulted the judges about the legality of the surrenders. The majority of the judges thought they had been illegal, but the House resolved to remove a statement to that effect and the bill failed to complete its passage.[54] The Whigs in the Commons made one last attempt to remove Tories from the corporations, by including in the indemnity bill a provision that some might be excluded for procuring surrenders and new charters; the Tories proposed the exclusion of those involved in regulating corporations and promising to take off the penal laws and Test Acts. Perhaps surprisingly, the House agreed that both should be included in the bill, which had not completed its progress through the Commons when the session ended on 27 January.[55] The Whig attempt to gain control of corporations through legislation had failed.

The failure to pass legislation to resolve the legal confusion facing many corporations left them to seek redress where they could. William had no desire to intervene actively in municipal affairs and sought to respond even-handedly to petitions; the privy council's usual response was to leave petitioners to

---

[52] *CJ*, x. 329–30; Morrice MS R, p. 84; *HP 1660–90*, iii. 731; Grey, ix. 510–20. This is the only debate on this bill that Grey recorded.

[53] *HMC House of Lords 1689–90*, 422–9; the provision about the Corporation Act is on p. 427.

[54] *LJ*, xiv. 419, 423–4; Morrice MS R, pp. 94, 98; Luttrell, ii. 8–9; Halliday, *Body*, 273–5.

[55] *CJ*, x. 341, 345. The Tories had tried unsuccessfully to move that the bill should specify persons rather than 'crimes' and had named Sir William Williams as the first to be excluded from indemnity: Grey, ix. 538–47; *CJ*, x. 338.

the law.[56] The problems of some corporations were resolved by issuing new charters. Some inhabitants of Saffron Walden petitioned for a new charter in 1690, claiming that they had lost their charter in 1684 and been 'destitute of government' since then. (In fact the town received a new charter in 1685.) Now it asked to be reincorporated, with a smaller corporation. The king did not respond, perhaps because he was informed that the old charter should have been restored. In January 1694 the mayor and aldermen petitioned for a confirmation of James II's charter, with some amendments; it was granted in December.[57] Colchester's surrender had been enrolled and so the old charter could not legally be restored. The corporation continued for a while to act under the charter of 1688, but then the mayor and eighteen others resigned, as they were not legally qualified, not having received the sacrament. The remainder could not raise a quorum, so government ceased. The king ordered the remainder of the corporation to elect a mayor and to continue to act under the 1688 charter, to preserve the peace. In March 1693 the attorney general recommended that the king regrant the town's old privileges in a new charter.[58] Nottingham's surrender had also been enrolled. The corporation continued to function, without a charter. In 1690 the magistrates put out in 1682 secured a *mandamus* to reinstate them; several Tory magistrates followed suit a few weeks later.[59] The lack of a charter remained problematical and in 1692 the mayor and burgesses petitioned for a charter to restore the liberties enjoyed before 1682. The attorney general found the point of law very tricky—was there now a legal corporation in Nottingham?—and recommended consulting the judges. A new charter was issued some months later.[60]

Only a minority of the uncertainties were resolved by issuing new charters. Sixteen were issued during William's reign, of which nine were to towns whose surrenders had been enrolled.[61] Of the remaining seven, Eye needed a new charter because its magistrates had neglected to subscribe the association.[62] All the members of Warwick corporation had been removed in April 1688. The

---

[56] Halliday, *Body*, 277.

[57] *CSPD 1685*, nos. 675, 778, *1690–1*, 199, *1694–5*, 354; PC 2/75, p. 321; Carte MS 76, fos. 600–1.

[58] PC 2/75, pp. 120–1; *CSPD 1689–90*, 225.   [59] Morrice MS R, pp. 154, 176.

[60] PC 2/74, pp. 332, 367, 427, 474–5; Halliday, *Body*, 278.

[61] Halliday, *Body*, 352–3; *London Gazette*, 15–18 Oct. 1688. The nine were Nottingham, Ludlow, Tewkesbury, Colchester, Plympton, Plymouth, Dunwich, Fowey, and Malmesbury. For petitions for new charters from Plymouth and Plympton, see *CSPD 1691–2*, 135, 387.

[62] PC 2/77, pp. 78, 81–2. The same happened at Malmesbury, where the surrender had been enrolled; the king ordered in November 1696 that it be granted a new charter, PC 2/76, p. 533. Halliday, *Body*, 353, dates the new charter 14 Nov. 1695.

town was left without a government until December, when Brooke and the last members of the corporation began to act again, 'to keep the inferior people in awe, who were very tumultuous'. They had hoped that the problem would be resolved by Parliament, but as no Act was passed, they were advised that legally they could no longer act, so that now (December 1691) there was 'no face of a corporation'. They petitioned for a new charter; the king granted one in March 1693.[63] A new charter for Liverpool was granted in an effort to resolve a long-running dispute whether the franchise for elections to the corporation belonged to the freemen or the common council; the privy council decided in favour of the freemen.[64] Deal was a new incorporation.[65] There was no policy of using charters as a means of intervening in towns and most towns where there were disputes or confusions preferred to take their cases to King's Bench. Thetford regained its old charter following a decision of the Commons committee of elections, and a suit in Chancery, but more common were requests for a writ of *mandamus* to reinstate members who had been put out. Having recourse to King's Bench helped to take the partisan heat out of disputes: the court decided cases on their legal merits, but was also concerned that effective government should be carried on.[66] One consequence of this use of the courts was the use, by litigants rather than the crown, of actions of *quo warranto*; another was that it became somewhat easier for Dissenters to become members of corporations.[67] With the crown ceasing to intervene in boroughs, local interests were left to fight it out as best they could, in the courts or the Commons' committee of elections and privileges.

IV. PARTISAN CONFLICT

The legacy of animosity from the 1680s, uncertainties about charters (and hence the mode of election), and disputes about who were the legal members

---

[63] *CSPD 1691–2*, 22; Halliday, *Body*, 353.

[64] PC 2/76, p. 139; *CSPD 1695*, 339; Carte MS 239, fo. 5; *HP 1690–1715*, ii. 330–1. The Commons committee of elections and privileges had recently decided a disputed by-election in favour of the candidate elected by the freemen: ibid. 330. For the background to the 1677 charter, see J. R. B. Muir, *A History of Liverpool* (Liverpool, 1907), 150–3.

[65] PC 2/77, p. 323.

[66] Halliday, *Body*, 289–95. Hayton sees the Commons' decision as effectively settling the matter: *HP 1690–1715*, i. 250, ii. 422–3. Liskeard regained its charter following a hearing at the assizes: ibid. i. 248.

[67] Halliday, *Body*, 296–9, 302–3.

of corporations could all lead to acrimonious disputes.[68] Lords Chandos and Coningsby fought a duel over the place of steward at Hereford.[69] At Oxford there was an attempt in 1689 to heal past wounds. The council invited Robert Pauling to resume his place on the corporation, but changed its mind when Pauling sent a long bitter letter, expatiating on his alleged maltreatment by Abingdon, who had had him expelled from the city.[70] The council proved equally accommodating towards Richard Carter, forced on the city as an alderman and mayor in 1688. He was chosen as an assistant in Pauling's place and in 1690 he was elected mayor.[71] The city soon became divided on party lines, with Abingdon's influence challenged by Lord Wharton.[72] The struggle focused on the place of town clerk. In 1694, Job Slatford was elected by a small majority, but the mayor refused to swear him, claiming he had not qualified under the Corporation Act. A fresh election was held and Samuel Thurston was declared the winner by 464 votes to 457. It was alleged, however, that Abingdon had summoned several country gentlemen to vote for Thurston. The commons called Abingdon and his son Jacobites; their inn had to be guarded by constables, to save them from the populace.[73] The church bells rang to celebrate Slatford's carrying the election, and again at his being sworn. There is no reference to this in the council acts, but it is possible that the king had approved Slatford's election, in the belief that he had then taken the necessary oaths.[74] The mayoral election in 1695 was hotly contested, as the mayor would act as returning officer in the forthcoming parliamentary election. Abingdon and Wharton mobilized all their resources. Abingdon's candidate won; Wright's supporters got drunk and went round abusing Tories and breaking their windows.[75]

As far as the council was concerned, the town clerk was Thurston.[76] In June 1696 both Slatford and Thurston brought writs of *mandamus*. The council resolved to defend both and appointed an acting town clerk until the matter could be resolved. In August the mayor was threatened while riding the franchises by masked men who demanded Slatford's salary.[77] In 1697 first Slatford and then Thurston secured a peremptory *mandamus* to be admitted to the place. Slatford took all the necessary oaths and it seems that he was admitted.

[68] See for example those at Colchester (*CSPD 1693*, 157, 296, 344) and Orford (Luttrell, iii. 382, 385; *Post Boy*, 18–20 July 1695).

[69] Luttrell, iii. 532.   [70] *OCA*, iii. 211, 213; BL, Egerton MS 3337, fos. 109–10.

[71] *OCA*, iii. 205, 214, 221. The seven assistants were among the more senior members of the corporation, ranking just below the aldermen, who were usually four in number.

[72] *HP 1690–1715*, ii. 481–2; *Post Boy*, 20–2 July 1697.

[73] *OCA*, iii. 245–6; Wood, iii. 462.   [74] Wood, iii. 478, 479.

[75] *HMC le Fleming*, 338; Wood, iii. 489.

[76] *OCA*, iii. 258, 266, 273.   [77] Ibid. 263–5.

When Thurston's *mandamus* was presented, and the council (having taken legal advice) admitted him, Slatford refused to hand over the town clerk's books. Undeterred, the council resolved to start new books and ordered the sergeants at mace to take orders from Thurston.[78] In an effort to resolve the matter the council held another election. Slatford refused to stand and Thurston was 'elected' by 316 votes to 6.[79] Slatford took his case to the privy council; several members of the council claimed that Thurston was not qualified, because his election had not been approved by the king as the charter required. The matter was referred to the attorney general, with instructions to safeguard the king's right of approval.[80] In November the attorney general brought an information against the mayor and Thurston in the Court of Exchequer and the following April Thurston was arrested.[81] The litigation dragged on until 1700, when the court gave its verdict. It seems to have been in Thurston's favour, because in October 1701 Slatford surrendered the office of town clerk. Thurston was then elected: he said that he regarded it as already his by right of the original election, but he was ready to qualify himself again.[82] The dispute had lasted seven years.

Animosities were, if anything, greater at Bristol. According to James II's proclamation of October 1688, the city reverted to its charter of 1664.[83] With the corporation reverting to the membership in place in 1683, the Tories were still dominant and Hart and Knight were elected to Parliament in 1689. However, the corporation does not seem to have transacted any substantive business between November 1688 and August 1689 and partisan divisions persisted.[84] In August Sir Thomas Earle, whose election in 1681 and removal in 1683 had been equally contentious, was declared to have been duly elected. Eston, who had replaced him, was removed; as he was in gaol for debt, he was in no condition to protest.[85] In September the mayor, William Jackson, who had been put into the corporation by James II, complained that some members of the corporation disrupted business by wrangling about precedence; most had supported the surrender of the charter and he suspected that they were disaffected.[86] The mayor was supported by the lord lieutenant, the earl of Macclesfield, a strong Whig. In Cheshire, where he was also lord lieutenant,

---

[78] *OCA*, iii. 271–2.   [79] Ibid. 275, 276.
[80] PC 2/77, pp. 161, 197.   [81] *OCA*, iii. 284, 286–7.
[82] Ibid. 296, iv. 4. The first says only that the verdicts are to be placed among the city's records, but not what they were.
[83] Latham, *Bristol Charters*, 57.   [84] BRO, 04264/8, fos. 28–30; *CSPD 1689–90*, 159.
[85] BRO, 04264/8, fos. 31–2; Latimer, i. 454.   [86] *CSPD 1689–90*, 241, 247–8.

Macclesfield was accused of mobilizing and drilling armed men, of using the militia to influence a by-election, and of showing undue favour to Dissenters. The commission of the peace was said to be divided on party lines.[87] Macclesfield was, therefore, the last man to bring peace to a volatile city. He turned out all the militia officers (who were presumably Tories) and replaced them (according to the corporation) with Dissenters and men who had been obnoxious to the Church and the government of the city.[88] In November 1689 Sir John Knight II claimed that he had been mocked and abused by Macclesfield's son, Lord Gerard of Brandon, and that he feared for his life.[89]

In the run-up to the next parliamentary election, in February 1690, accusations of dirty tricks multiplied. Sir Thomas Earle, who was planning to stand against Knight and Hart, was accused of obtaining a French pass for one of his ships; Knight claimed that this amounted to high treason. Earle complained that the accusations were false and alleged that his opponents were Jacobites, who cast aspersions on those who had appeared early for William in 1688.[90] Earle felt compelled to stand down and Hart and Knight were re-elected after a close contest.[91] Macclesfield's militia officers were active on the Whigs' behalf; later, following an alleged Jacobite conspiracy, they imprisoned some Tories and talked of imprisoning hundreds more. The mayor complained that Earle and his allies had affronted and obstructed him. Earle demanded to see the common council book, in Macclesfield's presence, to see if a rumoured order against him had in fact been made. The common council voted to expel him.[92] Undeterred, Earle obtained a writ of *mandamus* from King's Bench, but the mayor was reluctant to act on it.[93] Feelings continued to run high. In 1692 the Tories carried the election of Edmund Arundell as mayor, but in the following year the Whigs narrowly carried it for Robert Yate, one of the defeated parliamentary candidates in 1690, after which the Whigs were confident of sending 'good men' to Parliament.[94] Knight's extremism and vindictiveness were losing him support in the city. In 1695 he and Hart were comfortably defeated by Yate and Sir Thomas Day.[95]

[87] *HMC Kenyon*, 222–3, 234–5, 249, 273–4, 291, 411–12.
[88] PC 2/73, p. 85; BRO, 07831, under 1689, 04264/8, fo. 39.   [89] Morrice MS Q, p. 646.
[90] BRO, 04262/8, fos. 54–5 (another copy BCL, B7950, fo. 42); BL, Add MS 5540, fo. 27.
[91] *HP 1690–1715*, ii. 210–11.
[92] BL, Add MS 5540, fo. 28; BCL, B11154, Robert Henley to Sir Robert Southwell, 4 Aug. 1690; BRO, 04264/8, fos. 45–7, 53–4, 57.
[93] BRO, 04264/8, fos. 58, 64.
[94] *HMC Finch*, iv. 461; Luttrell, iii. 188; BL Add MS 28878, fo. 129.
[95] *HP 1690–1715*, ii. 212; BRO, 07831, 1695.

The Tories remained defiant. Some 'lewd persons' rang the church bells, or went round the streets with fiddles, when news came of Queen Mary's death; the government ordered that those responsible should be prosecuted and sent more troops to the city.[96] The assassination plot completed the Tories' discomfiture. Knight and Hart were sent to gaol. Papers were set up on the Tolzey, threatening to kill 'Captain Earle', who had arrested Knight.[97] Nothing could be proved against them, but the Bristol Whigs argued (as James II's privy council had in 1686) that the public safety required that Knight should not be released, as he would try to frustrate measures to secure 'good' magistrates. The privy council agreed that he should remain in custody, on suspicion of treason.[98] He was eventually discharged on health grounds at the beginning of September. Although seriously ill, he got to Bristol for the mayoral election. At first the Tories tried to abort proceedings, by staying away so that the mayor could not get a quorum, but those present chose ten 'well-affected' councillors in the place of those who had failed to subscribe the association, creating a clear Whig majority.[99] The Tories remained strong in the city as a whole. Hart and Knight contested the parliamentary election of 1698, but were again defeated. Thereafter, with the exception of 1705, no Tory candidate appeared until 1710. The Whigs were in control.

[96] Carte MS 76, fo. 585; Luttrell, iii. 423; Wood, iii. 476. See also *HMC Downshire*, i. 446–8; P. K. Monod, *Jacobitism and the English People 1688–1788* (Cambridge, 1989), 170.

[97] Bodleian, MS Gough Somerset 2, p. 121; Luttrell, iv. 25, 31; PC 2/76, p. 302; *Flying Post*, 28–31 Mar. 1696; Latimer, i. 483.

[98] *CSPD 1696*, p. 193; Carte MS 239, fo. 90; PC 2/76, p. 433.

[99] *CSPD 1696*, p. 258; PC 2/76, p. 506; Luttrell, iv. 106; BL, Add MS 28880, fo. 330; *Flying Post*, 3–5 and 17–19 Sept. 1696; *HP 1690–1715*, ii. 212–13.

12

The Rage of Party, 1700–1714

I. CROAKERS AND TACKERS

If partisan divisions receded into the background in the 1690s, they returned to the fore in 1700–1. The death of the duke of Gloucester reopened the issue of the succession. The Act of Settlement of 1701 was passed by a Parliament with a Tory majority, and showed that, however necessary the Hanoverian succession might be, the Tories viewed it with profound distaste. It imposed a series of novel restrictions on a future foreign monarch: its title was 'An Act for the further limitation of the crown and better securing the rights and liberties of the subject'. All future monarchs had to 'join in communion' with the Church of England (Sophia and George were Lutherans); they could not leave the realm or make war without Parliament's permission; no foreigner was to be admitted to any office.[1] Very few publicly questioned the inevitability of the Hanoverian succession—Tory addresses referred routinely to 'the Protestant succession in the illustrious House of Hanover'—but the Tories were deeply unhappy about the imminent demise of the Protestant Stuart dynasty and the traditional form of monarchy. This found expression in effusive loyalty to Queen Anne and emotional wallows in the Royalist past. Charles I featured prominently in Tory political iconography and Tory crowds chanted 'down with the Roundheads' or 'down with the Rump'.

Such gestures were not usually marks of Jacobitism. After Louis XIV recognized 'James III' as king of England on the death of his father, Tories as well as Whigs accepted the need for England to become involved in another war against France, which lasted from 1702 to 1713. This war did less damage than the last to English trade and industry, but it made necessary even higher taxes and the recruiting of far more soldiers. Although both parties accepted the need for the war, there developed considerable disagreement as to how it

[1] Browning, *Docts*, 129–35.

should be fought. The root cause was the invitation to Louis XIV's grandson to become king of Spain, which created fears of a Franco-Spanish super-power. The Whigs argued that much of the war effort had to be devoted to preventing France from gaining control of the Low Countries. The Tories preferred a strategy based on harassing French trade, seizing French colonies, and conquering Spain. The question of war aims became critical in 1709 when the Whig ministry adopted a policy of 'no peace without Spain'. Louis XIV was ready to discuss terms, but the Whigs insisted that he join the allies in driving his grandson out of Spain; he refused. This unrealistic demand led to claims that the Whigs wanted to continue the war indefinitely, in the interests of the Dutch and the London moneyed interest, who made handsome profits lending money to the government.[2] To make matters worse, 1709 saw a bad harvest and widespread dearth.

A third divisive issue, along with the nature of monarchy and the war, was the Church. Resentment of occasional conformity and the perceived growth of heterodoxy had led to the revival of convocation. Anne's undoubted commitment to the Church added to the High Churchmen's confidence, and helped secure the election of a Tory House of Commons in 1702, which passed three bills against occasional conformity. In 1702 and 1703, the bill was rejected by the Lords. In 1704 the Commons tried to prevent this by 'tacking' a clause against occasional conformity to a major money bill. Money bills could not be amended by the Lords, only accepted or rejected, so the Commons were putting in jeopardy money urgently needed for the war, in pursuit of a partisan measure. The queen was angry; her ministers canvassed moderate Tory MPs and the 'tack' was rejected. The issue was debated around the country; in Norwich Whigs called the Tories 'tackers', Tories called the Whigs 'croakers'. In 1708, after a minor Jacobite rising in Scotland, the Whigs won their only clear-cut election victory of the reign. The queen was forced to appoint Whig ministers, some of whom pursued a vendetta against the Church. This led the Tories to claim that the Church was in danger, a claim that had explosive consequences in 1710.

These issues create significant divisions in many towns. The Triennial Act meant that general elections were now far more frequent—there were ten between 1695 and 1715. Contested elections were by definition divisive: voting was a public act and poll books were public documents, which were often printed.[3] Frequent parliamentary elections meant partisan divisions also

---

[2] Holmes and Speck, *The Divided Society*, 135–6.
[3] See for example, *The Alphabetical Draft of the Poll of Robert Bene . . . and Richard Berney* (1710); *An Alphabetical Draft of the Poll of . . . William Bacon and Robert Britiffe* (1716).

affected elections of mayors and corporation members; where the corporation was evenly divided the election of one or two members could tip the balance. It should not be assumed that all towns were divided all of the time. Defoe remarked in 1705, of Leeds, Wakefield, and Sheffield, none of which sent representatives to Parliament: 'Frequent elections having no influence here to divide the people, they live here in much more peace than in other parts.'[4] There were also parliamentary boroughs, even with large electorates, which enjoyed relative peace. Hull returned two moderate Whig members in six consecutive elections.[5] Oxford, strongly Whig in the early 1680s, returned two Tories in each election of Anne's reign; when the Whigs offered a contest, they never came close to winning.[6] Leicester returned two High Church Tories in every election from 1705 to 1715. Although the town returned high Tory members, in October 1701 the corporation resolved *nem. con.* to address the king, deploring Louis XIV's recognition of 'the pretended Prince of Wales' as James III.[7]

Other towns, however, were divided by factionalism for years on end. The weapons used in these conflicts had changed since 1689. The crown no longer intervened in disputes and issued few new charters.[8] However, contending groups could still embark on litigation or appeal to Queen's Bench for writs of *mandamus* or *quo warranto*; the judges had resolved that the latter could no longer lead to forfeiting the charter, but it could be used to remove members for misconduct. It generally took a long time to secure a *mandamus*, but an Act of Parliament of 1711 speeded proceedings considerably. Litigation was always divisive, but the judges based their rulings on legal arguments, and showed concern for the public good. They were far less swayed by partisanship than the House of Commons committee of elections.[9] When all else failed factions fell back on force and fraud, especially if their party had a majority in the Commons.

In the Wiltshire borough of Devizes, contested parliamentary elections led to a disputed mayoral election in 1706 and the setting up of two rival corporations, which continued for sixteen years. In 1707 the mayors came to blows

---

[4] Defoe, *Letters*, 102.   [5] *HP 1690–1715*, ii. 732–4.

[6] Ibid. 481–4.   [7] LHP 39, fo. 63.

[8] The charter issued to Bristol in 1710 was designed to resolve uncertainty about whether the 1684 charter was still in force and to make it easier to punish those refusing office: Latham, *Bristol Charters*, 57–60; BRO, 04264/9, pp. 161–2, 176–7, 182–3, 224, 227; PC 2/83, pp. 10–11; PC 1/3030. However, the new charter issued to Bewdley was politically motivated and very contentious: Styles, *Studies*, 67–8; *HP 1690–1715*, ii. 705–8.

[9] Halliday, *Body*, 311–21, 347–8.

over the mayoral pew in the church; both sides spent heavily on elections and lawsuits and mobilized their friends in the county and the central government. The dispute was finally ended in 1722 by the mediation of the town's MPs; the reunited corporation celebrated with a handsome feast and the ringing of bells.[10] Winchester and Portsmouth had shown few signs of division hitherto. Winchester needed gentry custom, so found it prudent to avoid partisan extremes; Portsmouth was dominated by the dockyard and garrison. In Winchester, and possibly in Portsmouth, contention was stimulated by the efforts of the Whig second duke of Bolton to build an electoral interest. His brother, Lord William Poulett, had been returned for Winchester, with a Tory, in 1690, 1695, and 1698, but in January 1701, the first election after Bolton succeeded to his dukedom, a second Whig, George Rodney Brydges, was chosen as well; Bolton and his allies had managed to increase the number of Whig honorary freemen. The recorder, Thomas Coward, was Bolton's election agent; he and the duke were accused of intimidation in the January 1701 election and there were complaints that Bolton and other Whig peers were present at elections, to awe the voters.[11] More Whig freemen were created early in Anne's reign, and Poulett and Brydges were returned unopposed in four general elections. The corporation, in 1704, expressed the hope that it could preserve the unity, peace, and friendship that should exist among them; it expressed a similar resolution to 'live in unity and amity' in an address of 1707.[12] It also passed a resolution that all creations of freemen had to be approved in a full assembly and in 1707 rejected the proposal to elect Sir Thomas Hoby to the freedom.[13] In August 1710, however, the tide turned. It was carried by thirty-nine votes to thirty-two to admit six Tory freemen, although twenty-seven of the thirty-five honorary freemen present (including four Pouletts) voted against. The Poulett interest was further weakened when Bolton was replaced as lord lieutenant of the county by the Tory duke of Beaufort, who wrote that the county was delighted to be free of Bolton, whose management had depended on fear, bullying, and lies.[14] After the six freemen were chosen, the bells rang to celebrate 'the recovery of their liberties and privileges after twenty years servitude to a party'.[15] Coward was told that, as recorder, he had

[10] *HP 1690–1715*, ii. 659–64; *Post Boy*, 6 Oct. 1722.
[11] *HP 1690–1715*, ii. 254–5. Coward was at the centre of a dispute in 1682, in which he referred sneeringly to the 'tradesmen' in the corporation: Hants RO, W/B1/6, fos. 144–9; *CSPD 1682*, 411.
[12] Hants RO, W/B2/5, 22 Sept. 1704, W/B1/8, fo. 3.
[13] Hants RO, W/B2/5, 8 Dec. 1705, 28 Feb. 1707.
[14] Hants RO, W/B1/8, fos. 48–51; *HMC Portland*, iv. 599.
[15] *Post Boy*, 19–22 Aug. 1710 (also *Norwich Gazette*, 19–26 Aug. 1710).

no right to attend and vote at meetings. In October, Thomas Lewis, one of the new freemen, was returned to Parliament, along with Brydges; Poulett decided not to contest the seat.[16]

Portsmouth had also several times returned one Whig and one Tory member, but from 1703 contention appeared; Coward was elected recorder and Bolton became a burgess.[17] A group of five Tories, eventually reduced to three, monopolized the mayoralty from 1703 to 1709, thanks to a solid majority of Tories among the burgesses, who chose the mayor. At the end of 1709 the Tory mayor died and the Whigs seized control, admitting more aldermen and burgesses. In September 1710 Henry Seager was elected mayor and presided over a parliamentary election in which two Whigs were returned. The defeated Tory candidates petitioned against the return, alleging that Seager was not legally mayor. The Commons, now strongly Tory, agreed. Five Whig aldermen were convicted at Winchester assizes of holding office contrary to law (they had not taken communion within the required period).[18] The Tories, with the backing of the central government, the Commons, and Beaufort, were now firmly in command.

Party feelings also ran high in Norwich. In a by-election of 1703, a Tory, Thomas Palgrave, a brewer, won by only eighty-nine votes, in a contest marred (in the eyes of Prideaux, but not perhaps those of the electors) by two weeks of furious drinking.[19] Prideaux thought 'Torisme' [*sic*] was the 'prevailing humour' in the city and a correspondent of Defoe's remarked that the tradesmen of the city would be more likely to subscribe towards publishing a book in favour of divine right than one against it.[20] Party rancour ran high. In May 1704 a man who said he was for the current MPs was beaten by three men who drank confusion to all 'tackers'. In the Tom of Bedlam alehouse in 1710, a Jacobite said that the present Parliament were all 'croaking rogues'.[21] In August 1704 one of the aldermen for Conesford ward died. The Tory mayor, William Blyth, delayed holding an election for his replacement, because he feared that the freemen would elect Thomas Dunch, a leading Whig. In anticipation of the election both sides spent heavily: Dunch's supporters allegedly spent £700. The mayor

---

[16] Hants RO, W/B2/5, 11 Sept. 1710; *HP 1690–1715*, ii. 255–6.

[17] Portsmouth RO, CE 1/11, 13 Mar. 1703; East, 373.

[18] East, 207–13, 762–72; *Post Boy*, 9–11 Aug. 1711; *Pol State*, ii. 504–5; BL, Add MS 70421, fos. 221–2; *HP 1690–1715*, ii. 244.

[19] NRO, DCN 115/2, p. 14.

[20] NRO, DCN 115/1, p. 224; Defoe, *Letters*, 64.

[21] NCR, Case 12b/2, information of James Daglis and Thomas Barnham, 14 May 1704, information of Richard Callow, 19 Oct. 1710.

eventually called the election, at short notice, on 14 March 1705. Dunch defeated Benjamin Austin by twenty-one votes. There were various allegations of sharp practice. Some Tories called for a scrutiny, to give a pretext to delay swearing Dunch, which the mayor granted, but did not proceed with.[22]

On 22 March, after the mayor's court had appointed a committee to examine the charters, the mayor and some of the aldermen disallowed Dunch's election on the grounds that he was an unfit person, because of his 'uncivil behaviour' and 'malicious, turbulent, contentious temper'. They claimed that the freemen of the ward had a right only to nominate, not to elect.[23] The mayor held another election, again with very little notice, on 23 April. According to Dunch's supporters, when it seemed clear that Dunch was likely to win, Blyth sent orders to stop the poll, declared Austin elected, and had him sworn. According to the mayor, Dunch's supporters tried to insist on the previous election. Several of those present (which the mayor was not) told him that Austin seemed to have the majority of votes, and the next mayor's court declared Austin duly elected.[24]

According to Dunch's supporters, the mayor's court had no legal right to reject his election. The recorder initially thought that the court had such a right, but changed his mind after reading Charles II's charter.[25] Others had come to the same conclusion, but the mayor and his supporters stood their ground. Blyth initially alleged that Dunch had failed to produce evidence that he had taken communion, as required by law, and that he had set up the Exchange to further his own private interests, much to the annoyance of the city's traders. On reflection, he omitted these allegations. He retained a claim that workmen who would not vote for Dunch were threatened with dismissal.[26] Dunch went to Queen's Bench to seek a *mandamus* and his supporters petitioned the privy council. They sought the advice of Lord Townshend, the lord lieutenant and an active Whig; he was uncertain how to proceed, but was willing to present their petition and promised to do his utmost to secure their rights.[27] He wrote to the mayor, urging him to swear Dunch and warning him that he had no legal

[22] Prideaux, 175, 176, 196; MCB 26, fo. 185; NRO, MS 453, 'A Description', under 1704; NCR, Case 8h/1, petition to the queen, 1705 (another copy SP 34/6, no. 8, fo. 15 [VN]); Case 12b/2, information of Samuel Sparke and Robert Turner, 15 Mar. 1705.

[23] MCB 26, fo. 189; SP 34/6, nos. 25A, 25B, fos. 46–7 (VN); NCR, Case 8h/1, petition to the queen, 1705.

[24] NCR, Case 8h/1, petition to the queen and 'observations on the charters of Norwich'.

[25] MCB 26, fo. 196 (VN).

[26] Prideaux, 196; NCR, Case 8h/1, 'observations on the charters of Norwich' and draft of same. The final version of the letter is SP 34/6, no. 25, fos. 42–4 (VN).

[27] BL, Add MS 63079, fos. 3–4.

reason not to.[28] Meanwhile, the freemen of the ward of Over the Water refused to elect anyone to the livery of the Company of St George; the normally apolitical Company voted to thank Blyth for his efforts to preserve the honour of the city.[29] Partisanship was becoming all-pervasive.

In the midst of this contention, the parliamentary election for the city was held. A Whig newspaper claimed that the clergy preached 'Jacobitism, tacking and high church raillery' and that the mayor and 'his brewers called aldermen' tyrannized over the city, ignored the law, and lined their own pockets.[30] The mayor's court refused to allow the Whig candidates, Waller Bacon and John Chambers, to have tents or booths built for them by the city, as was the norm, on the grounds that they were not freemen. Townshend was active on their behalf and they gained a majority of over 100, but the sheriffs made a double return on the pretext that they were unsure whether Bacon and Chambers were legally qualified to stand. In December the committee of elections decided that they were duly elected and imprisoned Blyth for electoral irregularities.[31] Meanwhile, to Townshend's disgust, the privy council refused to consider the petition concerning Dunch's election; he was eventually granted a *mandamus* and was sworn alderman on 27 April 1706.[32] In October Townshend made Dunch a major in the city trained bands; Blyth and the former MP Palgrave were merely captains.[33] In January 1707 the mayor's court ordered the razing of records of the differences involving Blyth, Dunch, and Austin, including the statement that Dunch was contentious, seditious, and unfit. In the 1708 general election, which saw a swing to the Whigs nationwide, Bacon and Chambers were returned with an increased majority.[34] But although the city elected Whig MPs in 1705 and 1708, the prevailing, or at least the most vocal, sentiment among the citizens and assembly remained Tory, and strongly pro-Church. In 1704, encouraged by Townshend to draw up an address congratulating the queen on the victory at Blenheim, the assembly also thanked her for her 'princely munificence' to the Church. A similar address in 1706 thanked her for her care of the Church and her bounty to the clergy. In March 1708 an address deploring the attempted Jacobite invasion stated: 'the revenues of

[28] Raynham Hall, B2/2, draft from Townshend to [mayor], placed under *c*.1709.
[29] SGCR, pp. 558, 560.
[30] 'Reflections on the Present State of Norwich', *London Post*, 14 May 1705.
[31] MCB 26, fo. 196; C(H) corr., no. 423; *HP 1690–1715*, ii. 421; NRO, MS 79, pp. 236, 247.
[32] C(H), corr, no. 423; NRO, MS 453, 'A Description', under 1705; MCB 26, fo. 220; Guth, 'Croakers', 362–84.
[33] C(H), corr, nos. 503, 538, 588 (the year is clearly 1706).
[34] MCB 26, fos. 199, 236; Defoe, *Letters*, 80; *HP 1690–1715*, ii. 419.

the Church have been enlarged by your bounty, its hierarchy and worship are secured by your piety.'[35]

II. SACHEVERELL AND AFTER, 1710–1714

The Whig ministers whom Anne was forced to take into office in 1708 seemed to go out of their way to enrage the Tories in general and the High Church clergy in particular. They found their nemesis in Dr Henry Sacheverell. On 5 November 1709 he preached before the lord mayor of London, on the theme of 'in peril among false brethren'. In an impassioned and somewhat incoherent rant, he suggested that the Church was in danger under the present ministry and attacked the idea that the people possessed a right of resistance, claiming that there had been no resistance in 1688. The sermon was printed and was said to have sold 100,000 copies. The ministry rose to the bait and impeached him on a charge of seditious libel. The trial aroused enormous public interest. In the first days there were so many people in the streets that the doctor's coach had difficulty getting through; he played to the crowd, waving and allowing his hand to be kissed. On 1 March 1710 there was serious rioting in London, in which several Dissenting meeting houses were destroyed. The government reacted sharply, and there were no further significant disorders. The Lords found Sacheverell guilty, but handed down a light sentence: he was to be suspended from preaching for three years. At Wrexham a crowd celebrated the mild sentence; marching to beat of drum they broke the windows of meeting houses and leading Dissenters.[36] A Tory patron offered Sacheverell a lucrative living in North Wales. His journey there became a quasi-royal progress; at every town he was met by large cheering crowds (according to the Tory press) or a few parsons, paupers, and boys (according to Whig newspapers).

In the following weeks, many towns addressed the queen with expressions of loyalty and support for her and the Church, and denunciations of 'atheism', disaffection, and claims of a right of resistance; the addresses usually concluded with a promise, when her majesty thought fit to summon a new Parliament, to choose men loyal to the monarchy and Church. Appreciating the change in the public mood, the queen dismissed her Whig ministers, appointed Tories,

[35] FAB 8, fos. 270, 283, FAB 9, fo. 8.
[36] SP 23/12, fos. 59–60. This seems to have been the only attack on a meeting house outside London, although one at Westbury was burned down in 1711: *Pol State*, ii. 453.

and called a general election, which produced a House of Commons with a large Tory majority.[37] The new ministry secured the passage of a bill outlawing occasional conformity in 1711 and the Schism Act, against Dissenting schools, in 1714. It also negotiated the treaty of Utrecht, in 1713, on terms which the Whigs claimed were too generous to France and which ignored the interests of Britain's allies, including Hanover. In addition it negotiated a commercial treaty with France, which the Whigs alleged damaged British economic interests, especially the textile industry. The Commons were sufficiently concerned about some aspects of the treaty to reject two of its provisions.

It would be difficult to overstate the impact of the doctor and his trial on the public mood, or the depth of emotion generated, particularly among Tories, who saw him as a martyr for the Church. One contemporary wrote that, apart from elections, Anne's reign had been a continual series of rejoicings until the Sacheverell trial.[38] At Salisbury the mayor and corporation walked out of the church as Bishop Burnet was about to preach, after he had made some reflections on them in a sermon on Romans 13.[39] Henry Crossgrove, the author and publisher of the *Norwich Gazette*, had hitherto avoided partisan expressions; after the trial, his language became more forceful. Shortly before 30 January 1712 he wrote that Charles I had been 'sacrilegiously' murdered by 'those furies the Whigs', who maintained the 'damnable' principle of resistance.[40] On 1 May 1710 Robert Bene was elected mayor in a closely fought contest in which 3,174 freemen voted. Sacheverell's picture was hung out of a window opposite the hall. Tories huzza'ed when they saw it and passers-by were made to doff their hats to it. Hundreds followed Bene to his house chanting 'the Church and Bene, High Church and Sacheverell'.[41] Two days later the assembly approved an address to the queen which forthrightly denounced the principle of resistance. The people of Norwich, it said, had learned their principles of loyalty from their venerable mother, the Church of England. They promised that in the next election they would choose truly loyal and religious MPs, who would defend monarchy and true religion against 'the insults of impiety, profaneness and republican principles'.[42] A rival address was presented in the name of the deputy lieutenants, militia officers, gentlemen, and others. It

[37] The classic study of the trial and its consequences is Holmes, *Sacheverell.*
[38] R. Ferguson, *A History of All the Mobs, Tumults and Insurrections* (London, 1715), 52.
[39] BL, Add MS 61610, fo. 43.
[40] *Norwich Gazette*, 15–19 Mar. 1707, 18–25 Dec. 1708, 29 Dec. 1711–5 Jan. 1712.
[41] *Norwich Gazette*, 29 Apr.–6 May 1710.
[42] FAB 9, fo. 21. Printed in *Post Boy*, 13–16 May 1710; *Collection*, 32.

complained that malicious persons kept up divisions and criticized the queen's loyal and prudent (Whig) ministry, claiming that obedience was due even to the worst of princes. The signatories promised to defend the queen against the Pretender and his open and secret supporters.[43] It was significant that the petition was based very much on the trained bands, commanded since 1701 by Townshend.

The city's mood was better captured on guild day, when Sacheverell's picture was displayed between those of Charles I and Charles II. After George Gobbett was elected as freemen's sheriff, 'loyal boys' cried 'the Church and the queen, the Church and the doctor, Gobbett and Sacheverell, huzza!'[44] In view of this seeming prevalence of Toryism, it is perhaps surprising that the Tories, Bene and Richard Berney, carried the parliamentary election by only about 200 votes. The Tories carried around a pair of leather breeches, which some of 'the faction' had allegedly given to 'a poor honest fellow' to vote against the Church party; people cried out that the loyalists had defeated the 'Oliverians' and captured their standard. Pictures of Charles I, Anne, Sacheverell, and the six bishops who voted for the doctor were carried before them.[45] In the next two years Tory aldermen and sheriffs were chosen either unanimously or with minimal opposition.[46]

Since the Whigs had gained control of Bristol corporation in 1696, the city had enjoyed an unaccustomed peace. During the Jacobite scare of 1708, the magistrates were ordered to send for those they suspected of being disaffected. In 1689–91 the Whigs had alleged that the Tories were at least Jacobite sympathizers. Now they wrote that there were no more than twenty suspect persons in the city; they duly tendered them the oaths.[47] Things were soon to change. One of the Bristol annalists later wrote (of 1710): 'This year amongst ourselves began the unhappy distinction of High Church and Low Church.'[48] In the general election in October the Tories won a sweeping victory, to general surprise, as one of their candidates, the philanthropist Edward Colston, did not even appear. His colleague, Joseph Earle, was carried through the streets with a mitre and streamers before him. The Anglican clergy were active in

[43] *Collection*, 47.   [44] *Norwich Gazette*, 17–24 June, 26 Aug.–2 Sept. 1710.
[45] Ibid. 14–21 Oct. 1710
[46] Ibid. 16–23 Dec. 1710, 24–31 Jan., 31 Mar.–7 April, 25 Aug.–1 Sept. 1711, 26 Apr.–3 May, 17–24 May, 23–30 Aug. 1712.
[47] BL, Add MS 61607, fo. 177. In 1705 Defoe wrote that at Bristol, Gloucester, and Bath 'moderation prevails amain': Defoe, *Letters*, 104.
[48] BRO, 07831, 1709–10.

the election; the Quakers were not allowed to vote, because they would not swear the oath of abjuration. There were bonfires, bells, and illuminations; the common people broke the windows of 'several factious persons' who 'had not their lights'.[49]

There is little doubt that the Tory victory marked a triumph of the freemen over the corporation, which remained predominantly Whig. It also seems that, while the size of the Whig vote was similar to that in 1698, the Tories had mobilized many new voters.[50] They established a new focus for their activities, the Loyal Society, which held its first annual dinner on 2 November, Colston's birthday. At its second, in 1711, there were about 400 diners. Large crowds watched as they processed through the streets to the cathedral, accompanied by music, bells, and guns. The people (according to a Tory newspaper) gave vent to great expressions of joy, to the mortification of those calling themselves the sober party. Only five members of the corporation were present; the duke of Beaufort was elected president. The story was much the same in 1713, when it was alleged that there was not a Whig to be seen.[51] The Society was probably involved in an address, claiming to be from the clergy, merchants, and principal inhabitants, in June 1712, which praised the current ministry and its efforts to obtain peace; it denounced those who sought to encroach on the queen's prerogative, which she had received from God.[52]

In the years after the Sacheverell trial, addresses became increasingly partisan. Earlier addresses had celebrated military victories, with an occasional reference to the queen's support of the Church. The addresses after the trial served an obvious partisan purpose; many were printed (although not usually in the *Gazette*) and there was clearly an element of copying and emulation among towns, although most tried to make similar points using different words.[53] As at Norwich, there were Whig addresses as well, praising the present ministry. The corporation of Gloucester expressed indignation that anyone could suggest that the Church was in danger. Later it agreed an address condemning those who had shown respect for Sacheverell, a dangerous person, impeached by the Commons; Nonconformist preachers urged citizens to subscribe it.[54] The Whig corporation of Coventry stressed the need to compel the enemy to lay

[49] *Post Boy*, 28–31 Oct., 31 Oct.–2 Nov. 1710; Latimer, ii. 85; *HP 1690–1715*, ii. 213–14.
[50] Latimer, ii. 85; *HP 1690–1715*, ii. 214.
[51] BCL, B10163, Annales Bristolliae, 2 Nov. 1710; *Post Boy*, 3–6 Nov. 1711, 7–10 Nov. 1713.
[52] *Post Boy*, 26–8 June 1712. An address of 1714 in the name of the clergy, gentlemen, merchants, and principal inhabitants explicitly mentions the Loyal Society: *Post Boy*, 20–3 Nov. 1714.
[53] Knights, *Representation*, 153.   [54] *Collection*, 4; BL Add MS 70421, fo. 194.

down his arms. It promised to continue to send members who best understood the queen's and nation's interests.[55] A rival address from the deputy lieutenants, clergy, and principal inhabitants emphasized the queen's hereditary title and support for 'our holy religion'; they called on God to help her to preserve its doctrine, discipline, and worship. They promised to return MPs who would secure the 'holy faith' against atheists and heretics, and suppress schism, as well as defending the best of constitutions against republicanism.[56] At Canterbury some aldermen protested that the address from the city had not mentioned the Glorious Revolution, William (their 'deliverer'), or the need for charity towards all Protestants. The burghmote declared that the protest was false and scandalous and ordered that it be burned by the common hangman.[57] There was another surge of loyal addresses in 1712, thanking the queen for her 'condescension' in informing her people and Parliament of her attempts to secure peace with France.[58] The deputy lieutenants, 'loyal magistrates', clergy, gentry, and inhabitants of Coventry declared that the people would welcome peace after a long and tedious war and a great expense of blood and treasure. No one could oppose it but those who had made immoderate gains from the war, or had something to hide.[59] This address made no reference to the Protestant succession or the 'illustrious House of Hanover', but many did, and also praised the current ministry. There were fewer references to the Church than in 1710. Another wave of addresses greeted the news of the peace in 1713. At Gloucester, the Whig corporation did not thank the queen for the peace; the citizens, gentry, clergy, and other 'loyal inhabitants' did, declaring that those who obstructed the peace promoted faction, blasphemy, and rebellion.[60]

Just as the wording of addresses became more partisan, so civic celebrations grew in scale and became increasingly divisive. We have seen that Sacheverell's picture was displayed on guild day in Norwich in 1710. What should have been a celebration of civic unity became just the opposite. Celebration of the queen's birthday should have been non-partisan. At Gloucester in 1712 the city's Tory MP and garrison celebrated, with huzzas from the soldiers and the 'common, but honest part of the town'. The mayor did nothing until he was shamed into it by the loyalists, and then he invited only Whigs.[61] Celebration

[55] *Flying Post*, 27–9 Apr. 1710.   [56] *Post Boy*, 18–20 Apr. 1710; *Collection*, 8.
[57] *Flying Post*, 11–13 May, *Post Boy*, 6–8 June 1710; Knights, *Representation*, 142–3.
[58] See for example, *Post Boy*, 26–8 June, 28 June–1 July, 3–5 July, 8–10 July 1712.
[59] *Post Boy*, 8–10 July 1712; *Pol State*, iv. 36.
[60] *Pol State*, iv. 37; *Post Boy*, 30 Apr.–2 May 1713.
[61] *Post Man*, 9–12 Feb., *Post Boy*, 16–19 Feb. 1712.

of the peace of Utrecht was often exuberant, with large numbers of participants, but the peace itself was a source of contention, and in many places there was at least a partisan tinge to the occasion; the use of maypoles could be seen as offensive to Dissenters.[62] The drinking of healths could lead to acrimony. At Dursley they drank to Sacheverell, at Tamworth to the 'honest part' of the corporation.[63] There were a few celebrations of a different kind, when the Commons rejected the two clauses of the commercial treaty. At Frome and Kidderminster, both cloth towns, the people celebrated with bonfires, bells, and healths to the queen and the Protestant succession.[64] At Coventry cloth-workers went in procession around the city, with drum and trumpet. They carried the weavers' streamers and long poles dressed with greenery and garlands, bound with ribbons of jersey; many had jersey round their waists and necks and all had greenery in their hats. The journeymen had plenty of ale or money given them by their masters and the evening concluded with bonfires.[65] There was little overt opposition to the celebrations. At Lichfield, the chancellor of the diocese tried unsuccessfully to prevent the peace being proclaimed in the close.[66] But at Halstead even those regarded as disaffected gave at least a show of satisfaction. Although people at Tavistock feared that the commercial treaty would damage their already decayed cloth industry, they participated in the official day of celebration. A report from Sherborne stressed that 'all were innocently and peaceably merry'.[67]

Some celebrations could not but be divisive. The day that Sacheverell's three-year suspension was to end, in many towns the bells began tolling shortly after midnight and continued all day. In the evening there were bonfires and illuminations and healths to the queen, the Church, the ministry, and the doctor.[68] The Whigs tried to respond to the popularity of Sacheverell by reviving the practice of burning the pope (together with the Pretender) in effigy in London on 17 November 1711, but they were prevented from doing so,[69]

---

[62] *Post Boy*, 19–21, 23–6 May 1713.
[63] Ibid. 21–3 May, 2–4 June 1713.
[64] *Flying Post*, 23–5, 25–7 June 1713.
[65] Ibid. 27–30 June 1713.
[66] *Post Boy*, 2–4 June 1713.
[67] Ibid. 23–6 May, 16–18 July, 8–11 Aug. 1713. The prominence of clothworkers and the cloth industry in many celebrations may have been designed to counter claims that the peace would harm it.
[68] Ibid. 28–31 Mar. 1713; *Flying Post*, 7–9 Apr. 1713.
[69] *An Account of the Mock Procession of Burning the Pope* (1711); *A True Relation of the . . . Intended Riot and Tumult* (1711); *Flying Post*, 17–20 Nov. 1711; *Post Boy*, 17–20 Nov. 1711. The only reference I have found between 1688 and 1711 to a pope-burning dates from 1696: *Post Boy*, 17–19 Nov. 1696.

much to the queen's relief.[70] They were more successful in 1713 on 6 February, the queen's birthday, and 17 November, when the pope, Pretender, and devil were burned, again in London; there do not seem to have been any pope-burnings in the provinces at this stage.[71] Election victories were celebrated with partisan exuberance and sometimes violence. In February 1711 the Commons decided a disputed election for Rye in favour of the Whig candidates. The 'fanatics' rang the bells all day; at night two of the jurats led a mob that 'insulted' the houses of 'honest Churchmen'. They pulled a small cannon round the streets and fired it, breaking many windows, and fired a musket at the parson's windows. Next day, they rambled round the streets, saying that they were hunting the Church and would drive their high-flying parson out of town.[72] Such Whig celebrations were uncommon. The strongly Tory House of Commons decided most disputes in favour of the Tories. At Stafford the Tories celebrated for a week the news that a Tory candidate had been declared elected; the celebrations spread to neighbouring towns. A Whiggish churchwarden refused to hand over the keys or allow the Tories to ring the bells, until they pursued him to his house with 'rough music'.[73] At Devizes the resolution of the disputed election in favour of the Tories was celebrated with the ringing of bells. An effigy of one of the Whig candidates was paraded around the town and burned.[74] At Birmingham there were great celebrations, also lasting several days, on the news that William Bromley, a Warwickshire man, had been elected speaker of the Commons.[75]

There was also a heightened level of partisanship and violence in elections in 1710. At York the clergy voted Tory in a body and boys made a flag, with a picture of Sacheverell, which they paraded around the city and waved in the Whig candidates' faces.[76] At Coventry the Tories took both seats, despite the fact that the corporation was dominated by Dissenters and Whigs, and had recently elected the Whig earl of Sunderland as their recorder; both sheriffs were Whigs. Many gentlemen and clergy from the county appeared for the Tory candidates. Sunderland came to town but met with much rude language and was driven out by a large crowd.[77] At Taunton, once a bastion of Whiggism and Dissent, the Tory candidates were escorted to the town by 1,500 men on horseback from the county, and were met by as many from the town; all wore laurels of gold and silver, with the motto 'God save the Church and queen'. The

[70] *HMC Bath*, i. 217.   [71] *Flying Post*, 7–10 Feb., 17–19 Nov. 1713.
[72] *Post Boy*, 24–7 Feb. 1711.   [73] Ibid. 8–10 Feb. 1711.
[74] *Norwich Gazette*, 23–30 Dec. 1710.   [75] *Post Boy*, 7–9 Dec. 1710.
[76] BL, Add MS 70421, fo. 250. See Speck, *Tory and Whig*, 42–3.
[77] *Post Boy*, 24–6 Oct. 1710: BL, Add MS 70421, fos. 235–6; *HP 1690–1715*, ii. 630–1.

Whig candidates were attended by 'a great rabble of combers and redcaps', who were set upon by a Tory mob, which broke windows which were illuminated; the Tories won by over 200 votes.[78] In the Cheshire county election, held at Chester, men and women alike cried, 'No more Rump Parliaments, up with the Tackers, down with the Presbyterians and tub preachers'. To ridicule 'anti-loyal' (in other words, Low) Churchmen, tubs of all sizes were beaten around the streets.[79] The Whigs had the Hampshire election adjourned from Winchester to the Isle of Wight. The mayor and corporation of Southampton, in their formalities, welcomed George Pitt, one of the Tory candidates, attended by twenty-five clergy and at least 1,000 people ('not a Dissenter, non-juror or Hoadlyite among them'), and escorted them to the harbour, amid cries of 'God bless the Queen, the Church and the doctor'. When the duke of Bolton and the Whigs arrived, few turned out to meet them and they slunk to their boats through the side streets. On the news that the Tories had won, the mayor and aldermen came down to the quayside to meet the victorious candidates. They were greeted by salutes from the ships and gun platforms. Later the streets were full of torches and the windows full of candles, except for a few 'fanatics', 'who are like to pay the glaziers for their singularity'. The people shouted for the High Church and the meeting house might have been attacked, but for the care taken by the magistrates.[80]

After the bruising general election of 1710, both sides sought to gain control of corporations before the next election and the mutual hatred of High and Low Church if anything increased. At Chichester High Churchmen depicted the collapse of the cathedral steeple in a thunderstorm as God's judgement on the dean and chapter, who had suspended the organist for refusing to drink confusion to Sacheverell or the pious memory of King William.[81] At Exeter the Whig dean refused to allow the cathedral bells to be rung to celebrate the taking of Dunkirk. Next day the bishop and Tory gentlemen boycotted his sermon and, when he rose to preach, three-quarters of the congregation walked out.[82] At Colchester the newly elected mayor brought in a minister from outside the town to preach at his inauguration. It was said that this minister voted with the Dissenters and blamed the Church party for Charles I's death. None of the town's clergy would let him into their churches, so the mayor had to do without his sermon.[83] There were several attempts to prosecute Dissenters for

---

[78] *Norwich Gazette*, 14–21 Oct. 1710; BL Add MS 70421, fo. 244; *HP 1690–1715*, ii. 526, 528.
[79] *Post Boy*, 2–4 Nov. 1710.   [80] Ibid. 9–11 Nov. 1710.
[81] *Norwich Gazette*, 29 Sept.–6 Oct. 1711.   [82] *Post Boy*, 17–19 July 1712.
[83] *Norwich Gazette*, 6–13 Oct., *Flying Post*, 9–11 Oct. 1711.

keeping 'illegal' schools.[84] The Occasional Conformity Act of 1711 was designed to winkle partial conformists out of corporations. At Bristol only three members resigned and it was said to make little difference at Colchester and elsewhere.[85] Gloucester corporation remained firmly in Whig hands, despite Beaufort's effort to establish his influence there.[86]

The government and law courts broke the Whigs' control of Coventry corporation. The lord chancellor ordered that it should hand over the administration of Sir Thomas White's charity, which had a revenue of £900 a year, to trustees. As all of the trustees were Tories, a major source of patronage in the city was transferred from the Whigs to the Tories. It was alleged that seven Dissenters had received communion from a chaplain of Sunderland's, so that they could elect him recorder, and that only five members of the corporation were legally qualified to serve.[87] In 1712 the Whig pretender to the mayoralty absconded, faced with the threat of prosecution for holding office illegally, and of a *quo warranto* against the charter. Chancery issued an order of sequestration for over £2,200, which it was alleged that the corporation had embezzled from White's charity; commissioners were appointed to take possession of the sword, mace, and city lands. Some members of the corporation resigned and nine aldermen were adjudged by the courts to have forfeited their places because they were not qualified under the Corporation Act.[88] In 1713 the sword and mace were seized on a commission out of chancery, as the mayor and sheriffs were on their way to quarter sessions. The mayor resisted violently and the court ordered that he and eleven others be gaoled for contempt.[89] The discomfiture of Coventry's Whigs was shown by their putting up only one candidate against two Tories in 1713. In the first hour of polling the five electors who dared to vote for the Whig were hauled to a 9-foot high wooden horse and made to ride it, while several men hung on each leg. The Whig candidate withdrew and the Tories were returned. A petition that the election should be voided because of the violence used against Whig voters was, predictably, ignored by the new House of Commons, in which the Tories had an even larger majority.[90]

[84] BL, Add MS 70421, fo. 186; *Norwich Gazette,* 22–9 Mar. 1712; *Post Boy,* 26–8 Mar. 1713.
[85] BRO, 04264/9, fos. 286–7; *Post Boy,* 30 Oct.–1 Nov. 1712; Hurwich, ' "Fanatick Town" ', 30.
[86] *HP 1690–1715,* ii. 221–3.
[87] *HP 1690–1715,* ii. 631; *Post Boy,* 26–8 Apr., 9–11 Aug., 20–3 Oct., *Flying Post,* 25–7 Oct. 1711; BL, Add MS 61655, fos. 153–6. For rival mayors at Chichester, see *Norwich Gazette,* 6–13 Oct., 10–17 Nov. 1711.
[88] *Post Boy,* 4–6, 9–12 Dec. 1711, 9–12 Feb., 17–19 Apr., 2–5 May, 31 May–3 June 1712.
[89] Ibid. 8–10 Oct., 12–14 Nov. 1713, 9–11 Feb. 1714.   [90] *HP 1690–1715,* ii. 631.

There was also extensive violence at Bristol in 1713. The Whigs put forward only one candidate, Sir William Daines, against Earle and Thomas Edwardes. The Tories claimed that the corporation had created several hundred freemen to boost their vote and had hired others, with oak cudgels, to 'mob'. When Daines ran out of voters, the sheriffs sent to ask if there were more to poll, but those whom the Whigs had procured said that they had good food and drink and would stay where they were. The Whigs claimed they were initially denied the use of St George's chapel, which gave easy access to the hustings, and had to take a hall further away, from which voters had to run a gauntlet of blows and insults. When they eventually gained access to the chapel, stones were thrown through the windows and those inside locked themselves in, fearing for their lives. The next day Daines brought 500 men to secure access to the hall. The Tories agreed that all should be free to vote, but soon Tories were rampaging through the streets, with ribbons in their hats. Kingswood colliers, armed with flails, stood outside the houses where Daines's men were waiting to vote, so that they were too scared to move. The polls were closed with fewer than 700 votes cast; Daines received only 189.[91] The Tory victories in 1710 and 1713 owed much to fraud and intimidation, but also reflected the formidable surge of Tory and High Church sentiment, at all levels of society, following the Sacheverell trial. There were a few signs in 1713, however, that the Tories' popularity had been damaged by the commercial treaty. At Norwich, Bene and Berney were re-elected, but by fewer than 200 votes. The Whigs claimed that the treaty would damage the cloth industry and the mayor's court issued an order against people wearing in their hats wool, cloth, or other 'marks of distinction'.[92] Fraud and intimidation, moreover, begat fraud and intimidation. For the moment the Tories controlled the government, the Commons, and the legal system. When the Whigs regained control of all three, they were to use similar methods.

[91] *Post Boy, Flying Post*, both 15–17 Sept. 1713.

[92] MCB 27, fos. 127; *Post Boy*, 24–6 Sept. 1713. For hostility to the commercial treaty in Liverpool, see *HP 1690–1715*, ii. 332–3. The Tories too wore 'marks of distinction'—oak leaves: *Pol State*, vi. 189.

13

The Triumph of the Whigs? 1714–1722

I. A WHIG KING

Anne's death on 1 August 1714 brought George I to the throne. He had no first-hand experience of England, so was dependent on what his English advisers told him; he deeply resented the failure of Anne's Tory ministry to consider Hanover's interests when negotiating the peace of Utrecht. For years Whig politicians had been feeding George their perception that the Tories were actual or concealed Jacobites.[1] They had made similar claims under William III, but William soon came to realize that the allegations were at best exaggerated. George I knew that some Tories had actively supported his accession to the throne and, not wishing to become the prisoner of one party, he appointed several Tory ministers. Events, however, discredited the Tories in his eyes. From the day of his coronation riots and other disorders showed widespread disaffection. The Jacobite rebellion of 1715 confirmed this impression and the defection of such leading Tories as Ormond and Bolingbroke to the Pretender made him less willing to trust the rest. He dismissed the last of his Tory ministers early in 1716 and high politics henceforth centred on struggles for power among the Whigs.[2]

Meanwhile, the Whigs had won a general election early in 1715—as in 1708 fear of Jacobitism was their one electoral trump card. With a substantial majority in the Commons and an increasing monopoly of ministerial power, the Whigs sought to make their dominance permanent. They set out to exploit systematically the anomalies and inequalities in the electoral system. They could do little about the counties, where the franchise was fixed and the electorate large, but there was far more scope for gerrymandering in the boroughs, especially the smaller boroughs.[3] Often the franchise was open to dispute, but even

---

[1] Colley, *In Defiance of Oligarchy*, 177–8.   [2] Ibid. 179–88.
[3] Plumb, *Political Stability*, chs. 3–4, 6; Colley, *In Defiance of Oligarchy*, 120–2.

where it was not the final arbiter was the House of Commons, which could now be relied upon to decide disputes in favour of Whig candidates. Before 1689, when the franchise was disputed, the Commons had generally preferred the wider option, to reduce the scope for electoral interference by the crown. In the 1690s the Commons sometimes still opted for the wider franchise, but this became less common under Anne. After 1715 the Commons normally reduced the size of the electorate, making it easier to manage.[4] The Whigs made full use of the personal 'interests' of Whig borough-mongers—magnates like the dukes of Bolton, Bedford, and Newcastle, but also wealthy gentry and merchants; some even served as mayors of small towns.[5] And they exploited the 'government interest'. With the growth of the armed forces and the administration—especially the revenue administration—since 1689, there were far more government employees in towns, who could be persuaded to support Whig candidates.[6] William and Anne had refused to exploit this 'government interest' because they did not want either party to become too dominant: party leaders with an unassailable majority in the Commons would try to dictate to the monarch in matters of policy and patronage. George I, faced with what he saw as massive disaffection, was eager to help secure the election of 'loyal' men. This was made easier by the Septennial Act of 1716, which laid down that the maximum interval between general elections should be increased from three years to seven, so members did not have to face the voters too often. The repeal of the Occasional Conformity Act in 1719 and a series of court decisions made it easier for Dissenters to be admitted to offices in corporations; an Act of 1719 effectively removed the need to take the sacrament.[7]

These changes did not render the electoral process meaningless. In the counties and larger towns elections were often still vigorously contested; the Tories' popular support remained resilient, despite decades of exclusion from power. But the Whigs controlled enough small boroughs, which outnumbered the large, to maintain a majority in the Commons. They could never be certain of victory and worked extremely hard. They spent heavily on town halls, assembly rooms, and other amenities; at Rochester, Sir Cloudesley Shovell and Sir Joseph Williamson built a new town hall, the latter adding a 'mathematical school' for good measure.[8] They used their influence in high places to advance

---

[4] *HP 1690–1715*, i. 251–4.   [5] *Weekly Journal or British Gazetteer*, 13 Oct. 1722.
[6] For Townshend's building up his 'interest' in Yarmouth, see Gauci, *Yarmouth*, ch. 7, esp. 249–54.
[7] Halliday, *Body*, 306, 328–9; *Pol State*, xvi. 607, 628, xvii. 212.
[8] Plumb, *Political Stability*, 91.

or protect the towns' interests and secured favours for influential townsmen; and they dispensed lavish hospitality.[9] Appointments in the Church, armed forces, and administration were strongly influenced by party considerations; High Church clergymen could no longer hope for promotion.[10] The Whigs also used the law, fraud, and armed force to intimidate their opponents.[11] In this, they were merely replicating the tactics used by the Tories in 1682–5 or the last years of Anne's reign.[12] But in some ways they took them further. The Riot Act of 1715 empowered troops to fire on rioters if they failed to disperse, after due warning;[13] the use of the military to cow civilians in 1714–18 was extensive and brutal, and found parallels only in the reign of James II. The tactics worked: the widespread disaffection of 1714–16 was contained, leaving only localized shows of defiance.[14] The Whigs' control over the electoral system was demonstrated by their victory in the general election of 1722.

II. RIOT AND REBELLION

The proclamation of the new king was generally greeted with joy. Partisan feelings were laid aside and there were few signs of division and disaffection.[15] By the time of the king's coronation, on 20 October, he had appointed a predominantly Whig ministry and Whig attempts to celebrate were often disrupted. At Chippenham a procession with coronation favours in their hats was attacked by a mob with guns and clubs, which marched to the beat of drums. At Nuneaton a large crowd appeared at the Whigs' bonfire, asking for money to drink Sacheverell's health. When this was refused, the crowd destroyed the bonfire, broke windows, and assaulted a constable, as well as the daughters of one of the town's leading Whigs.[16] At Bedford the maypole was

[9] Plumb, *Political Stability*, chs. 3–4.

[10] Bishop Gibson of London, who was in some respects a High Churchman, was a Whig in politics.

[11] Wilson, *Sense of the People*, 96–101.

[12] Knights, *Representation*, 369–72. The question of the politicization of the legal process in 1710–14 needs investigation, but it is noticeable that the Tories obtained some favourable verdicts at the assizes (for example, against the Whig aldermen of Portsmouth: *Pol State*, ii. 504–5).

[13] Stevenson, *Popular Disturbances*, 6–8, 29.

[14] Kathleen Wilson argues that popular Jacobitism remained vigorous after 1715 (especially in comparison to the largely impotent Tory leadership) and was seen especially in the press, ballads, and seditious words: *Sense of the People*, 108–17.

[15] *Flying Post*, 7–10, 12–14, 14–17, 19–21 Aug. 1714; *Post Boy*, 5–7 Aug. 1714. For evidence of opposition, see *Post Man*, 12–14 Aug., *Flying Post*, 31 Aug.–2 Sept. 1714.

[16] *An Account of the Riots, Tumults and Other Treasonable Practices* (1715), 6–7, 9–12.

put into mourning, and remained so for three weeks,[17] and there were violent disruptions of the celebrations at Worcester, Reading, Birmingham, Frome, Norwich, and Taunton.[18] The rioters rarely used explicitly Jacobite language and their slogans were essentially Tory and High Church.[19] The most serious disorders were in Bristol, following a rumour that the Whigs planned to burn an effigy of Sacheverell. A large crowd attacked the house where the effigy was alleged to be. The rioters ransacked the house, carrying away goods and money; one of them was fatally shot as he tried to force his way upstairs; a Quaker was killed when he tried to persuade the rioters to disperse. Several meeting houses and private houses were badly damaged. The privy council was determined to inflict exemplary punishment, appointing a commission of oyer and terminer to try the rioters; it was greeted with cries of 'Down with the Roundheads!' The corporation and government hoped to find that leading Tories were behind the riot, but those arrested were generally poor and were condemned to only minor punishments.[20]

The punishment of the Bristol rioters failed to prevent further disorders. At Chichester a small bonfire to celebrate the conviction of the rioters led a crowd to assemble, which assaulted the duke of Richmond, with cries of 'No lord of the bedchamber, no Papist turned Protestant!'[21] However, election disorders apart, towns remained relatively calm until the end of May 1715. George I's birthday fell on the 28th, the day before 'Restoration day', celebration of which was required by Act of Parliament. The Tories celebrated it far more exuberantly than the 28th, a clear snub to the king.[22] Sometimes they disrupted Whig celebrations of the 28th. At Manchester a mob broke up the bonfire, throwing the embers into Whigs' houses and breaking windows which had been illuminated. On the 29th the Tories dressed their hats and houses with oak branches; the celebrations continued until 1 June, when they

[17] Ibid. 12; *Pol State*, viii. 365–8. The Dissenters responded by burning the Pretender and Sacheverell: *HP 1690–1715*, i. 209. The Pretender was also burned at Dorchester: Underdown, *Fire from Heaven*, 262.

[18] PC 2/85, pp. 133–4; *Account of the Riots*, 8–9, 13–15. For disturbances elsewhere, see P. Rae, *The History of the Rebellion Raised against . . . King George* (London, 1726), 108; Rogers, *Whigs and Cities*, 366–72.

[19] Monod, *Jacobitism*, 173–6, 178; Rogers, *Crowds, Culture and Politics*, 30.

[20] *The Bristol Riot* (1714); *A Full and Impartial Account of the Late Disorders in Bristol* (1714), 2–10; PC 2/85, pp. 108–9; Rae, *History of the Rebellion*, 112; Latimer, ii. 107–8.

[21] *Account of the Riots*, 15. This was the son of the duchess of Portsmouth, who had been chosen high steward of York in 1683.

[22] *Weekly Journal or British Gazetteer*, 7 June 1718; *Flying Post*, 3–5 June, 1–3 July 1718. Some towns tried to celebrate the two days equally: *Flying Post*, 2–5, 14–16 June 1716.

set the Dissenting meeting house on fire.[23] The most serious disorders came at Oxford. Both university and city had greeted George's accession with an enthusiasm that was, at best, muted. The council anxiously ordered that the occasion should be marked with loyal healths and hearty acclamations, but one observer commented on the 'meanness' of the bonfires.[24] The first outbreak of serious trouble came on 28 May. A newly formed group of university Whigs, the Constitution Club, met at the King's Head, in the High Street, and had a large pile of faggots erected in the street. The Club called on the common people to light the fire, but instead they carried the faggots away for their own use. It was alleged that the Club had intended to burn effigies of Queen Anne, Sacheverell, and Ormond (still, despite his disgrace, chancellor of the university; he was replaced by his brother in September). Deprived of its bonfire, the Club placed many candles in the windows, which the crowd promptly broke. People roamed the streets in their thousands: many had come from the country in expectation of 'sport'. They cried out for Ormond and Sacheverell, and 'down with the Roundheads'. About 10 p.m. they attacked and gutted the Presbyterian meeting house, put the preacher in the stocks, and burned part of the pulpit. The senior proctor judged that the only way to appease the mob was to disperse the Constitution Club; he escorted the members back to their colleges. Once there, they fired several shots at the crowd, who responded by breaking windows.[25]

The next day the city was quiet until 10 p.m., when the crowd gutted the Quaker meeting house, burning the benches in the street; it spoiled the goods of the Quakers' 'speaker', and wrecked a room used by the Baptists. Having broken windows that were illuminated the previous night, the people now broke those which were not.[26] Opinions differed as to how far students were involved. Some suggested that there were relatively few, because the university

---

[23] An Account of the Dreadful Mob at Manchester and Other Places (Edinburgh, 1715), 3 (much of this is based on a letter in Flying Post, 18–21 June 1715).

[24] OCA, iv. 87; HMC Portland, vii. 198.

[25] Post Boy, 2–4 June 1715; A Full and Impartial Account of the Oxford Riots (1715), 2–4; HMC Portland, vii. 222–3; St James's Post, 30 May–1 June 1715. For the members of the Club, see Full and Impartial Account, 8–9. The two letters in HMC Portland, vii. 222–3 are assigned to 1717, but clearly relate to 1715, not least because the first introduces the Constitution Club, which is referred to in passing in letters from 1716: HMC Portland, vii. 218. The report in St James's Post also appeared in Weekly Journal with Fresh Advices, 4 June 1715.

[26] Post Boy, 2–4 June 1715; Full and Impartial Account, 4–6; HMC Portland, vii. 223; St James's Post, 30 May–June 1715. The claim that the crowd was egged on by agents provocateurs from the Constitution Club is implausible: Full and Impartial Account, 4. The claim in St James's Post that the rioters were given money is rather less so.

authorities enforced the 9 p.m. curfew; others referred to the 'scholastic mob', but added that it had been joined by the 'black guard' from the city.[27] In March 1716 a grand jury found bills against three scholars for pulling down meeting houses and against two for scandalous words against the king.[28]

The university authorities tried to show that they had acted responsibly, and declared their determination to find out and punish those responsible. All members of the university were to avoid 'odious and contumelious words of reproach and distinction'.[29] Others claimed that Jacobitism was rife throughout the university and city.[30] At the assizes in August the judge called on the grand jury to enquire diligently into the cause of the disorders. The grand jury presented the Constitution Club as a set of men opposed to monarchy and good order, who met armed.[31] On 1 August, the anniversary of the king's accession, the mayor, vice chancellor, and heads of colleges made no bonfires. Recorder William Wright put several hundred lighted candles in his windows, on which a mob of students and 'rascally fellows' broke them, crying down with the Rump and the Roundheads, 'an Ormond, an Ormond'.[32]

The crowds which had assembled in Manchester continued for three weeks. Sometimes they broke Whigs' windows, but their main task was destroying the meeting house, breaking the slates from the roof so that they could not be reused. Having completed their work, they moved out into the surrounding countryside. Many dressed in women's clothes, to hide their identities. It was alleged that they drank the Pretender's health on his birthday, 10 June; they were eventually dispersed by soldiers.[33] But the riots spread. At Leeds those who celebrated the Pretender's birthday threatened to pull down the meeting houses; the mayor refused to suppress them. It was alleged that the inhabitants had lived as 'loving peaceable neighbours' until 'high-flying Scaramouche clergy' stirred up the multitude.[34] At Wolverhampton a crowd celebrated the town fair by pulling down the meeting house.[35] At Shrewsbury a crowd, with many dressed as women, pulled down a meeting house, over two or three

---

[27] *Post Boy*, 2–4 June 1715; *St James's Post*, 6–8 June 1715.

[28] *Weekly Journal or British Gazetteer*, 24 Mar. 1716.

[29] *Post Man*, 14–16 June 1715; *Weekly Journal with Fresh Advices*, 11 June 1715.

[30] C (H) corr., no. 693a; *Flying Post*, 9–11 June 1715.

[31] *Full and Impartial Account*, 10–12.   [32] *Flying Post*, 4–6 Aug. 1715.

[33] *Account of the Dreadful Mob*, 3–5; *Flying Post*, 14–16 and 25–8 June, 5–7 and 12–14 July 1715; *Weekly Journal with Fresh Advices*, 18 June 1715; J. D. Oates, 'Jacobitism and Popular Disturbances in Northern England, 1714–19', *Northern History*, xli (2004), 115–16.

[34] *Account of the Dreadful Mob*, 5 (*Flying Post*, 18–21 June 1715).

[35] *Flying Post*, 7–9 July 1715; *Weekly Journal with Fresh Advices*, 9 July 1715.

nights; when some were arrested they were rescued from gaol by their fellows.[36] At Worcester a crowd made a breach in the meeting house wall, but were beaten off by the mayor, sheriff, and constables, with some soldiers; the rioters took out their frustration on the Whigs' windows. It was said that the rioters knew that the Riot Act was due to come into force at the end of July and were determined to destroy all the meeting houses before it did.[37] The Act made failure to disperse on command a felony, without benefit of clergy. Shortly before it came into force, a royal proclamation asserted that the riots constituted a Jacobite rebellion. All civil and military officers were ordered to use their utmost efforts to suppress them. If anybody killed any of the 'rebels', they would be indemnified.[38]

Throughout July and August, there were riots in towns throughout Staffordshire and Shropshire; by 5 August only one Staffordshire meeting house remained undamaged.[39] At Shrewsbury the 'loyal mob' issued a 'proclamation' warning other Dissenters to have nothing to do with the Presbyterians, whose meeting houses were normally the main target.[40] At Wrexham the crowd destroyed the Baptist meeting house as well and cried 'Down with the Rump and the German'; the demolition work was carried on by men at night and by boys during the day.[41] The Whigs naturally seized on evidence of Jacobite rhetoric, but it is impossible to tell (and probably fruitless to speculate) how far the rioters were driven by Jacobite principles.[42] It seems more probable that they were fuelled by frustrated High Church and Tory sentiment, a response to the government's harassment of leading Tories; but there were more Jacobite slogans than in the coronation day riots, perhaps because the crowds knew that these would give greater offence.[43] There was a considerable copycat element; the riots were widely reported in the press. The attitude of many magistrates—ambivalent or even sympathetic—adds to the impression that (in the rioters' eyes) the destruction of meeting houses was a justified punishment: note the term 'proclamation' at Shrewsbury. It was alleged that the riots at Newcastle-under-Lyme started each night after the parish clerk or a churchwarden rang a bell.[44]

---

[36] *Flying Post*, 9–12, 14–16 July 1715; *Weekly Journal with Fresh Advices*, 16 July 1715.
[37] *Flying Post*, 16–19 July 1715. The Act was published on 23 July, perhaps in the hope of deterring the rioters: ibid. 21–3 July; *Weekly Journal with Fresh Advices*, 23 July 1715.
[38] *Pol State*, x. 105–6.   [39] *Flying Post*, 1–3 Sept. 1715.
[40] Ibid. 30 July–2 Aug. 1715.
[41] Ibid. 26–8 July, 30 July–2 Aug. 1715; *Weekly Journal with Fresh Advices*, 30 July 1715.
[42] Oates, 'Popular Disturbances', 120–1.
[43] Monod, *Jacobitism*, 185–94; Rogers, *Crowds, Culture and Politics*, 34–6.
[44] *Flying Post*, 13–16 Aug. 1715.

The riots did not spread far outside the West Midlands, west Yorkshire, and south Lancashire, although a meeting house was destroyed at Stamford and one was attacked at Bath.[45]

Faced with disorder, town authorities had limited resources, although Worcester had shown what could be achieved if they were sufficiently determined. Some preferred to rely on persuasion.[46] With many JPs sympathetic, the law was of limited use, even after the passing of the Riot Act. At Wem the magistrates seized several of the rioters, but a jury of substantial inhabitants, some of whom had been present at the riot, brought in ignoramus.[47] At Stafford the Dissenters had to bear all the trouble and cost of prosecuting rioters, because the authorities would do nothing.[48] The law, moreover, could be invoked only after the event, although the execution of two rioters at Worcester in September may have helped bring the riots to an end.[49] What the Dissenters wanted was effective protection. The owners of the meeting houses at Dudley, West Bromwich, and Oldbury consulted lawyers, who told them they might lawfully use force to defend them; to make doubly sure they obtained a warrant from a JP to the constable of West Bromwich to have watch and ward sufficient to disperse the rioters. When rioters attacked the meeting house, they were driven off with whips and cudgels. The rioters returned next day, armed with scythes, reaping hooks, and clubs, but fled when they saw that those defending the building had firearms. Later shots were exchanged and several of those guarding the meeting house were wounded.[50] In the following days the scale of the clashes grew; one account said that fourteen were killed or mortally wounded and thirty others were missing; others said that the 'rebels' had lost forty, or even 140. Later reports put the number killed at three.[51] In Staffordshire the nobility and gentry armed their friends and servants, and Lady Mohun's servants drove off a mob attacking a meeting house at Congleton.[52] The militia was also revived, to some effect; the *posse comitatus* was mobilized in Staffordshire and Warwickshire.[53] But it was generally agreed that there

[45] *Weekly Journal with Fresh Advices*, 23 July, 6 Aug. 1715. For West Yorkshire, see *Flying Post*, 23–5 June 1715. For an account of an attack on a meeting house in Bath, which may be wrongly dated (other letters in this volume are), see *HMC Portland*, vii. 237–8.

[46] *Flying Post*, 19–21 July 1715; Oates, 'Popular Disturbances', 121.

[47] *Flying Post*, 16–19 July 1715.   [48] Ibid. 8–10 Sept. 1715.

[49] Ibid. 13–15 Sept. 1715.

[50] Ibid. 16–19 July 1715; Oates, 'Popular Disturbances', 121–2.

[51] *Flying Post*, 23–6 July, 6–9 Aug. 1715.

[52] BL, Add MS 38507, fo. 138; *Flying Post*, 1–3 Sept. 1715.

[53] BL, Add MS 38507, fos. 138–9; *Weekly Journal with Fresh Advices*, 30 July 1715; *HMC Townshend*, 159.

was no substitute for regular troops. When two troops of cavalry arrived in Manchester, the rioters offered to fight them if they would lay down their arms, but the soldiers refused and the rioters dispersed.[54] A regiment of dragoons was stationed in Leeds after the disorders there. In August a troop of horse was quartered in Shrewsbury.[55] Since the passage of the Riot Act, the soldiers were entitled to fire if rioters failed to disperse after being ordered to do so; in Manchester on 28 May the soldiers' muskets had been charged only with powder and the crowd had defied them to their faces.[56]

III. THE ROLE OF THE MILITARY

The outbreak of the 1715 rebellion in September confirmed (in the eyes of the Whigs) the Jacobite character of the riots and the seriousness of the threat from 'the disaffected'. The new forces raised against the rebels gave the authorities the military resources to police and suppress them. These new forces were all kept in England; the forces needed to suppress the rising in Scotland were raised there or brought from the continent. The reprisals against the rebels after the defeat of the English Jacobites at Preston in November were severe and the trials and executions were widely reported.[57] In retrospect one can see that the rising had much less support in England than in Scotland and that most of the rebel soldiers were mobilized in the countryside rather than the towns.[58] The predominantly urban character of the riots led the government to see urban Jacobitism as a serious threat. Apart from the army, the militia was mobilized and volunteers raised; in some towns—Norwich, Derby, Nottingham, Shrewsbury, and Colchester—these were organized in artillery companies, which performed a role similar to that of the Tory artillery company in Bristol in 1682–5.[59] At Norwich the artillery company was established by Townshend, the lord lieutenant, early in 1715, as a means of countering the strongly Tory corporation. According to Crossgrove, its members were all

[54] *Flying Post*, 5–7 July 1715.
[55] *Weekly Journal with Fresh Advices*, 23 July; Raynham Hall, B1/1, Cabinet minutes, no. 25; *St James's Evening Post*, 23–5 Aug. 1715.
[56] *Account of the Dreadful Mob*, 3; Oates, 'Popular Disturbances', 122–3.
[57] D. Szechi, *1715: The Great Jacobite Rebellion* (New Haven, 2006), ch. 8.
[58] Oates, 'Popular Disturbances', 126.
[59] *Weekly Journal or British Gazetteer*, 10 Mar. 1716 (Shrewsbury); *Flying Post*, 7–9 June 1716 (Nottingham), 20–2 Aug. 1717 (Derby); *Pol State*, x. 438 (Colchester).

'of Oliverian cut' and insulted and dragooned the Tories. A Whig described them as substantial tradesmen who maintained order and put down tumults.[60] The company was armed and authorized and had no qualms about using violence against Tories, as in the disputed mayoral election of 1716.[61] One of its captains, William Hall, was given much of the credit for turning the city from Tory to Whig, through his 'active spirit and artful contrivance'.[62]

At Bristol, the corporation was still strongly Whig, so there was no need to create a paramilitary force to undermine it. In the eyes of both the corporation and the national government, the city was riddled with Jacobitism, an impression apparently confirmed by the coronation day riot. For the parliamentary election in January, the mayor appointed sixty extra constables and other officers. They were accused of fraud and of arresting Tory voters, but initially the Tory candidates seemed to have a slight majority. The Whigs overturned this through a scrutiny, for which they laid down the rules; they disallowed the votes of Tory voters who had children in any of the hospitals (especially Colston's). On the third day of the scrutiny, the constables kept out almost all of the Tories. Two Whigs were returned.[63] Following claims that a plot had been discovered to seize the city for the Pretender, the lord lieutenant, Lord Berkeley, appointed new officers for the city militia. A regiment of foot arrived to secure the city, and the militia was raised; the Whig press claimed that the richer citizens, normally reluctant to serve in the militia, did so with alacrity. Two volunteer troops of horse were also raised, with Berkeley's approval.[64] The mayor provided the necessary money and the council retrospectively approved his action.[65]

The Whigs claimed that harmony reigned between the military officers and the citizens.[66] The Tories did not agree. Most were loyal to the regime and, as Bishop Smalridge explained, deeply resented being aspersed as Jacobites. Smalridge went out of his way to assure the military authorities of the clergy's loyalty, stressing the subject's duty of obedience, but this cut no ice with the civic authorities. Tories faced arbitrary imprisonment on unsupported accusations of disloyalty, but their real 'offence' (the bishop thought) had

[60] BL, Add MSS 5383, fo. 107, 38507, fo. 133; MCB 27, fo. 198; NRO, MS 79, pp. 137–8.
[61] Wilson, *Sense of the People*, 382.   [62] NRO, Rye MS 18, pp. 30–1.
[63] *Weekly Journal, with Fresh Advices*, 12 Feb. 1715; *A Letter to a Member of Parliament from a Gentleman of Bristol*, 2nd edn. (London, 1715), *passim*.
[64] BRO, 07831, 30 Sept. and 2 Oct. 1715; *Post Man*, 25–7 Oct. 1715; BRO, 04264/9, pp. 399–400; *Pol State*, xi. 176.
[65] BRO, 04264/9, p. 390.   [66] *Post Man*, 19–22 Nov. 1715.

been to oppose the Whig candidates in the recent election.[67] The authorities shut the gates and guarded them with cannon; the entire militia regiment remained on foot for over two months: 'This city for several months was kept in manner of a garrison.'[68] The Loyal Society failed to hold its feast and never met again. The militia stood down in December but the volunteers and two regiments of regular troops continued, amid rumours that Ormond might attempt to seize the city.[69]

Another city where Jacobitism was believed to be strong was Oxford. A messenger who came to arrest two suspected Jacobites was besieged in his inn by crowds shouting Jacobite slogans.[70] Several hundred townsmen and students rescued a man taken by recruiting officers; again they shouted Jacobite slogans.[71] In October an infantry regiment was quartered in the city, which kept the students quiet. The officers made it clear that they regarded the students and citizens with loathing and contempt.[72] On 6 February 1716, the anniversary of Anne's succession, some gentlemen lit bonfires and drank 'certain healths'. They were dispersed by musketeers; two were seriously injured.[73] The soldiers' presence gave new confidence to the university Whigs. Some gentlemen of Merton invited some of their colleagues, and army officers, to celebrate the king's birthday. They lit a bonfire and illuminations and gave beer and money to the common people. Next day the Tories wore oak leaves; the Whigs did the same and provided as big a bonfire and as much beer as they had the previous day. Tory townsmen hissed and threw squibs, but were chased away by soldiers. The Whigs then drank to the 'reformation' of the university and the soldiers cleared the streets.[74] In the days around 10 June, the Pretender's

[67] Leics RO, DG7 (Finch MSS), uncalendared correspondence, bundle 24, Smalridge to Sir Roger Mostyn, 8 Oct. 1715; LPL MS 1741, fo. 4. It was reported that Smalridge refused to subscribe a declaration of loyalty submitted to the bishops and lost his place as lord almoner to the king: *Pol State*, x. 453.

[68] BRO, 04264/9, p. 396, 07831, 2 Oct. 1715; BCL, B10154, 2 Oct. 1715.

[69] Latimer, ii. 111–12; *St James's Evening Post*, 7–10 Jan. and 24–7 Mar. 1716; *Weekly Journal or British Gazetteer*, 4 Feb., 10 and 31 Mar. 1716; BRO, 04264/9, pp. 399–400.

[70] SP 35/2, fo. 40. This is undated, but was written after the passing of the Riot Act and before troops were quartered in the city.

[71] SP 35/4, fos. 31–2.

[72] *Pol State*, x. 338; Raynham Hall, B1/9, Papers relating to the Jacobite invasion, letter from Oxford, 6 Nov. 1715; *HMC Portland*, vii. 214.

[73] *News Letter*, 11 Feb. 1716.

[74] *Weekly Journal or British Gazetteer*, 9 June 1716. At Cambridge, which does not seem to have been garrisoned, the 29th was celebrated far more vigorously than the 28th (when a meeting house was attacked). 'Thousands' of students and townsmen cried 'down with the Hanoverians, down with the Rump' and broke the windows of 'moderate' Churchmen and Dissenters: ibid. 9 June 1716; *Flying Post*, 7–9 June 1716.

birthday, there were repeated clashes between students and soldiers, with casualties on both sides.[75] In August, after stones were thrown at soldiers, a captain sent to four students, who he believed were responsible, to drink to the king and Marlborough. They replied 'God bless King George and Ormond', whereupon the soldiers beat them with clubs. The soldiers were pulled off by passers-by and the Star Inn, where many of them lodged, was besieged. The mayor and vice chancellor with difficulty prevented the crowd from demolishing the inn and killing the soldiers.[76] On coronation day turnip tops and dirt were thrown at the soldiers.[77]

By 30 October, the birthday of the prince of Wales, the soldiers were in a belligerent mood. Not a bell was rung—not surprisingly as the day was not widely celebrated. Major d'Offranville complained to the mayor, who said he did not know that it was the prince's birthday. At 5 p.m. the soldiers were deployed along the High Street, to cries of 'down with the Roundheads'. Most of the officers met the Constitution Club at the Star Inn, where they ordered a bonfire and drank loyal healths. A crowd threw stones and broke the windows, whereupon soldiers broke those windows that had not been illuminated. Later a patrol was attacked by a mob and fired; according to an officer, the muskets were loaded only with powder, but others said that bullets were fired at the mayor and his entourage.[78]

Accounts of these events varied. Some said the soldiers broke windows as a spontaneous response to the attack on the Star, others accused d'Offranville of ordering his men to break them. The major claimed that he had ordered the soldiers to stop breaking windows. They had obeyed, but when the stone-throwing started again, the soldiers began breaking windows again. The major sent orders 'to suppress all disorders and disperse all mobs', an ambiguous command, which the soldiers could interpret as applying to the townsmen but not to them. He admitted that he had remarked earlier that people who failed to celebrate the prince's birthday deserved to have their windows broken.[79] The vice chancellor, the mayor, Thomas Rowney MP, and others were adamant that he had ordered the soldiers to break windows.[80] Rowney wrote that the soldiers marched around the city, beating citizens and breaking windows. When the magistrates tried to suppress them, the mayor and vice chancellor were insulted, Sir Daniel Webb was beaten, and the mace bearer was shot through

[75] *HMC Portland*, vii. 215.   [76] Ibid. 216.
[77] *OCA*, iv. 326; *The Several Papers*, 16–17.
[78] *OCA*, iv. 326–7; *Weekly Journal or British Gazetteer*, 10 Nov. 1716; *HMC Portland*, vii. 217–18; *Pol State*, x. 508.
[79] *OCA*, iv. 326–7.   [80] Ibid. 328, 330–1; *HMC Portland*, vii. 217.

his hat.[81] Whatever the facts of the case, the Whig regime in London was going to blame the Tories, not the soldiers. D'Offranville secured affidavits from soldiers and members of the Constitution Club justifying his conduct. The Whig recorder, William Wright, advised the mayor and vice chancellor to endorse them, without reading them or examining witnesses. The major also kept the originals of the depositions, which enabled the prince of Wales to suggest that d'Offranville's depositions were more authentic than the copies of others sent by the mayor and vice chancellor.[82]

The mayor and vice chancellor sent a set of affidavits to Lord Abingdon, to present to Townshend, the secretary of state. These, the major's affidavits, and other documents were referred to a committee of the privy council, chaired by the prince of Wales. Before it could consider the documents, some of the city's affidavits were printed; the mayor denied any part in this.[83] The committee decided that the mayor and heads of colleges had neglected to order rejoicing on the prince's birthday; that those who wished to celebrate were assaulted, which was the occasion of the riots that ensued, involving both soldiers and townsmen; and that d'Offranville's affidavits justified his conduct.[84] The matter was then taken up by the House of Lords, which asked to see the documents. On 3 April 1717, the House resolved to agree with the report of the committee. It condemned the printing of affidavits taken by the city, and ordered that other papers relating to the riots, including its own resolutions, should be printed, together with those printed earlier. A protest against the resolution, questioning the veracity of many of the testimonies, was signed by twenty-seven peers. It argued that, even if the account of breaking windows at the Star was accurate, it could not justify inciting or allowing soldiers to break windows or insult civil magistrates. It suggested that soldiers were above the law and exempt from the civil power.[85]

This seems to have been exactly the message received by the soldiers, who behaved as if they had been sent to Oxford to break the Jacobites.[86] Some

[81] *OCA*, iv. 330; *Weekly Journal or British Gazetteer*, 10 Nov. 1716. D'Offranville referred to Sir Daniel as Mr Daniel Webb: *OCA*, iv. 326.

[82] *HMC Portland*, vii. 218; *OCA*, iv. 353–5, 360.

[83] *Weekly Journal or British Gazetteer*, 1 Dec. 1716; *OCA*, iv. 100, 325, 332–3, 359. They were printed as *The Several Depositions Concerning the Late Riot in Oxford: Pol State*, xii. 510–31; they were later reprinted in *The Several Papers*, 2–14.

[84] *LJ*, xx. 436–7.

[85] Ibid. 432, 436–7; *OCA*, iv. 358–60; *Pol State*, xiii. 440–4. Some witnesses said that the windows at the Star were broken before 30 October: *OCA*, iv. 349–50; *The Several Papers, passim*.

[86] *OCA*, iv. 347, 352–3; *HMC Portland*, v. 525, vii. 219.

officers planned to burn effigies of the devil, pope, Pretender, and Ormond to celebrate the king's return to England in January 1717. The secretary at war agreed to forbid this, on condition that the university marked the day by ringing all its bells, which it did.[87] A Whig newspaper claimed that it was to the soldiers, 'under God, [that] we owe the preservation of both our religion and civil liberties', and soldiers throughout the country may well have believed this.[88] Others saw them differently. The people of Stamford complained bitterly that misrepresentations by a clergyman had brought soldiers on them.[89] At Worcester in 1721, when there was talk of building a new town hall, the officers took offence at figures of Charles I, Charles II, and Anne over the door of the old one.[90] Soldiers played a prominent, indeed dominant, role in civic celebrations. On the first anniversary of the coronation day riot in Bristol, the regular troops were exercised in Queen Square and fired volleys of shot. In the evening the regular, militia, and half-pay officers dined in the council house with the magistrates and clergy, with troops outside firing volleys at each health to the royal family. Wine was later distributed among the soldiers—there is no reference to the people—and the evening concluded with illuminations and bonfires. There were no disturbances.[91] There was a similar report from Hertford, with the comment 'heretofore the mayor and aldermen were wont to assemble in the council chamber to rejoice on such occasions, but this day they made no appearance at all'.[92] The regiment quartered at Bridgwater celebrated the prince of Wales's birthday in 1715; the officers drank healths to the royal family, on their knees, at the head of the regiment.[93] It became the norm for the military to be the organizers and main participants, with the corporation in an auxiliary role and the ordinary people reduced to mere spectators, who were allowed to cheer, and for whom beer might be provided. At Ashbourne, on 1 August 1716, the commanding officer gave orders at 9 p.m. (when many people were in bed) for drummers to go around the town telling householders to illuminate their windows. Soldiers and town Whigs broke the windows of

---

[87] *Pol State*, xiii. 233–5.

[88] *Weekly Journal or British Gazetteer*, 1 Dec. 1716.

[89] Leics RO, DG7, uncalendared correspondence, bundle 25, Countess of Nottingham to her husband, 12 Nov. 1718.

[90] *Weekly Journal or British Gazetteer*, 23 Sept. 1721; Borsay, *Urban Renaissance*, 107.

[91] *Flying Post*, 25–7 Oct., *Post Man*, 22–5 Oct. 1715. However, the celebrations at Colchester seem to have been widely supported, as were those at Worcester on 1 Aug. 1720: *Pol State*, x. 438–9, xx. 151–2.

[92] *Flying Post*, 20–2 Oct. 1715. There were similar celebrations at Boroughbridge, Chester, and Hoddesdon: ibid. 27–9 Oct.

[93] *Flying Post*, 5–8 Nov. 1715.

those who had not done so.[94] At Manchester on 20 October 1717 'nothing was done but in a truly military way'.[95] At Worcester on 28 May 1716 the regiment was drawn up outside the cathedral, while the officers attended a service. As the officers came out, the soldiers fired three volleys. They invited several of the cathedral clergy, 'hearty lovers of King George', and the mayor and loyal members of the corporation to join them. As they drank loyal healths, patrols were sent out to ensure that there were no disorders.[96] The marching and volleys were a clear statement of military power.

Celebrations were often nakedly partisan. Sometimes the Whigs wore distinguishing cockades or ribbons, often orange.[97] At Bridgnorth and Stamford they formed 'loyal societies', a conscious riposte to the Tory loyal societies in towns like Bristol and Gloucester.[98] At Kidderminster a 'loyal association', the majority of whose members were Dissenters, was formed to protect the meeting house and oppose the Jacobite rebels.[99] After the defeat of the rebels, the Pretender was burned in effigy, sometimes accompanied by Mar or Ormond; at Aylesbury the pope was burned as well.[100] Often reports referred to the loyal part of the corporation, or claimed that the Tories left town, or stayed at home, on a day of celebration.[101] At Nottingham, on 28 May 1716, after the artillery company had marched around the town, and mustered in the market place, the soldiers accompanied the 'loyal' part of the corporation to church; then there were more volleys and a feast, culminating in a bonfire where the officers provided wine for the soldiers to drink loyal healths.[102] The healths were also often party statements: at Shrewsbury, on 28 May 1718, the participants drank to Hoadly, whom they called the 'true supporter' of the Church, 'and all the

[94] SP 35/6, fos. 35–45. The depositions of the soldiers involved were less than convincing: SP 35/8, fos. 5–7, 11.

[95] *Weekly Journal or Saturday's Post*, 26 Oct. 1717. The celebrations in Manchester on 28 May 1716 seem to have involved only the military: *Flying Post*, 7–9 June 1716.

[96] *Flying Post*, 2–5 June 1716.

[97] *Weekly Journal or British Gazetteer*, 24 Nov. 1716; *Flying Post*, 7–9, 12–14 June, 1–3 Nov. 1716, 5–7 Aug. 1718; *Pol State*, xii. 545–6 (first anniversary of the defeat of the Jacobites at Preston).

[98] *Weekly Journal or British Gazetteer*, 10 Nov. 1716, 26 Jan. 1717. For the Gloucester Loyal Society, see *Post Boy*, 4–6 Nov. 1714. There were two Tory loyal societies in Norwich: N. Rogers, 'Popular Jacobitism in Provincial Context: Eighteenth-Century Bristol and Norwich', in E. Cruickshanks and J. Black (eds.), *The Jacobite Challenge* (Edinburgh, 1988), 131.

[99] *Flying Post*, 2–4 Feb. 1716.

[100] Ibid. 29–31 May, 2–5, 12–14, 14–16 June 1716. An effigy of Bolingbroke was burned at Cirencester: *Flying Post*, 2–5 June 1716. At Wells an inn sign of St Christopher was reportedly burned 'for a pope', with the child in his arms standing for the Pretender: *Post Boy*, 30 June–3 July 1716; the *Flying Post* denied that the story was true (7–9 Aug. 1716).

[101] *Flying Post*, 12–14, 14–16 June 1716; *Weekly Journal or British Gazetteer*, 9 Aug. 1718.

[102] *Flying Post*, 7–9 June 1716.

loyal Whig healths'.[103] However, some Tory magistrates exacted a revenge of sorts by quartering most soldiers on Dissenters; if they complained, they were told 'you sent for them, you love them and you shall have enough of them'.[104]

IV. POLITICS AND THE POOR

Political conflict affected even the poorest of the population, and children, as both parties sought to capture the next generation. In Norwich, the corporation tried to ensure that its captive poor, old and young, attended Anglican services. In 1675 the father of a boy admitted to the Great Hospital was asked to explain why his son had not been baptized.[105] In 1682 the keeper of the Great Hospital was ordered to report any man or woman who failed to attend the Tuesday lecture or their parish church on the 'usual days'.[106] In 1695, amid concerns that not many hospital boys and girls went to church, a committee was appointed to find convenient seats for them in the cathedral; a man was employed to take care of them during services; they were to attend the cathedral on 30 January.[107] In 1700 the court ordered that no one was to be admitted to the hospitals without a certificate of their date of birth from the parish register. The ostensible purpose of this order was to check on their ages, but the requirement would also tend to exclude Dissenters.[108] In 1713 inmates of the Great Hospital were threatened with expulsion if they did not receive communion within ten days; no one was to be admitted without a certificate that they had received in the last twelve months.[109] This requirement was extended to the other hospitals in 1714,[110] but in 1718 the assembly rescinded the order requiring sacrament certificates. The requirement that the inmates of the Great Hospital should attend their parish church continued.[111]

One reason for the corporation's concern with the hospitals was electoral; in 1705 and 1710 the mayor's court ordered that the inmates of the Great Hospital were not to vote.[112] Places in hospitals were useful pieces of patronage, enabling a supporter to provide for their elderly father or mother. There was

---

[103] *Weekly Journal or British Gazetteer*, 7 June 1718.
[104] *Flying Post*, 28–30 Mar. 1717.   [105] MCB 24, fo. 310.
[106] Ibid. 110.   [107] Ibid. 335, MCB 26, fos. 2, 8, 9.   [108] MCB 26, fo. 80.
[109] MCB 27, fo. 129: this was clearly enforced: ibid. 133–5, 138, 142, 147, 151, 184, 201, 202.
[110] FAB 9, fo. 49.   [111] FAB 9, fo. 73; MCB 28, fo. 113.
[112] MCB 26, fo. 211, MCB 27, fo. 36, MCB 28, fos. 57, 60. (The first occasion was just before the disputed aldermanic election of 1705.)

also competition for the hearts and minds of the young. The first four charity schools in Norwich were founded in 1700, by Presbyterians. In 1707 a group of Anglican divines, gentlemen, and inhabitants established funds to set up schools teaching reading, writing, and arithmetic. They wore distinctive uniforms, so could be identified if they misbehaved. By 1717 there were eleven schools teaching a total of 202 boys and 112 girls.[113] In Bristol, too, religious competition extended to schooling. The Tory philanthropist Edward Colston decreed that any boy from any of his foundations whose parents attended a Dissenting meeting should be expelled, and that no boy should be apprenticed to a Dissenter.[114]

Partisanship also extended into the treatment of the poor. The Bristol corporation of the poor contained a substantial proportion of Dissenters; most of the rest were Low Churchmen.[115] Of eight signatories of a letter of 1696, about the decision to press for a corporation of the poor, three were Quakers and at least one other was a Dissenter.[116] The corporation of the poor was strongly opposed to parish-based charity schools, which it saw as church schools; it also tried to draw up a non-denominational catechism.[117] One of its staunchest Anglican supporters, the Revd Arthur Bedford, eventually broke with the corporation on the issue of parish schools.[118] With the conspicuous exception of Edward Colston, most charitable donations to the poor came from Whigs (including the bishop, John Hall) and Dissenters, including at least eight Quakers (and this despite the fact that the Quakers also maintained their own poor).[119] Whereas in some towns corporations of the poor had been set up in opposition to Tory town governments, Bristol's was set up to wrest control of the poor from Tory parish vestries.[120] Both Tory churchwardens and the corporation of the poor were accused of using their control of poor relief for electoral purposes.[121]

[113] NRO, MS 79, pp. 211–12; *An Account of the Charity Schools in Norwich* (1717), copy in NRO MS 453.

[114] Fissell, in *Stilling*, 138; *Some Considerations Offered to the Citizens of Bristol* (n.p., 1711), 5–6.

[115] At least fifteen of fifty-eight members listed in *Ref and Revival*, 56–62 can definitely be identified as Dissenters. See *Some Considerations Offered*, 8–9; *Ref and Revival*, 4.

[116] BL, Add MS 5540, fo. 100. The Quakers were Charles Jones, Richard Coddrington, and Thomas Goldney. Of the remainder, Nathaniel Wade was definitely a Dissenter and John Duddleston was sympathetic to Dissent. Six of the eight were founder members of the Bristol Society for the Reformation of Manners.

[117] *Ref and Revival*, 7–8, 16, 23–7, 29–30, 32–40, 45 and n. 73.   [118] Ibid. 11–13.

[119] *HP 1690–1715*, iii. 653–4; *Ref and Revival*, 11, 29 n., 40, 45; C. Brent, *Persuasions to a Public Spirit* (London, 1704), 23–4; R. Mortimer, *Early Bristol Quakerism*, Bristol Historical Association (1967), 18; Watts, *The Dissenters*, 340–1.

[120] Slack, *From Reformation to Improvement*, 115–17; Barry, 'Reformation City', 266–7.

[121] *Ref and Revival*, 10; *Some Considerations Offered*, 8.

Partisan politics led to religious intolerance. In 1711 the Bristol Merchant Venturers, whose policy towards membership had hitherto been inclusive, formally excluded Quakers.[122] In 1714 an Act of Parliament to increase the funding of Bristol corporation of the poor required guardians and other officers to take communion in an Anglican church. Now Dissenters who might be willing to serve were unable to do so and (presumably) those who did not wish to serve had a way of avoiding it.[123] This was unusual: generally no religious tests were required of members of such bodies.[124] The clause had been added by a strongly Tory House of Commons as a condition of allowing the bill to go through. In an additional move to weaken the perceived Whig hold on the corporation, the Act laid down that all churchwardens should be ex officio members of the board of guardians. These measures appear to have given the Tories control over the corporation, as in 1718 a Whig Parliament removed half of the churchwardens from the board of guardians and also the sacramental test; the bill was strenuously opposed by Bishop Smalridge.[125] Such conflict was replicated elsewhere. In 1712 the election of the guardians of the corporation of the poor in Colchester was bitterly contested, on party lines: twenty-seven guardians were chosen, all from the 'church party'.[126] Their Whig predecessors were accused of favouritism in assessments and of assessing many poor people (who, if assessed for the poor rate, would be entitled to vote) and then failing to collect any money from them. They were also accused of spending money levied for the poor on feasting and drinking.[127] The Whigs countered with claims that the Tories sought control of the corporation solely in order to create more Tory votes.[128]

V. THE WHIGS AND THE TOWNS

The military gave the government, and the local Whigs, an additional weapon in bringing towns under control, but there was no centrally directed policy towards towns. George issued only three new charters and routinely approved new town clerks.[129] Sometimes, as at Bristol, the Whigs were already in control.

---

[122] McGrath, *Venturers*, 103 n. 8.
[123] Butcher, *Corporation*, 92–3; *The Case of the Workhouse and Hospital of the City of Bristol* (1718).
[124] *CUHB*, ii. 539.　　　[125] Latimer, ii. 103; *Pol State*, xv. 191, 218, 325–6.
[126] *Post Boy*, 8–10 July 1712. See also Brockett, *Nonconformity in Exeter*, 72–3.
[127] *Post Boy*, 30 Oct.–1 Nov. 1712.　　　[128] *Flying Post*, 7–9 Oct., 13–15 Nov. 1712.
[129] Halliday, *Body*, 324–30.

Other towns seem to have managed to avoid partisan divisions. A local historian wrote in 1798 of Hull in the reign of George I: 'during this whole reign no public transactions worthy of notice happened here.'[130] At Portsmouth the government interest, through the dockyard and garrison, was such that the town normally avoided partisan disputes. The divisions under Anne were unusual and did not last long. The Tories became divided over the choice of parliamentary candidates in 1713. One faction secured the support of the Whigs in return for a promise to elect two Whig aldermen.[131] In June 1716 they finally kept their promise. (Seager, elected mayor by the Whigs in 1710, was not reinstated.) Relations between Whigs and Tories never entirely broke down: even in 1710 Whigs and Tories frequented the same coffee house.[132] From 1716 to 1722 the annual election of the mayor and three justices always produced a mixture of Whigs and Tories, at times three Tories to one Whig; only in 1722 were there three Whigs to one Tory.[133]

Leicester's corporation became firmly Tory under Anne, and remained so, but it was careful to show that it did not harbour Jacobite sympathies. In an address on the peace of Utrecht, the corporation stressed that the peace had secured the Protestant succession in 'the illustrious House of Hanover'.[134] But the same address also emphasized the queen's undoubted title to the crown, as did another, which condemned restless spirits who questioned her title and traduced the 'apostolic' doctrines of the Church.[135] The corporation publicly applauded the peace, complaining of 'the unequal burdens of a tedious war'. Others in the town were less enthusiastic, especially about the implications of the French commercial treaty for the hosiery trade.[136] The corporation was careful to show its loyalty to George I, celebrating his coronation with ale, wine, bonfires, and expressions of joy suitable to the occasion.[137] It continued to celebrate the appropriate royal anniversaries, but there were hints that its enthusiasm was not unmixed. In 1716 the corporation resumed celebrating 29 May; it had stopped doing so in 1692.[138] The perceived strength of Jacobitism (or at least Toryism) probably explains the decision (as in the 1690s) to quarter soldiers in the town.[139] The

---

[130] Tickell, *Hull,* 600.   [131] *HP 1690–1715,* ii. 245.   [132] East, 774, 775, 779–81.
[133] Portsmouth RO, CE 1/13, pp. 98, 106, 112, 118, 130. (This assumes that James Harman, unlike his father, was a Whig.)
[134] *Post Boy,* 16–19 May 1713.
[135] Ibid. 6–9 May 1710, 16–19 May 1713. The former was reprinted in *Collection,* 23.
[136] LHB 4, fo. 74; *Post Boy,* 16–19 May 1713; *HP 1690–1715,* ii. 353.
[137] *RBL,* v. 71.   [138] LHP 37, fo. 95; LHB 5, fos. 41, 67, 85, 103, 152; *RBL,* v. 77.
[139] *RBL,* v. 79; *Flying Post,* 26–9 Jan. 1717. For the military presence in the 1690s, see LHP 38, no. 135; *CSPD 1694–5,* 253. In the latter, Stamford argued that it was unreasonable to burden the town unduly because it was 'growing honest'.

soldiers had arrived by January 1717 and were still there in 1721. At the celebration of George's return to England, in January 1717, the soldiers burned an effigy of the Pretender. In 1719 there were references to disturbances in the street and in May 1721 the corporation celebrated both royal birthdays on the 29th, at the Gainsborough, while allowing 40s. for drink for the soldiers at the Horse and Trumpet.[140] In 1722 there were disturbances on the Pretender's birthday; the duke of Rutland and the JPs for the county petitioned the king to join some of their number to the town justices, claiming that (left alone) the latter ignored Jacobite activity.[141] The king referred the petition to the attorney general; no action seems to have been taken.[142] The government and the local Whigs presumably saw Leicester, like Oxford, as irredeemably Tory; the most they could hope for was to prevent the Tories from becoming too disruptive or disorderly. Other towns were so evenly divided that the parties had to compromise. At Ipswich the election of bailiffs in 1722 was hotly contested and ended in the election of one Whig and one Tory.[143]

Other towns where the Whigs had lost control to the Tories were recaptured after 1714. At Winchester the Tory ascendancy in the corporation was brief and fragile. In 1712 and 1713 the city presented addresses strongly supporting the peace, while also expressing commitment to the Protestant succession and Hanover.[144] In 1712 the corporation elected four more honorary freemen, despite the opposition of the majority of gentlemen present.[145] Brydges and Lewis were re-elected without a contest in 1713, but the accession of George I revived the Whigs' fortunes. The corporation quickly produced a tactful address, with favourable mentions of William III and the new king's ministers, as well as his promise to uphold the Church and the rights of his people.[146] Bolton was reappointed lord lieutenant of Hampshire on Beaufort's death and in November 1714 and January 1715 the Whigs among the honorary freemen were able to secure the election of twenty-eight new freemen, despite the opposition of the majority of the corporation. William Poulett and George Brydges, son of George Rodney, were elected to Parliament.[147] Edward Hooker, supported as candidate for mayor by Poulett in 1710, and defeated in each of the next four years, was finally elected in 1715.[148] The Whig hold on the city

[140] *Flying Post*, 26–9 Jan. 1717; *RBL*, v. 84, 92.

[141] *RBL*, v. 94–5; Greaves, *Corporation* (1939 edn.), 160.   [142] Greaves, *Corporation*, 93.

[143] *Post Boy*, 1–4 Sept. 1722; *Weekly Journal or Saturday's Post*, 18 Sept. 1722; *Weekly Journal or British Gazetteer*, 15 Sept. 1722; Defoe, *Tour*, ii. 46–7.

[144] Hants RO, W/B1/8, fos. 88, 116 (the second address is described as unanimous).

[145] Ibid. 91–3.   [146] Ibid. 154–5.   [147] Ibid. 156–9, 164–5, W/B2/6, 21 Jan. 1715.

[148] Hants RO, W/B1/8, fos. 57, 72–4, 96–8, 127–9, 151–3, 178–81.

was strengthened by the election of more gentlemen to the freedom.[149] In 1722 the third duke of Bolton succeeded his father as high steward and Poulett and Brydges were re-elected to Parliament. Both continued to represent the city for the remainder of their lives.[150]

Breaking the Tory hold on Norwich proved much tougher. Toryism had been strong among the freemen since the early 1680s and the annual election of common councillors made the composition of the corporation volatile. The strength of Toryism explains Townshend's creation of the artillery company. Two Whigs were returned to Parliament in 1715, after a fierce contest in which the 'church party' were driven off Castle Hill with brickbats and stones.[151] The assembly produced loyal addresses on the king's accession and the Pretender's invasion, but gave them a Tory twist. The first stressed George's unquestionable right to the throne, but also said that the loss of Anne was almost 'insupportable'. The second suggested that the Jacobites had been encouraged by the divisions at home stirred up by those of anti-monarchical principles, and stressed that George had repeatedly promised to protect the 'lovely church'.[152] The artillery company petitioned to have the *Norwich Gazette* suppressed. Crossgrove was arrested in July 1715 and accused of plotting to disarm the company and attack meeting houses; he claimed that the witnesses against him were a convicted felon and an idiot; he was acquitted by a sympathetic jury.[153] Violence begat violence, or at least defiance, and George I's early years were full of reports of seditious papers and Jacobite healths and slogans.[154] Jacobites attacked 'croakers' in alehouses and raised mobs against them.[155]

In May 1717, after the Whigs had captured the common council, the tone changed. An address condemned the 'inglorious peace' and those cool towards the king's accession.[156] There followed a protracted struggle between the court of aldermen, which still had a Tory majority, and the common council. For over a year, the assembly effectively did not meet.[157] The mayor's court 'elected' its

[149] Hants RO, W/B1/8, fos. 201–2, 230–1, 245, 252–4, 257, 277.

[150] Hants RO, W/B1/9, fos. 73, 79; *HP 1690–1715*, iii. 373–4, v. 190–7.

[151] BL, Add MS 5383, fo. 107.

[152] FAB 9, fos. 50, 55. The former was printed in *Post Boy*, 9–12 Oct. 1714; *Pol State*, viii. 318–19.

[153] BL, Add MS 5383, fos. 107–8; Wilson, *Sense of the People*, 385–6; D. O'Sullivan, 'Politics in Norwich, 1701–1835', M.Phil. thesis (University of East Anglia, 1975), 72.

[154] MCB 27, fo. 306, MCB 28, fo. 117; Case 20a/18, 30 Apr., 8 Oct. 1715, 14 Jan., 14 Apr., 6 Oct. 1716; NRO, Rye MS 18, p. 11; Wilson, *Sense of the People*, 383–5.

[155] NCR, Case 12b/2, informations of Elias Medcalfe, 8 Oct., Robert Urwen, 18 Oct. 1722.

[156] FAB 9, fos. 65–6.

[157] No assembly is recorded in FAB between 3 May 1717, when the address was drawn up, and 3 May 1718. There are one or two entries in the minutes, but they are crossed out: NCR, Case 16c/8, pp. 62–3. The assembly held on 16 June 1718, guild eve, is marked 'no assembly': ibid. 73.

own town clerk; the Whig councilmen had the election quashed by the courts.[158] Meanwhile, two Tory mayors died in office in the latter part of 1717 and the third mayor for that year, Anthony Parmenter, was a Whig.[159] Parmenter held an election to fill one of the aldermanic vacancies, which the Whigs won using various tricks, including committing many of their supporters to gaol, because part of the gaol fell within the ward in question. When the new alderman came to be sworn, nine Tory aldermen walked out in protest.[160] The Tories secured a *mandamus* on behalf of the defeated candidate and others who claimed to have been wronged, but Parmenter refused to comply and the election stood.[161] The Whigs gradually strengthened their grip on the corporation. In 1720 they swept the board in the common council elections and two Whig sheriffs were chosen unopposed.[162] They secured a majority on the city committee, which was responsible for public works contracts, which were now awarded on party lines.[163] They gained control over the hospitals and reversed the order excluding Dissenters. They built up their electoral strength, creating new freemen. In 1722 the two sitting Whig MPs were returned without a contest.[164]

The Tories were far from finished. After four years in which Whigs were chosen as mayor without a contest, in 1722 Thomas Newton was chosen mayor in a very high turnout and Edward Weld, after two narrow defeats, was elected an alderman in August. The Tories were said to have taken control of the stairs leading to the room where the poll was held and to have prevented many Whigs from voting, beating some, terrifying others, and throwing some downstairs; Weld was declared the winner by about fifty votes.[165] When sent complaints of his conduct of the poll, the mayor replied blandly that he had done his utmost to keep the peace.[166] The Whigs looked forward to the annual election of sheriffs with trepidation. Weld was initially declared elected, amid allegations that many who voted were ineligible and that some had voted twice. The Tory mayor and the steward (the former Tory MP Richard Berney) rejected requests for a scrutiny; the mayor claimed (incorrectly) that the scrutiny had to take place on the day of the poll.[167] After the result was announced Tories rampaged around the streets, blowing trumpets, beating drums, and firing guns; they roared their support for Bishop Atterbury, accused of Jacobite plotting,

[158] Wilson, *Sense of the People*, 386–7.

[159] MCB 27, fos. 267–8, 277–80. The suggestion that he was a Whig derives from his remaining in the room when the Tory aldermen walked out in December: ibid. 285.

[160] MCB 27, fos. 277–80, 285; Halliday, *Body*, 304–5.   [161] Halliday, *Body*, 305.

[162] NRO, Rye MS 18, pp. 9, 12–13.   [163] O'Sullivan, 'Politics in Norwich', 78–9.

[164] *HP 1715–54*, i. 291.   [165] SP 35/32, fos. 255–9.   [166] Ibid. 282.

[167] Ibid. 253; SP 35/75, fos. 86–8; *HP 1690–1715*, i. 187.

and cried 'Down with the Hanoverians!' Almost a month after the election, it was said that Whigs scarcely dared appear in the streets, for fear of being insulted or assaulted. One Whig suggested that the only way to secure the city was to issue a new charter, confirming the current court of aldermen, which had a Whig majority, and giving it the power to nominate the common council, which should serve for life. The artillery company also needed a more dynamic commander.[168] Townshend took legal advice, which was that the only way to proceed was through the law; he was also advised to repeat the demand for a scrutiny of the poll in the shrieval election. When the scrutiny was eventually held, the Tories obstructed it as much as they could, but in the end the result was reversed.[169]

As the Whigs struggled to hold their own in the city, they could rely on their friends 'above'. In January 1723 the Whigs in the assembly petitioned Parliament for an Act to require all resident adult males in the worsted industry to take up the freedom, thus qualifying themselves to vote in elections. They calculated that the majority of those enfranchised would vote Whig, which they did.[170] But the Tories proved remarkably tenacious. They were defeated in the general election of 1727 by fewer than 400 votes in a turnout of almost 3,000. In 1728 they won control of the common council, which led to a Tory riot; a Tory was elected mayor and the Whigs boycotted the assembly for almost a year. Again, the Whigs had recourse to Parliament. The Norwich Elections Act of 1730 was designed to reduce both the number of voters and their influence over the outcome of elections; the aldermen were given a veto over the resolutions of the common council.[171] Still the Tories were not finished. Increasingly they made common cause with dissident Whigs, notably in opposition to Walpole's excise bill of 1733. In the 1734 general election the official Whigs scraped through amid the usual accusations of electoral chicanery. Not until 1747 were two Whig candidates returned unopposed.[172] As the examples of Coventry and Norwich show, although the Tories were excluded from power at a national level, they continued to compete at a municipal level and in parliamentary elections. The ideals of unity and consensus voiced at the Restoration seemed, by 1722, hopelessly anachronistic. Political competition, and conflict, were there to stay.

---

[168] SP 35/32, fo. 333; SP 35/33, fo. 161.
[169] SP 35/33, fos. 61, 162; Guth, 'Croakers', 444; NRO, MS 453, 'A Description', 28 Aug. 1722.
[170] Wilson, *Sense of the People*, 388; Rogers, *Whigs and Cities*, 319–20.
[171] *HP 1715–54*, i. 291; Wilson, *Sense of the People*, 389–91; Rogers, *Whigs and Cities*, 320–3; Knights, in *Norwich since 1550*, 172–4.
[172] *HP 1715–54*, i. 291; Wilson, *Sense of the People*, 392–5; Rogers, *Whigs and Cities*, 324–8.

Conclusion

In retrospect, the contrast between the seventeenth and the eighteenth centuries seems striking. In the middle of the seventeenth century, England, Scotland, and Ireland were convulsed by bloody civil wars. In the middle of the eighteenth, Great Britain, according to Namier, was largely free of divisions of political principle and so politics focused on 'a fierce, though bloodless, struggle for places'.[1] In the seventeenth century the English feared that their kings wished to overthrow their traditional liberties—safeguarded by trial by jury and Parliaments—and establish an absolute monarchy. Under the Georges Parliaments were safe, the powers of the monarch were effectively limited, and the law was used only sporadically against the government's political opponents. The archaic and slavish doctrine of the divine right of kings had been replaced by a pride in Britain's constitution, mixed and elegantly balanced. The religious fanaticism of the civil wars had given way to formal toleration of (almost) all Protestants; religion was not discussed in polite society and people kept their beliefs to themselves. Visceral fear of God's wrath and a painful conviction of human inadequacy gave way to faith in human reason; the laws making witchcraft a crime were repealed. The claims of university-trained clergy to unquestionable authority in matters religious were undermined and educated laypeople assumed the right to think for themselves. The things of this world were no longer dismissed as valueless and sinful. From seeing life as a painful journey through a hostile world, people came to accept that it was something to be enjoyed; in towns (for some) pleasure became the prime concern. Just under a century separated the publication of *Pilgrim's Progress* and the American Declaration of Independence, with its ringing endorsement of 'the pursuit of happiness'.

This is, of course, very much a Whig narrative, pervaded by a smug sense of British superiority and belief in 'progress'. It is a partial picture, in more senses than one. True, by the 1720s the English people were, in general, better fed and had more disposable income than their forebears a century before. They had a far larger choice of consumer goods, foods, beverages, and leisure activities on which to spend their money, and for this they came to towns. The growth

---

[1] L. B. Namier, *The Structure of Politics at the Accession of George III* (London, 1929), 21.

of spending power brought more extensive and varied social interaction. To reduce the potential friction that came from this there was a growing emphasis on 'politeness'. Self-restraint and rules of conduct were designed to control the passions. The growth of leisure facilities and spaces to which access was restricted —by limited membership, an entrance fee, or a dress code—was designed to enable 'polite', or 'genteel', society to mingle uncontaminated by the unsightly and uncouth poor. These spaces were not the exclusive preserve of civic or county elites, but those who entered were expected to abide by the elite's rules of behaviour. At the same time, by the 1720s there was a growing concern for the aesthetic aspects of urban living, seen in the creation of walks (and occasionally squares) and a growing interest in architectural style.[2]

And yet, as we have seen, this was only part of the picture. Much of the 'urban renaissance', particularly in terms of new building and specialist leisure facilities, took place after 1722. In general it affected only those parts of towns where the wealthy lived: the crowded extra-mural suburbs and the back alleys remained much as before.[3] Moreover, improvements in the infrastructure lagged well behind developments in architecture. If water supplies improved in many towns, the methods of disposing of sewage and rubbish did not: if anything, the problems became worse as urban populations grew. The increase in the size and trade of towns put greater pressure on streets that were still much as they had been in the middle ages; they were also maintained in much the same way—by individual householders, inadequately. Heavy iron-shod carts broke the road surfaces, sleds made them slippery; their passage—and that of pedestrians—was impeded by goods, dirt, building materials, and (in Bristol) coal, piled up in the streets. Privies overflowed, dirt and sewage clogged the gutters and sewers. Walking in towns at nights must have been at best unpleasant and at worst dangerous, especially as street lighting was either rudimentary or non-existent.[4] In other words, urban life was a good deal rougher than the veneer of style and politeness might suggest. Violence was commonplace, even among the elite, and it was not usually subject to the 'rules' of the duel. Gangs of Bristol apprentices routinely fought on Shrove Tuesday and tavern brawls were common. Sports and amusements were violent too, often involving extensive cruelty to animals. Those unfortunate enough to stand in the pillory

---

[2] Borsay, *Urban Renaissance*, chs. 6, 11; R. Porter, *English Society in the Eighteenth Century* (Harmondsworth, 1990), 225–33 and *passim*; P. Burke, *Popular Culture in Early Modern Europe* (London, 1978), ch. 9.

[3] Ellis, *Georgian Town*, 105.   [4] Ibid. 88–90, 98, 101.

could suffer serious injury, and the repeal of the laws against witchcraft did not stop angry neighbours from 'punishing' suspected witches.

The picture of the 'triumph of reason' in the eighteenth century is also only partially true. Pope might write 'God said "Let Newton be" and there was light' and Newton's scientific writings did indeed open up (to those who could understand them) the prospect that one day man day would be able to understand the world and the cosmos. Similarly Locke argued for the unlimited potential of the human intellect for learning and virtue—and in the process rejected original sin. Both Newton and Locke applied their formidable intellects to theology, refusing to take on trust traditional Christian teachings that had no basis in reason or Scripture. This did not involve a rejection of God, or of religion, but rather (in their eyes) the removal of unnecessary complications or inventions. Their ideas were attacked, as tending to atheism and immorality— for the clergy, people were inherently sinful and needed the wholesome moral discipline of the magistrate, and the Church. This viewpoint was advanced most stridently by the High Church clergy, but their moral stance was shared by many Low Churchmen and Dissenters, and found expression in the Societies for the Reformation of Manners. Meanwhile, a legal toleration did not end religious differences; the vehemence of civil war Puritans was replicated in the clashes of Low and High Church. If religious vituperation gradually diminished after 1714 this was partly because Low Church clergymen increasingly controlled the Church and denied preferment to High Churchmen; the end of convocation also removed one arena where the latter's voice could be heard. The prevailing ethos of the Church became 'moderate', no longer a pejorative term.[5] But enthusiasm was not dead, only sleeping, as was shown by the emergence of Methodism. The ferocious hostility which the Methodists provoked, from both Churchmen and Dissenters, should warn against complacent assumptions about eighteenth-century England being 'tolerant'. Anti-Catholicism also remained strong, as shown by the Gordon riots of 1780. By the 1710s there are signs that some leading Jewish families were winning a degree of acceptance in London. Newspapers reported Jewish weddings and religious festivals, but the attempt in 1753 to make it easier for Jews to become naturalized provoked a wave of anti-Semitic revulsion and the Jew bill was hastily repealed.[6]

---

[5] J. Walsh and S. Taylor, 'Introduction', in Walsh et al., 51–60.

[6] *English Post*, 1–3 Oct. 1701, 2–5 Mar. 1702; *Weekly Journal or British Gazetteer*, 15 Oct. 1720, 8 Apr. 1721; T.W. Perry, *Public Opinion, Propaganda and Politics in Eighteenth-Century England: The Jew Bill of 1753* (Cambridge, Mass., 1962).

Advances in scientific and philosophical understanding did not sweep away traditional religious beliefs, or destroy the traditional authority of the clergy. Jonathan Clark may have exaggerated the hold of the Church of England over the people—the extraordinary success of the Methodists showed that many felt that something was lacking—but his is a useful corrective to the traditional picture of overfed pluralist vicars and underfed curates ministering to indifferent congregations.[7] In towns like Bristol and Leicester, the established Church was vigorous and played a significant role in cultural life.[8] If England's two universities stagnated in the eighteenth century—especially in comparison with Edinburgh and Glasgow—they produced many scholars of distinction, and not just theologians. Many advances in science were made by clergymen. Sometimes, their discoveries might seem to undermine Scripture: developments in geology called into question the account of the creation in Genesis, for example, but this does not seem to have concerned them unduly. Assumptions that reason must triumph over ignorance and superstition ignore people's capacity for inconsistency, for not applying the same approach to all areas of belief and understanding. Historians may feel that their reason should have led Locke and Newton to question the existence of God, but it did not. Similarly, belief in magic, even among the educated, was much more tenacious than later writers thought it should have been. Many continued to believe in witchcraft, including leading members of the Royal Society, like Joseph Glanvill, who argued that its existence was 'proved' by the confessions of many of those accused. The witchcraft laws were repealed because of the difficulty of proving that harm had been done by occult means, not because the educated no longer believed in witches.[9]

Similarly, as we have seen, belief in the divine right of kings, the sanctity of the hereditary succession, and the royal touch was far more resilient than Whig writers thought it should have been. One reason why the first two Georges won limited popular support was that they had a weak hereditary claim to the throne. Another was that they, like William III, did not touch for the king's evil and largely abandoned the ceremonial traditionally associated with monarchy.[10]

---

[7] J. C. D. Clark, *English Society, 1688–1832: Ideology, Social Structure and Political Practice during the Ancien Regime* (Cambridge, 1985); Walsh and Taylor, in Walsh et al., 10–12, 24–9.

[8] J. Barry, in Walsh et al., especially 193–4.

[9] I. Bostridge, *Witchcraft and its Transformations, c.1650–1750* (Oxford, 1997); J. A. Sharpe, *Instruments of Darkness: Witchcraft in England 1550–1750* (Harmondsworth, 1997).

[10] L. Colley, *Britons: Forging the Nation 1701–1837* (New Haven, 1992), ch. 5. For Charles II's careful use of ceremonial see Anna Keay, 'The Ceremonies of Charles II's Court', Ph.D. thesis (London, 2004).

George I's accession marked the beginning of a new sort of monarchy, lacking the sacred and mystical attributes associated with the Stuarts and their predecessors. The sense of loss was felt most acutely by the Jacobites, too often dismissed by historians as 'troglodytes',[11] rooted in an irrecoverable and perhaps imaginary past. Defining who was, or was not, a Jacobite is (I think) ultimately a futile endeavour.[12] It is nevertheless true to say that a small, but significant minority in England was prepared to conspire against William III, George I, and even Anne, and to appear in arms in 1715. A much larger body of Tories shared the Jacobites' emotional attachment to traditional monarchy and sometimes drank the Pretender's health or shouted Jacobite slogans. But whatever their sympathies, Jacobites and Tories had to contend with a government which controlled the machinery of law and order, and, under George I, an army which was used to crush 'disaffection'. The English landed elite possessed few weapons and could no longer summon its tenants to arms; rebellion was simply not an option. (In Scotland the nobility possessed far more weapons and greater power over men, which is why the 1715 and 1745 rebellions were far more formidable in Scotland than in England.)

The bitter political conflict of the 1710s suggests that in the eighteenth century political passions had not been tamed, any more than religious emotions had been. Namier's view of the eighteenth century as an ideology-free zone was comprehensively attacked by J. H. Plumb and Geoffrey Holmes (among others), particularly in relation to 1689–1715.[13] Both, however, argued that the political world became calmer after 1715. Holmes emphasized the implosion of the Tory party, following the internal feuds of 1710–14.[14] Plumb placed more stress on Walpole's management and manipulation of every part of the political world: the court, Parliament and the electoral system. He was well aware that Walpole's regime was widely unpopular, but dissatisfaction could find no expression at the national level so long as he maintained a Whig majority in the Commons and managed that majority through the distribution of places and pensions, and by following the sort of policies that Whig MPs wanted.[15] His success was such that the issues of principle so important under Anne (or

---

[11] D. Cannadine, 'British History: Past, Present—and Future?', *P & P* 116 (1987), 189–90.

[12] See the comments of David Hayton: *HP 1690–1715*, i. 476–8.

[13] Holmes, *British Politics*; Plumb, *Political Stability*.

[14] G. Holmes, 'Bolingbroke, Harley and the Downfall of the Tory Party', in Holmes (ed.), *Britain after the Glorious Revolution*, ch. 10.

[15] Plumb, *Political Stability*. Colley, however, argued that politics became less stable after 1714: *In Defiance of Oligarchy*, ch. 1.

Charles II)—the nature of monarchy, religion—were replaced by attacks on Walpole's methods of political management—or 'corruption'.

Yet the Whigs' seemingly impregnable control of Parliament was only part of the story. They never assumed that it was unassailable and prepared for elections with meticulous care and intensive use of the press, exploiting fears of Jacobitism and popery. If a policy proved unexpectedly unpopular, it was abandoned, as with the general excise in 1733 and the Jew bill in 1753.[16] The need to do so is an indication that, while one party might be firmly in control at Westminster, that was not the case in the localities. This has been shown by studies of local politics after 1715, notably those by Kathleen Wilson, Nicholas Rogers, and Linda Colley. Paul Monod, while judiciously rejecting some of the more extravagant claims of the strength of Jacobitism, showed that it was far from a spent force after 1715 or even 1746.[17] The Tories may have been excluded from power at the centre, in county government, and the Church, but they remained resilient in the constituencies; periodic conflicts within the Whig party kept alive hopes that one day their time in the wilderness would end. They remained especially active in towns, where opportunities for meeting and discussion were greatest, and where most information was available. Where municipal elections involved the wider body of freemen—and sometimes even where they did not—these could be fought on party lines. Whig Parliaments passed Acts designed to improve their supporters' chances in towns like London and Norwich, but even then the Tories continued to fight; in Norwich they were finally ground down by the cost of fighting elections.[18]

The period 1660–1722 saw political debate, and discord, become a normal part of English urban life. National politics impinged far more on townspeople's lives than in the sixteenth century, when few parliamentary elections were contested, so there was no need to place issues before the electors. It is hard to tell when political issues began to play a significant part in elections, but one could make a case for the 1620s: in five general elections, candidates campaigned on issues—and often on their records in the Commons—which invited discussion among the electors. But these were hardly 'normal' times: there was a mounting sense of alarm, which led to talk of a 'crisis of parliaments'. This was even more true in 1640. The 1640s saw an explosion of printing and debate, as the settlement which moderates on both sides longed for became

---

[16] P. Langford, *The Excise Crisis* (Oxford, 1975); Perry, *Jew Bill*.
[17] Monod, *Jacobitism*. See also Rogers, *Crowds, Culture and Politics*, ch. 1.
[18] Wilson, *Sense of the People*, 388, 391–7; Rogers, *Whigs and Cities*, 37–42, 319–24.

more and more elusive and England moved further and further away from the traditional order in Church and state. The Restoration seemed to bring a return to normal, including press censorship, but the itch for news and public interest in politics continued, as alarm grew about the king's intentions.[19] The debates of 1679–81, stimulated by three general elections and the ending of censorship, brought partisan politics back to England's towns, but despite the Tories' rhetoric this was not a re-run of the civil war. The battles were political rather than military, fought out on the hustings rather than the battlefield. The debates and contests clarified the issues and hardened identities. People knew where they stood and where other people stood.[20] In the years after 1681 the Tories affirmed their identity and principles through loyal addresses; the Whigs kept their heads down. As towns were seen as centres of opposition to the regime, the crown embarked on an unprecedented campaign of intervention; the issuing of new charters offered opportunities to purge Whigs from the corporation and, occasionally, to alter the franchise.

The clear-cut division between Tories and Whigs was thrown into turmoil by James II, but in late 1688 it reappeared as Whigs and Tories jostled for power under the new king. In Parliament, the Whigs sought revenge for their sufferings in 1681–5, and tried to purge Tories from corporations. This lust for vengeance was replicated in some towns, notably Bristol, which had seen exceptionally vicious faction-fighting. In other towns the corporation tried to recapture the solidarity that it had shown before the Exclusion Crisis: there were no purges and apparently no recriminations in Norwich, but the solidarity was fragile, as shown by the dispute about the association in 1696. After 1689 the crown generally eschewed intervention in towns' affairs. On the other hand, the Triennial Act of 1694 made general elections regular and predictable for the first time, which drew the attention of the landed elite and the London plutocracy to those towns which were represented in Parliament. For many townspeople, their attention was welcome, as it meant beer, bribes, and excitement. But frequent elections, many of them contested, also brought political issues into urban life. With the revival of the newspaper press, and the growing number of places where its contents—news *and* comment—could be discussed, political debate became a normal part of urban life. Meanwhile, elections offered an opportunity even to the unenfranchised to express their views. As the political

---

[19] Miller, *After the Civil Wars*, ch. 4.

[20] In contrast to the position in 1647–8: J. H. Hexter, 'Presbyterians, Independents and Puritans: A Voice from the Past', *P & P* 47 (1970), 135–6.

temperature rose, emotions ran high and violence became more common, with some contests being decided by clubs or fists rather than votes. Even after the Whigs tightened their hold on the national government, and elections became less frequent, party divisions and rivalries remained strong.

The divisions remained strong, but they did not tear communities apart. True, Whigs and Tories often did not meet socially: there were Whig and Tory inns, clubs, coffee houses, race-meetings, and even doctors.[21] But their differences did not end in war. It suited the Tories in 1679–81 to accuse the Whigs of trying to start a civil war. It suited the Whigs under George I to claim that the Tories wanted to put 'James III' on the throne. Many of them may have believed it, but it did not happen. Party rivalry was expressed through name-calling, symbols and effigies, missiles and blows, but not through armed conflict: the nearest thing to it were the battles between Whig and Tory mug-houses in London, or the assaults on Dissenting meeting houses in 1715, or elections like those at Bristol in 1713 or Coventry in 1722; these all ended with broken heads rather than fatalities.[22] This is due in large part to the fact that the English, despite their reputation for rebellion, were a 'governable people' and, to a considerable extent, governed themselves.[23] This was especially apparent in towns. Town elites and populations had often tried hard to avoid becoming embroiled in the civil war, because war was bad for business and set neighbour against neighbour. At the Restoration many corporations tried to keep ejections to a minimum, partly because the pool of suitable members was limited, but also because ejection was divisive. In many towns, members ejected in 1662 found their way back and civic rulers were lax about enfor-cing the Corporation Act. Magistrates were often reluctant to enforce the laws against Dissenters. This solidarity and moderation owed much to the nature of towns, where rulers and ruled lived close together and traded with one another. Residential zoning was already apparent in London by 1722, with obvious social and architectural differences between East End and West End.[24] But the sort of new developments that were becoming a feature of the West End —squares and streets for the better off, without back alleys and courts—were

---

[21] Holmes, *British Politics*, 20–6.

[22] One person was killed in the election at Queenborough in 1705: *HP 1690–1715*, i. 87.

[23] Miller, *After the Civil Wars*, ch. 1.

[24] L. Stone, 'The Residential Development of the West End of London in the Seventeenth Century', in B. C. Malament (ed.), *After the Reformation: Essays in Honour of J. H. Hexter* (Manchester, 1980), 167–212.

still rare in provincial towns. Similarly, during the eighteenth century some corporations became notorious for self-seeking oligarchy and corruption—Leicester was a prime example[25]—but such vices were less apparent in the early part of the century. I do not wish to suggest that there were no divisions. There were, especially between employers and employees, and these probably became more serious, as the economy became more complex and the distance between entrepreneur and wage-earner grew. But there remained large areas of common interest: in maintaining law and order, relieving the deserving poor (and disciplining the undeserving poor), managing the markets, and keeping the streets as clean and well repaired as was possible under the circumstances. These were everyday concerns—undramatic compared to elections, but necessary for urban life to function—and perhaps, in the larger scheme of things, more important than religious differences or party politics.

[25] Greaves, *Corporation, passim.*

Select Bibliography

(Not including items listed under 'Abbreviations'.)

Abney, J. R. (ed.), *The Vestry Books and Accounts of St Mary's, Leicester, 1652–1729* (Leicester, 1912).

An Account of the Dreadful Mob at Manchester and Other Places (Edinburgh, 1715).

An Account of the Riots, Tumults and Other Treasonable Practices since his Majesty's Accession (London, 1715).

Ailesbury, T. Bruce, earl of, *Memoirs*, ed. W. E. Buckley, 2 vols., Roxburgh Club (1890).

An Appendix to the Chronological History of Norwich (Norwich, 1728).

Austin, R., 'The City of Gloucester and the Regulation of Corporations, 1662–3', *Transactions of the Bristol and Gloucestershire Archaeological Society*, lviii (1936).

Barry, J., 'Bristol as a Reformation City, *c.*1640–1780', in N. Tyacke (ed.), *England's Long Reformation, 1500–1800* (London, 1998).

—— 'Bristol Pride: Civic Identity in Bristol, *c.*1640–1775', in M. Dresser and P. Ollerenshaw (eds.), *The Making of Modern Bristol* (Tiverton, 1996).

—— 'The Parish in Civic Life: Bristol and its Churches, 1640–1750', in S. J. Wright (ed.), *Parish Church and People* (London, 1988).

—— 'Popular Culture in Seventeenth-Century Bristol', in B. Reay (ed.), *Popular Culture in Seventeenth-Century England* (London, 1988).

—— (ed.), *The Tudor and Stuart Town: A Reader* (London, 1990).

—— and Brooks, C. (eds.), *The Middling Sort of People, 1550–1800* (Basingstoke, 1994).

Baxter, R., *Calendar of the Correspondence of Richard Baxter*, ed. N. Keeble and G. Nuttall, 2 vols. (Oxford, 1991).

Beattie, J. A., *Crime and the Courts in England, 1660–1800* (Oxford, 1986).

Beloff, M., *Public Order and Popular Disturbances, 1660–1714* (London, 1963).

Bennett, G. V., *The Tory Crisis in Church and State, 1688–1730* (Oxford, 1975).

Blomefield, F., *An Essay towards a Topographical History of Norfolk*, 11 vols. (London, 1805–10).

Borsay, P., ' "All the Town's a Stage": Urban Ritual and Ceremony, 1660–1800', in Clark (ed.), *The Transformation of English Provincial Towns*.

—— (ed.), *The Eighteenth-Century Town: A Reader* (London, 1990).

—— *The English Urban Renaissance: Culture and Society in the Provincial Town, 1660–1770* (Oxford, 1989).

—— and McInnes, A., 'Debate: Leisure Town or Urban Renaissance?', *P & P* 126 (1990).

Boyle, J. R. (ed.), *Charters and Letters Patent Granted to Kingston upon Hull* (Hull, 1905).

Braddick, M. J., *State Formation in Early Modern England, c.1550–1700* (Cambridge, 2000).

Braithwaite, W. C., *The Second Period of Quakerism* (York, 1979).

Bramston, Sir J., *Autobiography*, ed. Lord Braybrooke, Camden Society (1845).

Branford, C. W., 'Powers of Association: Aspects of Elite Social, Political and Cultural Life in Norwich, 1680–1760', Ph.D. thesis (University of East Anglia, 1994).

Brockett, A., *Nonconformity in Exeter, 1650–1875* (Manchester, 1962).

Browne, J., *History of Congregationalism in Norfolk and Suffolk* (London, 1877).

Browne, Sir T., *Works*, ed. G. Keynes, 4 vols. (London, 1964).

—— *Works*, ed. S. Wilkin, 4 vols. (London, 1836).

Burnet, G., *Supplement to Burnet's History of his own Time*, ed. H. C. Foxcroft (Oxford, 1902).

Butcher, E. E. (ed.), *Bristol Corporation of the Poor, 1696–1898*, BRS iii (1932).

Cartwright, T., *Diary*, ed. J. Hunter, Camden Society (1843).

Cary, J., *An Account of the Proceedings of the Corporation of Bristol* (1700).

Childs, J., *The Army, James II and the Glorious Revolution* (Manchester, 1980).

—— *The Army of Charles II* (London, 1976).

—— *The British Army of William III* (Manchester, 1987).

Clark, P., *British Clubs and Societies, 1500–1800* (Oxford, 2000).

—— (ed.), *Country Towns in Pre-industrial England* (Leicester, 1981).

—— (ed.), *The Transformation of English Provincial Towns* (London, 1984).

—— and Slack, P. (eds.), *Crisis and Order in English Towns, 1500–1700* (London, 1972).

—— —— *English Towns in Transition, 1500–1700* (Oxford, 1976).

Clifton, R., *The Last Popular Rebellion: The Western Rising of 1685* (London, 1984).

Coleby, A. M., *Central Government and the Localities: Hampshire, 1649–89* (Cambridge, 1987).

—— 'Military–Civilian Relations in the Solent, 1651–89', *HJ* xxix (1986).

Colley, L., *In Defiance of Oligarchy: The Tory Party, 1714–60* (Cambridge, 1982).

Cooper, C. H., *Annals of Cambridge*, 4 vols. (Cambridge, 1842–52).

Corfield, P., *The Impact of English Towns, 1700–1800* (Oxford, 1982).

Corie, T., *Correspondence*, ed. R. H. Hill, NRS xxvii (1957).

Cozens-Hardy, B. (ed.), *Norfolk Lieutenancy Journal, 1676–1701*, NRS xxx (1961).

Davies, A., *The Quakers in English Society, 1655–1725* (Oxford, 2000).

Davies, R., *An Account of the Convincement of Richard Davies* (London, 1771).

Davis, J. R., 'Colchester 1600–1662: Politics, Religion and Office-Holding in an English Provincial Town', Ph.D. thesis (Brandeis University, 1981).

Delapryme, A., *Diary*, ed. C. Jackson, Surtees Society (1870).

—— *A History of Kingston upon Hull*, 2 vols. (Hull, 1986).

Eddington, A. J., *The First Fifty Years of Quakerism in Norwich* (London, 1932).

Ellis, J. M., *The Georgian Town, 1680–1840* (Basingstoke, 2001).

Evans, J. T., *Seventeenth-Century Norwich* (Oxford, 1979).

Evelyn, J., *Diary*, ed. E. S. de Beer, 6 vols. (Oxford, 1955).

Falkus, M., 'Lighting the Dark Ages of English Economic History: Town Streets before the Industrial Revolution', in D. C. Coleman and A. H. John (eds.), *Trade, Government and Economy in Pre-industrial England* (London, 1976).

Foyle, A., *Bristol*, Pevsner Architectural Guides (New Haven, 2004).

A Full and Impartial Account of the Oxford Riots (1715).

Gauci, P., *Politics and Society in Great Yarmouth, 1660–1722* (Oxford, 1996).

Gent, T., *Annales Regioduni Hullini, or the History of the Royal and Beautiful Town of Hull* (York, 1736).

Gillett, E., and MacMahon, K. A., *A History of Hull* (Hull, 1980).

Glines, T., 'Politics and Society in the Borough of Colchester, 1660–93', Ph.D. thesis (University of Wisconsin, 1974).

Goldie, M., 'James II and the Dissenters' Revenge: The Commission of Enquiry of 1688', *HR* xlvi (1993).

—— 'The Theory of Religious Intolerance in Restoration England', in O. P. Grell, J. I. Israel, and N. Tyacke (eds.), *From Persecution to Toleration: The Glorious Revolution and Religion in England* (Oxford, 1991).

—— 'The Unacknowledged Republic: Office-Holding in Early Modern England', in T. Harris (ed.), *The Politics of the Excluded, 1500–1850* (Basingstoke, 2001).

Granville, D., *Remains*, ed. G. Ornsby, Surtees Society xxxvii (1861), xlvii (1867).

Greaves, R. W., *The Corporation of Leicester, 1689–1836* (Leicester, 1970).

—— 'The Earl of Huntingdon and the Leicester Charter of 1684', *HLQ* xv (1952).

Griffiths, P., Fox, A., and Hindle, S. (eds.), *The Experience of Authority in Early Modern England* (Basingstoke, 1996).

Gutch, J., *Collectanea Curiosa*, 2 vols. (Oxford, 1831).

Guth, G., 'Croakers, Tackers and Other Citizens: Norwich Voters in the Early Eighteenth Century', Ph.D. thesis (Stanford, Calif. 1985).

Haley, K. H. D., *The First Earl of Shaftesbury* (Oxford, 1968).

Harris, T., *Politics under the Later Stuarts, 1660–1714* (London, 1993).

—— *Restoration: Charles II and his Kingdoms, 1660–85* (London, 2005).

Hembry, P., *The English Spa, 1560–1815* (London, 1990).

Hirst, D., *The Representative of the People? Voters and Voting under the Early Stuarts* (Cambridge, 1975).

Holmes, G., *British Politics in the Reign of Anne* (London, 1967).

—— *The Trial of Dr Sacheverell* (London, 1972).

—— and Speck, W. A. (eds.), *The Divided Society: Parties and Politics in England, 1694–1716* (London, 1967).

Horwitz, H., *Parliament, Policy and Politics in the Reign of William III* (Manchester, 1977).

Hudson, W., and Tingey, J. C. (eds.), *Records of the City of Norwich*, 2 vols. (Norwich, 1910).

Hurwich, J. J., 'A "Fanatick Town": The Political Influence of Dissenters in Coventry, 1660–1720', *Midland History*, iv (1977).

Hutton, R., *The Rise and Fall of Merry England: The Ritual Year 1400–1700* (Oxford, 1994).

Innes, J., 'Prisons for the Poor: English Bridewells, 1555–1800', in F. Snyder and S. Hay (eds.), *Labour, Law and Crime* (London, 1987).

Jackson, G., *Hull in the Eighteenth Century* (Oxford, 1972).

Jones, E. L., and Falkus, M. E., 'Urban Improvement and the English Economy in the Seventeenth and Eighteenth Centuries', in Borsay (ed.), *Eighteenth-Century Town*.

Jones, J. R., 'James II's Whig Collaborators', *HJ* iii (1960).

Kennett, D. H., 'Mayor Making in Norwich in 1706', *Norf Arch* xxxv (1971).

Kenyon, J. P., *Revolution Principles: The Politics of Party, 1689–1720* (Cambridge, 1977).

Key, N., and Ward, J. P., ' "Divided into Parties": Exclusion Crisis Origins in Monmouth', *EHR* cxv (2000).

Kilmartin, J. G., 'Popular Rejoicing and Public Ritual in Norwich and Coventry, 1660–1835', Ph.D. thesis (Warwick, 1987).

Kirby, J. W., 'Restoration Leeds and the Aldermen of the Corporation', *Northern History*, xxii (1986).

Kishlansky, M., *Parliamentary Selection: Social and Political Choice in Early Modern England* (Cambridge, 1986).

Knights, M., *Politics and Opinion in Crisis, 1678–81* (Cambridge, 1994).

—— *Representation and Misrepresentation in Later Stuart Britain* (Oxford, 2005).

Landon, M. de L., 'The Bristol Artillery Company and the Tory Triumph in Bristol', *Proceedings of the American Philosophical Society*, cxliv (1970).

Langford, P., *Public Life and the Propertied Englishman, 1689–1798* (Oxford, 1991).

Latham, R. (ed.), *Bristol Charters, 1509–1899*, BRS xii (1946).

Lee, C., ' "Fanatic Magistrates": Religious and Political Conflict in Three Kent Boroughs, 1680–4', *HJ* xxxv (1992).

McGrath, P. (ed.), *Bristol in the Eighteenth Century* (Newton Abbot, 1972).

—— *The Merchant Venturers of Bristol* (Bristol, 1975).

McInnes, A., 'The Emergence of a Leisure Town: Shrewsbury, 1660–1760', *P & P* 120 (1988) and 'Debate', with P. Borsay, *P & P* 126 (1990).

—— *The English Town*, Historical Association (London, 1980).

Mackerell, B., 'Account of the Guild of St George', *Norf Arch* iii (1852).

Mackintosh, Sir J., *History of the Revolution of 1688* (London, 1834).

McNulty, L., 'Priests, Church Courts and People: The Politics of the Parish in England, 1660–1713', Ph.D. thesis (London, 2005).

Miller, J., *After the Civil Wars: English Government and Politics in the Reign of Charles II* (Harlow, 2000).

Miller, J., *Charles II* (London, 1991).

—— 'Containing Division in Restoration Norwich', *EHR* cxxi (2006).

—— 'The Crown and the Borough Charters in the Reign of Charles II', *EHR* c (1985).

—— *James II* (New Haven, 2000).

—— 'The Militia and the Army in the Reign of James II', *HJ* xvi (1973).

—— *Popery and Politics in England, 1660–88* (Cambridge, 1973).

—— 'Proto-Jacobitism? The Tories and the Revolution of 1688', in E. Cruickshanks and J. Black (eds.), *The Jacobite Challenge* (Edinburgh, 1988).

—— ' "A Suffering People": English Quakers and their Neighbours, *c.*1650–1700', *P & P* 188 (2005).

Monod, P. K., *Jacobitism and the English People, 1688–1788* (Cambridge, 1989).

Mullett, M., 'Conflict, Politics and Elections in Lancaster, 1660–88', *Northern History*, xix (1983).

—— ' "Deprived of our Former Place": The Internal Politics of Bedford, 1660–88', *Publications of the Bedfordshire Historical Society*, lix (1980).

Newton, S., *Diary*, ed. J. E. Foster, Cambridge Antiquarian Society (1890).

Nichols, J., *History and Antiquities of Leicestershire*, 4 vols. (London, 1793–1815).

Oates, J. D., 'Jacobitism and Popular Disturbances in Northern England, 1714–19', *Northern History*, xli (2004).

O'Sullivan, D. S., 'Politics in Norwich, 1701–1835', M.Phil. thesis (University of East Anglia, 1975).

Outhwaite, R. B., 'Dearth and Government Intervention in English Grain Markets, 1590–1700', *Economic History Review*, 2nd series, xxxiii (1981).

Parkin, C., *History and Antiquities of the City of Norwich* (Norwich, 1783).

Patterson, A. T., *A History of Southampton, 1700–1914*, i: *An Oligarchy in Decline*, Southampton Records Series xi (1966).

Pickavance, R. G., 'The English Boroughs and the King's Government: A Study of the Tory Reaction, 1681–5', D.Phil. thesis (Oxford, 1976).

Plumb, J. H., *The Growth of Political Stability in England, 1675–1725* (London, 1967).

Pound, J., *Tudor and Stuart Norwich* (Chichester, 1988).

Price, J. L., *Holland and the Dutch Republic in the Seventeenth Century* (Oxford, 1994).

Ramsbottom, J. D., 'Presbyterians and "Partial Conformity" in the Restoration Church', *JEH* xliii (1992).

A Relation of the Inhumane and Barbarous Sufferings of the People Called Quakers in . . . Bristol (1665).

Reliquiae Baxterianae, ed. M. Sylvester (London, 1696).

Rogers, N., *Crowds, Culture and Politics in Georgian Britain* (Oxford, 1998).

—— 'Popular Jacobitism in Provincial Context: Eighteenth-Century Bristol and Norwich', in E. Cruickshanks and J. Black (eds.), *The Jacobite Challenge* (Edinburgh, 1988).

—— *Whigs and Cities: Popular Politics in the Age of Walpole and Pitt* (Oxford, 1989).

Rosen, A., 'Winchester in Transition', in Clark (ed.), *Country Towns in Pre-industrial England*.

Rosenfeld, S., *Strolling Players and Drama in the Provinces, 1660–1765* (Cambridge, 1939).

Roy, I., 'The English Republic, 1649–60: The View from the Town Hall', in H. G. Koenigsberger (ed.), *Republiken und Republikanismus im Europa dem frühen Neuzeit* (Munich, 1988).

Sacks, D. H., *The Widening Gate: Bristol and the Atlantic Economy, 1450–1700* (Berkeley, 1991).

Schilling, W. A. H., 'The Central Government and Municipal Corporations in England, 1642–63', Ph.D. thesis (Vanderbilt University, 1970).

Scott, D., 'Politics, Dissent and Quakerism in York, 1640–1700', D.Phil. thesis (York, 1990).

The Several Papers . . . Relating to the Riots at Oxford (London, 1717).

Seyer, S., *Memoirs Topographical and Historical of Bristol and its Neighbourhood*, 2 vols. (Bristol, 1821).

Sharpe, J. A., *Crime in Early Modern England* (London, 1994).

Shephard, A., and Withington, P. (eds.), *Communities in Early Modern England* (Manchester, 2000).

Short, M. J., 'The Corporation of Hull and the Government of James II, 1687–8', *HR* lxxi (1998).

Simmons, J., *Leicester: The Ancient Borough to 1860* (Gloucester, 1983).

Slack, P., *From Reformation to Improvement: Public Welfare in Early Modern England* (Oxford, 1999).

—— *Poverty and Policy in Tudor and Stuart England* (London, 1988).

—— 'Poverty and Politics in Salisbury, 1597–1666', in Clark and Slack (eds.), *Crisis and Order in English Towns*.

Spaeth, D. A., *The Church in an Age of Danger: Parsons and Parishioners, 1660–1740* (Cambridge, 2000).

Speck, W. A., *Tory and Whig: The Struggle in the Constituencies, 1701–16* (London, 1970).

Spufford, M., 'Puritanism and Social Control?', in A. J. Fletcher and J. Stevenson (eds.), *Order and Disorder in Early Modern England* (Cambridge, 1985).

Spurr, J., 'The Church of England, Comprehension and the Toleration Act of 1689', *EHR* civ (1989).

—— *The Restoration Church of England, 1649–89* (New Haven, 1991).

Stevenson, J., *Popular Disturbances in England, 1700–1832*, 2nd edn. (London, 1992).

Strong, S. A. (ed.), *A Catalogue of Letters and Other Historical Documents at Welbeck* (London, 1903).

Styles, P., *Studies in Seventeenth-Century West Midlands History* (Kineton, 1978).

Sweet, R., *The English Town, 1680–1840: Government, Society and Culture* (Harlow, 1999).

Thompson, J., *History of Leicester from the Romans to the End of the Seventeenth Century* (Leicester, 1849).

Tickell, J., *History of the Town and County of Kingston upon Hull* (Hull, 1798).

Underdown, D., *Fire from Heaven: Life in an English Town in the Seventeenth Century* (London, 1992).

—— *Revel, Riot and Rebellion: Popular Politics and Culture in England, 1603–60* (Oxford, 1985).

Watts, M., *The Dissenters from the Reformation to the French Revolution* (Oxford, 1978).

Webb, S. and B., *English Local Government: The Manor and the Borough*, 2 vols. (London, 1908).

Whitaker, W., *One Line of the Puritan Tradition in Hull: Bowl Alley Lane Chapel* (London, 1910).

Wilson, K., *The Sense of the People: Politics, Culture and Imperialism in England, 1715–85* (Cambridge, 1995).

Withington, P., 'Two Renaissances: Urban Political Culture in Post-Reformation England Reconsidered', *HJ* xliv (2001).

—— 'Views from the Bridge: Revolution and Restoration in Seventeenth-Century York', *P & P* 170 (2001).

Wrightson, K., 'The Politics of the Parish in Early Modern England', in Griffiths, Fox, and Hindle (eds.), *The Experience of Authority in Early Modern England.*

—— and Walter, J., 'Dearth and the Social Order in Early Modern England', *P & P* 71 (1976).

Index

Index